Sport and Democracy in the Ancient and Modern Worlds

This book explores the relationship between sport and democratization. Drawing on sociological and historical methodologies, it provides a framework for understanding how sport affects the level of egalitarianism in the society in which it is played. The author distinguishes between horizontal sport, which embodies and fosters egalitarian relations, and vertical sport, which embodies and fosters hierarchical relations. He also differentiates between societies in which sport is played and watched on a mass scale and those in which it is an ancillary activity. Using ancient Greece and nineteenth-century Britain as case studies, he analyzes how these variables interact and finds that horizontal mass sport has the capacity to both promote and inhibit democratization at a societal level. He concludes that horizontal mass sport tends to reinforce and extend democratization.

Paul Christesen is Professor of Classics at Dartmouth College. He is the author of *Olympic Victor Lists and Ancient Greek History* (Cambridge, 2007) and co-editor (with Donald Kyle) of the *Wiley-Blackwell Companion to Sport and Spectacle in Greek and Roman Antiquity* (forthcoming).

Sport and Democracy in the Ancient and Modern Worlds

PAUL CHRISTESEN
Dartmouth College

CAMBRIDGE
UNIVERSITY PRESS

CAMBRIDGE UNIVERSITY PRESS
Cambridge, New York, Melbourne, Madrid, Cape Town,
Singapore, São Paulo, Delhi, Mexico City

Cambridge University Press
32 Avenue of the Americas, New York, NY 10013-2473, USA

www.cambridge.org
Information on this title: www.cambridge.org/9781107012691

Paul Christesen 2012

First published 2012

Printed in the United States of America

A catalog record for this publication is available from the British Library.

Library of Congress Cataloging in Publication data
Christesen, Paul, 1966–
Sport and democracy in the ancient and modern worlds / Paul Christesen.
p. cm.
Includes bibliographical references and index.
ISBN 978-1-107-01269-1 (hardback)
1. Sports – History. 2. Sports – Sociological aspects. I. Title.
GV573.C57 2012
306.4'83–dc23 2011049737

ISBN 978-1-107-01269-1 Hardback

Contents

List of Figures

List of Maps

List of Tables

Acknowledgments

In the course of bringing this project to completion I have been immeasurably aided by more individuals than I can properly thank. The Humanities Research Center at Rice University generously provided a fellowship that made it possible to write much of the text of this book. The Dean of the Humanities at Dartmouth College was kind enough to supply funds to defray the costs of acquiring publication rights for the images reproduced herein.

Numerous people, most notably Allen Guttmann, Richard Holt, Donald Kyle, Ned Lebow, Aurora McClain, and Stephen Miller read earlier drafts and made suggestions that contributed markedly to the final product. My colleagues in the Department of Classics at Dartmouth, Margaret Graver and Jeremy Rutter, also provided helpful comments for which I am grateful. Special thanks are due to James Tatum, who provided invaluable notes on a near-final version of the manuscript. Along the way I have received advice on specific points and assistance from Paul Cartledge, Danny Diceanu, Matthew Guterl, Stephen Hodkinson, Claire Hornig, Samuel Kahng, Zara Martirosova Torlone, Ellen Millender, and Max Weiner. Jennifer Carey edited the manuscript and notably improved it in the process. The debt I owe to my family in general and my parents in particular defies simple expression but is no doubt well known to readers from their own experience. Finally, special thanks are due to my wife Cecilia and my son Michael for their unswerving patience and support.

Hanover, New Hampshire
January 1, 2012

Preface

Living on top of a fault line tends to make people uneasy. Consciously choosing to do so may seem more than a bit perverse, and the architecture of this book, which is built astride two distinct fault lines, merits brief explanation.

In general terms, scholars who study sport fall into two broad groups: historians and sociologists. Given that they share a passionate interest in a similar body of material, one might well expect there to be a constant, fruitful interchange between sport historians and sport sociologists, but in practice such interchanges occur with less than optimal frequency. The divide between the two groups is evident in the existence of two separate professional associations, the North American Society for Sport History and the North American Society for the Sociology of Sport, which hold annual conferences, at different times and in different cities. In 2011, for example, sport historians came together in May in Austin, sport sociologists in November in Minneapolis. Sport historians are few and far between at the conferences organized by the North American Society for the Sociology of Sport, and sport sociologists equally scarce at North American Society for Sport History gatherings.[1]

This situation is less inexplicable than it might seem at first glance. The relationship between history and sociology has been complicated ever since these disciplines coalesced in a formal fashion in the nineteenth century. Despite the fact that scholars in both disciplines explore and seek to explain human social activity, particularly within the bounds of complex, literate societies, and despite repeated calls for a symbiotic relationship between the

---

[1] I am aware that the preferred usages are "sociology of sport" and "sociologist of sport" and will, throughout the text that follows, regularly (though not exclusively) employ the former but not the latter. The reason for this is purely stylistic – "sociologist of sport" is less than an entirely elegant phrase. On the reasons why these are the preferred usages, see Malcolm 2012, 27.

two,[2] history and sociology remain largely separate enterprises.[3] Among the many reasons why this is the case, two stand out.

First, historians tend to emphasize human agency as a key factor shaping social activity, whereas sociologists stress the importance of social structures. A satisfactory resolution for what might be called the agency/structure dilemma has remained elusive. As Philip Abrams put it more than three decades ago:

It is the problem of finding a way of accounting for human experience which recognizes simultaneously and in equal measure that history and society are made by constant, more or less purposeful, individual action and that individual action, however purposeful, is made by history and society. How do we as active subjects make a world of social objects which then, as it were, become subjects making us their objects?

Abrams concluded that the dilemma "is easily and endlessly formulated but, it seems, stupifyingly difficult to resolve."[4]

Second, historians tend to have an idiographic orientation, sociologists a nomothetic one. Although there is enormous variation among individual scholars, it is probably safe to say that historians typically focus on "the meanings of the complexity of lived experience" and assume that "God is in the details." Sociologists, on the other hand, "aim to cut through the messy details that make up real life" and seek "to find underlying general structures and principles."[5] That is not to say that historians are disinterested in theoretical approaches and that sociologists are disinterested in detailed factual information, but that historians tend to see theory as a means to the end of understanding the material they study, whereas many sociologists see the generation of theories as an important goal of their work. Historians and sociologists can thus have considerable difficulty in agreeing on either what to do or how to do it.

Nonetheless, the potential value of a hybridized approach incorporating both history and sociology remains significant. This book seeks to untangle the relationship between democratization in society and democratization in sport by using an approach that draws heavily on both sport history and the sociology of sport. Thus, Chapters 1 to 7 draw heavily on the sociology of sport, Chapters 8 to 16 on sport history. As a result, the work that follows rests directly on the fault line between the history of sport and the sociology of sport.

---

[2] See, for instance, C. W. Mills 1959, 143–64.

[3] There are of course a number of notable exceptions, including much of the scholarship produced by *Annalistes* such as Braudel, on which see L. Hunt 1986. For a discussion of the relationship between the history of sport and the sociology of sport, see Malcolm 2012, 117–34 (with the caveat that this discussion was written by a sport sociologist).

[4] Abrams 1980, 7, 8, respectively.

[5] Morris 2002, 8. On idiographic and nomothetic approaches, see Windelband 1894.

This book also sits atop another fault line, this one within sport history itself, because it incorporates and juxtaposes both ancient and modern material. Chapters 8 to 10 explore sport in ancient Greece, Chapters 11 to 15 sport in nineteenth-century Britain and Germany, Chapter 16 sport in the United States in the twentieth century. Classicists specializing in the study of ancient Greek history have since the nineteenth century evinced an interest in sport, based on an awareness of the great importance of sport in ancient Greek society.[6] It was, however, not until the 1960s that the study of sport in more recent periods emerged as a distinct subfield.[7] Since that time, sport historians who focus on ancient and modern material have for the most part formed two distinct groups, with an amicable but functionally distant relationship. That distance reflects a commonly held belief, perhaps most evident in the influential work of Allen Guttmann,[8] that ancient and modern sport were fundamentally different, not just with respect to the sports that were played, but also with respect to the very nature of sport.

My decision to write a book that sits astride these two disciplinary fault lines was not driven by a quixotic quest to seek out and bridge scholarly divides. Rather it reflects my conviction that it is impossible to study the relationship between democratization in society and in sport in a satisfactory manner without drawing on a broad range of methodologies and material. Indispensable analytical benefits flow from simultaneously bringing empirical and theoretical perspectives to the same questions, and the juxtaposition of ancient and modern material makes it possible to clarify issues of causation in ways that would be otherwise impossible.

In carrying out this project I have had both the disadvantage and advantage of being in many ways an outsider. I was trained as an ancient historian, with a particular focus on the economic history of ancient Greece, and in the past decade I have worked extensively on the historiography and history of ancient Greece in the Archaic and Classical periods (700–323 BCE). I would describe myself as neither a sport historian nor a sport sociologist, but as a social historian with a strong interest in ancient Greece. My point of entry for this project had significant disadvantages, among them the need to familiarize myself with a considerable body of theoretical and historical material. On the other hand, I had the advantages of not being invested in any particular approach to studying the relationship between sport and democratization and of having a grounding in economic history, a field in which the intermingling of theoretical and empirical approaches is almost a given. Moreover, my familiarity with ancient Greek sport conferred a certain breadth of vision when it came to dealing with modern-day sport. As an outsider, I was in perhaps a better position than I otherwise would have been

---

[6] See, for instance, Gardiner 1910.
[7] See Struna 1985.
[8] See in particular Guttmann 1978.

when it came to thinking about the most productive fashion of exploring the complicated interconnections between sport and democratization.

To endeavor to bring together sport history and the sociology of sport and ancient and modern material inevitably entails certain risks and could easily be construed as (and might well be) foolhardy. A text that draws on a diverse array of methodologies and material may attract the approbation of none and the ire of all, and individual readers, with varying areas of expertise, may find some parts of the text overly simplified, other parts overly complex. My hope is that each part of the discussion that follows has done sufficient justice to the subject matter as to satisfy specialists and enlighten nonspecialists. Rather than attempting to provide a comprehensive bibliography, I have cited only those pieces of scholarship that are most directly relevant. My expectation is that, for any given point, specialists will already be familiar with the full spectrum of pertinent sources, and that nonspecialists are best served by being guided to good starting points for further reading.

The appeal and the importance of the questions addressed in this book are, I think, apparent, and I hope that the same can be said about the possibilities created by bringing together sociology and history and ancient and modern material. Whether the promise inherent in subject matter and approach is realized is of course a matter for the reader to decide.

A Note on the Title

The title on the cover of this book is something of a relic. When I originally conceived this project, I imagined it to be an exploration of the relationship between sport and democracy. As the project moved forward, I discovered that it was much more productive to consider the relationship between sport and democratization. However, by the time I made that discovery the manuscript was already under contract, and a title had been irrevocably chosen. If I had to do it over again, I would give this book a different title: *A School for Democracy: Sport and Democratization in the Ancient and Modern Worlds*. Democracy and democratization are sufficiently closely related that the title as given is not, I think, fundamentally misleading. However, the reader should be aware that this is a book about democratization rather than democracy, an important distinction that is discussed in detail in the text that follows.

Introduction

I.I. SETTING THE SCENE

Democratic societies rest on foundations that extend far beyond governmental institutions. In *Democracy in America* Alexis de Tocqueville observes that "The most democratic country on earth is found to be, above all, the one where men in our day have most perfected the art of pursuing the object of their common desires in common and have applied this new science to the most objects. Does this result from an accident or could it be that there in fact exists a necessary relation between associations and equality?" Tocqueville supplies a strongly affirmative response to his own question and argues that the cooperative, face-to-face interactions that take place in voluntary associations have important effects on the individuals involved: "sentiments and ideas renew themselves, the heart is enlarged, and the human mind is developed only by the reciprocal action of men upon one another." He concludes that voluntary associations are an indispensable component of egalitarian, democratic societies:

Among the laws that rule human societies there is one that seems more precise and clearer than all the others. In order that men remain civilized or become so, the art of associating must be developed and perfected among them in the same ratio as equality of conditions increases.[1]

The associations that Tocqueville has in mind are not solely or even primarily those that are overtly political in nature, but those formed for a variety of other purposes, ranging from distributing books to founding hospitals. Although Tocqueville has nothing to say about sport, Robert Putnam, whose widely-read work on social capital builds directly on Tocqueville's

---

[1] de Tocqueville 2000 (1835–40), 490, 491, 492, respectively. For current thinking about voluntary associations and democracy, see Warren 2001. For the intellectual background to Tocqueville's work, see Lebow and Lebow, forthcoming.

ideas, makes the case that the voluntary associations that contribute in a significant and positive fashion to democratization include soccer clubs and bowling teams.[2]

Seen from the perspective outlined in Tocqueville's and Putnam's work, the relationship between democratization in society and in sport might seem too obvious to warrant extended discussion. Sports teams, as Putnam points out, are a form of voluntary association, and if voluntary associations are a vital part of democratic societies, it would seem to follow that sport should be seen as a meaningful underpinning of democratization. There are, however, complicating factors that need to be taken into account in considering the relationship between sport and democratization. To begin with, sport is not necessarily an archetypal voluntary association. Sport can be a context in which participants regularly experience face-to-face interactions, a defining component of voluntary associations. On the other hand, some forms of sport, such as running every morning entirely alone, are devoid of such interactions. In addition, sport is seen by many people as little more than a pastime, a harmless diversion that has no noteworthy effects. From this perspective, a discussion of the relationship between sport and democratization is roughly akin to a discussion of the relationship between the hobby of collecting antique bottle caps and democratization. Finally, even if one accepts that sport, especially in times and places where it is played and watched with great seriousness and regularity by large numbers of people, might have an impact on society as a whole, the notional democratizing capacity of sport is not always immediately apparent. Sport was, for example, immensely popular in both Nazi Germany and the Soviet Union during the Stalinist era, neither of which is likely to be held up as a model democratic society.[3] For all of these reasons one cannot blithely conclude that sport promotes democratization.

There is, nonetheless, good reason to think that there may well be a connection of some sort between democratization in society and democratization in sport. Consider the following statistics. The 91st Congress of the United States, which was in office from 1969–71, had 524 male representatives and 11 female representatives.[4] In 1970, there were in the United States 308,627 male physicians and 25,401 female physicians. When the National Federation of State High School Associations conducted its annual survey of the number of athletes on varsity sports teams in the United States in 1971–72 it found 3,666,917 male athletes and 294,015 female athletes. In the early 1970s females thus represented roughly 2% of all members of

---

[2] Putnam, Leonardi, and Nanetti 1993, 91–99; Putnam 2000, 109–14.

[3] This observation echoes much recent research that has emphasized that not all voluntary associations exert a positive, democratizing influence on society. See Warren 2001, 3–16.

[4] All dates are CE unless otherwise specified, with the exception of Chapters 8–10, in which the reverse is true.

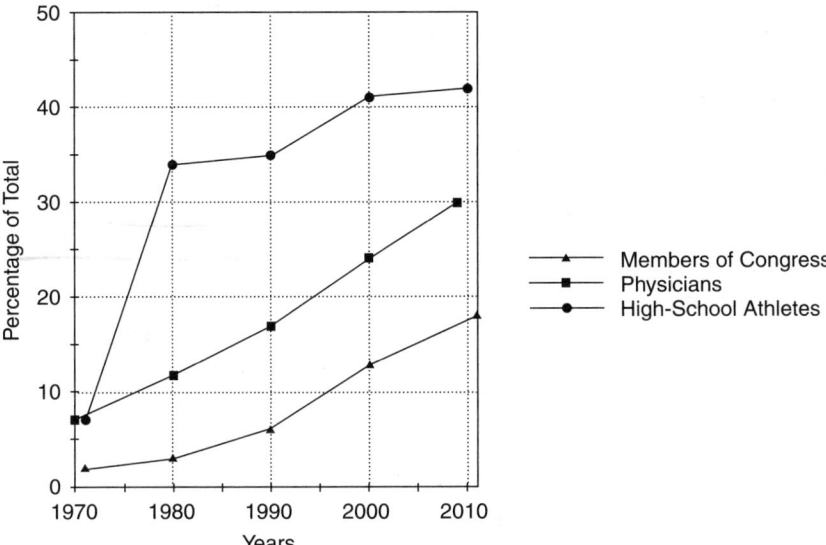

FIGURE I. Percentage of Females among Total Number of Individuals in Various Fields and Activities in the United States, 1970 to Present, by Decade

Congress, 7% of all physicians, and 7% of all varsity high school athletes. The 112th Congress of the United States, which will be in office from 2011–13, has 94 female representatives. In 2009, there were in the United States 684,219 male physicians and 287,683 female physicians. When the National Federation of State High School Associations conducted its annual survey of the number of athletes on varsity sports teams in the United States in 2009–10 it found 4,455,740 male athletes and 3,172,637 female athletes. Females thus currently represent roughly 18% of all members of Congress, 30% of all physicians, and 42% of all varsity high school athletes.[5] This data is presented graphically (with figures for intermediate decades included) in Figure 1. The progress of American women in achieving more equal rights and opportunities in society as a whole has thus been closely paralleled in their growing participation in sport.

This is but one example of a much larger phenomenon, which can be understood in four different ways:

[5] Information about the number of female members of the United States Congress is taken from http://womenincongress.house.gov/historical-data/representatives-senators-by-congress.html; about the number of female physicians from http://www.ama-assn.org/ama/pub/about-ama/our-people/member-groups-sections/women-physicians-congress/statistics-history.page? and from the American Medical Association's publication *Physician Characteristics and Distribution in the U.S., 2011*; about the number of female high school athletes from http://www.nfhs.org/content.aspx?id=3282.

(1) democratization in society is cause, democratization in sport effect, or, to put it differently, the nature of sport reflects and is determined by the nature of the society in which it is played, whereas the nature of sport has little or no effect on the nature of society;

(2) democratization in sport contributes meaningfully to the democratization of society;

(3) democratization in both society and sport is more apparent than real, and society and sport function primarily as mutually reinforcing systems of domination and oppression; sport, to the extent that it acts on society in this regard, typically inhibits democratization;

(4) democratization in society and in sport are both determined by one or more exogenous factors such as capitalism, industrialization, urbanization, Protestantism, or modernization.

All of these views of the relationship between sport and democratization, which are by no means entirely mutually exclusive, have been much discussed among both scholars and the general public for well over a century. The attention that has been paid to this subject is not surprising given the practical and ideological importance of democracy in the Western world and widespread devotion to sport, both in the present day and in the past, stretching back to ancient Greece. The nature of the relationship between sport and democratization is of interest to a wide array of scholars, ranging from sport historians and sport sociologists to political scientists and social historians.

Moreover, the relationship between sport and democratization is a matter of considerable significance well beyond the academic community. If sport does indeed have the capacity to affect and effect democratization in society as a whole, the expenditure of resources on sport can be understood and explained as a worthwhile investment in sustaining and extending democracy. If sport has no capacity to promote democratization, then one of the basic justifications for spending time, energy, and money on sport vanishes. If sport actually inhibits democratization, it becomes, from one perspective, a pernicious activity that needs to be reconstructed or curbed.

The nature of the relationship between sport and democratization thus has significant public policy ramifications because in much of the world, most notably in liberal democracies in Europe, North America, and Australasia, the expenditure of vast amounts of time, energy, and public and private funds on sport is legitimized in part by appeals to the capacity of sport to foster democratization. Daniel Tarschys, Secretary-General of the Council of Europe, proclaimed in 1995 that:

The hidden face of sport is…the tens of thousands of enthusiasts who find in their football, rowing, athletics, or rock-climbing clubs a place for meeting and exchange, but above all the training ground for community life. In this microcosm, people learn to take responsibility, to follow rules, to accept one another, to look for consensus, to take on voluntary tasks – in a word, to take an active part in building the environment they like, thus living their very own democracy. Seen from this angle, sport is, *par excellence*, the ideal school for democracy.[6]

The current official position of the Council of Europe is that "sport is a fundamental pillar of society" and that sport, if played properly, promotes "democracy and participation."[7] This position helps justify, and is reflected in, consistently high levels of public funding for sport by European governments; for instance, national and local governments in France spend the equivalent of more than $15 billion per year on sport, in Germany more than $8 billion.[8]

Belief in the democratizing powers of sport is also widespread in the United States, where public spending on sport comes primarily through the financing of athletics in public school systems. Some sense of scale can be had from the fact that the 218 public universities in America that field sports teams competing at the highest level (Division 1) spent $6.2 billion on athletics in 2010. Of that total, roughly $4 billion came from revenue sources such as television rights and ticket sales, and $2 billion came from subsidies in the form of fees paid by students and transfers from schools' general budgets.[9] If one keeps in mind that there are approximately 4,000 institutions of higher learning in the United States and 7.5 million high school athletes, the scale of public spending on sport begins to become clear.

That spending is justified in a variety of different ways, among the most important of which is the claim that sport participation (and to a lesser extent spectatorship) has strongly positive effects that are valuable to American society. For example, a recent study by the United States Anti-Doping Agency characterizes sport as "a national asset" on the grounds that:

We know that sport, at its best, can build character and promote the virtues of honesty, respect, selfless teamwork, dedication, and commitment to a greater cause. Sport lessons (good and bad) transcend the playing field, spilling over into the classroom, the business world, and the community, and contribute to shaping the character and culture of America's citizens.

The study included a survey of 8,934 individuals that collectively constituted a representative sample of the population of the United States, and found that:

---

[6] Tarschys 1995, 5. The characterization of sport as a "school in democracy" is found in Betts 1974, 330, but it was in regular use long before Betts' time. It appears, for example, in an article on physical education in Germany written by Carl Diem in 1948 (Diem 1948, 431), and it in all probability was in circulation well before then. The roots of this usage likely can be found in Pericles' Funeral Oration, a paean to Athenian democracy, in which he declared that Athens was the "school of Greece" (Thucydides *The Peloponnesian War* 2.41.1).

[7] http://www.coe.int/t/dg4/epas/about/history_En.asp. On recent developments in government sport policies, see Bergsgard, Houlihan, Mangset, Nødland, and Rommetvedt 2007 and Nicholson, Hoye, and Houlihan 2011.

[8] For government expenditures on sport, see Humphreys, Maresova, and Ruseski 2010.

[9] Berkowitz and Upton 2011.

The majority of adults agree that sport provides a source of fun and enjoyment (80%), can reduce youth crime and delinquency (84%), can teach valuable life lessons (80%), and can bring people together in ways that strengthen communities (76%).[10]

The survey did not ask about the relationship between sport and democratization per se, but the results leave little doubt that most Americans subscribe to the belief that sport plays a key role in maintaining a healthy democratic society in the United States.[11]

1.2. LOOKING FORWARD

Despite its importance, the relationship between sport and democratization has rarely been discussed in a systematic or entirely satisfactory fashion. All of the four views outlined earlier about the nature of that relationship have been intermittently defended or attacked, either explicitly or implicitly, but a methodical treatment of the subject does not appear to exist.

In addition, much of the earlier work on this subject has been vitiated by a number of terminological and methodological shortcomings, four of which merit specific mention. First, the words "democracy" and "democratization" can take on an enormous range of meanings, and discussion of the relationship between sport and democratization has sometimes been clouded by confusion resulting from the use of similar terms to designate disparate phenomena. Second, sport has frequently been treated as a monolithic phenomenon that has uniformly positive or negative effects, an approach that fails to consider the possibility that different kinds of sport might have different impacts on democratization or that even particular kinds of sport might have the capacity to both foster and inhibit democratization. Third, a considerable fraction of the work, scholarly and otherwise, supporting the idea that sport fosters democratization has suffered from a "black-box" problem, which is to say that it postulates a causal relationship without specifying mechanisms responsible for the presumed result. This has been a factor of some importance in the frequently skeptical reception that work has received. Fourth, most previous treatments of sport and democratization have worked within limited temporal horizons determined by a presentist bias, and that has impeded consideration of a range of material that can clarify many of the relevant issues.

My goals in this book are to formulate terminology and methodology more refined than that used in the past and to draw on a more temporally diverse collection of evidence in the service of exploring

---

[10] United States 2011, 3, 7, respectively.

[11] The view that sport is an essential training ground for democratic citizenship in America is nicely articulated in Gillespie 2010. For an earlier articulation of the same position, see Tunis 1941.

each of the four possible views of the relationship between sport and democratization. I will argue that certain kinds of sport do indeed foster societal democratization.

Chapter 2 lays the groundwork for what follows by considering four key terms: democratization, mass sport, vertical sport, and horizontal sport. Democratization is here defined as either a condition in which the balance between egalitarian and hierarchical relationships in a given situation is tilted strongly toward the former, or the process that brings such a balance into being, maintains it, or extends it further toward egalitarianism. Democratization can characterize a society as a whole as well as the specific sphere of sport. Although the participation of a small percentage of a society's populace in sport might conceivably contribute significantly to democratization on a societal level, participation on a mass scale is inherently more likely to do so and its effects are much easier to trace. It is, therefore, prudent to focus on mass sport, which can be defined as a situation in which large numbers of people from a broad socioeconomic spectrum are regularly involved in sport as participants and spectators. Another essential distinction is between what are here called horizontal and vertical sport. Horizontal sport is organized and conducted in an egalitarian fashion, vertical sport in a hierarchical fashion. The former tends to foster democratization, whereas the latter tends to inhibit it. The discussion in the remainder of the book thus concentrates on horizontal mass sport.

Chapter 3 is devoted to a review of previous work that has posited a causal connection between sport and democratization. This review, which starts with the American Progressives at the beginning of the twentieth century and finishes with the work of Robert Putnam at the end of that century, focuses on familiarizing the reader with methodologies that have been used in the study of sport and democratization. Functionalism, which stresses the interconnection between activities in various spheres of any given society, is given particular attention because it implicitly or explicitly lies at the heart of virtually all scholarly work on the relationship between democratization in sport and society.

Chapter 4 explores one possible view of the relationship between sport and democratization, namely that democratization in society is cause, and democratization in sport effect. This view rests on the ideas that the nature of sport reflects and is determined by the nature of the society in which it is played and that the nature of sport has little or no effect on the nature of society. We will see that sport does indeed reflect society, but that sport also affects society, by shaping the behavior of participants and spectators both on the playing field and off it.

Chapter 5 probes the possibility that democratization in sport contributes meaningfully to the democratization of society. It identifies and, on the basis of evidence from modern-day democratized societies in Europe, North America, and Australasia, substantiates the operation of four separate mechanisms by means of which horizontal mass sport fosters democratization in society:

- the facilitation of the formation of small-scale, tightly bonded horizontal groups that literally enact democratization;
- the cultivation of particularized and generalized trust;
- the cultivation of a sense of political efficacy;
- the cultivation of self-disciplined individuals with a predisposition to obey rules and legally constituted authorities.

It is argued that these mechanisms are operative in all societies with horizontal mass sport.

Chapter 6 examines the possibility that sport inhibits societal democratization. It shows that horizontal mass sport can engender docility, exclusion, hostility, and status differentials and, as a result, has the capacity to act as an impediment to democratization. Here again, the effects of horizontal mass sport appear to be independent of historical context.

Chapter 7 takes up the problem of assessing the cumulative impact of the various components of the relationship between democratization in sport and society. The preceding discussion shows that sport both reflects and shapes society and that horizontal mass sport can both foster and inhibit democratization. This means that democratization in sport is to some extent a reflection of democratization in society, but that horizontal mass sport also has the capacity to exert an influence on democratization in society as a whole, both positively and negatively.

The capacity of horizontal mass sport to both foster and inhibit democratization alters the nature of the inquiry because it means that considering the relationship between democratization in sport and society becomes in large part a matter of determining overall effect. In other words, the question becomes whether horizontal mass sport, *on balance*, helps or hinders democratization at the societal level.

The sheer complexity of the interactions involved and the lack of suitable quantitative data make it impossible to establish the relative weight of each relevant factor and on that basis reach a conclusion about the overall effect of horizontal mass sport on societal democratization. There are, however, a variety of different ways of evaluating the relative efficacy of the various mechanisms by means of which horizontal mass sport promotes and inhibits societal democratization. Horizontal mass sport has the capacity to facilitate the formation of a plethora of tightly bonded, egalitarian groups, which exert a powerful democratizing effect on society that is not easily counteracted. In addition, four of the mechanisms by means of which sport fosters and inhibits societal democratization form two antithetical pairs, and the relative strength of the mechanisms within these pairs can be established with some confidence. In both instances, the positive effects of sport on democratization appear to outweigh its negative effects. Further clarity can be achieved by studying outcomes, which means looking at democratization in societies with horizontal mass sport.

Data from the present day shows a strong correlation between rates of participation in horizontal sport and levels of societal democratization, which suggests that horizontal mass sport fosters societal democratization. This data is not, however, conclusive because it cannot show how that correlation came into being. More persuasive evidence can be found in data from countries that in recent decades have instituted government-sponsored programs to increase sport participation. In those countries, increasing levels of participation in horizontal sport show a strong positive correlation with increasing levels of societal democratization. However, here again there are interpretive difficulties. If, as hypothesized, democratization in society and sport are mutually determinative, the influence of society on sport is particularly strong in instances in which increases in sport participation are the product of official sport-for-all programs. In such instances, the correlation between democratization in sport and society may well be largely the product of the influence of society on sport.

The most illuminating cases, therefore, are those in which significant changes in participation in horizontal sport have occurred without government intervention. Due to the relative rarity of mass sport until recently, there are only two obvious examples of that occurring: Greece in the sixth and fifth centuries BCE and Britain in the nineteenth century CE. In both of those times and places systems of horizontal mass sport emerged spontaneously, and they thus represent essential test cases for the relationship between democratization in sport and society. The United States in the first half of the twentieth century represents a similar but not identical case. In that instance horizontal mass sport emerged in the absence of an official sport-for-all program, but due in part to a mix of private and public initiatives intended to increase sport participation.

Chapters 8–16 thus contain detailed historical case studies of democratization in sport and society in Greece and Britain. Two other historical examples of mass sport are examined in a more cursory fashion in Chapters 10 and 14: Germany, where mass sport before World War II was primarily vertical, and the United States. Taken together these chapters provide an outline of the early history of mass sport. The absence of detailed statistical information for all of these times and places makes it difficult to establish the level of societal democratization directly, and so democratization is tracked primarily through changes in political institutions and practices. Such changes do not represent the only or even the most important form of democratization, but they are, given the available evidence, the most easily documented form of democratization and offer a useful if imperfect proxy for democratization broadly construed. As will become obvious, whereas Chapters 2–7 have a strong tincture of the sociology of sport, Chapters 8–16 are more typical exercises in sport history in particular and social history in general.

The result of these case studies is clear: in Greece, Britain, and the United States the emergence of horizontal mass sport, and the resulting democratization of sport, were closely associated with powerful democratizing trends in society as a whole. In Greece and Britain horizontal mass sport fostered societal democratization, by means of the four mechanisms identified earlier, and by three further, contextually specific means: by serving as an arena for meritocratic status competition that undermined systems of ascribed rank, by serving as a model of and for emergent horizontal relationships, and by promoting group closure. The cumulative effect of these mechanisms appears to have outweighed the inhibiting effect of the docility, exclusion, hostility, and status differentials generated by horizontal mass sport. In Germany, vertical mass sport was associated with a strongly authoritarian sociopolitical system.

In Chapter 17 the preceding discussion is summarized, and the four possible views of the relationship between democratization in sport and society are assessed. One of those views, that democratization in both society as a whole and in sport is determined by one or more exogenous factors such as industrialization, urbanization, capitalism, Protestantism, or modernization, is addressed. This view can be evaluated relatively simply because none of the exogenous factors that have been suggested as determinative of democratization in society and sport were operative in ancient Greece. The fact that the correlation between democratization in sport and society held good in that context strongly suggests that democratization in society and sport are not determined by an exogenous factor.

The other three views of the relationship between democratization in sport and society are all at least partially valid and all need to be taken into consideration to formulate a nuanced understanding of that relationship. I will argue that:

- democratization in sport reflects, but is not entirely determined by, democratization in society;
- horizontal mass sport can, in and of itself, be an important form of democratization;
- horizontal mass sport can both foster and inhibit democratization on a societal level, but its cumulative effect is significantly weighted to the former; horizontal mass sport thus reinforces democratization in society as a whole.

It is important to bear in mind that it is impossible to achieve complete certainty about the relationship between democratization in sport and society. There can be no doubt that democratization in sport reflects democratization in society and that the level of democratization in society is influenced by a variety of factors. It remains possible that democratization in sport either has no significant effect on democratization in society or actually inhibits societal democratization and that the consistent correlation between increases in democratization in society and sport is solely the result of the effect of society on sport. The evidence does not appear to support this interpretation, but it cannot be excluded entirely. In order to do so, it would be necessary to run something like a series of experiments in which the level of societal democratization was measured after repeatedly adding or subtracting horizontal mass sport to or from otherwise identical societies. That is, of course, not within the realm of possibility; as E. P. Thompson noted, history "affords no laboratory for experimental verification." Here, as in almost all cases involving complex societal interactions, the most one can hope for is what Weber called "a particularly plausible hypothesis."[12]

Despite these interpretive challenges, the evidence pertaining to sport and democratization makes it possible to reach something that could reasonably be described as a particularly plausible hypothesis. The existence of seven separate mechanisms by means of which sport can foster societal democratization, the relative weighting of the mechanisms by means of which sport promotes and impedes democratization, and the consistent correlation between increases in democratization in sport and in society all strongly support the conclusion that democratization in sport has a significant positive effect on democratization in society. There is nothing particularly surprising about that conclusion insofar as it posits that an activity involving a great deal of cooperative, face-to-face interaction possesses democratizing capacity, which aligns with a well-established school of thought rooted in Tocqueville's work on American democracy. Furthermore, in positing a connection between activities in different spheres of society, this conclusion aligns with the basic tenets of functionalism, one of the most widely used methodologies in the social sciences. It is in fact probably fair to say that the conclusion that horizontal mass sport does *not* have a positive effect on societal democratization would be significantly more surprising and difficult to defend than the conclusion that it does so. There is, therefore, good reason to believe that horizontal mass sport is indeed a school for democracy.

[12] E. P. Thompson 1995 (1978), 51; Weber 1962, 37.

2

Terms and Concepts

2.1. DEMOCRATIZATION

Defining "democratization" would seem to be a straightforward task in that it can be understood as referring to a process that brings democracy into being. The immediate difficulty, however, is that "democracy" is an enormously complicated concept. A standard approach is to define democracy in institutional terms and, more specifically, as a form of government characterized by equality with respect to decision-making processes. A good example of this approach can be found in the work of David Beetham, who writes:

Democracy I take to be a mode of decision-making about collectively binding rules and policies over which the people exercise control, and the most democratic arrangement to be that where all members of the collectivity enjoy effective equal rights to take part in such decision-making directly – one that is to say, which realizes to the greatest conceivable degree the principles of popular control and equality in its exercise. Democracy should properly be conceptualized as lying at one end of a spectrum, the other end of which is a system of rule where the people are totally excluded from the decision-making process and any control over it.[1]

From this perspective democratization is an attempt "to subject government to popular control and to make states work in ways that favor the broad mass of the people."[2]

A major difficulty with the institutionalist approach to defining democracy and democratization is that it ignores the important ramifications of nonpolitical forms of inequality on two separate levels. First, it fails to take into account the political effects of spheres of activity that are not overtly

---

[1] Beetham 1992, 40. There is a considerable body of work that adopts the same perspective but that also provides detailed lists of institutional prerequisites for identifying a state as democratic. For perhaps the best known work of this type, see Dahl 1971 and Dahl 1989.

[2] Grugel 2002, 1.

political. For example, two citizens of an institutionally democratic state that enjoy identical political rights but who have very different levels of economic resources at their command have very different capacities to exert control over the state's political processes. Gender is another relevant issue; a highly patriarchal social system can deeply undercut notional political equality even in a nation with the sort of political institutions associated with democracy, including universal adult suffrage. Second, the institutionalist approach implies that the significant exercise of power is limited to the political realm, but there has been a growing recognition in recent decades that power is diffused throughout a social structure and is present in virtually all human relationships. Foucault, for instance, argued that:

> This problem of power…is too often reduced…to the problem of sovereignty.…Between every point of a social body, between a man and a woman, between the members of a family, between a master and his pupil, between every one who knows and every one who does not, there exist relations of power which are not purely and simply a projection of the sovereign's great power over the individual; they are rather the concrete, changing soil in which the sovereign's power is grounded, the conditions that make it possible to function.[3]

Fundamental inequalities in the exercise of power can, therefore, exist among the citizens of a state with impeccable democratic machinery.

The shortcomings of the institutionalist approach suggest an alternative approach, in which democracy is seen, not as a system of government, but as a commitment to equality that is enacted throughout a society. John Dunn has pointed out that the latter approach:

> is bound to attach special weight to the sense that democracy can only be adequately seen not as a form in which individual states are or are not governed, but as a political value, or a standard for justifiable political choice, against which not merely state structures, but every other setting or milieu in which human beings live, can and should be measured. Democracy, so viewed, promises (or threatens) the democratization of everything (work, sex, the family, dress, food, demeanor, choice by everyone over anything which affects any number of others). What it entails is the elimination of every vestige of privilege from the ordering of human life. It is a vision of how humans could live with one another, if they did so in a context from which injustice had been eradicated.[4]

One might, therefore, choose to define democracy in a way that requires not only political equality, but also equality in all other dimensions of social existence. Such a definition has the advantage of recognizing that each society is a complex, interdependent web of relationships in which personal and institutional interconnections that involve the exercise of power exist in a variety of different forms. It has the disadvantage of setting a very

---

[3] Foucault 1980, 187.
[4] Dunn 2005, 168–69.

high standard for identifying a state as a democracy. Indeed, defined in those terms it is debatable whether there are any democratic states anywhere in the globe. From this perspective democratization would require "socio-economic reform, cultural and social change, and a transformation in gender relations" of a particularly thoroughgoing kind.[5]

The understanding of democracy and democratization adopted here acknowledges the importance of aspects of society that are not overtly political while remaining agnostic as to the precise kinds and degrees of equality that must be achieved in order to label a society as democratic.

This will be done by conceiving of societies as mixtures of vertical and horizontal relationships. Vertical relationships are hierarchical and unequal; the parties (either individuals or groups) involved have very different degrees of social power (the ability to affect the behavior and beliefs of others). The dominant party in the relationship is in a position, in some if not all instances, to compel the subordinate party to comply with its wishes. Horizontal relationships are nonhierarchical and involve individuals or groups that are on a relatively equal footing with respect to social power. The parties in the relationship can influence each other's behavior by interacting in a cooperative and collaborative manner that emphasizes solidarity, trust, and reciprocity. Although horizontal relationships are by definition significantly more egalitarian than vertical relationships, they do not necessarily involve parties with identical statuses or social power. Indeed, horizontal relationships frequently include a considerable degree of fluidity, springing in large measure from meritocratic competition. Individuals or groups can move up and down a status and power hierarchy, with the critical caveat that at no point do any of the parties involved accumulate sufficient social power to dominate the others.[6] (Should that happen the relationship obviously becomes vertical rather than horizontal in nature.)

Both horizontal and vertical relationships are present in all societies; the key issue is the balance between the two. Consider, for example, France in the decades immediately preceding the revolution of 1789. This was an unusually vertical society, but horizontal relationships did exist, both among members of subordinate groups and among members of the aristocracy. A good contrasting example can be found in the Scandinavian social democracies of the present day, in which horizontal relationships are prevalent, but in which significant social inequalities persist and in which the election of governmental representatives necessarily creates vertical relationships, albeit temporary ones.

Democratization will be conceptualized here in two ways: as either a condition in which the balance between egalitarian and hierarchical

---

[5] Grugel 2002, 5.

[6] For clear, concise delineations of horizontal and vertical relationships, see K. Davis 1980 (1936), 161–63 and Granovetter 2002, 35–38.

relationships in a given situation is tilted strongly toward the former, or the process that brings such a balance into being, maintains it, or extends it further toward egalitarianism. The two senses of the term are closely related because democratization as a condition is both brought into being and sustained by democratization as a process. Incessant societal change, not least in the form of birth and death, means that relationships, and hence the condition of democratization, need to be constantly renewed. In other words, democratization as a condition, even in times and places where the balance between horizontal and vertical relationships is static, depends upon democratization as a process.

This understanding of democratization is based on Robert Putnam's work on the functioning of democratic institutions in modern-day Italy. Putnam found that democratic institutions were, by a variety of different measures, much more effective in northern than in southern Italy. He argued that this was because northern Italy had a highly developed civic community "marked by an active, public-spirited citizenry, by egalitarian political relations, by a social fabric of trust and cooperation" and by "networks of civic engagement…[that] represent intense horizontal interaction."[7] Putnam found that southern Italy, on the other hand, was "cursed with vertically structured politics, a social life of fragmentation and isolation, and a culture of distrust." He concluded that "these differences in civic life turn out to play a key role in explaining institutional success."[8]

If one adopts an understanding of democracy as a commitment to equality in all spheres of social life, a shift from vertical toward horizontal relationships outside of the governmental sphere in and of itself represents a form of democratization. In addition, there is, as Putnam points out, good reason to believe that democratization in one sphere of activity can eventuate in democratization in other spheres, including overtly political activities.

2.2. MASS SPORT

"Mass sport" is impossible to define without first defining "sport." It has proven difficult for scholars to agree upon a definition for "sport," and, in view of the large number of different forms sport can take, it is probably true that no one definition is appropriate for all times and places. In his book on the birth of modern sport in the Western world, *Ritual to Record*, Allen Guttmann proposes a definition that works well for the

---

[7] Putnam, Leonardi, and Nanetti 1993, 15, 173, respectively.

[8] Putnam, Leonardi, and Nanetti 1993, 15. Putnam was not, of course, the first to draw a connection between relationships in civil society and governmental form and functioning. That line of thought goes back at least as far as Tocqueville and was continued in the twentieth century in the work of Sidney Verba and others. See the discussion in Section 3.5.

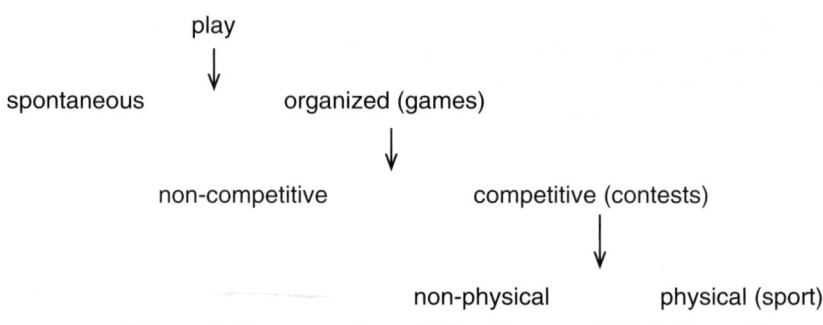

FIGURE 2. Schematic Representation of Allen Guttmann's Definition of Sport

subject matter covered here.[9] Guttmann starts by differentiating between two kinds of play, spontaneous and organized (see Figure 2). He labels organized play "games" and identifies two kinds of games, noncompetitive and competitive. He assigns the term "contests" to competitive games and finds two categories of contests, intellectual and physical. Sport is defined as physical contests. In the discussion that follows we will use Guttmann's definition of sport, with one difference. Under the heading of sport we will also put physical activities that are directly based on sport or that are undertaken in preparation for competition. Sport thus includes such things as someone throwing a football informally with a few friends and someone lifting weights in order to compete more successfully in organized games of football.

A few further nuances require brief discussion. Guttmann in fact uses the term "sports" instead of "sport." The latter is employed here because it avoids unnecessary confusion between the larger phenomenon of physical contests on one hand and specific activities on the other. Hence, "sport" designates physical contests and closely related activities in a general sense, and "sports" designates individual activities, such as rugby, that fall under the heading of sport. The terms "sport" and "athletics," which are sometimes assigned different meanings, are used interchangeably throughout the rest of the text, simply for the sake of variety. Finally, we will also look at activities positioned along the continuum stretching from sport to military

[9] Guttmann 1978, 1–14. Philosophers of sport have had an extended and still unresolved debate over defining the terms "sport," "sports," "athletics," and so on. The articles collected in Holowchak 2002, 7–98 offer a good sense of the range of definitions that have been proposed. Much has been made of the differences between activities that are overtly competitive and those that are not, between "sport" and "recreation." A more inclusive understanding of sport is, however, more appropriate for present purposes, and, in any case, there is much to be said for Richard Holt's refusal to draw a line between sport and recreation on the grounds that "we commonly use the word 'sport' to refer both to casual play and to the highest levels of performance" (Holt 1992, 10). Furthermore, the trend in recent scholarship has been to employ a more inclusive understanding of sport (Malcolm 2012, 155–56).

drill; these activities consist of regimented forms of physical exertion that do not fit neatly under the heading of sport because the element of play is largely absent and because they are typically conducted in a noncompetitive fashion. They are, however, closely related to sport in that they represent organized, physical actions and in that some elements of them are frequently incorporated into sport. Two examples of such activities are choral dance in ancient Greece and gymnastics as practiced in nineteenth-century Germany.

Mass sport can be defined as a situation in which large numbers of people from a broad socioeconomic spectrum are regularly involved in sport as participants and spectators.[10] With respect to the study of the relationship between sport and democratization, the element of participation is essential. Of the three basic elements in sport practice – participation, organization, and spectatorship – participation has the most powerful and direct effect on shaping behavior, and democratization requires active participation by a society's populace in shaping their own lives. As a result, a society with mass spectatorship of sport but without mass participation in it, would not, as the term is used here, be a society with mass sport.

Some sort of sport seems to be part of every known human society,[11] but even in places where mass sport exists involvement in athletics is never universal. The presence or absence of mass sport does not, therefore, involve a contrast between societies in which everyone is involved in sport on one hand and no one is involved in sport on the other. There is, however, a fundamental difference in the quantity of time, energy, and money that societies with mass sport invest in athletics. Some statistics may help clarify this point. Mass sport clearly exists in the modern-day United States. In 2009–10 roughly half of all American high school students played organized sports, with the total number of high school athletes reaching nearly 7.5 million. In 2006, 25 million Americans participated in organized softball, and there were 24 million tennis players. In 2008, college football teams sold 44 million tickets, college basketball teams 43 million. In the same year, the four major professional sports leagues – baseball, football, basketball, and hockey – sold nearly 140 million tickets and had a combined total revenue of roughly $18 billion. Sporting goods manufacturers sold $66 billion

[10] Three essential insights – that mass sport is relatively rare historically, that it existed in ancient Greece, and that it did not, after its disappearance from the Greek world, re-emerge again until the nineteenth century – are taken from a single, invaluable article by H. W. Pleket (Pleket 1998). These insights are mentioned in passing as part of a discussion of sport in Asia Minor in the Roman period and are not further developed elsewhere in Pleket's extensive body of scholarship. It is a pleasure to acknowledge the importance of these insights, while, for better or worse, taking responsibility for how they are used here.

[11] Susan Brownell notes that "sports, loosely defined, are found everywhere in the world in which anthropologists work" and points to the statement by the eminent ethnologist George Peter Murdock that sport is a human universal (Brownell 2000, 43).

worth of products in the United States in 2008.[12] In addition, American communities of all sizes continue to make massive investments in facilities for sport. To give but one example, the Department of Youth and Recreation for the city of Colorado Springs, Colorado (population 360,000) maintains six outdoor swimming facilities, two indoor pools, forty-five tennis courts, seventy-seven soccer fields, eighty basketball courts, and over one hundred softball and baseball fields.[13]

Societies with mass sport pour substantial fractions of the resources at their disposal into athletics. This is not simply a matter of having a surplus to spend, because virtually every society has some resources beyond the bare minimum needed for survival. Most societies have historically used only a small portion of their surplus resources on sport, whereas a few have spent lavishly on constructing a system in which a substantial fraction of the populace is regularly involved in sport.

Mass sport is such a familiar feature of the modern world that it is easy to lose sight of how rare it has been historically. Mass sport first came into being in ancient Greece in the sixth century BCE. Greek families that could afford the expense hired tutors to teach their sons how to play sports. The typical Greek city provided training and competition facilities for its citizens and organized athletic contests with valuable prizes. For instance, by the end of the sixth century BCE Athens had three large-scale, publicly maintained exercise facilities and an unknowable but substantial number of smaller, privately owned facilities. The man who won the short footrace at the Panathenaic Games in Athens received a prize worth about $60,000, the runner-up took home well over $10,000. Athens rewarded its athletes who won a victory at the Olympic Games with a cash payment worth well over $100,000, as well as free meals for life in the town dining hall.[14] People spent literally months journeying from all over the Greek world to participate in and watch the Olympic Games. In the middle of the fifth century BCE, a new stadium was built at Olympia to hold more than 40,000 people, at a time when the city of Athens, the largest urban center in the Greek world, had a population of no more than 100,000. Mass sport remained characteristic of Greece until the gradual suppression of athletics due to the spread of Christianity. After the disappearance

[12] These data come from Plunkett Research, the U.S. Census Bureau, and the Women's Sport Foundation. See http://www.plunkettresearch.com/Industries/Sports/SportsStatistics/tabid/273/Default.aspx, http://www.census.gov/compendia/statab/, and http://www.womenss-portsfoundation.org/Content/Articles/Issues/Participation/M/~/media/Files/PDFs%20and%20other%20files%20by%20Topic/Issues/Participation/A/2007%202008%20HS%20Gap%20Chart.pdf.

[13] These figures come from Fullinwider 2006, 7.

[14] On the current-day value of the monetary rewards offered to Athenian athletic victors, see D. Young 1984, 115–33.

of mass sport in Greece at the end of the sixth century CE, it was unknown anywhere in Europe until it reappeared in Britain and Germany in the nineteenth century.[15]

The idea that mass sport was until recently the exception rather than the rule runs so directly counter to our lived experience that it may be difficult to accept. It is true beyond doubt that humans have played sports in many different times and places, sometimes quite seriously. But in the majority of those times and places one or more elements of mass sport have been missing. In many cases regular participation in sport was limited to a small part of the population, usually elites. Nonelites might play games casually but in a way that made sport into nothing more than an occasional pastime. In other cases, spectatorship existed on a grand scale but participation in sport was limited.

Ancient Rome is an example of a society with mass spectatorship but without mass sport. Roman citizens neither played sports in a serious way nor showed much interest in watching them. They did, however, prodigally expend resources in staging and attending public spectacles. The Colosseum and the hundreds of other amphitheaters built by the Romans were designed to allow comfortable viewing of performances put on mostly by condemned prisoners, war captives, and slaves, performances that had little to do with sport. In view of the frequently mortal consequences of the activities that took place in the Roman arena, the identification of gladiators as athletes and gladiatorial combat as a form of sport requires a problematic and probably unsustainable definition of sport, in which the element of play is absent.[16] The chariot races in the Circus Maximus and other places like it were wildly popular and much closer to being sports. However, these races were about the speed of the horses and daring of the drivers, not about the sort of direct, physical competition between humans that lies at the heart of sport. Moreover, here again active participation was not something that held any attraction for respectable people. Roman citizens were found in the seats of amphitheaters and circuses, not on the arena floor or on the track.[17]

The evidence at our disposal makes it possible but not certain that something approximating mass sport may have existed in a handful of times and places other than those discussed here. A particularly well-known example

---

[15] For an overview of athletics in ancient Greece, see Miller 2004a and Miller 2004b. On athletics in ancient Athens, see Kyle 1987. On the monetary rewards of athletic success in ancient Athens, see D. Young 1984, 115–27. On the stadium at Olympia, see Romano 1993, 17–24. On the population of Athens, see Hansen 2006. Athens as an entire political unit probably had a population of about 200,000, about half of whom lived not in the city of Athens but in the surrounding countryside. For more on Greek sport, see the discussion in Chapters 8 and 9.

[16] For an exploration of gladiatorial combat as a sport, see Golden 2008, 68–104.

[17] On sport and spectacle in ancient Rome, see Kyle 2007, 251–339.

is Mesoamerica and the Mesoamerican ballgame. Various versions of that game, which had some similarities with modern soccer, basketball, and volleyball, were played for nearly 3,000 years starting around 1500 BCE. The remains of 1,700 ballcourts spread over much of Central America and ceramic models showing courts surrounded by spectators attest to the popularity of the game. However, in at least some versions of the game, players were habitually victims of human sacrifice at the end of the contest, and this suggests that it may have had more in common with Roman gladiatorial combats than ancient Greek or modern-day sport. There is thus unambiguous evidence for mass sport in only three times and places before the twentieth century: ancient Greece, and Britain and Germany in the nineteenth century.[18]

2.3. HORIZONTAL AND VERTICAL SPORT

When it comes to democratization, not all sport is created equal. A pair of contrasting examples will help illustrate this point. In a recent study of a group of seven elite Australian female gymnasts, Natalie Barker-Ruchti and Richard Tinning concluded that their athletic training prevented the gymnasts "from developing independence and self-determination. Instead they developed into docile athletes."[19] Compare this conclusion with the following passage from a memoir published in 1983 by Caryl Rivers, about playing basketball in high school:

To play basketball in the '50s was to step out of woman's inherited role, to cast off docility for ferocity, to control, if not your destiny, at least the arc of one particular piece of cowhide for a slice of eternity. Even as I made the sign of the cross, I knew damn well that it was my own control that would seal the fate of the foul shot, and Divine Will had precious little to do with it. If you have played basketball – really played it with pride and passion – you can never really be docile again.[20]

Any analysis of the relationships embedded in sport and of the effects of sport on athletes and spectators needs to take this sort of complexity into account. The difficulty is finding a degree of nuance that does justice to that complexity without getting lost in a sea of details. In the discussion that follows this challenge is addressed by differentiating between what are here labeled horizontal and vertical sport.

   This system of categorization is employed because it is helpful in exploring the connection between sport and democratization. It focuses attention on the nature of the relationships fostered by sport and on the form of sports

---

[18] On the Mesoamerican ballgame, see Scarborough and Wilcox 1991. On the date of the emergence of mass sport in the United States, see Chapter 16.

[19] Barker-Ruchti and Tinning 2010, 243.

[20] Rivers 1983, 311.

activity, participation, that has the most powerful and direct effect on shaping behavior. Organization and spectatorship will not be ignored entirely, but will not be treated with the same degree of detail as participation.

The use of this system of categorization should not be understood as an implicit statement that this is the only possible or useful means of breaking down the kaleidoscopic complexity of sport into more analytically manageable pieces. Although the number of different categories that could be used to subdivide sport is not infinite, it is certainly quite large. Different systems of categorization are helpful in answering different questions.[21]

At the most basic level, horizontal and vertical sport can be understood as enshrining horizontal and vertical relationships, respectively. That is, horizontal sport embodies egalitarian relationships, whereas vertical sport embodies hierarchical relationships.

It is essential to bear in mind that horizontal and vertical sport are concepts formulated in the tradition of Weberian ideal-types. They represent two ends of a spectrum, and no real-world sports activity is purely horizontal or vertical; put another way, all sport partakes of both the horizontal and the vertical. The balance between the two can be influenced by a variety of factors, including such things as the sport in question, how a sport is played in a given time and place, and the inclinations of coaches.

Of particular interest here is the balance between the horizontal and vertical elements in any particular sports activity, how this shapes relationships, and the concomitant effects on democratization. Sports activities in which the balance is tilted strongly toward the horizontal are the site of egalitarian relations that promote democratization. Sports activities in which the balance is tilted strongly toward the vertical are the site of hierarchical relations that inhibit democratization.

In order to differentiate between horizontal and vertical sport it will be helpful to have a list of criteria that distinguish one from the other (see Table 1). These criteria can be clarified further by applying them to two examples of sport, both taken from nineteenth-century Britain. Starting in the middle of the nineteenth century a number of modern sports such as soccer and rugby began to take shape at elite boarding schools in England. In 1845, the students at the Rugby School drew up the first set of written rules for a game that they called "foot-ball" and that had been regularly played at the school for a considerable period of time. These rules, which formed the basis of the game that eventually became rugby, were produced at the initiative of the students themselves, through a formal democratic process. Rugby students had a system of holding assemblies to deal with issues of concern to them, and the 1845 rules were drafted by an assembly of the oldest students at the school and were ratified by an assembly of all the boys in the upper

---

[21] A brief discussion, with helpful bibliography, of various means of dividing sport into analytically useful subcategories can be found in Heinemann 1992, 383.

TABLE 1. *Characteristics of Horizontal and Vertical Sport*

	Horizontal Sport	Vertical Sport
Organizational Structure	Organizers and participants are either one and the same or have similar status or social power	Organizers have significantly more status or social power than participants
Degree of Regimentation in Playing of Sport	Low (emphasis on autonomy of participants)	High (emphasis on conformity among participants)
Stated Goals	Emphasis on benefits to individual participants	Emphasis on benefits to collectivities such as the state

grades. The rules included enforcement mechanisms that relied entirely on the players themselves; Rule XXIV stated that "Heads of sides, or two deputies appointed by them, are the sole arbiters of all disputes."[22]

Although these rules imposed some limits on the players' freedom of action, those limits were minimal and games were in practice chaotic, frequently violent affairs, as is evident from an illustration that was published in 1845 (see Figure 3). The freedom of action enjoyed on the foot-ball fields at Rugby is described vividly by Thomas Hughes, who attended Rugby from 1834 to 1842 and who wrote the classic novel *Tom Brown's Schooldays*. Tom Brown finds foot-ball matches to be wild free-for-alls punctuated by breaks for snacks and beverages, including beer.[23]

As one might expect, Rugby students were not prone to philosophizing on the goals they pursued in playing sport, but Hughes did have some things to say on the subject. After Tom Brown has a brutal fistfight with an opponent named Slogger Williams, Hughes offers the following advice to his readers:

Learn to box, then, as you learn to play cricket and foot-ball. Not one of you will be the worse, but very much the better for learning to box well. Should you never have to use it in earnest, there's no exercise in the world so good for the temper, and for the muscles of the back and legs.

When Tom Brown is about to graduate, he tells one of his teachers that foot-ball has helped him learn discipline and how to cooperate effectively with others.[24]

[22] On the creation of the Rugby rules of 1845, see Dunning and Sheard 2005, 75–84. For further discussion, see Sections 11.5 and 12.3.
[23] Hughes 1858 (1857), 121.
[24] Hughes 1858 (1857), 334, 394, respectively.

FOOT BALL AT RUGBY.—(SEE NEXT PAGE.)

FIGURE 3. "Foot Ball at Rugby" Engraving (From the *Illustrated London News*, December 20, 1845)

A counterpoint to foot-ball at the Rugby School can be found in the physical activities of students in publicly funded schools in Britain. These schools, which were populated primarily by children from working-class families, were overseen by members of the upper class, and neither the students nor their families were given much of a voice in their operation. Over the course of the nineteenth century it became increasingly common that students in these schools were required to participate in military drill or highly regimented forms of gymnastics (typically of one of two types, German or Swedish). A student who went to a publicly funded school in the 1870s later recalled:

When…a boy in my ninth year, I marched with the boys of my own class to a small village drill hall…once a week, for a half hour's drill under the direction of an ex-military sergeant….The instructions consisted in "standing to attention," "standing at ease," "standing easy," "falling in," "falling out," "dressing in line," "eyes right," "eyes left," "eyes front," "left turning," "right turning," "about turning," "slow marching," "quick marching," "double marching," "halting," "right wheeling," "left wheeling," "about wheeling," "breaking off," "numbering," etc. You can easily imagine that to boys such as we were, novel as this seemed in the first few lessons, it soon became unbearably boring, and we had to relieve the monotony by naughtiness.[25]

Some sense of what Swedish gymnastics looked like can be had from Figure 4, which reproduces a picture taken in a publicly funded English school in the early part of the twentieth century.

[25] On the history of physical education in nineteenth-century Britain, see McIntosh 1968, 11–142. The quote given here comes from pages 109–10 of McIntosh's book. On the specific subject of drill and its use in British schools in the closing decades of the nineteenth century, see also Mangan and Hickey 2006. For further discussion, see Section 14.3.

FIGURE 4. Swedish Gymnastics at the Hague Street School, Miles Platting, Manchester, 1911 (DPA 301/1 from the Documentary Photo Archive, reproduced with permission from Greater Manchester County Record Office)

Drill and gymnastics were overtly intended as a means of reinforcing hierarchical relationships between school authorities and students and of rendering the students obedient and in this way securing the prevailing social order. J. P. Kay (later Sir James Kay-Shuttleworth) and E. Carleton Tufnell, in an 1839 report on a publicly funded school for children of paupers, noted that the students were given regimented exercises "to introduce regularity into the movement of so large a body of children, to secure prompt obedience to the direction of the teacher, and to maintain personal cleanliness and propriety." Kay observed that "the moral training pervades every hour of the day, from the period when the children are marched from their bedrooms to the washhouse in the morning, to that when they march back to their bedrooms at night."[26] In 1862 Lord Elcho speaking in Parliament proposed that the government supply funds to provide drill and gymnastics in schools that served the poor. He noted that military drill was already being given to boys in some schools of this sort in London and stated that he himself had visited one such school:

in which children of the very lowest and most criminal class...were being educated, and it was really astonishing to see what tidy, obedient, orderly, and respectable boys the military training to which they were subjected made them.[27]

Foot-ball at the Rugby School involved participants organizing and policing their own sports activity and engaging in a sport that gave athletes

[26] Quoted in Hurt 1977, 169.
[27] Parliament 1862, 24.

a great deal of autonomy and that was understood to benefit the individual players. Foot-ball embodied and fostered egalitarian relationships and is thus a particularly clear-cut instance of horizontal sport. Drill and gymnastics involved the imposition of activities by members of the upper class on frequently unwilling students from the working class, activities that left individuals very little autonomy and the benefits of which were felt to accrue to society as a whole. Drill and gymnastics embodied and fostered hierarchical relationships and are thus particularly clear-cut instances of vertical sport.

Drill does not represent sport per se, but it and similar activities merit attention because they are intensely physical practices that are frequently paired with sport and that clearly manifest vertical tendencies that are present in all but the most horizontal sport. The essence of drill is highly synchronized movement by the members of a group in response to verbal commands. Drill continues to be a staple activity for training soldiers because it is highly effective in creating a sense of unity and a disciplined habit of instant obedience. The United States Army issues a 277-page long field manual on drill and ceremonies, which includes the following observations:

The purpose of drill is to enable a commander or non-commissioned officer to move his unit from one place to another in an orderly manner, to aid in disciplinary training by instilling habits of precision and response to the leader's orders; and to provide for the development of all soldiers in the practice of commanding troops.

Once the elements of discipline have been instilled through drill on the parade square, it develops, naturally, into various forms of crew drill, gun drill, and battle drill but the aim of discipline remains unchanged. This aim is the conquest of fear. Drill helps to achieve this because when it is carried out men tend to lose their individuality and are unified into a group under obedience to orders. If men are to give their best in war they must be united. Discipline seeks through drill to instill into all ranks this sense of unity, by requiring them to obey orders as one man.[28]

Drill thus serves an important purpose in adjusting individual behavior to suit the needs of a hierarchical system.[29]

There is a spectrum of activities that stretch from drill to horizontal sport, in all of which there is an emphasis on the inculcation of hierarchy and obedience through coordinated group movement instigated by verbal commands issued by an authority figure. German gymnastics,

---

[28] Department of the Army 2003, Sections 1–1 and 10–1, respectively. The second passage is a quote from General Sir Harold Alexander.

[29] The observed effects of synchronized activity by large numbers of people may have a biological basis. Ethological studies suggest that rhythmic movement by groups of humans can elevate social cohesion by triggering physiological responses that lower inhibitions that normally restrain contact between individuals and that may in turn render individuals more susceptible to demands made upon them. This subject has been only cursorily studied so any conclusions are preliminary and speculative. See d'Aquili and Laughlin Jr. 1979.

FIGURE 5. Coach Danny Diceanu Looks on as the Boys' Soccer Team at Franklin Monroe High School in Arcanum, Ohio, Does Caterpillar Pushups, 2010 (From Coach Danny Diceanu)

which took shape in the first half of the nineteenth century and bore a close resemblance to military drill, was part of the curriculum of German public schools almost from their inception, and became widely popular outside of Germany. Swedish gymnastics, which took shape at roughly the same time, was less overtly militaristic and was thought to be more suitable for females, but was still highly regimented. George Mélio's *Manual of Swedish Drill*, published in 1889, contains the following statement in its preface:

> The School Drill herein set forth has been adopted to a very considerable extent in the English schools, where it has been found of great utility, not only as a purely physical exercise, but as one promoting cheerfulness, erectness of carriage and general alertness and promptitude in the school work. The whole tendency of the drill is to produce a love of order and an actual liking for discipline, lightening at once the teacher's labors and brightening and awakening the pupil.[30]

The program of mass calisthenics instituted by the Chinese government in the 1950s, which continues to operate in diluted form, is similar in many ways to German and Swedish gymnastics.[31]

[30] Mélio 1889, 5.
[31] On Chinese calisthenics, see Section 4.1.

All of this may seem temporally or spatially distant, but the same tendencies manifest themselves in much sports activity in the present day, typically more in training than in competition. A standard component of training for team sports is synchronized exercise by all members of the team at the command of their coaches. American football coaches have shown a consistent fondness for group calisthenics as a form of warm-up exercise. Another illustrative practice can be found in what are called caterpillar push-ups, in which the members of a team form a circle with their feet on each other's shoulders and do push-ups on command (see Figure 5). This practice is a useful reminder that horizontal sport virtually always has at least some vertical elements and that drill is not quite as different from sport as it might seem at first glance. The synchronization and regimentation of movement is not the only element of verticality in vertical sport, but it has particular importance and, as we will see, a long history.

3

Previous Work Positing a Causal Relationship between Sport and Democratization

The relationship between sport and democratization has been a subject of discussion for more than a century. Over the course of time, several different approaches to studying that relationship have come into being, and some degree of familiarity with those approaches is an indispensable prerequisite for any new research. What follows is by no means an exhaustive summary of all previous work, but rather a resumé of some key contributions and methodologies.

3.1. SOURCES OF SOCIAL ORDER

An exploration of the relationship between sport and democratization requires a basic grasp of the sources of social order. All societies must generate a system of interlocking institutions, practices, and norms that creates social order by shaping the behavior of individuals and hence enabling coordinated actions by large groups of people. There are, in abstract terms, a limited number of means for shaping individual behavior, and any argument positing a causal relationship between sport and democratization, which entails sport shaping behavior in particular ways, either explicitly or implicitly, presumes the involvement of one or more of those means.

To talk about social order raises an immensely complex set of questions that cannot be discussed in any sort of depth here. It is sufficient for our purposes to understand the problem in terms of the need to strike a balance between order and autonomy. Every society needs to find a way to get its members to adhere with some consistency to a set of explicit and implicit rules and expectations – thus ensuring order – while also leaving individuals a certain degree of freedom to do as they wish – thus granting them autonomy. Autonomy is essential because individual human beings do not typically enjoy having others control every detail of their lives, and they may resist, sometimes violently, attempts to impose that level of control on them. In addition, exerting that level of control requires the devotion of time and energy to micromanaging people's lives. It is, as a result, necessary to give individuals some freedom of action. Different societies strike different balances between order and autonomy. The most obvious examples are totalitarian societies with a powerful, centralized state on one hand, and liberal democracies that give their citizens a considerable amount of freedom on the other. Think North Korea and the United States; one emphasizes order, the other autonomy.[1]

Ensuring a sufficient level of compliance with rules and expectations, that is, with what are here called, for the sake of convenience, social rules, is a challenge that must be met by every society. R. P. Cuzzort puts it nicely: "A socio-cultural system cannot rely on random individual responses to create the structure and the cohesiveness required for organized effort. A society cannot, in other words, rely on people simply 'doing *their* thing.' A society must, in effect, generate ways that ensure that what gets done is 'society's thing.'"[2] It need hardly be said that social rules are not rigid prescriptions and that individuals choose from among various courses of action in any given situation. However, social rules do encourage some forms of behavior and inhibit others, and in so doing generate regular patterns of activity that form the basis of social order.

There are three basic ways that people are induced to obey social rules: socialization, consensus, and coercion.[3] Teaching children social rules virtually from birth, that is, socialization, goes a long way toward making those rules second nature to the point where people adhere to them literally without thinking about it. Consensus occurs when the members of a group come to broad agreement about social rules they will voluntarily obey and are rewarded for adherence to those rules and sanctioned for noncompliance. Coercion can range from the brutal to the subtle; it can take the form of pressure, threats, intimidation, or outright force, or it can be a gradual indoctrination in the habit of obeying rules and authority figures.[4] Every

---

[1] A discussion of the need to balance order and autonomy in the specific context of ancient Greece can be found in Farrar 1988. The existence of self-aware individuals capable of truly autonomous action has been called into question by thinkers such as Lacan and Foucault. This school of thought is not without interest, and it is quite probable that individuals in the Western world tend to imagine themselves as being significantly more autonomous than they are in reality. However, the concept of the self-aware individual capable of autonomous action is such a fundamental part of modern-day scholarship in the social sciences that there is no need to provide a lengthy defense of it here. A brief discussion of the issues can be found in Thomas May 1994. For a book-length treatment, see Dworkin 1988.

[2] Cuzzort 1989, 179.

[3] An excellent brief introduction to past and current thinking about the basis of social order can be found in Cohen 1968, 18–33. For a more up-to-date and scholarly work on the same subject, see Wrong 1994. For a collection of important pieces of earlier scholarship on social order, see Hechter and Horne 2009.

[4] The summary given here represents a modified version of the three standard schools of thought on societal order, which are typically called coercion theory (associated with Thomas

society uses a combination of varying kinds and degrees of socialization, consensus, and coercion to ensure compliance with social rules and hence order, without which it simply could not exist.

Democratization, especially when seen as a process rather than as a condition, generates large challenges in achieving social order. It entails the creation of horizontal relationships that require cooperation among individuals who function as relative equals; sustained conflict within the bounds of those relationships poses a fundamental threat to a democratized social order. This in practice means that groups small and large need to achieve some form of consensus, an end-point that can be particularly difficult to reach when, as is typically the case, horizontal relationships came into being in part because vertical relationships collapsed despite the best efforts of elites to defend the status quo. Vivid recollections of those late, lamented vertical relationships and lingering resistance can make cooperation and consensus elusive. The difficulties are further heightened because horizontal relationships typically encompass limited but meaningful differences in status and social power that regularly shift as the result of ongoing meritocratic competition and other processes of change. Shifts in the relative standing of individuals create resentments that can easily erode cooperation and consensus. Furthermore, as relationships move from vertical to horizontal and social and political privilege is diffused, those who have reaped the benefits of democratization become less liable to overt forms of coercion while also enjoying greater autonomy. Those individuals must learn how to manage

Hobbes), value-consensus theory (associated with Émile Durkheim and Talcott Parsons), and interest theory (associated with John Locke and Friedrich von Hayek). Coercion theory holds that societal order comes into being when people surrender some of their freedom to a state that they invest with coercive powers. Value-consensus theory holds that societal order exists primarily because people share norms and ways of thinking about the world. There are two variants of interest theory. One holds that order results from a consciously made "contract" between people who find it in their best interests to make certain binding social arrangements with each other. The other holds that order is an unintended consequence of people separately pursuing their own interests. The basic ideas of value-consensus theory are here put under the heading of socialization because this is the single most important means of transmitting and inculcating shared norms and ways of thinking about the world. The basic ideas of interest theory are here put under consensus because, whether people intentionally or unintentionally create social order in pursuing their interests, that order can only be sustained if they coordinate their actions and cooperate. That, in turn, requires that they implicitly or explicitly agree to adhere voluntarily to some set of norms, or, put another way, that they reach consensus. As von Hayek noted, societal order rests on individuals' "propensity to obey certain rules of conduct in which the order of action of the group as a whole rests" and "in any group of men of more than the smallest size, collaboration will always rest both on spontaneous order as well as on deliberate organization" (quoted in Hechter and Horne 2009, 147 and 149, respectively). Von Hayek was keenly aware that free choice, what is here called autonomy, can create order but cannot in and of itself sustain it. The approach used here in studying social order reflects our focus on locating the specific mechanisms by means of which sport fosters democratization.

that autonomy, which means learning how to exercise an enhanced degree of personal freedom within the bounds created by the social rules that govern the society in which they live. In sum, democratization means that consensus becomes more important as a basis for social order but also becomes more difficult to achieve and that overt coercion becomes less viable, at the same time that individual autonomy is increasing. Even when viewed from a purely institutionalist perspective, many democratization processes fail and are reversed. Hence the emphasis political scientists of an institutionalist bent put on the need to distinguish between pseudo-democracies, partial democracies, and consolidated democracies.[5]

3.2. THE AMERICAN PROGRESSIVES

Sport and democratization became a subject of regular discussion at a relatively late date, for the simple reason that mass sport and democracy were, until quite recently, exceedingly rare. Mass sport and forms of governance that could reasonably be labeled democratic were both widespread in the Greek world from the sixth through the fourth centuries BCE.[6] This was also a period in which Greeks produced a considerable corpus of political theory, and Plato and Aristotle, among others, gave careful thought to how education systems shaped political practice and to the role of sport in education.[7] No extended treatment of the relationship between sport and democratization is to be found in the extant Greek sources, but virtually no prodemocratic political theory survives from ancient Greece (neither Plato nor Aristotle were advocates for contemporary forms of democracy),[8] so it is entirely possible, even likely, that that topic received due consideration. After the end of the fourth century BCE, governance throughout Europe was more autocratic than democratic, and, leaving aside a brief florescence in some Italian city–states in the twelfth through fifteenth centuries, it was not until the eighteenth century CE that democracy again became a significant factor in Western political history.[9] By the end of the sixth century CE mass sport – which had always been something that remained peculiarly Greek – had gone out of existence, and although Europeans continued to play sports after the sixth century CE, they did so in a much more casual fashion and

---

5 Grugel 2002, 32–45.
6 As is evident from Section 2.1, it can be difficult to decide what should or should not be labeled a democracy, but there can be no doubt that the governments of many Greek communities fit most if not all definitions of democracy.
7 On the role of sport in education, see Aristotle *Politics* 1337a4–9a10; Plato *Laws* 764c-66c, 795e-66e, *Republic* 403d-12a.
8 See, however, Aristotle's comments on the relationship between sport and political systems, which are discussed in Section 10.1.
9 On the developmental trajectory of democratic governance in the Western world, see Dunn 2005 and the articles collected in Dunn 1992.

on a much smaller scale than had been the case in ancient Greece.[10] It was only in the second half of the nineteenth century that mass sport reappeared in Britain and Germany. It is, as a result, easy to understand why the relationship between sport and democratization was not a topic that attracted much attention for a long period of time.

Both mass sport and democratization were important features of the British social landscape of the second half of the nineteenth century, but Britons did not evince much interest in how sport might interact with democratization. Over the course of the nineteenth century, sport became increasingly common in Britain and was viewed in an increasingly positive light. A particularly important development was the emergence of Muscular Christianity, a belief that it was a religious duty to maintain a healthy, strong body, typically by means of playing sports, and that playing sports built personality traits and behavioral tendencies appropriate for good Christians. However, the idea that the relationship between sport and democratization was an important one did not take hold in Britain in the nineteenth century, perhaps because British sport was characterized by strong class-based divisions.[11]

It was members of the Progressive Movement in the United States who were responsible for popularizing the idea that sport could play an important role in fostering democratization. The Progressive Movement coalesced at the end of the nineteenth century in response to economic, political, and social problems created by industrialization and urbanization (among other things). One of the issues that exercised the minds of many Progressives was what they saw as an increasingly virulent dedication on the part of both individuals and corporations to the pursuit of their own selfish interests and a concomitant disdain for the common good. They were concerned that efforts to reform political and economic institutions would end in failure without a revival in what might be called civic virtue. For instance, in 1911 George Forbes, president of the Board of Education in Rochester, New York, published an article with the title "Buttressing the Foundations of Democracy," in which he wrote that:

No inborn endowment of a human being develops except in response to its appropriate stimulus....It is, therefore, an absolutely essential condition of democracy that the ethical spirit shall be aroused in the average citizen by appropriate stimulation. This can not be left to haphazard influences. The existing dominant influences are those which appeal to selfish instincts. Modern individualism with its "each for himself" has abnormally stimulated the spirit of unscrupulous competition on the one hand and monopolistic greed on the other. It has repressed and atrophied the sense of brotherhood and developed to an inordinate extent the selfish impulses....We are now intensely occupied in forging the tools of democracy, the direct primary, the initiative, the referendum, the recall, the short ballot, commission

---

[10] See Section 10.5 and Chapter 11.
[11] See the discussion in Chapters 11–12, 14–15.

government. But in our enthusiasm we do not seem to be aware that these tools will be worthless unless they are used by those who are aflame with the sense of brotherhood.[12]

Concerns about the disappearance of civic virtue were also grounded in the challenges presented by assimilating immigrants who were arriving in America in large numbers, frequently from places without anything resembling a democratic political culture.

Many Progressives became convinced that sport could be an important means for inculcating values that would help remedy America's social and political ills. The belief in the character-building capacity of sport enshrined in Muscular Christianity took hold in the United States at an early date, and Progressives took a logical step by connecting the character-building capacity of sport to democratization. Mark Dyreson, who has written insightfully about what came to be an almost religious dedication to sport on the part of Progressives, makes the case that:

Many Americans came to see sport as a powerful reform instrument that could revitalize their rapidly modernizing nation.... They announced that sport would reconstitute popular representative government, restore equity in American society, and rejuvenate public virtue. They argued that sport could create a common set of values. In short, in the grand tradition of American political philosophy, they made universal promises about the power of sport to reinvigorate the republican experiment.[13]

The idea that sport was a key source of civic virtue is found in much Progressive writing, including a 1910 article by Otto Mallery titled "Social Significance of Play": "It seems a far cry from the ideal of fair play in boys' games to the ideal of fair play in the political life of our democracy, yet it can be demonstrated that the ideals of fair play and team play are important in forming the character of a community."[14]

Some Progressives also portrayed sport as an important equalizing force that eroded class-based social distinctions and hence reinforced democracy. This is evident from Calvin Coolidge's assertion that:

In the case of a people which represents many nations, cultures, and races, as does our own, a unification of interests in recreations is bound to wield a telling influence for solidarity of the entire population. No more truly democratic force can be set off against the tendency to class and caste than the democracy of individual parts and prowess in sport.[15]

The Progressives' beliefs led them to create programs intended to democratize American sport by helping to make it available to people throughout the

---

[12] Forbes 1911, 590. On the history of the Progressive Movement, see McGerr 2003.

[13] Dyreson 1998, 3. Dyreson's book includes a thorough treatment of the subject of the Progressives and sport.

[14] Mallery 1910, 156.

[15] Coolidge 1926, 10.

socioeconomic spectrum from an early age. For instance, the Public School Athletic League, founded in New York in 1903 and widely imitated elsewhere in the United States, collected funds from wealthy donors and made opportunities to play sports available outside of school hours to both boys and girls who were enrolled in public schools. The Playground Association of America, founded in 1906, established an immensely successful program to create public playgrounds, many with hired staff to organize sports activities. In 1906 there were eighty-seven playgrounds in twenty-four American cities. By 1916 there were 3,940 playgrounds in 481 cities.[16]

Progressives envisaged, and to some extent effected, a democratization of American society that looked to sport as an important mechanism for achieving their goals. The outcome of the Progressives' attempt to shape sport into a mechanism for democratization was a mixture of failure and success. On one hand, the Progressives were content to accept what were, by current standards, high levels of social exclusion in sport, so that, for instance, sport participation opportunities for females and African Americans remained sharply circumscribed. In addition, the Progressive Movement lost momentum in the aftermath of World War I, and overt discussion of the connection between sport and democratization became less common.[17] On the other hand, the steps Progressives took to democratize sport have had a lasting influence on the nature of athletic activity in the United States, and their beliefs have had an enduring impact on Americans' attitudes toward sport.

What the Progressives did not do is create a carefully thought out body of research and writing that supported their claims about sport. They made nothing like a concerted effort to collect evidence that could convincingly demonstrate that sport fosters democratization, and their explanations of how sport shaped behavior were intuitive rather than rigorously empirical or theoretical.

Nonetheless, the Progressive view of sport was based on an implicit understanding of how sport contributed to the creation of a democratized social order. Although they did not put it in such terms, Progressives believed that sport, because it was a powerful form of socialization, promoted widespread acceptance of shared values associated with democratic political culture and thus helped generate a stable consensus on a societal scale around a particularly desirable set of norms. In current social science parlance, the Progressives saw sport in functionalist terms. Functionalism has a long, complex, and controversial history in social thought and will be employed in the analysis undertaken here, so it warrants detailed discussion.

---

[16] On children's sports and playgrounds in the United States in the early years of the twentieth century, see Guttmann 1988, 82–100 and Wood 1913. The figures on playgrounds come from Guttmann 2004, 156–57.

[17] Dyreson 1998, 199–208.

3.3. FUNCTIONALISM

Functional analyses in the social sciences are based on assumptions that can vary significantly in number and kind and that are more often than not left unstated. As a result, there has been and continues to be a great deal of confusion about functionalism. The most basic assumption, shared by all functionalist analyses, is that a given social practice or institution has one or more characteristic effects. A standard corollary of that assumption is that, because social practices and institutions have effects external to themselves, societies are at least to some extent interdependent wholes in which activity in one sphere influences activity in other spheres. An additional trait of many, though by no means all, functional analyses is a focus on those social practices and institutions that are understood as contributing to social stability.

After that, matters get rapidly more complicated because functionalist analyses can differ in regard to both the object and nature of the presumed effects of social practices and institutions. In regard to the former, the social practice or institution in question can be understood as affecting individuals, relationships between individuals, or larger social groups as a whole. In regard to the latter, many functionalist analyses include what might be called existence or persistence assumptions of ascending levels of complexity. They may presume that social practices or institutions *come into existence* because they cause social effects, cause social effects that contribute to social stability, or cause social effects necessary to achieve social stability that would not otherwise be possible. They may also presume that social practices or institutions *persist* because they cause social effects, cause social effects that contribute to social stability, or cause social effects necessary to achieve social stability that would not otherwise be possible. In addition, existence and persistence assumptions can be combined, so, for instance, some functionalist analyses assume that social practices or institutions both come into existence and persist because they cause social effects that contribute to social stability. The number of possible permutations and combinations of these various assumptions, and hence the number of different varieties of functionalist analysis, is obviously quite large.[18]

"Nearly every tradition in the social sciences...employs functional explanations,"[19] but in the second half of the twentieth century one specific variety of functionalism achieved particular prominence, that associated with

---

[18] Helpful treatments of functionalism can be found in Barnes 1995, 37–60; Kincaid 1996, 101–141; and Mouzelis 1995, 127–47.

[19] Kincaid 1996, 101. Robert Merton made the larger claim that "the central orientation of functionalism – expressed in the practice of interpreting data by establishing their consequences for larger structures in which they are implicated – has been found in virtually all of the sciences of man – biology and physiology, psychology, economics and law, anthropology and sociology" (Merton 1957, 46–47).

Talcott Parsons (1902–79). Parsons' work is complex and even a bare summary would take up a good deal of space; for our purposes it is sufficient to highlight four key features.[20] First, Parsons subscribed to a notably strong form of functionalism in that he saw social practices and institutions as persisting because they cause social effects necessary to achieve social stability that would not otherwise be possible. Second, Parsons conceptualized societies as integrated wholes that he compared to organisms on the grounds that "the very definition of an organic whole is one within which the relations determine the properties of its parts."[21] Third, Parsons argued that social order is achieved primarily through consensus built around a shared value system inculcated through socialization and that coercion, because it provoked negative reactions, is "an inadequate and inefficient method of maintaining order in society."[22] Finally, in his late work Parsons articulated an evolutionary theory of social change that emphasized what he called "adaptive upgrading" in which societies tended to become better able to respond to challenges; contemporary North American societies were presented as the most advanced in the world.

Parsonian functionalism achieved great popularity in the 1940s and 1950s, but it met with virulent criticism starting in the 1960s and is now largely discredited. Three of the basic grounds on which Parsons' work was critiqued are worth reviewing because they need to be taken into account in considering functionalist analyses of all kinds. First, C. Wright Mills and Ralf Dahrendorf, among others, argued that Parsons put too much emphasis on integration and consensus and too little on conflict and coercion. Second, Anthony Giddens and many others charged Parsons with making no allowance for self-determined action on the part of individuals; one of the most regularly suggested alternative viewpoints is rational choice theory, which presumes that behavior is largely a product of preference-driven choices made by individuals. Finally, Alvin Gouldner and others censured Parsons for propounding views that functioned to reinforce a decidedly unsatisfactory status quo, both in the United States and the world.[23]

---

[20] On Parsonian functionalism and its critics, see Holmwood 2005 and Ritzer 2008a, 457–80.

[21] Quoted in Holmwood 2005, 94.

[22] Ritzer 2008a, 469.

[23] After the wave of criticism of functionalism that appeared in the 1960s and early 1970s, further debate took place over the utility of functionalist analysis. For instance, Anthony Giddens argued that "the concept of 'function' has no place in the social sciences, and it is best to jettison it altogether" (Giddens 1990, 102). Giddens and others felt that functionalism, by its very nature, led sociologists to underestimate the role of agency and that, ultimately, the crux of social analysis was causal mechanisms, something that was easily obscured in functionalist approaches. I am persuaded by the arguments of those scholars who have taken the position that functionalism, when properly conceived and executed, remains an indispensable methodology in the social sciences (see the sources cited in n. 18). A key proviso is that functionalist analyses need to incorporate both questions of effect (i.e., function) and of cause (i.e., mechanisms by which that effect is produced).

Parsons' work remains important in large part because it became the prototypical form of functionalist social analysis and remains a key point of reference in many recent, almost invariably critical, discussions of functionalism.[24] This is unfortunate because there are a substantial number of other forms of functionalism that are less problematic than that of Parsons. One such version of functionalism, a version that offers insights that will be used in the discussion that follows, is that of Parsons' student Robert Merton (1910–2003).[25]

Merton highlighted three debatable assumptions present in many functionalist analyses and suggested alternative perspectives. The first of these was "the postulate of the functional unity of society," by which Merton meant the assumption that societies are highly integrated wholes in which the effects of social practices and institutions are the same for all members of a society. He argued instead that "not all societies have that *high* degree of integration in which *every* culturally standardized activity or belief is functional for the society as a whole and uniformly functional for the people living in it."[26] This meant that, "social usages or sentiments may be functional for some groups and dysfunctional for others in the same society" and that "various groups and strata in the structure of a society have *conflicting* interests and values as well as *shared* interests and values."[27] The "postulate of universal functionalism" referred to the assumption that all social practices and institutions have positive functions. Merton insisted that social practices and institutions can either be partially or wholly dysfunctional or can have no functional consequences at all. Finally there was the "postulate of indispensability," the paired assumptions that:

there are certain *functions* which are indispensable in the sense that, unless they are performed, the society (or group or individual) will not persist. This then sets forth a concept of *functional prerequisites, or preconditions functionally necessary* for a society...and...it is assumed that *certain cultural or social forms* are indispensable for fulfilling each of these functions.[28]

[24] See, for instance, on the specific subject of functionalist analyses of sport, Loy and Booth 2000.

[25] Parsons published on functionalism over a period of decades, and Merton's work on the subject was both influenced by and influenced Parsons' ideas. On Merton's work, see Elwell 2009, 137–68 and the articles collected in Clark, Modgil, and Modgil 1990. His ideas about functionalism are explicated in Merton 1957, 19–84. In the later part of his career Merton championed what he called "structural analysis" (see Merton 1975). As Piotr Sztompka has pointed out, structural analysis is "a natural outgrowth of functional analysis, complementing but not all supplanting it." Sztompka adds that "functional analysis specifies the consequences of a social phenomenon...structural analysis searches for the determinants of the phenomenon in its structural context" (Sztompka 1990, 56). The nature of the present inquiry is such that we will focus on Merton's ideas about functional analysis.

[26] Merton 1957, 27.

[27] Merton 1957, 27; Merton 1996, 97.

[28] Merton 1957, 33.

Merton argued that this assumption was mistaken because *"just as the same item may have multiple functions, so may the same function be diversely fulfilled by alternative items."*[29]

The functionalism advocated by Merton is in many ways more nuanced than the Parsonian version and does not suffer from some of the latter's problems. Parsons and Merton are sometimes seen as representatives of two distinct flavors of functionalism, strong and weak, with the key difference being that strong functionalism assumes that societies are highly integrated systems that operate like organisms with homeostatic processes that assure stability, whereas weak functionalism assumes that the various components of a society are to some degree interdependent, but integration is always imperfect and dysfunction and conflict are always present.[30] Moreover, weak functionalism does not necessitate, though it can include, either existence or persistence assumptions.

3.4. CRITICAL SPORT SOCIOLOGY

As we have seen, Progressives' beliefs have had an enduring influence on the views of sport held by a considerable fraction of the American public, but until relatively recently the idea that sport can be a democratizing force has not gained much traction in the scholarly community. The reasons for that start from the fact that serious study of sport did not become common until the 1960s, when two academic subfields developed, sport history and the sociology of sport.[31] Early practitioners of sport history who wrote about American sport of the early twentieth century for obvious reasons discussed in some detail the relationship between the Progressives, sport, and democratization,[32] and a few sport historians carried on the Progressive tradition and argued that sport fostered democratization.[33] Sport history was, however, at that point a new and not terribly methodologically sophisticated field, and attempts by sport historians to connect sport and democratization met with sharp, and justified, criticism.[34]

Sport sociologists, who were better equipped methodologically to deal with the relationship between sport and democratization, tended either to show little interest in the subject or to approach it from a perspective grounded in critical theory. One reason why investigating the relationship between sport and democratization had little attraction for many sport sociologists was that drawing a causal connection between sport and

[29] Merton 1957, 33–34.
[30] For more on the distinction between weak and strong functionalism, see Ritzer 2008a, 219.
[31] On the history of sport history, see Struna 1985. On the history of the sociology of sport, see Coakley and Dunning 2000a and Malcolm 2012.
[32] See, for instance, Riess 1999.
[33] See, for instance, Betts 1974.
[34] See, for instance, Guttmann 1979.

democratization entailed making a functionalist argument, and by the 1960s functionalism, which was closely associated with Parsonian functionalism, was under heavy attack.[35] Another factor was that democratization was a fuzzy notion that eluded easy quantification. A considerable amount of scholarly work was done on the effects of sport participation, but that work focused on outcomes such as increased educational attainment or decreased delinquency. These outcomes were amenable to quantification and hence of greater interest to many sociologists trained in a discipline that stresses the analysis of quantitative data.[36]

The sport sociologists who did evince an interest in the relationship between sport and democratization were for the most part proponents of critical sociology, which took shape in the 1950s and 1960s, in large measure as a reaction against functionalism in general and Parsonian functionalism in particular. Parsons, whose work was more subtle than some of his critics allowed, was seen by many social scientists as promoting what Dennis Wrong in 1961 called an "oversocialized" view of behavior. Wrong argued that Parsons and others of like mind portrayed humans as "overwhelmingly sensitive to the opinions of others and obedient to the dictates of consensually developed systems of norms and values, internalized through socialization."[37] That understanding of human behavior, and the concomitant emphasis on socialization and consensus as the bases of social order, was subjected to increasingly virulent criticism. As Mark Granovetter has pointed out, "Most sociologists...veered away from theoretical arguments based on actors' shared value commitments because of the excesses of mid-twentieth century sociology. This view, which has been called 'oversocialized,'...leaped from observing that such commitments are a significant force in social life to the conclusion that all social action flows from them."[38]

Social scientists who explicitly or implicitly rejected the importance of socialization and consensus as bases of social order were left with two options: they could emphasize either the autonomy of individuals within social systems or the power of coercion. Many political scientists chose the former option and poured their energies into developing rational choice theory and exploring how uncoordinated, preference-based choices of autonomous individuals could produce ordered collective action.[39]

Sociologists, for the most part, took a different road, one that led to the development of critical sociology. They drew on the critical theory of the Frankfurt School, which was heavily influenced by Marx and Freud, and developed a deep interest in the social structures by means of which people

---

[35] Various varieties of functionalism have, however, been regularly used, almost always implicitly rather than explicitly, in scholarly work on sport.

[36] For an overview and critique of the relevant research, see Miracle and Rees 1994.

[37] This summary of the position outlined in Wrong 1961 comes from Granovetter 1985, 483.

[38] Granovetter 2002, 41.

[39] For an introduction to rational choice theory, see Voss and Abraham 2000.

are subjected to domination and oppression. This almost inevitably led them to focus on coercion as the primary source of social order. It is also important to bear in mind that adherents of critical theory, and of what became known as critical sociology, were from the outset, and continue to be, committed to attacking the social structures responsible for domination and oppression in order to create a fundamentally egalitarian and just social order.[40]

Critical sociology rapidly became the dominant paradigm in the subfield of the sociology of sport. As Jay Coakley and Eric Dunning put it in their survey of the history of that field:

Marxist/neo-Marxist, feminist, and Marxist-feminist scholars became increasingly vocal and powerful, if not hegemonic, figures in the sociology of sport. As they grew more influential there was an associated change in the dominant professional self-image among sociologists of sport. Rather than seeing themselves as technocratic servants of sport-forms which they uncritically accepted as "good," many began to see themselves as critics whose principal goal was to use research and action to "purify" the "pathological" sport-forms produced under capitalism. The ultimate goal was to secure more egalitarian articulations of sports into more egalitarian social frameworks.[41]

Proponents of critical sport sociology took existing sport practice as one of the social structures that underpinned domination and oppression. They typically did not explicitly address the relationship between sport and democratization, but they regularly produced scholarship on how sport reinforced gender-based and class-based inequalities. Critical sport sociologists interested in gender portrayed sport as a means by which hierarchical relationships between the sexes were reproduced and perpetuated.[42] Critical sport sociologists interested in social class initially favored a heavy-handed Marxism,[43] but rapidly gravitated toward a more subtle approach grounded in Antonio Gramsci's work on hegemony. Sport was portrayed as one of the means by which those in dominant positions in society imposed their will on their less empowered counterparts, primarily by communicating a set of values that served the interests of the privileged.[44] Foucault's immensely influential work on discipline played a role as well; starting in the 1980s, critical sport sociologists came to see sport as a disciplinary system that produced "docile bodies."[45]

---

[40] On the evolution of sociology in the decades after World War II, see Ritzer 2008b, 189–222. On critical theory, see Bronner 2011.

[41] Coakley and Dunning 2000a, xxix.

[42] See the discussion in Theberge 2000.

[43] See, for instance, Brohm 1981 and Hoch 1972.

[44] See, for instance, Hargreaves 1986.

[45] See the discussion in Section 5.5. Critical sport sociologists have typically adopted a view of sport that is significantly more pessimistic than that common among the general public. As the authors of a recent study point out, "Critical sport studies offered an important corrective to romanticized and uncritical acceptance of sport as an unambiguously positive

Critical sport sociologists thus developed an extensive and sophisticated body of theory and research that presented sport as a means of propping up existing hierarchical relationships and as an important impediment to the development of egalitarian social relations and hence, implicitly, as an impediment to democratization. In doing so they adopted a position that was diametrically opposed to that of the Progressives; the Progressives had argued that sport, in the terms used here, fostered horizontal relations, whereas critical sport sociologists saw sport as fostering vertical relations. There is a certain irony that critical sport sociologists, in arguing that sport had characteristic effects in spheres outside of sport, adopted an approach that was functionalist even though that terminology would have been anathema to them.[46]

3.5. ROBERT PUTNAM, SOCIAL CAPITAL, AND SPORT

In 1993, Robert Putnam, with assistance from two collaborators, published what turned out to be a highly influential book, *Making Democracy Work*, on the performance of democratic institutions in modern-day Italy. He developed a variety of quantitative measures to test the effectiveness of democratic institutions, showed that by all those measures local government functioned much better in northern than southern Italy, and then explored the reasons behind that strong regional difference. In doing so, he considered three basic categories of factors that had been used to explain the performance of government institutions: institutional design, socioeconomic factors, and sociocultural factors. His analysis of the data from Italy led Putnam to emphasize the importance of sociocultural factors in general and more specifically the existence of a civic culture "marked by an active, public-spirited citizenry, by egalitarian political relations, by a social fabric of trust and cooperation," a civic culture that he argued was fostered in part by vibrant associational activity in civil society.[47]

institution. The emphasis on critique, however, drove out any discussion of the potentially positive aspects of sport. Most athletes, coaches, parents, youth sports organizers, and spectators…know from experience that sport participation has offered them numerous moments of pleasure, healthy exercise, friendships, mentoring relationships, and lessons about achievement, cooperation, and competition that spill over into nonsport contexts" (Gatz, Messner, and Ball-Rokeach 2002, 5).

[46] The term functionalism retains for most social scientists strong overtones of Parsonian functionalism, which puts it in bad odor, but the basic approach remains in widespread use. As Barnes observes, "Many sociologists are inclined to believe that everything worth saying about functionalism has already been said, and to express that view in a way which implies that functionalism is as dead as a dodo. But whatever is worth saying about functionalism bears repeating, for it is the most misunderstood and misused of social theories. And it remains in any case clearly alive…functionalist forms of thought have penetrated so deeply into the culture of the social sciences that they are often employed without being explicitly recognized as such…" (Barnes 1995, 37).

[47] Putnam, Leonardi, and Nanetti 1993, 15.

The idea that civic culture and voluntary associations are important to underpinnings of democratic governance had a long history before Putnam's time.[48] Its roots lay in Alexis de Tocqueville's *Democracy in America* (1835–40), in which he argued that the "habits of the heart" that sustained American democracy were nurtured in a wide array of voluntary associations that helped create a participatory culture and belief in equality. In the 1950s and early 1960s, social scientists working in the functionalist tradition extended Tocqueville's work, in part by using quantitative data to study various components of civic culture. The best-known example of such work is Gabriel Almond and Sidney Verba's *The Civic Culture: Political Attitudes and Democracy in Five Nations* (1963), which was built around survey data taken from five separate 1,000-person samples. Almond and Verba argued that democracy was sustained by social structures and processes that generated a set of social and political attitudes, what they called a civic culture, "based on communication and persuasion, a culture of consensus and diversity."[49] They emphasized the importance of a robust associational life, and one of their more intriguing findings was that membership in nonpolitical organizations had a significant impact on political competence.[50] Unfortunately, Almond and Verba and other scholars working along the same lines largely ignored sport as a component of civic culture. As might be expected, scholarly interest in the connection between civic culture and voluntary associations on one hand and democracy on the other declined after the early 1960s as a result of the attacks on functionalism and the growing emphasis on coercion as a source of social order, though it at no point disappeared entirely.[51]

Putnam, therefore, worked in a well-established intellectual tradition in crafting *Making Democracy*, but he also introduced an important innovation through his use of the concept of social capital. That concept has a long and varied history, having been independently invented and reinvented over the course of the twentieth century; Putnam took it from the work of James Coleman on the sociology of education.[52] Putnam defined social capital as "features of social organization, such as trust, norms, and networks, that can improve the efficiency of society by facilitating coordinated actions."[53] He made the case that social capital facilitates effective democratic governance by instilling habits of collaboration, solidarity, and public-spiritedness that

---

[48] On the intellectual history of the civic culture concept, see Almond 1980. Lebow and Lebow forthcoming argue that Putnam's understanding of Tocqueville's work is impoverished in significant ways.

[49] Almond and Verba 1963, 8.

[50] Almond and Verba 1963, 319–22.

[51] Almond and Verba, for instance, published in 1980 a collection of essays on civic culture (Almond and Verba 1980).

[52] On the history of the concept of social capital, see Farr 2004.

[53] Putnam, Leonardi, and Nanetti 1993, 167.

make it easier for individuals to form cooperative relationships of all kinds and that thus carry over into and shape political activity.

The notion of social capital as articulated by Putnam, which contained little conceptual novelty and which was initially less than fully developed, proved to be a very useful "thing to think with." As Alejandro Portes noted in a 1998 article on social capital:

Despite its current popularity, the term does not embody any idea really new to sociologists. That involvement and participation in groups can have positive consequences for the individual and the community is a staple notion ... the term social capital simply recaptures an insight present since the very beginnings of the discipline.[54]

The idea of social capital could be understood as a rewriting of the ideas that socialization into specific values (Putnam's norms) and consensus born from participation in groups (Putnam's networks) are important sources of social order (Putnam's facilitating coordinated actions), and it is certainly not coincidental that in his discussion of social capital Putnam overtly critiqued rational choice and coercion as means of enabling coordinated actions.[55]

As articulated in *Making Democracy Work* the concept of social capital also had some flaws, including a failure to take into account the possibility that norms and networks could function in ways that inhibited democratization and a lack of differentiation between origins, substance, and effects.[56] Nonetheless, Putnam's work played a key role in making social capital into a concept that achieved wide circulation both in academic circles and among the general public. That outcome can be traced in part to the fact that social capital neatly captured a special case of more general ideas about the creation of social order, one that applied specifically to democratized societies. In addition, social capital was a convenient means of returning socialization and consensus to thinking about social order, after a period when social scientists had emphasized rational choice and coercion. Models of societal functioning that failed to take socialization and consensus into account were inherently incomplete, and social capital proved to be a useful means for remedying this problem.

Putnam's work on social capital is of overriding importance in the present context because it drew a direct connection between sport and democratization. In *Making Democracy Work* he followed in the footsteps of Tocqueville, Almond, Verba, and others in highlighting the importance of voluntary associations in democratic societies:

Networks of civic engagement, like the neighborhood associations, choral societies, cooperatives, sports clubs, mass-based parties, and the like ... represent intense

---

[54] Portes 1998, 2.
[55] Putnam, Leonardi, and Nanetti 1993, 163–67.
[56] We will see that Putnam subsequently offered a more nuanced understanding of social capital.

horizontal interaction. Networks of civic engagement are an essential form of social capital: the denser such networks in a community, the more likely that its citizens will be able to cooperate for mutual benefit.[57]

It is crucial for our purposes that Putnam included sports clubs among the forms of associations that nurtured horizontal relationships. In fact, he found that, apart from labor unions, sports clubs were by some distance the most popular form of voluntary association in Italy.[58]

Putnam went on to apply some of the basic concepts and findings from *Making Democracy Work* to the United States, starting with an article that appeared in the *Journal of Democracy* in 1995 with the title "Bowling Alone: America's Declining Social Capital." He supplied a considerable amount of quantitative data in an attempt to show that stocks of social capital in the United States were declining and closed with the following evidence taken from sport:

The most whimsical yet discomfiting bit of evidence of social disengagement in contemporary America that I have discovered is this: more Americans are bowling today than ever before, but bowling in organized leagues has plummeted in the last decade or so. Between 1980 and 1993 the total number of bowlers in America increased by 10 percent, while league bowling decreased by 40 percent. (Lest this be thought a wholly trivial example, I should note that nearly 80 million Americans went bowling at least once during 1993, *nearly a third more than voted in the 1994 congressional elections*...)....The broader social significance [of the rise of solo bowling]...lies in the social interaction and even occasionally civic conversations over beer and pizza that solo bowlers forgo. Whether or not bowling beats balloting in the eyes of most Americans, bowling teams illustrate yet another vanishing form of social capital.[59]

The same idea featured in a book Putnam published in 2000, *Bowling Alone: The Collapse and Revival of American Community*, that included detailed analysis of trends in sport participation and spectatorship in the United States.[60]

In the past two decades a number of governments have incorporated the concept of social capital into their official sport policies.[61] Government intervention in sport has a long history; for example, in 1863 the Norwegian Parliament allotted funds to a voluntary association that promoted exercise and training in the use of firearms.[62] Up through World War II most government sport policy was intended to heighten levels of physical fitness

---

[57] Putnam, Leonardi, and Nanetti 1993, 173.
[58] Putnam, Leonardi, and Nanetti 1993, 91–92.
[59] Putnam 1995, 70.
[60] Putnam 2000, 109–14.
[61] On sport policy in a variety of different countries, see Bergsgard, Houlihan, Mangset, Nødland, and Rommetvedt 2007; Coalter 2007; and Nicholson, Hoye, and Houlihan 2011.
[62] Bergsgard, Houlihan, Mangset, Nødland, and Rommetvedt 2007, 220.

for either military or public health purposes or to limit social unrest. In the 1960s and 1970s sport came to be seen in many industrialized nations as an important source of personal fulfillment and wellness and hence a matter of social welfare. A number of governments for this reason adopted "sport-for-all" policies that aimed to augment opportunities for sport participation for all citizens. This is evident in a report issued by the Council for Cultural Co-operation of the Council of Europe in 1970, *Sport for All*, which characterized sport as contributing to "development and expression of personality."[63]

Starting in the 1990s increased emphasis was put on sport as a means of enhancing social integration and hence democratization, a development in which Putnam's ideas about social capital played a central role. The authors of a newly published review of government sport policy point out that:

There is a recent but increasingly firmly established belief that sport is a vehicle for the creation of social capital and the associated benefits of social inclusion, social connectedness, community strengthening, community well-being, improved local governance, and greater civic participation and volunteerism.[64]

Official statements of sport policy in numerous countries, including but not limited to Australia, Canada, New Zealand, and the United Kingdom, now draw a specific connection between sport and social capital. For instance, a report with the title "Game Plan: A Strategy for Delivering Government's Sport and Physical Activity Objectives," issued by Britain's Department of Culture, Media, and Sport in 2002, contains the statement that, "Using sport to promote social inclusion can also help to build social capital through developing personal skills and enlarging individuals' social networks."[65] In some cases, the link to Putnam's work is explicit; "More than Winning: The Real Value of Sport and Recreation in Western Australia," issued by the Department of Sport and Recreation of the Government of Western Australia in 2008, offers the observation that:

International research shows that increasing community participation in organised sport and recreation contributes to what is known as "social capital," which is the "social fabric, or glue" that ties members together in a given locality....According to Putnam (2000) sports clubs and community organisations are important conduits for developing such capital and are good barometers of community strength.[66]

The claim that sport is a "school for democracy" has in the past two decades appeared in official statements of sport policy with considerable frequency. We have already seen that Daniel Tarschys, Secretary-General of the Council of Europe, proclaimed in 1995 that "sport is, *par excellence*, the

[63] Europe 1970, 7.
[64] Nicholson, Hoye, and Houlihan 2011, 2.
[65] Department of Culture 2002, 60.
[66] Western Australia 2008, 9.

ideal school for democracy."[67] Tarschys' views on sport are regularly quoted in government documents, for example in Sport England's "The Value of Sport."[68] Miklos Révész, writing in 1997 as the chairman of the Council of Europe's Steering Committee for the Development of Sport, stated that:

> Sport, particularly in voluntary clubs, with free elections and accountability, is a major "school for democracy."...All sports, all games are based on rules and laws generally accepted, and above all, grounded in an ethical approach, this surely is a training ground for Life and Citizenship.[69]

The current version of the Council of Europe's website includes the statement that, "Sport is a fundamental pillar of society....If played properly, sport makes for the promotion of the following in particular"; the list that comes immediately after is headed by "democracy and participation."[70]

The immense popularity of Putnam's books and articles and the incorporation of social capital into government sport policy have together generated a considerable body of recent research into the idea that sport can be an important source of social capital. In part this is because significant numbers of governmental initiatives inspired by that idea have been put into practice, and there is a concomitant interest in attempting to document outcomes.[71] This rapidly growing collection of research on sport and social capital represents the first substantive body of serious research that posits a causal connection between sport and democratization, in which the former fosters the latter.

---

[67] Tarschys 1995, 5.
[68] SportEngland 1999, 12.
[69] Révész 1997, 8.
[70] http://www.coe.int/t/dg4/epas/about/history_En.asp.
[71] See the discussion in Coalter 2007.

4

Congruence between Society and Sport

cause/effect works both ways

One of the four possible views of the relationship between sport and democratization is that democratization in society is cause, and democratization in sport effect. This view assumes that the nature of sport is determined by the nature of the society in which it is played, whereas the nature of sport has little or no effect on the nature of society. Both of these assumptions will be examined in this chapter. It will be shown that the nature of sport does indeed reflect the nature of the society in which it is played, but that sport, especially mass sport, can also shape society.

4.1. THE IMPACT OF SOCIETY ON SPORT

The definition of democratization proposed in Section 2.1 and the categorization of sport proposed in Section 2.3 both rely on the same classificatory criteria, horizontal versus vertical, and with good reason: systems of sport and the social systems within which they operate tend toward congruence. Put most simply, this means that societies in which horizontal relationships are prevalent usually have sport that is largely horizontal in nature, whereas the reverse is true of societies in which vertical relationships prevail. It is worth pursuing some of the reasons for the congruence of social and sport systems, because they will provide considerable insight into the relationship between sport and democratization.

To begin with, societies are always to some extent integrated wholes in which individual components' structure and operation exert a mutual influence on each other; this represents one of the fundamental assumptions of functionalist analyses (see Section 3.3). It would, in fact, be surprising if there were not some degree of congruence between a social system as a whole and the sport that takes place within it.

Another good reason to expect sport and social systems to be congruent is that organized games are in many ways small-scale societies. In both cases the individuals involved are oriented toward the achievement of certain goals and are constrained in doing so by an interlocking set of institutions, practices, and norms, which shape, though do not determine, behavior by means of socialization, consensus, and coercion. For instance, Americans are, among other things, oriented toward the accumulation of wealth and are constrained in doing so by institutions, practices, and norms that establish legitimate (e.g., running a small business) and illegitimate (e.g., armed robbery) means of making money, that are enforced through socialization, consensus, and coercion, and that channel but do not determine behavior (e.g., a businessman may choose to work part-time in order to pursue goals other than the acquisition of wealth).

Compare this to a game of American football. The goal of American football is to score more points than one's opponent in sixty minutes of playing time. A set of written rules constrains behavior by specifying that points can only be scored in certain ways – the ball can be kicked through the uprights for three points but no points are awarded if the ball is thrown through the uprights. Constraints extend beyond formal, written regulations to practices and norms. A professional football team leading its opponent by thirty points late in the fourth quarter will typically make an effort *not* to score any more points.[1] This practice is of course not required by the formal rules of the game, but both players and spectators are familiar with it. At the same time, written rules and unwritten expectations leave a good deal up to the players. In order to get the ball across the goal line, teams can choose from a variety of plays, depending on their strengths and inclinations. "Three yards and a cloud of dust" and a spread passing formation both serve the purpose of getting the ball over the goal line, but in very different ways. Conformity with written rules and unwritten expectations is assured through familiarity developed by unstructured exposure to the game and structured instruction in it (socialization), through agreements between the participants (consensus), and through enforcement backed by the threat of sanctions (coercion). Hence, an experienced football player is unlikely to have ever sat down and read the official rule book, but nonetheless is deeply familiar with the rules of the game, has played in both "clean" and "dirty" games in which the constellation of players on the field reached an implicit or explicit agreement to interact in certain ways, and has been penalized by an official for rule infractions.

The similarities between societies and organized games spring from the fact that both are to a large extent exercises in coordinated action by groups of individuals and hence entail the imposition of constraints that generate stable patterns of behavior. Coordinated action among groups of individuals is nearly impossible when individual behavior is not heavily constrained.

---

[1] Otherwise they would be accused of running up the score and seeking to humiliate the losing team. The situation might be different at a college football game because the point differentials between winning and losing teams can be important in some ranking systems.

The traffic in a large city would rapidly grind to a halt if every driver felt free to do what he or she wished upon arriving at every intersection, and a football game would disintegrate if the teams involved failed to establish legitimate and illegitimate means of scoring points. Constraints permit coordinated action by making the behavior of other participants largely predictable. Insofar as both societies and organized games involve coordinated action by groups of individuals, they bear a close resemblance to each other, albeit on very different scales of complexity, and are regularly analogized to each other. As Geertz noted, three of the more commonly employed analogies for society are game, drama, and text. He pointed out that, "Seeing society as a collection of games means seeing it as a grand plurality of accepted conventions and appropriate procedures."[2]

Insofar as organized games present organizational challenges that bear close resemblance to those faced by societies as a whole, the institutions, practices, and norms found in the latter almost inevitably tend to get transferred in one way or another to the former. As Richard Gruneau has observed:

> While one of the purposes of rules is to separate play from reality, the very act of rule construction has the effect of embedding play deeply in the prevailing logic of social relations and thereby of diminishing its autonomy. For this reason, the study of play is haunted by a fundamental paradox. Play gives the impression of being an *independent and spontaneous* aspect of human action or agency and at the same time a *dependent and regulated* aspect of it.[3]

This is the reason for the much repeated, still valid observation that sport reflects society. For example, the games of soccer, invented in Britain, and *kemari*, invented in Japan, both involve multiple players kicking a ball of about the same size. However, soccer is highly competitive, pitting one team against another in a contest to score points, whereas *kemari* privileges cooperation because the game involves a single group of players working together to keep the ball in the air for as long as possible. At a more subtle level, the same game can be played in very different ways. The behavior of players on Japan's professional baseball teams is by no means the same as that of their counterparts in the United States. Japanese players are expected to display a resilient stoicism, make an immense effort to improve, and to obey their managers. American players who go to Japan have been surprised by demanding and precisely organized training schedules. When Warren Cromartie joined the Yomiuri Giants, he remarked that, "I'd come to Japan to play baseball and discovered that I'd joined the Marines instead." In a similar vein, for many years unmarried Japanese players lived in barracks and

[2] Geertz 1983, 19–35 at 25–26.
[3] Gruneau 1999, 2–3.

had to seek permission from their manager to marry. American managers find their players much less receptive to their dictates.[4]

The congruence between society and sport with regard to horizontality and verticality is nicely illustrated in the case of China. The verticality of China's sociopolitical system is evident from the most comprehensive measure of degree of democratization currently available, the Unified Democracy Scores (UDS) calculated by James Melton, Stephen Meserve, and Daniel Pemstein for most countries for the years 1946–2008. Unified Democracy Scores are an aggregate of twelve different systems of measuring democratization that have been developed by various researchers. Most of those systems have a strong institutionalist bias, but some, most notably those compiled by Freedom House and, to a lesser extent, by the Polity Project, reflect a broader understanding of democratization. UDS are thus a reasonable if not perfect proxy for democratization as defined here.[5]

Unified Democracy Scores run from roughly −2.1 to 2.1, with a higher score indicating a more democratic system. China's UDS over the decades has hovered around −1, which puts it near the bottom of the democracy rankings. For example, in the UDS for the year 2000, China ranked 181st out of 191 countries.

China has also long had a strongly vertical system of mass sport that was constructed in the decades after World War II. Although sports of various kinds existed in China from an early date, nothing resembling mass sport existed until the 1950s. For an extended period, disdain, common among elites, for physical activity of all kinds acted to minimize the importance of sport. This is evident in the story told about a high-ranking Chinese government official of the early twentieth century who, having witnessed the English consul playing tennis, remarked to him, "It is a pity that you worked so hard....It would be much better if you could hire a man to come play in your place."[6] Foreign influences and modernization combined to bring gradual change beginning in the late nineteenth century. The Young Men's Christian Association (YMCA), which was dedicated to promoting sport participation (see Chapter 16), began to operate in China in 1895, and its arrival coincided with efforts at national renewal that gathered strength after China's defeat in the First Sino-Japanese War (1894–95). Successive

---

[4] On sports in Japan (including *kemari* and baseball), see Guttmann and Thompson 2001. Cromartie is quoted on page 171 of Guttmann and Thompson's book. For the original, see Cromartie and Whiting 1992, 104. Cf. John Tunis' observation that "The principles of real sport are the principles of democracy. And the principles of democracy are the principles of real sport" (Tunis 1941, 40).

[5] For an explanation of the UDS project, see Pemstein, Meserve, and Melton 2010. For the data, see http://www.unified-democracy-scores.org/. Quantifying democratization presents enormous methodological challenges, which are discussed with admirable clarity in Munck 2009.

[6] The story is related in Brownell 1995, 40.

governments came to see sport as a means of preparing China for war, and attempts were made to promote participation with that in mind. For example, when the Citizens' Physical Education Act, which was originally passed in 1928, was revised in 1936, its first clause read, "It is the responsibility of every young man and woman of the Republic of China to pursue physical exercise."[7] However, initiatives to promote sport were not as effective as they might have been, and participation remained relatively limited up through the middle of the twentieth century. Roy Clumpner and Brian Pendelton note that at "the time the Communist Party came to power in 1949, the vast majority of Chinese had never…participated in physical education or sport."[8]

An abrupt transformation came with the accession of a Communist government under the leadership of Mao Zedong, who had a strong interest in sport. Mao had written an article in 1917 calling for regular exercise and in 1952 exhorted the Chinese people to "promote physical culture and sport, and build up the people's health."[9] Steps were rapidly taken to construct a system of mass sport, including the establishment in 1949 of the All-China Sports Federation, which was charged with organizing recreation and sport programs for the entire populace, and the establishment in 1952 of the State Physical Culture and Sports Commission, which was responsible for policy, finance, personnel, and public relations.

The history of sport in China since that time is quite complex, and it is sufficient here to focus on a single issue, namely that the sport system constructed by the Chinese Communist government was strongly vertical. This is evident from even a cursory consideration of the three variables identified in Section 2.3: organizational structure, degree of regimentation, and stated goals. From the beginning, sport was organized from the top down and remained under close governmental control at all times. The central government promulgated detailed policies, and oversaw their implementation by regional and local sports commissions.

A wide range of sports was practiced, but a particular emphasis was put on highly organized group activity that reflected an ideal of regimentation. Mao oversaw the development of a calisthenics program, and in 1951 the government decreed that it be practiced by the entire populace twice a day, daily. Participation in calisthenics has, as the result of ongoing social, political, and economic change, declined, but the practice remains widespread in China. Figure 6 reproduces a picture, taken in 2002, of students at a

---

7 Quoted in Xu 2008, 63.
8 Clumpner and Pendleton 1978, 109. On sport in China, see Brownell 1995, Brownell 2000, Clumpner and Pendleton 1978, Hong and Zhouxiang 2011, Xiangjun and Brownell 1996, and Xu 2008. Xu (pp. 12–74) provides a detailed and insightful treatment of sport in China up through 1949.
9 Quoted in Clumpner and Pendleton 1978, 111.

FIGURE 6. Students Do Morning Calisthenics at the Wenxuan Middle School in Liaocheng, Shandong Province, China, 2002 (From Samuel Kahng)

middle school arrayed in orderly lines for mandatory morning calisthenics. Clumpner and Pendelton wrote in 1977 that, from the Western perspective, Chinese sport involved "regimented people following orders as to where, when, and how to engage in exercise."[10] The observations of Susan Brownell, who both studied and participated in athletic competitions in China in the 1980s, are worth quoting at some length. Brownell discusses body culture, which she defines as "the entire repertoire of things that people do to and with their bodies, and the elements of culture that shape their doing." She argues that:

The body culture that was promoted by the Party after 1949…was highly militarized. By that, I mean that military discipline was the ideal, the paradigm, which shaped body techniques in most other realms of life. The military paradigm was characterized by an ideology of strengthening the body in order to strengthen the nation for war. Its practices were characterized by highly rigid body movements performed in unison by large numbers of people, reminiscent of military marching displays. These techniques were normalizing and homogenizing in that they were the same for everyone, and did not vary by age, sex, ethnicity, and so on. Mass calisthenics were the most widespread example. For many Westerners, television images of thousands of green-clad androgynous Chinese performing them in unison became one of the enduring images of the

[10] Clumpner and Pendleton 1978, 122. They also pointed out that participation in the government's exercise program was, notionally at least, voluntary and that adherence varied quite a bit both regionally and among different age groups.

Cultural Revolution. Marching displays and mass calisthenics were also the performance genre used in opening and closing ceremonies of sports meets at every level, from the local elementary school to the National Sports Games.[11]

Brownell points out that the same body culture manifested itself in sports and in that vein discusses her own experiences as a member of the track team of Beijing University in 1985–86. A theme that ran throughout the Chinese sport system was "socialist spiritual civilization," which in practice primarily meant displaying self-discipline (*jilü*).[12]

The stated goals of the Chinese sport system were from the outset almost purely statist. Mao believed that sport was an essential means of preparing China's people for war and for productive labor, and the government understood sport programs as an important means of political indoctrination. The founding document of the All-China Sports Federation includes the following declaration:

The Federation is under the leadership of the central government and the CCP [Chinese Communist Party]. It follows rule 48 of the "Common Program of the Chinese People's Political Consultative Conference," and helps the government to organize and promote physical education and sports. The objective is to improve people's health and serve the national defense and state-building.

In an article that appeared in the *China Sports Daily* in 1975, sport was characterized as an "important approach to promote people's health, to attack the bourgeois and help socialism to take over the field of ideology and culture."[13] A picture from *Sports in China*, produced by the People's Sport Publishing House in Beijing in 1973, shows two girls reading a book and is captioned, "Chinese sportsmen and sportswomen conscientiously study Marxism-Lenin-Mao-Tsetung Thought and steadily raise their political understanding."[14]

The strongly vertical version of mass sport promoted by the Chinese government was thus very different from the horizontal mass sport found in some Western nations. A cautionary note is in order, because the government's aspirations and the reality on the ground were never identical. Even in the heyday of Communist Party control, there were divergent visions of sport within the Chinese bureaucracy, and individuals' motivations for playing sports by no means always matched those championed by the government. Moreover, sport in China always had some horizontal elements; mass calisthenics, for instance, imposed a form of equality and homogeneity on the participants. Nonetheless, mass sport in China was primarily vertical in nature. Here again Brownell's observations are incisive:

[11] Brownell 2000, 51, 52, respectively.
[12] Brownell 1995, 26–27.
[13] Quoted in Hong and Zhouxiang 2011, 161, 171, respectively.
[14] Sport Publishing House 1973, 42–43.

Mass calisthenics represent an equality that is made possible by ordered regimentation and systematic training administered by a centralized bureaucracy. The partiality of this equality is revealed by the presence of leaders of state on the rostrum in the grandstand and the emphasis on their presence in press reports.[15]

Significant changes in Chinese sport practice followed upon the program of economic liberalization launched by Deng Xiaoping in 1992. The Physical Culture and Sports Commission fell in line by setting forth a new vision of sport suitable for a market economy. Brownell characterizes the resulting changes as a shift in body culture from communism to consumerism and points to the reduced role of mass calisthenics in sports competitions held in China since the early 1990s.[16] Fan Hong and Lu Zhouxiang, considering the current situation, state that, "Compared to the 1970s and 1980s, mass sports activities have changed from being government-led to taking place on a voluntary basis."[17] Even now, however, sport in China remains significantly more vertical than sport in most Western liberal democracies. In August 2010, the Beijing People's Broadcasting Station announced that it would resume broadcasts of music and instructions for mass calisthenic programs, after they had been suspended in 2007 in order to devote more time to the upcoming Beijing Olympics. The Beijing Federation of Trade Unions expressed its hope that all workers in state enterprises would resume the former practice of exercising in groups at 10 AM and 3 PM daily.[18] One would be hard pressed to find an equivalent practice in North America or Europe.

Society and sport in China are, therefore, both notably vertical. An illuminating comparison can be found in the case of Norway, one of the most democratized societies in the world. In 2000, when China was ranked 181st out of 191 countries on the UDS scale, Norway was 5th. It is also interesting to note that whereas China's UDS has stayed at roughly -1 since 1946, Norway's score steadily improved starting in the mid-1960s (see Table 2).[19] Norway also has an extremely horizontal system of mass sport, a system that became more inclusive starting in the mid-1960s. This is clear from a rapid sketch of Norwegian sport in terms of the three criteria used here: organizational structure, degree of regimentation, and stated goals.

The Norwegian government has actively intervened in sport for over a century. Responsibility for sport was vested in the Ministry of Defense until 1929, then transferred to the Ministry of Social Affairs, to the Ministry of Church and Education, and finally, in 1982, to the Ministry of Cultural

---

[15] Brownell 1995, 26–27, cf. 151.
[16] Brownell 2000, 52–55.
[17] Hong and Zhouxiang 2011, 178.
[18] Branigan 2010; Zhihua 2010.
[19] During this same period Norway's global ranking also improved noticeably, from thirteenth in 1950 to fourth in 2008.

TABLE 2. *Unified Democracy Scores for Norway, 1946–2008, by Half Decade*

Year	UDS	Year	UDS
1946	1.24	1980	1.67
1950	1.19	1985	2.02
1955	1.20	1990	2.00
1960	1.19	1995	2.00
1965	1.32	2000	2.02
1970	1.58	2005	2.01
1975	2.10	2008	2.01

Affairs. In recent decades, the government has for the most part concentrated on financing and building sport facilities, which are used by locally organized and run sports clubs staffed almost entirely by volunteers. Norwegians show a distinct preference for nonregimented forms of physical activity. Favored activities are skiing, biking, jogging, hikes in the mountains, and swimming; less popular but still important are gymnastics, dance, aerobics, weight training, and soccer.[20]

Government policy on sport was focused originally on military preparedness and later on health and education. As was the case elsewhere in Europe, emphasis shifted in the 1960s to encourage broad-based participation in order to foster healthy lifestyles and personal development. In 1967 the Norwegian government instituted a sport-for-all program called Trim. This program was very successful, and participation rates climbed sharply; between 1960 and 1995, membership in sports clubs tripled, and the number of women in sports clubs quadrupled. Norway's sport system is in many ways the model of what horizontal mass sport looks like.[21] It is not coincidental that the launch of Trim and the growth in sport participation took place just at the time that Norway's UDS was climbing sharply.

The preceding discussion has reviewed two examples of congruence between a society's degree of democratization, conceptualized in terms of horizontality versus verticality, and the nature of its sport system. That congruence is, for reasons treated previously, what would be expected, and virtually certainly represents a generalized pattern.[22] Naturally, exceptions

[20] Skirstad 1999, 286–87.

[21] On sport in Norway, see Bergsgard, Houlihan, Mangset, Nødland, and Rommetvedt 2007; Bergsgard and Tangen 2011; Europe 1970, 55–89; and Skirstad 1999.

[22] This congruence has not escaped notice, and there have been efforts in the emerging field of comparative sport policy research to find consistent patterns in the relationship between sport policy and types of political system. See, for instance, Bergsgard, Houlihan, Mangset, Nødland, and Rommetvedt 2007.

exist; for example, a relatively rapid shift toward democratization at an institutional level might not be reflected in sport for a considerable period.

4.2. THE IMPACT OF SPORT ON SOCIETY

To say that the nature of sport reflects the nature of the society in which it is played is not tantamount to saying that, in the relationship between sport and society, sport is an entirely dependent variable. That is because there is incontrovertible evidence that sport shapes the behavior of participants and spectators, both on the playing field and off it.

In exploring the capacity of sport to shape the behavior of individuals off the playing field it is helpful to distinguish between micro, meso, and macro scales of analysis. At the micro scale, the level of the individual athlete, there is abundant documentation, primarily in the form of reflexive writing by athletes, of the effects of sport participation on behavior outside sport. We have already seen Caryl Rivers, in describing her experiences playing basketball, claim that, "If you have played basketball – really played it with pride and passion – you can never really be docile again."[23] Rivers' essay forms part of a rapidly growing collection of memoirs by female athletes, in which one of the dominant themes is that sport can be "an expression of the larger quest for female autonomy."[24] To give one other example of what is a very substantial body of literature, we can turn to John Gerdy's *Sport, the All-American Addiction*. Gerdy wrote this book as a call for major reform of the college sport system in the United States, so he is by no means an unquestioning apostle of sport. Yet in the introduction to the book he writes:

I love sports. I have been involved in organized athletics my entire life in virtually every capacity imaginable – as a player, a youth league coach, as a fan, and as a youth and college administrator. I believe very strongly that participation in athletics can teach valuable life lessons in ethics, discipline, and teamwork....I believe very strongly in the power and potential of athletics to mold people and change lives. It did mine....I have invested heavily in organized athletics because, other than my family, participation in them has influenced my life experience – the person I am and the values I hold dear – more than anything else.[25]

The micro-scale evidence, which is impressive in its cumulative weight, typically attracts less scholarly attention than it deserves. If athletes regularly express the opinion that their participation in sport has had a profound effect on the course of their lives, there is every reason to take that opinion seriously.

[23] Rivers 1983, 311.
[24] Bandy and Darden 1999, xii.
[25] Gerdy 2002, xi-xii.

Scholars have evinced less interest than they might in the testimonia of individual athletes for a variety of reasons, two of which merit mention here. First, although there is a great deal of such material, it is difficult to agglomerate these micro-scale testimonia in such a way as to make them useful in the study of sport. Second, individual athletes writing about their own experiences, like all emic observers, have a difficult time in separating manifest motives from latent functions. This distinction is most closely associated with the work of Robert Merton, who pointed out that it was necessary to distinguish between the subjective dispositions of individuals that motivate them to act in a given fashion and the consequences of that action for the individual and the society to which she or he belongs, consequences which are frequently unclear to the individual in question.[26] Foucault put it more stylishly when he wrote that "People know what they do; they frequently know why they do what they do; but what they don't know is what what they do does."[27] As a result, the testimonia of individual athletes are not necessarily useful for scholars interested in what sport does. However, they offer strong evidence that individuals' experiences in sport carry over to the rest of their lives.

Equally strong evidence that sport shapes society is available at the meso level, which in this instance means studies of small groups of athletes. The number of such studies that have been carried out by sport sociologists is substantial and continues to grow. Perhaps the best known example of this kind of work is Loïc Wacquant's *Body and Soul: Notebooks of an Apprentice Boxer* (2004). Wacquant, at the time of the study a sociologist at the University of Chicago, spent three years as a member of a boxing gym, trained there three to six times a week, fought in the Golden Gloves tournament, and kept a highly detailed diary that he used to write *Body and Soul*. He found that over the course of time individuals were fundamentally reshaped by the experience of regularly training in the gym. This is evident in the following passages from his work:

The gym is…a *school of morality*, in Durkheim's sense of the term, that is to say a machinery designed to fabricate the spirit of discipline, group attachment, respect for others as for self, and autonomy of will that are indispensable to the blossoming of the pugilistic vocation.…

These conversations [that take place daily at the gym] impregnate them with the values and categories of judgment in currency in the pugilistic universe, the core of which are those same ones that anchor the culture of the ghetto: a mix of peer-group solidarity and defiant individualism, physical toughness and courage ("heart"), an uncompromising sense of masculine honor, and an expressive stress on personal performance and style.

---

[26] Merton 1957, 60–82; cf. Holmwood 2005, 90–92.
[27] Cited as a personal communication in Dreyfus, Rabinow, and Foucault 1983, 187.

The gym functions in the manner of a *quasi-total institution* that purports to regiment the whole existence of the fighter – his use of time and space, the management of his body, his state of mind, and his most intimate desires. So much so that pugilists often compare working out in the gym to entering the military. [Wacquant then quotes from two relevant conversations with other members of the gym.]

Butch: in the gym, you learn discipline, self-control. You learn tha' you s'pose to go to bed early, git up early, do your road work, take care of yourself, eat the right foods. Uh, yer body is a *machine*, it's s'pose to be well-tuned. You learn to have some control so far as rippin' and runnin' the streets, social life. It jus' gives you kin' of like an *army, soldier mentality*, an' [chuckling] that's real good for folks.

Curtis: The average guy tha' trains in this gym, kid or man, he *matures 85 perzent*, 85 perzent more than if he was out on d'street. 'Cause it discipline him to try to be a young man, to try to have sportsmanship, ring generalship, you know, uh, I don' know....[stumbles] It's more like, I coul' sit up here an' give you a line of thin's, you know but [you can] break it down to: it works *like bein' in the military*, it show you how to be a *gentleman* and all, and learn respect.[28]

One of the recurrent themes of meso-level studies of the effects of sport on the larger behavioral patterns of athletes and spectators has been the power of sport to reinforce particular kinds of gender-role expectations among males. Much of the relevant scholarship has drawn on R. W. Connell's work on hegemonic masculinity, which Connell defines as a culturally exalted form of masculinity in which men are expected to be physically strong and tough, competent, and dominant and oppressive in their relations with women. Connell has argued that sport is one of the more important sites in which hegemonic masculinity is displayed and through which males are taught to conform to its expectations: "The cults of physicality, and especially of sport – the cult which is not only allowed to schoolboys but positively encouraged by their elders – give clear ideal definitions of how a male body should look and work."[29] Sport, especially violent contact sports, inculcates hegemonic masculinity in both participants and spectators. The former absorb relevant behavioral patterns and values through first-hand exposure to a hyper-masculine sport culture; the latter learn through displays of hegemonic masculinity on the playing field, particularly displays by individual athletes who serve as exemplars of masculinity.[30] These behavioral patterns and values, once learned from sport, are influential in a wide range of social interactions that extend well beyond the sphere of sport.

A good example of work that explores the connection between sport and hegemonic masculinity is Steven Schacht's participant-observer based study of the members of male rugby teams at two different American universities.

[28] Wacquant 2004, 14–15, 40, 56, respectively.
[29] Connell 1983, 20.
[30] Connell 1983, 17–32; Connell 1990. See also the discussion in Markula and Pringle 2006, 92–133.

Schacht argued that "the rugby 'pitch' is one social terrain situationally located among many where men's hierarchical conceptions of men *and women* are individually and collectively created, contested, and continually reconstructed." He found that in both clubs players were taught to value the ability to exert physical force and to endure pain as constitutive of masculinity and at the same time to reject anything understood as feminine, defined in large part by the absence of force and physical fortitude. These attitudes shaped the players' interactions with women. At the clubs of which Schacht was a member, women who attended practices were routinely ignored, while female passersby were consistently the target of explicit comments made by team members. Schacht noted that "These remarks serve as reminders to both the players and the women who pass by of the gender hierarchy being constructed in this setting: men at the center (the top), with women relationally being chased off and not even allowed on the sidelines." The masculine culture learned on the playing field extended to other environments, most notably at parties organized by the rugby team, parties at which "women are expected to attend and play an active role in their own denigration (women who attend parties often are called rugger-huggers, rugby hags, and rugby whores)."[31]

Douglas Foley carried out another such study, this one a detailed ethnography of a high school football team in Texas. Foley's work is particularly interesting because he examined how the entire community was drawn into the rituals associated with high school football games, rituals that included pep rallies, marching bands, cheerleaders, homecoming festivities, and the interactions of former and current players. Among other things, he found that those rituals symbolically staged decidedly unequal forms of gender relations. Of particular interest was a "powder-puff" football game held once a year. This involved female students from the junior and senior classes, dressed in football jerseys and helmets, playing a game of touch football before a sizeable audience. Male football players, having dressed as girls complete with padded breasts, lipstick, and high heels, served as cheerleaders and took great delight in sexually provocative play acting. Foley pointed out that this is a standard ritual of inversion and that "the power of these young males to appropriate and play with female symbols of sexuality was a statement about males' social and physical dominance." He concluded that his case study showed how sport could be "deeply implicated...in the reproduction of class, gender, and racial inequality."[32] The involvement of much of the town's population in the rituals associated with football games meant that those inequalities were enacted as much or more off the football field as on it.

---

[31] Schacht 1996, 551, 558, 559, respectively.
[32] Foley 1990, 119, 111, respectively.

Macro-level studies of large groups of athletes have not been typically successful in establishing any consistent, significant effects of involvement in sport. Perhaps the most obvious examples of such work are the literally dozens of studies that have been carried out on the effects of participation in athletics on American high school students. The results of those studies have been vitiated by three significant shortcomings. First, in many cases there was no reason to think that the groups of students surveyed were representative of any larger population, which meant that the significance of any results was unclear. Second, virtually all of these studies were unable to account for the role of self-selection; in cases in which studies did find significant differences between athletes and nonathletes, it was impossible to establish whether this was because the experience of playing sports was responsible for the differences in question (treatment effects) or whether individuals with certain personality traits chose to play sports (selection effects). This is a problem because research has shown that there is a considerable degree of self-selection in regard to sport participation, and it could be the case that any outcome associated with sport participation, e.g., increased educational attainment, was the result of the fact that individuals with particular qualities chose to become athletes, not because sport participation helped generate the qualities that resulted in the outcome in question.[33] Finally, in most cases, the data permitted no conclusions as to what specific aspects of participating in sports might cause changes in individual behavior. Moreover, the findings of such studies have varied widely, some concluding that athletic participation had positive effects such as heightened levels of academic aspiration and achievement, whereas other studies found no such effects.[34]

Herbert Marsh, who spent years examining and extending this body of work, sought to address these problems by using a database with detailed information on a nationally representative sample of American high school students, consisting of 12,084 individuals who were surveyed four times over the course of six years, starting in 1988, at which point all the students involved were in eighth grade. He argued that measuring a range of variables on multiple occasions helped make it possible to control for preexisting differences. Analysis of the data led him to conclude that "participation in high school sports had positive effects on many Grade 12 and postsecondary outcomes (e.g., school grades, coursework selection, homework, educational and occupational aspirations, self-esteem, university applications, subsequent college enrollment, and eventual educational attainment) after controlling background variables and parallel outcomes from Grades 8 and 10." He used his findings, particularly the fact that the positive effects

---

[33] For statistical data demonstrating self-selection in sport participation, see Stevenson 2010, 2–7.

[34] See the discussion in Coakley 1987 and Marsh and Kleitman 2003.

of athletic participation were linear (i.e., increased levels of participation were associated with better outcomes), to test three separate theories of how sport might shape behavior. Marsh concluded that his findings were consistent with the theory that athletic participation "fosters identification with the school and school-related values."[35]

An equally sophisticated study using an even larger dataset and with similar results was carried out by Betsey Stevenson, who analyzed data from the 1980 and 2000 censuses pertaining to American females aged 25–34, using a representative sample of 5% of the total (the Census Bureau's 5% Public Use Micro Sample).[36] Stevenson looked carefully at the changes that resulted from the passage of Title IX of the Education Amendments of 1972, which required that high schools and colleges in the United States make equal provisions for sports for male and female students.[37] Stevenson pointed out that sport participation rates for female students in the United States prior to 1972 were extremely low, that Title IX required the percentage of male and female students in school sports programs to be roughly equal, and that there were significant state-by-state variations in participation rates for male students. These three facts taken together meant that there were large state-by-state variations in sport participation rates for female students in the years after Title IX was implemented. In states with high rates of male sport participation, schools had to make available to female students much more in the way of opportunities for sport participation than schools in states with low rates of male sport participation. That in turn creates an invaluable opportunity to study the effects of sport participation on female students on a nationwide scale while also eliminating the distortions introduced by self-selection. State-by-state variation in rates of female sport participation in the years after the implementation of Title IX was not the result of self-selection but rather the result of variation in the opportunities offered for sport participation (which were in turn dictated by rates of male sport participation).[38]

Stevenson analyzed census data from before and after the enactment of Title IX, identified statistically significant changes in the areas of education and employment among females that varied on a state-by-state basis, and discovered that some changes in those areas correlated with high versus low rates of female sport participation. After controlling for a wide variety of

---

[35] Marsh and Kleitman 2003, 205, 206, respectively.

[36] Stevenson 2010.

[37] For the text of the Title IX Amendments, see http://www.dol.gov/oasam/regs/statutes/titleix.htm.

[38] Stevenson's approach is most productive when applied to female students in the years immediately after the implementation of Title IX, for two reasons. First, the sudden increase in female sport participation starting in 1972 makes it easier to trace treatment effects. Second, rates of sport participation have tended to equalize across the United States over the course of time (though there are still significant state-by-state variations, see Stevenson 2007).

other possibly relevant variables, she found that sport participation had a substantial positive effect on educational attainment, labor force participation, and participation in previously male-dominated occupations, especially high-skill occupations.[39] She estimated, for instance, that the sharp increase in female sport participation that resulted from Title IX was responsible for a 4.5% increase in labor force participation by females in the United States.

Unfortunately, Marsh's and Stevenson's work remains unusual in regard to the richness of the relevant dataset and the methodological sophistication with which the data is analyzed. In addition, there is good reason to doubt whether macro-level studies of the effects of playing or watching sports are likely in most cases to produce consistent or useful results. A key problem is that sport is not a monolithic phenomenon. For example, the effects of long-term participation in horizontal sport are very likely to be substantially different from those resulting from participation in vertical sport. Large-scale studies that agglomerate the experiences of thousands of athletes playing a variety of sports in a variety of settings tend to mask wide differences in outcomes for individual athletes. Furthermore, unless the dataset is very large and clearly representative of a given population, wide differences in outcomes for individual athletes are likely to produce results that vary significantly from one study to the next. Meso-level studies are almost always more valuable, because they focus on smaller groups of athletes whose experiences with sport are relatively homogeneous.

We have now had the opportunity to look at micro-, meso-, and macro-level studies of the effects of sport. Properly conducted macro-level studies, albeit few in number, find that participation in sport does indeed shape individual behavior outside of sport. Meso-level studies, which present etic perspectives informed by detailed research on small groups of athletes undertaken by trained social scientists, also indicate that playing or watching sports can shape the behavior of individuals outside of sport. The fact that this is precisely the same point that emerges from the emic perspectives expressed in the writings of former athletes working at the micro level leaves little doubt about the power of sport to affect behavior in a wide range of contexts that extend well beyond the sphere of sport.

The significance of the behavioral changes induced by sport participation is greatly magnified in societies with mass sport. We have already seen that something like half of all American high school students participate in organized sports, and the vast majority of these students began playing sports well before they entered high school. What this means in practice

---

[39] Stevenson ran a series of statistical analyses that eliminated the legitimate concern that "states that had higher rates of male athletic participation prior to the passage of Title IX were bad for women in ways that changed over time, perhaps as a result of Title IX, but not because of athletic participation" (Stevenson 2010, 20).

is that roughly half of all Americans arriving at adulthood have spent a considerable portion of their childhood playing sports. There is a downward shift in participation as these students become adults, but they continue to invest much time, energy, and money in playing, organizing, and watching sport. Norway, about which large amounts of statistical information is available, offers a useful comparandum that makes it clear that Americans are not unique in their dedication to sport. All competitive sport for people of all ages in Norway is organized through sports clubs. Roughly one-third of Norway's 4.8 million inhabitants are members of at least one sports club, and roughly three-quarters of all Norwegians are a member of a sports club at some point before age eighteen. Most of the work of running these clubs is carried out by members on a voluntary basis; Norwegians spend approximately 22 million hours per year volunteering in sports clubs, which are the most common form of voluntary organization in Norway. On any given day approximately one-third of Norway's population is engaged in some sort of sport-related activity.[40]

In societies with mass sport, a significant fraction of the populace spends a significant fraction of their time from an early age playing sports, an activity that has a proven capacity to shape their behavior in a variety of contexts outside of sport. As a result, sport, especially in societies with mass sport, not only reflects the nature of the society in which it is played, but also shapes the nature of that society.

[40] For these figures, see Bergsgard, Houlihan, Mangset, Nødland, and Rommetvedt 2007, 9; Seippel 2002, 258–60; Seippel 2006, 175; and Walseth 2008, 2–3.

5

Sport as a School for Democracy

The contributions of sport to social democracy have been significant.
John Betts, *America's Sporting Heritage*[1]

5.1. INTRODUCTION

The analysis of the relationship between sport and democratization undertaken in this book is somewhat unusual among the current scholarship on sport in being overtly functionalist. As we have seen, in recent decades functionalism has been associated with Talcott Parsons. The undoubted shortcomings of Parsons' version of functionalism have made scholars reluctant to label their own work as functionalist, but a substantial fraction of the ongoing scholarship in the social sciences could comfortably be placed under that heading. Indeed, there is something to be said for the idea that functionalism represents an essential component of social science methodology.

It is, therefore, helpful to move past the misleading habit of making functionalism equivalent to the Parsonian version and to look to less flawed, more nuanced forms of functionalism suitable for particular analytical tasks. The methodology employed here aligns closely with what is sometimes called weak functionalism in that it presumes that societies are interdependent wholes, but that they are imperfectly integrated and that dysfunction and conflict are inevitable. This version of functionalism is closely associated with Robert Merton, whose work on that subject was summarized in Section 3.3 and whose ideas have appeared intermittently throughout the preceding discussion. One of Merton's many insights is his refutation of what he called the "postulate of universal functionalism," by which he meant the assumption that all social practices and institutions have positive functions. Merton insisted that any given practice or institution can have a range of effects and

---

[1] Betts 1974, 326.

can be simultaneously functional and dysfunctional with respect to certain ends, most notably the maintenance of a stable social order.

This is a crucial insight in the present context because it suggests that the characteristic effects of horizontal mass sport include some that promote democratization and some that inhibit it. We will explore the former in this chapter, the latter in the next.[2]

The previous writing in which sport is presented as a "school for democracy" has frequently suffered from a failure to identify and substantiate in a thorough fashion the mechanisms by means of which sport might foster democratization. The Progressives created a series of programs to encourage sport participation, but they made only superficial attempts to articulate the specific mechanisms by which sport might foster democratization and to document the democratizing effects of sport participation.

Robert Putnam's books and articles have inspired an enormous body of scholarly work on social capital and a rapidly growing collection of research on the connection between sport and social capital. The latter is an invaluable resource for studying the relationship between sport and democratization, but it has not to this point typically been used to that end. Instead, the focus has been on the ways that sport might foster social inclusion or reduce undesirable behavior such as crime. Democratization as such is rarely mentioned, in part because of a persistent tendency to see democracy in institutionalist terms. In addition, many studies of the effects of sport on social capital have been driven by attempts to document the results of government-sponsored sport programs and have been – implicitly – concerned with the extent to which sport can increase extant levels of democratization; the extent to which horizontal mass sport is responsible for democratization that has already taken place is not addressed in those studies.[3] Furthermore, research on sport and social capital has for the most part focused on documenting the capacity of sport to generate social capital and has had relatively little to say about underlying mechanisms. Scholarly work on how voluntary associations generate social capital is relevant to some extent because horizontal sport can be seen as a form of voluntary association, but that work does not take into account the many features of sport that make it different from other kinds of voluntary associations.

There is, as a result, still no coherent body of argumentation that specifies, in a clear and convincing fashion, the mechanisms by means of which sport might foster democratization on a societal level. That issue is addressed in this chapter, in which four such mechanisms are discussed:

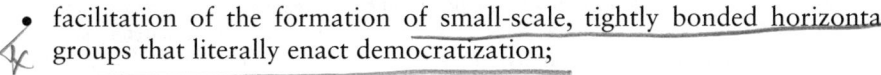

- facilitation of the formation of small-scale, tightly bonded horizontal groups that literally enact democratization;

---

[2] On the application of Merton's work to the study of sport, see Loy and Booth 2004.
[3] See the discussion in Coalter 2007.

- cultivation of particularized and generalized trust;
- cultivation of a sense of political efficacy;
- cultivation of self-disciplined individuals with a predisposition to obey rules and legally constituted authorities.

All four mechanisms will be explored in detail and substantiated on the basis of evidence from modern-day democratized societies in Europe, North America, and Australasia.

These mechanisms seem to be operative in all societies with horizontal mass sport, though their cumulative effect will vary widely depending on contextually specific factors. The claim of transhistorical validity cannot be proven beyond doubt on an inductive basis, both because the sources from many places and times are insufficient for that task and because a single exception could falsify it at any moment. That said, these mechanisms are tied directly to and rely on horizontal mass sport, and they should, therefore, function wherever horizontal mass sport is found. In addition, all the extant evidence supports the claim that they are in fact transhistorically valid (see the discussion in Chapters 10 and 15), and there is no evidence to the contrary.

What follows does not purport to be an exhaustive catalog of the positive effects of sport participation and spectatorship – many of which are causally null with respect to democratization – nor even a complete listing of possible ways that sport might foster democratization; rather it includes only those mechanisms that are relatively well-understood and well-documented.

5.2. SMALL-SCALE, TIGHTLY BONDED, HORIZONTAL GROUPS

Sport fosters democratization through facilitating the creation of small-scale, tightly bonded, horizontal groups that literally enact democratization. In order to understand this process, it is necessary to begin with social capital. The concept of social capital, as understood and used here, is not by any means identical to social capital as it appears in Putnam's work, though that work has exerted a continuing influence on subsequent scholarship, including the analysis undertaken here.

The concept of social capital has been repeatedly refined and redefined over the past two decades, and it is, therefore, necessary to specify precisely what it means in the present context.[4] It is useful to begin by making a

---

[4] The discussion that follows is a highly abbreviated synthesis of a complex corpus of theoretical thinking and empirical research. It is not possible here to treat the evidence that underpins each of the following claims about social capital, but it is important to bear in mind that such evidence does exist, in no small quantity, and can be located by pursuing the work cited in the footnotes. A good introduction to current thinking about social capital can be found in Field 2008. The discussion provided here also draws on the following sources: Adler and Kwon 2002, Burt 2005, Coffé and Geys 2007, Coleman 1988, Farr 2004, M. Leonard 2004, Portes 1998, Putnam 2000, and Woolcock 2001.

TABLE 3. *Types of Social Capital*

	Identity of Individuals	Nature of Relationship	Likely Intensity of Resulting Bonds	Orientation
Bonding	Similar in regard to social status and social identity	Horizontal	Strong	Exclusive
Bridging	Similar in regard to social status, dissimilar in regard to social identity	Horizontal	Intermediate	Inclusive
Linking	Dissimilar in regard to social power	Vertical	Variable	Inclusive

distinction between three different types of social capital: bonding, bridging, and linking.[5] The distinction between the three is based on the identity of the individuals involved, the nature of the relationship between them, the intensity of the resulting bonds, and the orientation of the group, as seen in Table 3. Specific examples will help clarify how this might work in practice. Bonding social capital would exist among the members of a local voluntary association that was made up entirely of engineers (who worked in the same North American office of a large company and who had for the most part been born, raised, and educated in the surrounding region) and that organized the teaching of science in after-school programs in inner city areas. Bridging social capital would exist between the members of that organization and the members of another voluntary association that was made up entirely of recent college graduates who came from families of recent immigrants, that organized the teaching of English as a second language, and that worked in the same schools as the engineers. Linking social capital would exist between those teaching science or English on one hand and their students on the other. As will become evident, sport is primarily associated with bonding capital and, to a lesser extent, bridging capital.

One of the most significant differences between bonding and bridging capital is that the former creates exclusive groups, the latter inclusive groups. Bonding capital builds in-group solidarity while sharpening the perceived differences between in-group and out-group. It can, therefore, bring both positive and negative social consequences; an example of the latter is the persistence of neo-Nazi groups that are tightly bound together by bonding capital and hence resistant to attempts to dissolve them. Bridging capital, which serves to bring together individuals who differ in some basic

[5] On this distinction, see Woolcock 2001, 13–14.

component of their social identity, is, for obvious reasons, inclusive. Bonding capital appears as a general rule to be more easily formed and stronger than bridging capital, which in turn can create difficulties in achieving unity among large groups of heterogeneous individuals.

A second helpful distinction in thinking about social capital is that between origins, substance, and effects.[6] There is considerable variation in these dimensions between the different kinds of social capital, and it will be most productive to focus on bonding capital. Bonding capital originates in iterated and cooperative interactions, which frequently focus on achieving a shared goal, between people of similar social standing. The substance of bonding capital consists of social networks built around horizontal relationships that simplify the sharing of information (particularly about members of the network), impart knowledge about how to work effectively as a member of a group, create trust between members and a cognitive bias toward trust, and socialize members in and enforce norms that typically include expectations of reciprocity, cooperation, and concern for the collective well-being of the members of the network. Social networks contain both structural and voluntaristic elements in that norms are inculcated and backed up by sanctions, while, at the same time, there are also opportunities for autonomous behavior. The formation of bonding capital has the effect of promoting solidarity, cooperative collective action, and consensus among the members of a network and hence the formation of tightly bonded, horizontal groups.

In the past decade, a number of studies have been carried out on the relationship between sport and social capital; the research methodologies employed in those studies remain a work in progress, and the results, particularly in regard to the magnitude of the effects associated with sport participation, need to be treated with some caution. Because social capital cannot be observed directly, most studies have employed measures of interconnectedness between individuals and trust as proxies for social capital. The connection between sport and social capital is traced by collecting qualitative or quantitative data to test the relative performance on those measures of sport participants versus nonparticipants.[7]

This approach has two important shortcomings. First, it treats sport participation as a monolithic phenomenon with uniform effects, whereas there

---

[6] This useful approach to thinking about social capital is taken from Adler and Kwon 2002.

[7] Putnam's idea that sport could be a source of social capital rapidly attracted attention. See, for instance, Uslaner 1999, 145–46. The best starting place for those interested in recent research on the relationship between sport and social capital is the collection of articles in Nicholson and Hoye 2008. There is a considerable body of scholarship on sport that does not employ the concept of social capital, but which, in terms of either projected effects or mechanisms or both, reaches very similar conclusions. See, for instance, Burdsey and Chappell 2003, in which it is argued that sport spectatorship has created strong in-group solidarity and equally strong out-group hostility in Northern Ireland and Scotland.

is every reason to think that the experiences of sport participants will differ meaningfully depending on the extent to which the environments in which they take place are horizontal or vertical. Although some researchers have realized that it is important to differentiate among divergent kinds of sport in examining the relationship between sport and social capital, to date no such studies have been carried out.[8] This, less than ideal, situation is ameliorated by the fact that most of the relevant work has been carried out in Australia, Canada, and Norway (all highly democratized countries with systems of mass sport that are strongly horizontal in nature), and so there is a priori reason to believe that most studies of sport and social capital are in fact testing the relationship between horizontal sport and social capital. A second shortcoming is that this approach does not take into account the existence of alternative means of generating social capital. We have seen that, from the perspective of Mertonian functionalism, the same effect can be produced by a variety of different mechanisms (Merton's "postulate of indispensability," see Section 3.3), and it is virtually certain that in a dataset of any size at least some of those not participating in sport are active in alternative activities that are excellent sources of social capital. Ideally, studies of the relationship between sport and social capital would compare sport participants with those not engaging in any functionally equivalent activities, but no such studies exist.

There is, therefore, good reason to think that the research carried out to date underestimates, to an unknowable degree, the capacity of sport to generate social capital. One might also bear in mind that social capital research has been heavily concentrated in countries that are already to a considerable extent democratized and in which horizontal mass sport is a long-established part of the social landscape. That is relevant with respect to the scale of changes one might expect to see in the many studies of the effects of government-sponsored sport programs on social capital.

We will, as a result, concentrate on the question of whether the research on sport and social capital does or does not indicate that sport can generate social capital, and we will not expend a great deal of energy examining the magnitude of any relevant changes associated with sport participation.

The body of research on sport as a source of social capital is too large to make an exhaustive survey possible in the present context. It will, however, be useful to have some sense of the kind of work that has been done on this subject. With this in mind, eight recent studies will now be briefly reviewed.[9]

---

[8] To be more precise, this author is aware of no such studies. For recognition that variations in kinds of sport should be taken into account in social capital research, see Henry 2006, 39 and Seippel 2006, 174.

[9] The ongoing debate about how to define the term "social capital" means that no two studies use the term in precisely the same way. However, all of the studies reviewed here employ it in a fashion that is consistent with the definition offered here.

In 2005, Liam Delaney and Emily Keaney published an analysis of the relationship between sport and social capital in the United Kingdom in particular and Europe in general. Their data was drawn from 30,000 face-to-face interviews conducted as part of the 2002 European Social Survey. They found that:

Participation in sport and social capital are linked. There are very strong correlations between a nation's level of sports membership and the levels of social trust and well being.[10]

In 2005, Matthew Tonts published the results of a study of sport practice in rural communities in northwestern Australia. Tonts constructed a dataset of 40 interviews and 285 survey responses. He concluded that "sport is an important arena for the creation and maintenance of social capital."[11] His findings indicated that bonding capital was particularly prominent, and he pointed out that:

High levels of participation in sport, together with the considerable time and resources that residents were willing to provide as volunteers or supporters, helps to emphasise the sense of reciprocity and altruism often found in sporting clubs and associations.[12]

The residents of the communities studied by Tonts regularly characterized sport as a means of transcending social barriers, and hence, as a source of bridging capital, and although there was some evidence that this was indeed the case, it was also true that "In a number of cases, the networks and bonds associated with some clubs or particular sports acted to exclude certain citizens on the basis of race, class, gender, and status."[13]

In 2006, Kim Atherley published the results of a study of the role of sport in rural communities in Western Australia. Her dataset consisted of information gathered from the records of 25 sports clubs and 169 survey responses. She concluded that "sport...plays an integral role in the formation of bonding and bridging capital."[14] Atherley found that sport generated bonding capital at the local level and bridging capital at the regional level.

In 2006, Cora Burnett published the results of an assessment of the impact of the establishment of community clubs in South Africa under the auspices of the Australia Africa Sport Development Programme. Sport was the primary activity sponsored by these clubs, though other programs were

---

[10] Delaney and Keaney 2005, 32. Delaney and Keaney were notably cautious in using their findings as the basis of causal inferences because the nature of the data (which were not intended to study the effects of sport participation) did not make it possible to determine if existing social capital encouraged sport participation, vice-versa, or both.

[11] Tonts 2005, 137.

[12] Tonts 2005, 147.

[13] Ibid.

[14] Atherley 2006, 348.

offered as well. The assessment examined one of five clubs and was based on interviews and focus groups, held both before and after its establishment, that involved 209 individuals in all. Burnett concluded that "From the evidence it is clear that the Siyakhula Community Club was a catalyst in the creation of social capital in the rural community of Tshabo." Her findings indicated that the club's activities generated bonding capital between the players, bridging capital between players and coaches, and linking capital between coaches and local stakeholders.[15]

In 2006, Ørnulf Seippel published the results of a study of the relationship between sport and social capital among members of sports clubs in Norway. He drew on data generated as part of the Johns Hopkins Comparative Nonprofit Sector Project, which provided him with 1,695 survey responses from a representative sample of the population of Norway. Seippel found that:

The analyses support previous studies and confirm that being a member of voluntary organizations in general…but also sport organizations in particular, has a positive effect on certain kinds of general social trust and some political attitudes and activity….[16]

He concluded that voluntary sport organizations generated social capital.

In 2007, Thomas Perks published the results of a study of the relationship between sport participation and community involvement in Canada. His dataset consisted of survey results from a representative sample of Canadians, comprising 14,724 responses in all. He concluded that:

The findings from this study support the general proposition that youth sport participation has a positive association with adult community involvement. This is consistent with the interpretation that sport participation early in life fosters social capital, and that this social capital pays off in access to higher levels of involvement in the community as an adult.[17]

In 2008, Kevin Brown studied the relationship between membership in community sport and recreation groups and social capital measures in Sweden and Australia. He made use of a dataset generated as part of a larger project on active citizenship in six countries. For the work in question Brown looked at 646 survey responses from Lund, Sweden and Ballarat, Australia. He concluded that:

Following discussion of Putnam's treatment of tolerance and social capital, a mix of indicators measuring aspects of trust, connectedness, civic activity, and tolerance was outlined as a potentially useful instrument for measuring broad aspects of comparative social capital. This analysis of the data from Lund and Ballarat shows that

---

[15] Burnett 2006, 291, 290, respectively.
[16] Seippel 2006, 178.
[17] Perks 2007, 393.

for both samples, members of sport/recreation organizations compared to all other types of community organization members scored significantly higher on some social capital measures. In addition they were not significantly different on the remaining measures.[18]

In 2009, Dwight Zakus, James Skinner, and Allan Edwards published the results of a study of the role of sport in Australian society from the perspective of social capital formation. Their dataset consisted of the results of two separate surveys that together produced 1,115 responses. They concluded that, "Sport, sport clubs, and other organisations comprising the sport delivery system play an important role in building local and national social capital...."[19]

Two further studies are also relevant because they show that sport can lead to social capital formation not only among athletes, but also among volunteers who help organize sports activities and among spectators. In 2008, Graham Cuskelly published a study of the effects of volunteer activity in sports clubs on social capital formation. He used data taken from the National Survey of Giving, Volunteering, and Participating conducted in Canada in 2000 and a report issued by the Australian Bureau of Statistics, "Australia's Sports Volunteers 2000" (which drew on the Voluntary Work Survey conducted in 2000). In both cases the surveys in question involved interviews with a representative sample of the adult population of the country (14,724 in Canada; 12,900 in Australia). Cuskelly concluded that, "The statistics presented here suggest that initial engagement and ongoing involvement in sport volunteering tend to reinforce the maintenance and development of bonding capital."[20] He added an important caveat to this finding, namely that volunteering in sport is closely connected to playing or spectating (i.e., volunteers typically get involved through their own sports activity or through watching the sports activity of family members or friends), so social capital formation through sport volunteering is something of a secondary process. That said, the scale of sport volunteering means that its cumulative effect is substantial. We have already seen (Section 4.2) that in Norway, a country with a total population of less than 5 million, 22 million hours are volunteered to sports clubs each year. In Australia, population c. 22 million, 187 million hours are given to sport volunteering annually.[21]

In 2007, Catherine Palmer and Kirrilly Thompson published a study of male fans of the North Adelaide Football Club in Australia. Their work was based on two focus groups and ninety-three in-depth interviews conducted with members of a loosely organized fan group that called itself the "Grog Squad." They concluded that social interactions within the Grog Squad

[18] Brown 2008, 181.
[19] Zakus, Skinner, and Edwards 2009, 994.
[20] Cuskelly 2008, 197. Cf. the similar conclusions reached in Bradbury and Kay 2008 and J. Harvey and Lévesque 2007.
[21] Zakus, Skinner, and Edwards 2009, 988.

reinforced an ethos of hegemonic masculinity (on which, see Section 4.2), but that "to concentrate on this alone…obscures the very real friendships and social supports that enable bonding and bridging social capital among the Grog Squad."[22] Here again it is important to bear in mind the scale of the activity in question; sports spectating is widespread around the globe.

Although there has been no significant research on the specific question of why sport is a good source of social capital, there is a considerable body of experimentally grounded work in social psychology that provides insight into the relevant processes. In the 1960s and 1970s, Henri Tajfel conducted a series of experiments in which individuals were asked to perform extremely mundane activities such as guessing the number of dots in a projected image and then given the task of dividing sums of money between two other subjects. In doing so, each individual knew whether he or she had under- or overestimated the number of dots and whether each of the other two subjects had under- or overestimated. However, none of the subjects had any first-hand interaction whatsoever and were identified by code numbers rather than names. Tajfel found that individuals who had underestimated the number of dots consistently allocated more money to other subjects who had done the same, and vice-versa. In a further series of experiments he required subjects to choose either to increase the differential between the amounts rewarded to those who were like themselves in under- or overestimating the number of dots or to increase the absolute amount collectively awarded to all subjects. Those experiments showed a consistent bias toward maximizing differentiation rather than the total amount awarded. Tajfel also conducted experiments in which subjects who had no contact with each other were assigned to groups formed on an explicitly random basis, in which circumstances subjects still showed a strong bias toward distributing rewards in favor of members of their own group. These results were repeatedly replicated in a variety of similar experiments.[23]

Tajfel found a propensity to construct groups even in the absence of any meaningful personal interaction. Experiments by other social psychologists found that the propensity to construct cohesive groups is strongly reinforced by the existence of a shared goal necessarily achieved through cooperation. In the 1960s, Muzafer Sherif and a number of collaborators performed an experiment in which individuals previously unknown to each other were formed into a number of groups, which were then required to interact. Sherif found that the presence of superordinate goals played a key role in group formation:

When the individuals interacted in a series of situations toward goals with common appeal value which required interdependent activity for their attainment, definite

[22] Palmer and Thompson 2007, 197.
[23] Tajfel 1981, 268–87.

group structures arose....As group structure was stabilized, it was unmistakably delineated as an "in-group."...Ways of doing things, of meeting problems, of behaving under certain conditions were standardized, permitting variation only within limits. Beyond the limits of the group norms, behavior was subject to group sanctions, which ranged from ridicule, through ignoring the offender and his behavior, to threats, and occasionally to physical chastisement.

Another significant finding from Sherif's experiment was that cohesion was increased further when a group was set a task that entailed competitive interaction with another group:

When two groups met in competitive and reciprocally frustrating engagements, in-group solidarity and cooperativeness increased....This heightened in-group solidarity and cooperativeness were observed at the very time when intergroup hostility was at its peak.[24]

Sport, especially in the form of competitive team sports, creates precisely this sort of situation.

Sherif and Tajfel's experiments showed that humans will tend to form groups with norms that shape the behavior of their members. Indeed, the "tendency for a group to converge on a norm" has been described as "the most elementary 'fact' known to the social psychologist."[25] Tajfel, in collaboration with John Turner and others, constructed what is now called social identity theory, which can be summarized as follows:

The core idea is that a self-inclusive social category (e.g., nationality, political affiliation, sports team) provides a category-congruent self-definition that constitutes an element of the self-concept. People have a repertoire of such discrete category memberships that vary in relative overall importance in the self-concept. The category is represented in the individual member's mind as a social identity that both describes and prescribes one's attributes as a group member.[26]

Hence, individuals construct their identities around and behave in a fashion consonant with membership in particular groups.

Social identity theory ties closely into horizontal sport and social capital because sport participants will tend to identify themselves as members of a group defined by that shared activity. The groups thus formed will tend to be highly cohesive because of the existence of a shared, superordinate goal. The members of those groups will tend to act in accordance with the behavioral norms of the group, which in the case of horizontal sport emphasize cooperative, egalitarian interactions between group members. Horizontal sport, as a result, has a strong tendency to generate the sort of

[24] Sherif, Harvey, White, Hood, and Sherif 1961, 206, 207, respectively.
[25] Heine 2008 (1971), 25.
[26] Hogg 1996, 66–67.

cooperative, egalitarian groups that are an essential part of social capital formation.

One might also point out that both the studies of the relationship between sport and social capital and the experimental work in the social psychology of groups echo a body of theoretical thinking that goes back to Plato and Aristotle and that found further expression in foundational work in the modern social sciences by Durkheim and others. That body of thinking stresses the power of iterated interaction to foster cooperative relationships among members of groups by means of socialization and consensus. As David and Richard Ned Lebow put it, Plato and Aristotle argued that "at the personal, society, and inter-state levels, cooperative relationships are created and sustained through a dense network of social interaction and reciprocal obligations that build common identities along with mutual respect and affection."[27] Plato and Aristotle saw those interactions as taking place in a variety of different social and political contexts. Durkheim wrote at length about the power of group activity, especially in the form of religious rites, to generate what he called *la conscience collective*.[28]

Moreover, the interactions that occur in the context of horizontal sport are precisely those that Tocqueville emphasized in highlighting the importance of voluntary associations in democratic societies. Tocqueville argued that, "In democratic countries the science of association is the mother science; the progress of all the others depends on the progress of that one."[29] We have already seen (Section 1.1) that he believed that "sentiments and ideas renew themselves, the heart is enlarged, and the human mind is developed only by the reciprocal action of men upon one another." For Tocqueville voluntary associations were an essential underpinning of democracy in large part because they provided a setting in which cooperative personal interactions took place. Horizontal sport is in that sense a particular manifestation of the broader phenomenon of voluntary associations.

Hence, the growing collection of studies on sport and social capital, experimental social psychology, and a related body of long-established social theory all point in precisely the same direction. Together they leave little doubt that sport can be an important source of what is here described as bonding capital and to a lesser extent bridging capital as well. Insofar as both bonding and bridging capital originate in interactions between people of similar social standing, it would be more precise to say that horizontal sport can be an important source of bonding and bridging capital.[30]

---

[27] Lebow and Lebow Forthcoming.
[28] See Durkheim 1949 (1893) and Durkheim 1965 (1912).
[29] de Tocqueville 2000 (1835–40), 492.
[30] It seems likely that vertical sport is a good source of linking social capital, though there does not appear to be any scholarly work on that subject.

The conclusion to be drawn from the preceding discussion is clear: the bonding and bridging capital formed in sport can be an important wellspring of democratization. More than anything else this is because social capital formation in sport involves the creation of social networks built around horizontal relationships. When democratization is understood as a process involving a shift in the balance between horizontal and vertical relationships toward the former, the capacity of sport to facilitate the growth of bonding and bridging capital and hence the growth of horizontal relationships means that sport has a corresponding capacity to facilitate democratization. The expansion of the practice of horizontal sport within any given society necessarily entails the expansion of horizontal relationships and hence *is* democratization, and so, for example, the implementation of a successful (horizontal) sport-for-all program in the 1960s did in fact increase the level of democratization in Norway. Conversely, the implementation of a system of vertical mass sport after 1949 *decreased* the level of democratization in China. This is a relatively simple point but one that merits particular emphasis: the expansion of the practice of horizontal sport, particularly on a mass scale, in and of itself represents a meaningful form of democratization.

A more subtle but equally important phenomenon involves conceiving of democratization as a condition that is maintained in part by sport participation. The balance between horizontal and vertical relationships in a given society at a given moment is to some extent the product of long-term processes, as is evident from Putnam's work on democracy in Italy.[31] On the other hand, relationships are actualized in the interactions between human beings, and the inevitability of change, especially aging and death, means that those relationships need to be constantly renewed. An established system of horizontal mass sport is an important means by which horizontal relationships are renewed in each succeeding generation, and for that reason plays an important part in perpetuating extant levels of democratization. The strong element of continuity makes sport's contribution to democratization in such situations less obvious, but no less significant.

In thinking about the relationship between social capital, sport, and democratization, the issue of scale requires careful attention. The formation of social capital takes place primarily through face-to-face interactions, which means that the networks involved in bonding capital are necessarily relatively small. Bridging capital creates connections between groups, but here again there are obvious constraints because the members of the different groups must interact in some meaningful fashion.

The small scale at which sport works in producing democratization through the formation of bonding and bridging capital does not diminish its importance. Gary Alan Fine and Brooke Harrington have recently made

---

[31] Putnam, Leonardi, and Nanetti 1993.

the case that small groups represent an essential part of civil society. They follow Robert Bales in defining a small group as "any number of persons engaged in interaction with each other...in which each member receives some impression or perception of each other member distinct enough so that he can...give some reaction to each of the others as an individual person."[32] Fine and Harrington point out that political theorists have in the past dwelled on the significance of small-group settings such as coffeehouses, secret lodges, salons, and literary societies. They argue that small groups are "the microfoundations of civil society" because they are "cause, context, and consequence of civic engagement."[33] Fine and Harrington highlight the role of small groups in framing issues of public concern and mobilizing resources to address them (and in the course of doing so forming civic identities); the emphasis here is instead on the horizontal relationships that exist within small groups.

For the vast majority of individuals in any given time and place, the most meaningful part of their social existence centers around their day-to-day realities, particularly their personal interactions, rather than membership in more abstract groupings, such as their identity as a citizen of a particular nation. The strongly felt horizontal relationships formed via sport can, therefore, exercise a powerful influence in creating a real sense of democratization in the everyday lives of people. To give but one example, for someone who comes from a disadvantaged ethnic group that has a problematic relationship with the prevailing, institutionally democratic but still sharply nonegalitarian sociopolitical system and who is employed as a low-wage worker in a corporation with a strongly vertical structure, being a member of a team in a bowling league is likely to be the most personally consequential element of democratization in his or her existence.

The democratizing effect of small groups formed around sports activity is greatly magnified by their sheer number. It is of course true that not all sport takes place within stable small groups, but a very significant fraction of it does; the sports teams of American schools and local soccer clubs in Europe are only the most obvious examples of a broad array of such groups. These groups ramify to an almost improbable extent in societies with horizontal mass sport, as is evident, for instance, in the fact that sports clubs make up 73% of all voluntary associations in Italy.[34] Sport thus exerts a powerful democratizing force within the bounds of societies with horizontal mass sport. As Putnam pointed out, many more Americans bowl than vote in national elections.[35]

---

[32] Fine and Harrington 2004, 343, quoting Bales 1950, 33.
[33] Fine and Harrington 2004, 341.
[34] Putnam, Leonardi, and Nanetti 1993, 91–92. Putnam excludes labor unions from the relevant calculations.
[35] See Section 3.5.

5.3. PARTICULARIZED AND GENERALIZED TRUST

There is good reason to believe that sport also contributes to democratization on a macro scale, because it cultivates particularized and generalized trust. It should be noted at the outset that the components of the relationships considered here – between social capital and democratization, between the horizontality of sport and the horizontality of society, between membership in voluntary associations and generalized trust – are mutually determinative. For instance, Pamela Paxton has argued, based on a careful analysis of a large amount of relevant data, that "social capital was found to promote democracy while a return effect from democracy to social capital was also established."[36] This makes sorting out cause and effect in these relationships a complex process.

One of the questions addressed by social scientists studying the relationship between social capital and democracy is how the formation of social capital, which is operative primarily in face-to-face interactions, promotes democratization at a societal level. A partial solution to this problem is found in bridging capital. Putnam and others have emphasized the role of bridging capital in democratic societies, and it is undoubtedly true that, because it can tie together two or more groups, bridging capital can work on a larger scale than bonding capital. Well before the current wave of social capital research, Mark Granovetter had argued that what he called "weak ties" played an important role in creating bridges between otherwise unconnected groups.[37]

Nonetheless, if one presumes that the formation of bridging capital requires active, personal interconnections among at least some members of the linked groups, there are still sharp limits on scale. This is evident from the examples of the operation of weak ties cited by Granovetter, which include schools with strong cliques, hospitals with strong departmental structures, and local community movements.

Moreover, sport seems to be more effective in generating bonding than bridging capital. This was implicit in some of the scholarly work discussed earlier, and is explicit in a recent study by Ørnulf Seippel that merits particular consideration because of Seippel's interest in clarifying the connection between sport and civil society (and hence democratization) and the care with which he distinguishes between bonding and bridging capital. Seippel's dataset consisted of a total of 4,475 survey responses, representing a representative sample of Norwegians aged 18–80, drawn from the World Values Surveys of 1982 and 1990 and the European Social Survey of 2002.[38] That

---

[36] Paxton 2002, 272. On generalized trust and associational membership, see Sønderskov 2011.

[37] Granovetter 1973, Granovetter 1982.

[38] Seippel dates the European Social Survey to 2003. Insofar as the ESS is conducted in even-numbered years, one must presume that he is referring to data gathered in 2002 and published in 2003.

data indicated that "sports organizations are influential due to size, but relatively weakly positioned in civil society." Seippel argued that:

Couched in theoretical terms, the influence of sports in civil society depends on a well-developed and balanced amount of the two kinds of social capital, bonding and bridging. Whereas voluntary sports have been shown to be relatively strong with respect to the bonding aspect.., this article tells a different story for the bridging side of sports as social capital. Relative to size, sports seem less embedded in civil society than most other organizations and thereby also to be weak in bridging-social capital. Sports consequently do not provide a strong opportunity structure for communication and persuasion, and thereby lack a most important precondition for a really influential position in civil society.[39]

It is, therefore, distinctly unlikely that sport promotes democratization at a societal level in a significant fashion through the creation of bridging capital.

A number of other explanations have been proposed with respect to how small-scale relationships might democratize other, larger-scale social relationships. Mark Warren has suggested that participation in voluntary associations fosters democratization in three possible ways, and, insofar as horizontal sport can be a form of voluntary association, his system of categorization can be usefully adapted to the issues under consideration here. Warren points to: (1) public sphere effects ("associations may contribute to the formation of public opinion and public judgment"), (2) institutional effects ("associations may contribute to *institutional* conditions and venues that support, express, or actualize individual and political autonomy as well as transform autonomous judgments into collective decisions"), (3) developmental effects ("associations may contribute to forming, enhancing, and supporting the capacities of democratic citizens").[40]

There is little reason to believe that sport has significant public sphere or institutional effects, but it is virtually certain that it has important developmental effects, which Warren places under the following five headings: (a) information (participation in voluntary associations provides members information that politically empowers them), (b) political skills (participation in voluntary associations helps members acquire competencies such as negotiation and bargaining), (c) critical skills (participation in voluntary associations helps members acquire cognitive capacities to form autonomous judgments), (d) civic virtues (participation in voluntary associations inculcates norms and behavioral tendencies that promote democratization), and (e) efficacy (participation in voluntary associations helps members develop self-confidence and hence empowers them to seek to influence collective actions at various levels).[41] If sport produces developmental effects

---

[39] Seippel 2008, 69, 77–78, respectively.

[40] The list and descriptions draw on Warren 2001, 61.

[41] Warren 2001, 72–75. Warren argues that three civic virtues nurtured by voluntary associations have democratizing effects: reciprocity, trust, and recognition. Reciprocity and trust are

(a)–(c) it does so almost accidentally, and so they can be put to the side. That leaves us with civic virtues and efficacy. We will deal with civic virtues in this section, efficacy in the next.

The idea that sport fosters civic virtues has been widely circulated since the time of the American Progressives (see Section 3.2), and, although that idea is not unsound, it has in the past been articulated in a distinctly imperfect fashion. The norms and behavioral tendencies ostensibly fostered by sport have typically been fuzzily defined and, more importantly, little effort has been made to explain precisely how playing sport inculcates those norms and behavioral tendencies, or to elucidate how norms and behavioral tendencies inculcated on the playing field affect democratization on a societal level. All those difficulties will be addressed in turn here. We will not attempt to explore the full range of civic virtues that have in the past been associated with sport and will focus on a single behavioral tendency, trust, that can be shown to play an important role in democratized societies and that can be convincingly connected with sport.

The value of cooperative relationships is difficult to exaggerate; to give but one example, cooperative relationships among a group of business associates facilitates economic activity by reducing the need for third-party enforcement and hence transaction costs. The importance of cooperation in a democratized society is too obvious to require extended explanation. Collective action at any scale in the context of horizontal relationships is virtually impossible in the absence of some degree of willing cooperation.[42]

Despite their value, cooperative relationships are not inevitable, especially in larger groups in which cooperation requires generalized rather than particularized trust. Cooperative relationships are very difficult to sustain in the absence of trust, because the individuals involved must do their part, which frequently requires some degree of self-sacrifice, without complete assurance that others will not defect.[43] For instance, if two neighbors agree that they will walk each other's children to the school bus stop in alternate weeks, one of the two has to do so for the first week without being certain that their neighbor will do the same in turn. In other words, the individuals

---

both discussed below. For Warren "recognition" entails cognizance of one's abilities, which is notionally important because it makes individuals secure in their identities and hence in a better position to become aware of their "own preferences and beliefs without threat of destabilizing the core of [their] personality" (Warren 2001, 75). This idea is both complex and vague and is not pursued here.

[42] For further discussion of the importance of cooperation in democratic societies, see Paxton 2002, Putnam 2000, Uslaner 1999.

[43] Cooperative relationships can be built around self-interested behavior or coercion, but the former limits the range of relationships that can be formed and the latter brings with it enforcement expenses that limit the utility of the resulting relationships. See the discussion in Gambetta 1988.

involved must have some level of trust in each other. Cooperation within small, tightly-bonded groups is founded on "thick ties," bonds based on a thorough familiarity with the other individuals involved and the ability of individuals within the group and the group as a whole to impose sanctions on those who fail to cooperate. If our two neighbors who have agreed to walk each other's children to the bus stop have known each other for years and regularly share the use of one's outdoor barbeque and the other's pool, it is unlikely that either one will defect. The issues get much more complicated, however, when the situation involves "thin ties," for example, if we imagine the adults of every household in the neighborhood, many of whom are almost total strangers, agreeing that there will be an adult present at the bus stop each morning to keep an eye on the children, with each household taking turns in supplying the requisite adult. Both arrangements require trust, but of different kinds. The agreement between two neighbors is founded on trust of specific people known to each other, particularized trust, whereas that among everyone in the neighborhood requires trust of relative strangers, generalized trust.[44]

There is a great deal of evidence that generalized trust plays a crucial role in democratic societies. This is because "generalized trust...helps to build large-scale, complex, interdependent social networks and institutions....Moreover, generalized trust is connected to a number of dispositions that underwrite democratic culture, including tolerance for pluralism and criticism."[45] As one would expect, there is a strong correlation between levels of generalized trust and levels of democratization. This is clear from a large body of scholarly literature, among the more important examples of which is Ronald Inglehart's study of survey data from forty-three societies over a period of three decades. Inglehart concluded that, "trust [is] crucial to the viability of democratic institutions."[46]

During the past two decades a considerable amount of research has been carried out on the subject of how generalized trust comes into being, and over the course of time two basic schools of thought have developed: psychological propensity and social learning. According to the former:

---

[44] On the importance of trust in making cooperation possible, see J. Walker and Ostrom 2009.

[45] Warren 1999, 9, summarizing the conclusions in Uslaner 1999.

[46] Inglehart 1997, 209. For a more skeptical view of the importance of trust in democratic societies, see Cleary and Stokes 2009. The challenges involved in defining trust and studying its effects on political behavior and systems are substantial, and many issues of fundamental importance remain unresolved. At the end of a lucid discussion of those issues Nannestad concludes that "the question of trust is a huge puzzle that is not even near solution" (2008, 432). It is thus important that the reader remain aware that the views on the sources and political ramifications of trust articulated here, though based on a large body of previous scholarship, would not meet with anything resembling universal approbation among political scientists.

Trust of all types [is] driven by a highly stable psychological propensity, unlikely to be appreciably modified by commonplace experiences. This perspective sees trust as a *psychological predisposition*, a propensity to trust other people that is innate or formulated early in life.

According to the advocates for the social learning perspective, levels of generalized trust are determined largely by the nature of individual experience. Adherents of this school acknowledge that trust can be domain specific, so that, for instance, trust in family members is not automatically extended to strangers, but argue that individuals, either consciously or unconsciously, tend to extrapolate opinions formed from their experiences with people known to them to form opinions about people unknown to them. Hence:

The social learning perspective suggests that individuals rely upon the trust developed with particular groups of people, such as family, neighbors, and fellow voluntary association members, in the formation of a more generalized sense of trust.[47]

It is likely of course that both psychological predispositions and social learning affect levels of generalized trust, but, insofar as the capacity of sport to engender generalized trust would be largely a matter of social learning, it is noteworthy that recent research has supplied strong validation of that position. Perhaps the best single piece of recent, relevant work was carried out by Jennifer Glanville and Pamela Paxton, who in 2007 published a sophisticated study of the sources of generalized trust. They analyzed information taken from the Social Trust Survey conducted by the Pew Research Center in 1998 and the national component of the Social Capital Benchmark Survey conducted by the Roper Center for Public Opinion Research in 2000, which together provided a dataset of survey responses from 6,523 adults. Glanville and Paxton reached the conclusion that "positive trust experiences in localized settings have a powerful influence on generalized trust…individuals generalize from experiences in particular domains in formulating their assessments of the trustworthiness of people in general."[48]

Glanville and Paxton added the important caveat that not all trust experiences are identical when it comes to nurturing generalized trust. In the early stages of social capital research it was assumed that particularized trust springing from social capital formation inevitably increased generalized trust. However, it rapidly became evident that this was a problematic assumption. In retrospect this should have come as no surprise. Sherif and his collaborators, as part of the experiments described in Section 5.2, concluded that:

---

[47] Glanville and Paxton 2007, 231, 232, respectively.
[48] Glanville and Paxton 2007, 238. See also Foddy and Yamagishi 2009. For a thorough defense of the alternative perspective, psychological propensity, see Uslaner 2002.

The nature of intergroup relations cannot be extrapolated from the nature of in-group relations. In-group solidarity, in-group cooperativeness, and democratic procedures need not necessarily be transferred to the out-group and its members. Intergroup relations cannot be improved simply by developing cooperative and friendly attitudes and habits within groups.[49]

Glanville and Paxton pointed out that trust formed among members of groups with shared norms based on highly pessimistic views of others would be unlikely to produce generalized trust. On the other hand, they found no evidence that particularized trust could diminish general trust, only that it might not elevate it.[50]

We have seen to this point that large-scale cooperative relationships are an essential component of democratized societies, that cooperative relationships on a large scale require generalized trust, and that generalized trust comes at least in part from particularized trust between the members of relatively small groups. The final piece of the puzzle is that horizontal sport is almost inevitably an important source of particularized trust that is likely to increase generalized trust and hence fosters a propensity for forming the large-scale cooperative relationships essential to democratization. We will see that sport cultivates trust through iterated face-to-face interactions, which means that we are primarily concerned here with sport participation rather than sport spectatorship.[51]

The capacity of horizontal sport to foster trust is beyond question. Horizontal sport generates bonding and, to a lesser extent, bridging capital. The substance of both bonding and bridging capital includes a social network consisting of individuals who place particularized trust in each other.

There is, moreover, good reason to believe that participation in horizontal sport is an unusually good means of cultivating particularized trust. One of the difficulties with trust is that, although it offers significant benefits, it also entails risk, especially in the initial stages of its formation, when the individuals involved lack reliable experiential information about the trustworthiness of their counterparts. The logical solution is to begin by engaging in cooperative action with relatively minimal risk. Sport is an ideal venue for doing just that because it offers abundant opportunities to test the trustworthiness of others with risk minimized because, in most cases, sport is a form of play. The most obvious example of the role of trust in sport is the relationship between members of a sports team, who rely on each other in achieving a shared goal. Trust is also important in any sport in which one individual or group is pitted against an opponent, because it becomes

---

[49] Sherif, Harvey, White, Hood, and Sherif 1961, 207.

[50] Glanville and Paxton 2007, 240. Cf. the discussion in Hooghe 2003, who concludes that "not all voluntary associations automatically produce democratic attitudes" (105).

[51] Sport volunteering is also no doubt relevant, but has not been thoroughly studied with respect to the creation of trust and hence is not discussed here.

possible to observe how opponents play the game, for example, whether they will seize the chance to break rules when there is no likelihood of sanction. Thus sport, because it represents a low-risk, iterated activity that offers significant information about the trustworthiness of others, might well be considered a seedbed of particularized trust, which can then form the basis of generalized trust.

The connection between sport participation and generalized trust is supported by the limited body of relevant research carried out to date. There are three studies, all already mentioned earlier, that have considered in some depth the relationship between sport participation and generalized trust. Delaney and Keaney, in their analysis of the data from the European Social Survey, looked at both social trust, i.e., trust in other people, and political/institutional trust, i.e., trust in institutions of government. They found that at a national level "countries with high levels of sports participation also tend to have high levels of social and institutional trust and vice versa. In particular the correlations are substantial for the level of sports participation in a country and measures of social trust."[52] With regard to individuals rather than countries, "membership of sports clubs is associated with being more satisfied with life, more trusting, more sociable, healthier, and more positive toward state institutions."[53] Delaney and Keaney noted that correlation is not the same as causation, and hence did further analyses controlling for age, income, gender, other associational memberships, years of full-time education, and self-reported levels of suffering from discrimination. They found that "the impact of sports participation on measures of political trust...remains statistically significant even after controlling for other factors....However, there is no relationship between participation in sport and trust in other people once we control for other factors."[54] Delaney and Keaney took this absence of a correlation between sport and social trust after controlling for other variables as a sign that the initial correlation was the result of self-selection, but that in a sense begs the question of how the individuals involved developed social trust in the first place. Their calculations show that the variable that had, by some margin, the largest effect was the number of associational memberships, precisely as one might expect.[55] Associational memberships help foster generalized trust,[56] and in that respect sport is just another form of associational membership.[57] The incremental

[52] Delaney and Keaney 2005, 26.
[53] Ibid.
[54] Delaney and Keaney 2005, 27.
[55] Delaney and Keaney 2005, 38–39.
[56] For discussion of this point, see Paxton 2007.
[57] In their discussion of the strong correlations at the national level between sport participation and various positive outcomes, Delaney and Keaney themselves suggest that "it may be associational membership in general rather than sports membership in particular which displays these positive correlations" (23).

benefit of participating in sport is limited in the case of individuals active in a variety of other voluntary associations. This brings us back to Merton's "postulate of indispensability," namely that "*just as the same item may have multiple functions, so may the same function be diversely fulfilled by alternative items.*"[58]

In their (separate) investigations of the relationship between sport and social capital, Seippel and Brown also found that sport participation generated generalized trust. Seippel's analysis used data from Norway and took into account a number of variables, such as age, gender, and education. It produced the finding that, "Being a member of a voluntary sport organization seems to contribute to generalized trust; less than for members of other organizations, but, nevertheless, with a significant positive effect."[59] Brown used data from Sweden and Australia and found the same positive correlation between sport participation and generalized trust.[60]

It thus seems safe to conclude that horizontal mass sport plays an active role in furthering democratization by serving as an important environment in which individuals develop particularized trust, which in turn leads to the development of generalized trust. By cultivating particularized and generalized trust, sport inculcates a propensity for forming cooperative relations on both a small and large scale, relations that are essential components of democratized societies.

5.4. POLITICAL EFFICACY

The extent to which a society's members actively engage in collective decision-making processes is, for obvious reasons, closely related to the prevailing level of democratization. The availability of opportunities to do so is critical in this regard, as is individuals' willingness to use and possibly augment existing opportunities. The latter is to a large extent determined by individuals' sense of political efficacy. In the discussion that follows, we will concentrate on political efficacy with respect to its deployment in overtly political activities, but the same combination of competence and confidence that enables involvement in such activities underwrites participation in collective decision-making processes of all kinds and hence democratization in the broad sense of that term.

Political efficacy is typically understood as having two dimensions: internal and external. Internal political efficacy concerns personal beliefs regarding the ability to achieve desired results in the political domain through personal engagement and an efficient use of one's own capacities and resources. External political efficacy concerns people's beliefs that the political system

[58] Merton 1957, 33–34. See Section 3.3.
[59] Seippel 2006, 179.
[60] Brown 2008.

is amenable to change through individual and collective influence. Whereas internal efficacy mostly concerns the degree of influence that people perceive to be able to exert, due to their own capacities, external efficacy concerns the degree of influence people perceive to be able to exert, due to the actual functioning of the political system."[61]

There is good reason to believe that sport participation can increase internal and external political efficacy and hence raise levels of active participation in collective decision-making processes and in so doing promote democratization. The evidentiary issues here are more complex than one might hope because, despite the fact that political efficacy has been a topic of active research for over a half century,[62] much more attention has been paid to the effects of political efficacy and its differential distribution within societies than its sources.[63] We will begin by very briefly reviewing the large body of scholarly work on efficacy in general and then focus on the more specific subject of political efficacy.[64]

Most discussions of efficacy focus on subjective efficacy (individuals' perceptions of their ability to produce desirable outcomes or prevent undesirable ones) rather than objective efficacy (their actual ability to do so), for the simple reason that subjective efficacy has been shown to be significantly more important in shaping behavior.[65] Individuals' determinations of subjective efficacy with regard to specific situations are strongly influenced by their estimates of their competencies and of the degree of contingency in the situation at hand.

Individuals' estimates of their competencies in a given situation, frequently referred to as perceived self-efficacy, are based on four sources of information: mastery experiences, vicarious observational experiences, related physiological states, and verbal persuasion. Mastery experiences, the most powerful source of perceived self-efficacy, consist of successes in dealing with the challenges presented by prior situations that are perceived as similar to the one at hand. The combination of experience and success confers contextually specific skills and knowledge as well as a concomitant confidence in one's ability to handle comparable challenges in the future. A vicarious observational experience is an opportunity for an individual to see or visualize others, whose abilities are understood as roughly equal to one's own, successfully confronting challenges similar to the ones at hand. The

---

[61] Caprara, Vecchione, Capanna, and Mebane 2009, 1002. On political efficacy, see also Almond and Verba 1963, 180–213; Caprara 2008; and Pateman 1970.

[62] The earliest important work on this subject can be found in Campbell, Gurin, and Miller 1954.

[63] Political scientists interested in the sources of political efficacy have typically focused on overtly political activities. See, for instance, Beaumont 2010.

[64] Invaluable guides to the scholarly literature on efficacy can be found in Gecas 1989 and Skinner 1996.

[65] Skinner 1996, 551 and 554.

physiological states generated by challenges, for example, fear, can affect perceived self-efficacy, as can verbal persuasion, which requires no special explanation.[66]

Estimates of degree of contingency, that is, the extent to which individual or collective action can influence the outcome of events, are based on a variety of factors, the most relevant of which in the present context is prior experience. Individuals who regularly encounter situations of noncontingency, that is, situations over which they understand themselves as being unable to exert any significant level of control, can develop a chronic habit of greatly underestimating the degree of contingency even in situations potentially subject to a high degree of control.[67] It is likely that success in situations of contingency, that is, mastery experiences, have the opposite effect, because of the feeling of control that results when an "individual intentionally exerts effort toward a goal and can feel the energy of the effort transmitted into the environment to produce the outcome."[68]

The key question in the present context is whether sport participation can have a positive effect on internal or external political efficacy. Although there has evidently been no research on this specific question, there are a number of indications that point toward an affirmative answer. The first relevant consideration is that perceived self-efficacy is particularly important in sport. Albert Bandura, whose work on efficacy has been immensely influential, has noted:

> That a firm sense of self-efficacy is a key to optimal performance has long been recognized in athletic circles. After capabilities are perfected and practiced extensively, perceived self-efficacy can be the difference between a good or poor showing in athletic contests.[69]

This is reflected in the fact that perceived self-efficacy is one of the primary loci of interest in the field of sports psychology.[70]

Furthermore, sport offers copious opportunities for the development of domain-specific perceived self-efficacy. The typically iterated nature of sport means that mastery experiences are a regular possibility, and vicarious observational experiences; positive, adrenaline-fueled physiological states; and affirming verbal persuasion from coaches, other players, family members, and friends are common. It is of course true that sport, especially in its more competitive forms, entails losing at least occasionally, but the resulting negative effects are strongly mitigated by a recognition that some degree of failure is virtually inevitable, and even losing efforts can be mastery

[66] Bandura 1995, 3–5; Bandura 1997, 79–115.
[67] Abramson, Seligman, and Teasdale 1978; Goffman 1961, 3–124, esp. 43–48; Seligman 1975.
[68] Skinner 1996, 551.
[69] Bandura 1986, 433.
[70] See, for instance, Feltz, Short, and Sullivan 2008.

experiences. Another important factor is that some of the most powerful sport experiences with respect to the development of perceived self-efficacy take place not in competitive settings but during practice; as Bandura has observed, "many practice routines are designed as much to boost perceived self-efficacy as to perfect skill."[71]

A very considerable body of research has shown that the relationship between perceived self-efficacy and sport participation is reciprocal: perceived self-efficacy improves athletic performance, and sport participation increases perceived self-efficacy. The single most helpful piece of relevant scholarship is a meta-analysis carried out by Sandra Moritz and several colleagues based on forty-five previous studies of self-efficacy and sport performance. They found a strong correlation between these two variables and that "self-efficacy is both a cause and effect of performance."[72]

Perceived self-efficacy is to some extent domain specific, so that, for instance, an engineer might express absolute confidence in her ability to design a bridge but would be apprehensive about baking a wedding cake. On the other hand, individuals do regularly generalize perceived self-efficacy with the result that success in one field nurtures confidence about the results of future endeavors in others.

There is some evidence that perceived self-efficacy developed in sport is prone to generalization to other domains. This has not been an active area of research, evidently because, among academics, self-efficacy in sport is primarily of interest to sports psychologists who, as a group, are interested in explaining and improving athletic performance. Most of the scholarly work on the generalization of perceived self-efficacy from sport to other domains is concerned with the potential use of sport participation to improve the lives of individuals and groups frequently excluded from sport. Some examples from a sparse field will suffice to give the flavor of the whole. One study focused on the effects of participation in a swimming program on a small group of adults over the age of sixty. The authors found that perceived self-efficacy increased both with respect to swimming and with respect to a range of other activities.[73] Another study looked at the effects on adolescent girls of participation in a four-month long strength-training program. The subjects of the study were broken into three groups, one of which took part in the strength-training program, one of which was given a light activity program, and one of which was nonactive (with a total of twenty-seven girls in all three groups). The authors of the study found that whereas the two control groups showed no significant change in physical capacity or self-efficacy, the girls who went through the strength-training program not only showed a sharp improvement in their physical skills, but also manifested

[71] Bandura 1986, 433.
[72] Moritz, Feltz, Fahrbach, and Mack 2000, 289, cf. Feltz 1992.
[73] Hogan and Santomier 1984.

marked increases in "perceived physical ability, physical self-presentation confidence, and general effectiveness in life."[74] Two separate studies have shown that physical self-defense training for women significantly enhances perceived self-efficacy not only with respect to ability to resist would-be attackers, but also with respect to a wide array of other behaviors.[75]

The evidence for the more specific possibility of self-efficacy in sport increasing external and internal political efficacy is more compelling. With regard to external political efficacy, which reflects the degree of influence people perceive themselves to be able to exert on political systems, sport is a high-contingency environment in which individuals have an unusual degree of control over outcomes. Just as prolonged exposure to low-contingency environments depresses individuals' estimates of contingency in all situations, it is probable that prolonged exposure to sport exerts a generalized positive effect on estimates of contingency. That generalized positive effect would include a heightened estimate of contingency in political systems and hence would heighten external political efficacy.

With regard to internal political efficacy, it is necessary to bear in mind that one of the key factors that enables the transfer of self-efficacy from one domain to another is the degree of similarity between the two domains, so that the domains in question either require similar skills or are understood by the individuals involved as encompassing similar activities.[76] Fundamental similarities between sports activity and political activity exist at both the operational and structural level. At the operational level, competitive sport and political activity both involve the exercise of power. Weber famously defined power as "the probability that one actor in a social relationship will be in a position to carry out his will despite resistance," and sports competitions can be seen as a test of the ability of one or more individuals to carry out their will despite resistance from an opponent.[77] Sport participation thus provides individuals with first-hand experiences in the exercise of power, experiences which in at least some cases must contribute to the development of a strong sense of internal political efficacy.

The connection between sport and power is evident in the fact that one of the more common themes in the reminiscences of former athletes is that sport was for them a source of empowerment. We have already seen Caryl Rivers stating that playing basketball made it impossible for her to be docile (see Section 2.3). An unnamed rugby player interviewed for a book on women in contact sports put it in the following terms:

---

[74] Holloway, Beuter, and Duda 1988, 699.
[75] Ozer and Bandura 1990; Weitlauf, Cervone, and Smith 2000.
[76] Bandura 1997, 50–54.
[77] Weber 1947, 152. On athletic competition as a matter of exercising power, see Shogan 1999, 11, 36.

I stay involved in the sport for so many reasons! I love playing on a team. With each game you learn something about yourself. Rugby keeps me active while encouraging me to push myself. I love the contact, I love tackling, mauling, rucking. . . . I love using my strength and strategies to improve my game. . . . Rugby empowered me.[78]

This theme has been particularly prominent among female athletes; meso-level research suggests that this is because sport presents many girls and women with opportunities to achieve high degrees of self-efficacy in a traditionally male sphere of activity and to develop behaviors and skills useful in other male-dominated spheres.[79]

There are also strong similarities between sports activity and political activity at the structural level. We have already seen that organized games and societies are both exercises in coordinated action by groups of individuals that involve the imposition of constraints in order to generate stable patterns of behavior. Sport tends to reflect society because institutions, practices, and norms found in the latter almost inevitably get transferred in one way or another to the former in order to solve similar organizational challenges (see Section 4.1). The parallel extends further because individual involvement in democratic political activity is typically based to some extent on the belief that one's own involvement is necessary to ensure a suitable outcome and that other individuals will do their part; research has shown that a belief that participation of all members is necessary for group success is an important determinant of political involvement.[80] The same expectation of active cooperation from everyone involved to achieve a shared goal is developed in individuals with experience in playing a team sport.

The present state of scholarly research on political efficacy does not permit any ironclad conclusions, but it seems highly probable that sport participation can and frequently does produce increases in internal and external political efficacy. Sport participation undoubtedly elevates domain-specific perceived self-efficacy. Fundamental operational and structural similarities between sports activity and political activity make the transfer of self-efficacy from the former to the latter a straightforward process. This is evident in the considerable body of literature attesting to the empowering effects of sport participation, which shows every sign of having the capacity to increase internal political efficacy. The same goes for external political efficacy, because regular participation in sport, which is unusually susceptible to control, probably creates a positive bias in individual judgments about the degree of contingency in political systems. Although both horizontal and vertical sport would seem to have the capability to boost feelings

---

[78] Quoted in Lawler 2002, 39.

[79] See, for instance, Blinde, Taub, and Han 1993 and L. Chase 2006. We have already encountered evidence that Title IX was responsible for a noticeable increase in the numbers of women in male-dominated professions (see Section 4.2).

[80] Finkel, Muller, and Opp 1989.

of efficacy, the presence of strongly hierarchical elements in vertical sport runs counter to political efficacy, and, as a result, here again it is horizontal sport that is the focus of attention.

The mooted connection between sport and political efficacy finds support in a study by Mark Hugo Lopez and Kimberlee Moore that specifically looked at the relationship between participation in high school sports and civic engagement. Lopez and Moore used a dataset consisting of 1,500 responses from a representative sample of Americans aged 15–25 to a survey that was carried out in 2002 and that was designed to test levels of civic engagement. The data showed that, even after controlling for a range of variables, "18–25 year olds who participated in sports activities while in high school were more likely than non-participants to have: volunteered, volunteered regularly, worked to solve a community problem, participated in a run/walk/ride charity fundraiser event, registered to vote, voted in 2000, boycotted a product or service, felt comfortable about making a statement in a public meeting, watched the news closely...."[81]

As Mark Warren put it in his work on voluntary associations and democracy, political efficacy should be seen as "the reflexive effects of experiences, sedimented in individuals' biographies over a lifetime and expressed as a psychological disposition....One can be trained, as it were, for confidence, assertiveness, and agency, primarily through experiences in which one does have some impact."[82] Sport is an excellent training ground for those qualities, and there is, therefore, yet another avenue by which sport promotes democratization – by elevating internal and external political efficacy sport promotes active participation in collective decision-making processes of all kinds.

5.5. DISCIPLINED CITIZENS

The fourth mechanism by means of which sport fosters democratization is that sport helps create disciplined individuals with a predisposition to obey rules and legally constituted authorities. That claim may seem paradoxical, particularly because it comes immediately after a lengthy discussion of sport's capacity to foster political efficacy. However, all societies need to strike a balance between order and autonomy (see Section 3.1), and a society that exercised no constraint on its members would not be a society at all but anarchic chaos. Democracies do not represent exceptions to this rule, despite Plato's famous jibe that in democracies "all things everywhere are just bursting with the spirit of liberty" such that "every man [has] licence to do what he likes," children have disdain for their parents, and even horses and donkeys move about as they please (*Republic* 563d, 557b, 563a, 563d, trans. P. Shorey).

[81] Lopez and Moore 2006, 2.
[82] Warren 2001, 71.

The reality is that the citizens of democratized societies face a set of demands riven by contradictions. Those contradictions are neatly summed up in the ancient Greek formulation "rule and be ruled," which is explained by Aristotle as follows: "The basis of a democratic state is liberty.... One principle of liberty is for all to rule and to be ruled in turn..." (*Politics* 1317a40–b2, trans. S. Everson). More recently, the conflicting expectations of democratic citizenship were a subject of extended discussion in Almond and Verba's *Civic Culture*,[83] in which the authors point out that "the democratic citizen is called on to pursue contradictory goals: he must be active, yet passive; involved, yet not too involved; influential, yet deferential." They note that the civic culture of their model democratic states, the United States and Britain, not coincidentally, is also mixed and represents "a balanced political culture in which political activity, involvement, and rationality exist, but are balanced by passivity, traditionality, and commitment to parochial values."[84]

One of the central problems in a democratized society is how individuals, many of whom are at least notionally empowered to participate in the adoption of laws and the selection of leaders, can be induced to adhere to the demands made by laws and leaders, particularly those demands that they would prefer to ignore. Noncompliance, beyond a relatively minimal level, represents an existential threat to the society as a whole. As Robespierre pointed out, "Democracy perishes by two excesses, the aristocracy of those who govern, or the contempt of the people for the authorities which it has itself established."[85]

The requisite compliance is to a significant degree ensured through the application of coercion.[86] Much of that coercion is unabashedly overt; there are over 700,000 police officers in the United States, along with an elaborate apparatus of courts and prisons.[87] Overt coercion is, however, an expensive and blunt instrument of social control and can be deployed only with great difficulty against the more privileged. There is, therefore, a pressing need for more subtle forms of coercion, capable of more gently but equally firmly compelling obedience from large numbers of people.

Michel Foucault produced seminal work on that type of coercion, which he labeled "discipline" and defined as follows:

"Discipline" may be identified neither with an institution nor with an apparatus; it is a type of power, a modality for its exercise, comprising a whole set of instruments, techniques, procedures, levels of applications, targets; it is a "physics" or an "anatomy" of power, a technology.

---

[83] On that work, see the discussion in Section 3.5.
[84] Almond and Verba 1963, 478–79, 32, respectively.
[85] From *Discours et rapports à la Convention*, quoted in Dunn 2005, 118.
[86] Socialization and consensus are not irrelevant, just insufficient.
[87] The information on the number of police officers in the United States comes from the Federal Bureau of Investigation. The data is usefully aggregated at http://nneindicators.unh.edu/ShowOneRegion.asp?IndicatorID=33&FIPS=33000.

The imposition of discipline creates a particular kind of person: "the obedient subject, the individual subjected to habits, rules, orders, an authority that is continually exercised around him and upon him, and which he must allow to function automatically in him."[88] Disciplined individuals have a powerful predisposition to adhere voluntarily to the dictates of rules and authority figures. Discipline can thus – without making any functionalist claims about origins or persistence (see Section 3.3) – be understood as an elegant solution to some of the challenges created by democratization.

Here again balance is a key issue, because too ready a willingness to be compliant is just as much a threat to a democratized society as complete unwillingness to be compliant. Discipline necessarily undermines individual agency, and an obvious question is the extent to which it does so. Foucault adopted an uncompromising position on this question; he saw the very idea of the autonomous individual as a cultural construct and portrayed human societies as closely resembling prisons writ large (see below).[89] A less pessimistic view would be that a due measure of discipline, though not determinant of behavior, does constrain it, by creating individuals with a deep-seated reluctance to transgress. This may not correspond to idealized treatments of the notionally wide-ranging freedoms accorded to the members of democratized societies, but it does leave ample space for the exercise of autonomy and is entirely compatible with an advanced degree of democratization.

Sport becomes part of this equation as one of the more important mechanisms for the imposition of discipline. Foucault argued that discipline is imposed through systemic arrangements that had three basic components. The first component consists of mechanisms for minutely regulating space, time, and activity so that individuals are carefully distributed in controlled spaces (e.g., barracks, factories) according to their place in classificatory systems, actions are organized according to strict timetables and seriated so that each ends with an examination and possible correction, and individuals are efficiently combined into larger wholes. The second component consists of procedures for proper training, specifically hierarchical observation, normalizing judgment, and examination. The last is surveillance, placing individuals in an environment in which they can always be observed and which thus induces self-policing (panopticism).[90]

[88] Foucault 1977 (1975), 215, 128–29, respectively. Foucault's work on discipline forms part of a much larger exploration of the nature of power and how it is exercised. For Foucault, discipline is not power itself but a means by which power is exercised. For a good introduction to Foucault and his work, see Downing 2008. On the specific subject of his ideas on power, see McHoul and Grace 1997.

[89] Foucault shifted toward a less pessimistic position on the possibility of individual autonomy in his late work.

[90] Foucault 1977 (1975), 135–228.

How sport can function as a disciplinary system is best understood by examining a specific example of how it works in practice. Natalie Barker-Ruchti and Richard Tinning, in a study mentioned earlier, examined the operation of a training center for elite competitors in women's artistic gymnastics. They used a multimethod ethnographic approach to track the activities of seven gymnasts, 10–15 years of age, and two coaches. Barker-Ruchti and Tinning argued that all the elements of a Foucauldian disciplinary system were present:

- controlled space/classificatory systems: the gymnasts trained in the controlled space of a gymnasium, within which they were separated according to age and distributed among apparatuses and kept apart from non-elite gymnasts; "the hall was organized as an 'analytical space,' an area in which the coaches could, with minimal effort, observe and train the gymnasts efficiently and effectively;"[91]
- controlled timetables/seriation/correction: training sessions consistently followed a set schedule and pattern (warm-up, strength and flexibility exercises, dance instruction, apparatus training, cool-down), with activities organized into a series of graded tasks through which individual gymnasts progressed as their strength and skills improved and with the coaches carefully observing and correcting the gymnasts; some exercises were carried out in synchronization with an audible count kept by one of the coaches;
- combination into wholes: each of the gymnasts was intimately familiar with the pattern of the training sessions, and the entire group moved smoothly and efficiently through the discrete stages of each session;
- hierarchical observation: the gymnasts were constantly subject to observation by each other and by the coaches, and expected to be subjected to the scrutiny of judges at upcoming competitions;
- normalizing judgment: the gymnasts were subject to the judgment of the coaches, who at all times set clear standards of what was and was not normative, both in terms of performance and in terms of effort;
- examination: the gymnasts' strength and skill were constantly tested and more challenging tasks were assigned when an individual demonstrated mastery of an activity;
- surveillance: the open space of the gymnasium and the spatial distribution of gymnasts allowed the coaches to see the gymnasts at all times, the presence of mirrors added an element of self-scrutiny in which the gymnasts observed and surveilled themselves; in addition, the gymnasts wore "tight and scanty training outfits" that "exposed the body to the coaches" and "allowed maximal visibility of body shapes and forms, which in turn facilitated surveillance and correctional interference."[92]

[91] Barker-Ruchti and Tinning 2010, 239.
[92] Barker-Ruchti and Tinning 2010, 240.

The training center studied by Barker-Ruchti and Tinning has the advantage of representing an almost Weberian ideal type of a sport program as a Foucauldian disciplinary system. Most sports activity occurs in environments that are significantly less structured and hence less effective in imposing rigid discipline. Barker-Ruchti and Tinning concluded that their training prevented the gymnasts "from developing independence and self-determination. Instead they developed into docile athletes."[93] The distinction between a predisposition to obey rules and legally constituted authorities on one hand and docility on the other is one to which we return.

An important contributing factor in the relationship between sport and discipline is the intensely corporeal nature of sport. The corporeal dimension of discipline is not something to which Foucault devoted much attention, though the body features in much of his work. For example, he argued in *Discipline and Punish* that:

the body is…directly involved in a political field; power relations have an immediate hold upon it; they invest it, mark it, train it, torture it, force it to carry out tasks, to perform ceremonies, to emit signs.[94]

However, it is easy to exaggerate the extent to which Foucault's concept of the body was corporeal. Though his usage of the term varied considerably both within individual works and across his *oeuvre* as a whole, in many cases what Foucault called the body was a substitute for the self-reflexive individual. As mentioned before, Foucault was resolutely opposed to the idea that there was such a thing as an autonomous and transcendent human subject on which society acted; he instead saw individual consciousness as a relatively recent illusion that resulted from a particular set of discursive formations. Hence his comment that, "Man is an invention of recent date. And one perhaps nearing its end."[95] He could not, however, avoid discussing individuals as such, and treating individual human beings as bodies was an effective means of implicitly rejecting humanism. This is evident in his frequent use of the term "social body" (*le corps social*) to refer to society as a whole. Foucault in fact tended to see discipline as something that was imposed on the body through the intermediary of the mind and for the most part took the body as a passive entity that received but did not initiate actions.[96]

The foundational work on the corporeal dimension of discipline in sport was done by Pierre Bourdieu, who took the position that discipline could be inculcated by means of bodily training and that the disciplined body as a corporeal entity could in and of itself shape individual behavior. He

[93] Barker-Ruchti and Tinning 2010, 243.

[94] Foucault 1977 (1975), 25.

[95] Foucault 1994 (1966), 387. On Foucault's antihumanism, see Paden 1987. On his substitution of the body for the self-reflexive individual, see Markula and Pringle 2006, 40–41.

[96] See the discussion in Lash 1991 and McNay 1999.

also argued that such training had far-reaching effects precisely because its physical nature made it resistant to conscious examination:

If all societies and, significantly, all the "totalitarian institutions" in Goffman's phrase, that seek to produce a new man through a process of "deculturation" and "reculturation" set such store on the seemingly most insignificant details of *dress, bearing, physical and verbal manners*, the reason is that, treating the body as a memory, they entrust to it in abbreviated and practical, i.e., mnemonic, form the fundamental principles of the arbitrary content of the culture. The principles em-bodied in this way are placed beyond the grasp of consciousness, and hence cannot be touched by voluntary, deliberate transformation, cannot even be made explicit; nothing seems more ineffable, more incommunicable, more inimitable, and, therefore, more precious, than the values given body, *made* body by the transubstantiation achieved by the hidden persuasion of an implicit pedagogy, capable of instilling a whole cosmology, an ethic, a metaphysic, a political philosophy, through injunctions as insignificant as "stand up straight" or "don't hold your knife in your left hand."... The whole trick of pedagogic reason lies precisely in the way it extorts the essential while seeming to demand the insignificant.[97]

Unlike Foucault, who evinced no direct interest in the subject, Bourdieu wrote at some length on sport. He made the case that:

If most organizations – the Church, the army, political parties, industrial firms, etc. – put such a great emphasis on bodily disciplines, it is because obedience consists in large part in belief, and belief is what the body... concedes even when the mind ... says no.... It is perhaps by considering what is most specific in sport, that is, the...manipulation of the body, and the fact that sport – as all disciplines in all total or totalitarian institutions, such as convents, prisons, asylums, political parties, etc. – is a way of obtaining from the body a form of consent that the mind could refuse, that one will best manage to understand the use that most authoritarian regimes make of sports. Bodily discipline is the instrument par excellence of all forms of domestication.[98]

The phrases "belief is what the body...concedes even when the mind says no" and "sports...is a way of obtaining from the body a form of consent that the mind could refuse" merit special consideration.

From Bourdieu's perspective, environments in which the physical disposition of individuals is subject to exterior control are strongly disciplinary and "domesticate" those subject to such control. The most obvious example of the imposition of discipline through physical means is drill, which involves minute control over the movements of individuals. For example, the United States Army field manual on drill includes the following guidelines for trainees:

On the command of...Forward, **MARCH**, step forward thirty inches with the left foot. The head, eyes, and body remain as in the *Position of Attention*. The arms

[97] Bourdieu 1977 (1972), 94–95.
[98] Bourdieu 1988, 161. On the application of Bourdieu's ideas to the study of sport, see Laberge and Kay 2002 and Tomlinson 2004.

swing in natural motion, without exaggeration and without bending the elbows, about nine inches straight to the front and six inches straight to the rear of the trouser seams. The fingers and thumbs are curled as in the *Position of Attention,* just barely clearing the trousers.[99]

Here again, we encounter something that approximates a Weberian ideal type, this time in the form of a training program that imposes strict corporeal discipline by means of highly detailed instructions that shape individual physical activity. This level of intervention is rare in sport, but less extreme manifestations of the same methodology of control are common. Less detailed but still significant control over individual movement is imposed in all systems of group calisthenics, such as that installed by the Chinese government in the 1950s and that used by many sports teams as a warm-up exercise.[100] Moreover, virtually all organized sports teams have regular practices in which coaches specify what exercises are to be done in what order. It is also by no means coincidental that participants in competitive sport, like soldiers and prisoners, are given little freedom over how they dress; the members of all three groups wear uniforms that homogenize their appearance. At least a partial surrender of control over physical disposition is thus a standard component of sport participation.

We are now in a position to reach some conclusions about the relationship between sport, discipline, and democratization. The idea that sport can be a disciplinary mechanism that cultivates compliance is something of an article of faith among many if not most sport sociologists, and there are numerous meso-scale studies that support this conclusion.[101] There have evidently not been any macro-scale studies of the disciplinary effects of sport participation, and any such studies would have to confront the reality that the disciplinary element in sport varies widely. The experience of being a member of a casually organized softball or soccer team that plays on weekends in warm weather has, in this respect, little to do with the experiences of the gymnasts studied by Barker-Ruchti and Tinning.

The degree of discipline present within sport can be productively aligned with the distinction between vertical and horizontal sport. Discipline is closely associated with vertical sport, for the simple reason that the maintenance of a strict disciplinary regime in sport is virtually impossible in the absence of a clearly articulated and enforced hierarchy. At the training center at which Barker-Ruchti and Tinning carried out their work, the

---

[99] Department of the Army 2003, Section 2–2.

[100] See Section 2.3 for further discussion of drill and calisthenics and their relation to vertical sport.

[101] The application of Foucault's ideas about discipline to the study of sport is explored at length in Markula and Pringle 2006. Other relevant work includes, but is by no means limited to, L. Chase 2006, G. E. Chapman 1997, Heikkala 1993, Rinehart 1998, and Shogan 1999. On the more general issue of sport as a form of social control, see Eitzen 2000.

coaches were "authoritative figures, with the gymnasts experiencing little responsibility and independence." When one of the gymnasts failed to perform a task to the satisfaction of one of the coaches, the coach shouted at her, "If I say something, you do it!"[102] It would be fair to say that sport at this training center – which consisted of preparing high-level competitors in a sport with a long history of regimentation – was predominantly vertical.

Although the disciplinary element in horizontal sport is relatively muted, it is by no means entirely absent, and this aligns with the needs of democratized societies. As has been pointed out, real-world activity never corresponds precisely to the ideal types of horizontal and vertical sport. To return to Norway as an example, even though both Norwegian society and sport are unusually horizontal, children playing on a soccer team organized by a local sports club are emplaced within a distinct hierarchy and are subject to a disciplinary regime. And even within a system such as Norway's, there are elite athletes subject to highly disciplined training programs, with the important caveat that their numbers are dwarfed by those whose involvement with sport is much more casual.[103]

There is a rough but not insignificant parallel between the existence of varying but generally restrained levels of discipline in horizontal sport and the need for some but not too much compliance on the part of the citizens of a democratized state. The discipline and resulting compliance instilled through sport inculcates a predisposition – but not a compulsion – to obey rules and legally constituted authorities. That in turn fosters democratization by contributing meaningfully to the resolution of one of the basic challenges faced by democratized societies: how to induce empowered individuals to submit willingly to authority.

This concludes our exploration of the mechanisms by means of which horizontal mass sport fosters democratization. The preceding discussion has pointed to the existence and importance of four such mechanisms, which show every sign of being capable, individually and collectively, of positively affecting levels of democratization on a societal level. It seems, therefore, safe to conclude that sport can in fact be an important school for democracy.

[102] Barker-Ruchti and Tinning 2010, 240, 236, respectively.
[103] On elite sport in Norway, see Augestad and Bergsgard 2008.

6

Sport as an Impediment to Democratization

From their formative studies it became clear, to some, that sport and exercise were not social practices that were fundamentally meritocratic and democratising.

Pirkko Markula and Richard Pringle *Foucault, Sport and Exercise: Power, Knowledge and Transforming the Self* [1]

6.1. INTRODUCTION

We now turn to an exploration of the ways in which horizontal mass sport inhibits democratization. This does not require the compilation of a complete list of the undesirable results of sport participation and spectatorship, any more than our exploration of the positive side of the relationship between sport and democratization required the compilation of a complete list of the positive effects of sport. [2]

The discussion that follows builds directly on the preceding chapters and is based on an extensive and sophisticated body of scholarly literature (see Section 3.4), and so it is possible to work through the issues relatively rapidly. The brevity of the treatment given these issues should in no way be read as a statement of their relative unimportance. [3]

Previous work on how sport inhibits democratization has generally focused on the capacity of sport to foster docility, exclusion, hostility, and

---

[1] Markula and Pringle 2006, 3.

[2] A thorough exploration of the reasons to be skeptical about claims for the positive effects of sport can be found in Miracle and Rees 1994. See also the much briefer but still valuable comments in Dyreson 2001.

[3] Some of the more important pieces in a substantial collection of scholarly literature are Eitzen 2009, Gruneau 1999, Hargreaves 1986, Markula and Pringle 2006, Miracle and Rees 1994, Sage 1998, and the articles collected in Coakley and Dunning 2000b. Democratization is rarely explicitly mentioned in this body of work, but it is implicit throughout in the consistent concern with equality and social justice.

inequalities springing from meritocratic competition.[4] Here again, the mechanisms in question appear to rely entirely on the existence of horizontal mass sport, and should, as a result, be transhistorically valid.

6.2. DOCILITY

We have already seen that sport can be an important means of inculcating a predisposition to obey rules and legally constituted authorities, and, within limits, that predisposition is useful in promoting democratization (Section 5.5). However, that same predisposition can develop to the point where it impedes democratization by enabling verticality and authoritarianism and by undercutting autonomy and political efficacy. That transition might be described as involving a change from compliance to docility, with the difference being that docility entails the near total absence of autonomy and self-efficacy.

Sport has the capacity to generate docility because athletes can find themselves in environments that bear more than a passing resemblance to what Erving Goffman called total institutions, such as prisons and asylums, in which individuals are placed in highly regimented environments that subject virtually every aspect of their lives to minute control. Total institutions are Foucauldian disciplinary environments pushed to their logical extreme, and consciously aim at making their inmates as docile as possible. Goffman noted that "total institutions disrupt or defile precisely those actions that in civil society have the role of attesting to the actor and those in his presence that he has some command over his world – that he is a person with 'adult' self-determination, autonomy, and freedom of action."[5]

Sport training programs can verge on totality, especially for deeply committed elite athletes. The training center for elite gymnasts studied by Barker-Ruchti and Tinning (see Section 5.5) clearly approximated a total environment, and less extreme versions of that same environment can be found in much high level sport. This is particularly evident in American football, which almost from its inception has included an unusually strong element of authoritarianism. Walter Camp, the "father" of American football,

---

[4] What is conspicuous by its absence here is any mention of sport as a mechanism of hegemony, which might be thought of as the propagation of ideologies that serve the interests of the dominant class so that the disadvantaged members of a society come to accept ideas and practices that perpetuate their subordination. A great deal has been written about sport and hegemony, but there are two enduring difficulties with this approach to the study of sport: levels of sport participation are consistently higher among privileged groups, and hegemony seems to do more to unite ruling groups than impose beliefs on subordinate groups (Abercrombie, Hill, and Turner 1980). It is not obvious, therefore, that sport inhibits democratization because it hegemonizes subordinate groups. That said, the discussion (below) of sport reinforcing social exclusion overlaps with hegemony theory in significant ways. For an insightful discussion of the complexities of applying hegemony theory to sport, see Hargreaves 1992.

[5] Goffman 1961, 43.

wrote a guide for the proper playing of the game, in which he expatiated at some length on the importance of discipline and obedience:

Discipline should receive the very earliest consideration. If there be not an established tradition strong enough to absolutely prevent anything like "talking back" to the coaches, such a rule should be put in effect, and with sufficient severity to kill once for all such tendency. It may be necessary to make an example by summarily dropping one such offender, in order to insure instant and unquestioning obedience.[6]

Richard Davies has noted that, "Throughout his career, Camp...wanted to create a game in which chance and spontaneity were sharply reduced by rules requiring team discipline and organized patterns of play....As Camp influenced the evolving structure of the game, athletes came to be viewed merely as cogs in an organized human machine, doing what industrial manager Camp liked to call the 'work' of football."[7]

Camp, who ran a clock factory, began a continuing tradition among American football coaches of the exertion of control through precise timing of activities during practices. The extent to which that tradition that began with Camp continues to permeate American football is evident in a memo from the football coach at the University of South Carolina, which is reproduced in the work of one of the pioneering figures in the sociology of sport, Harry Edwards (see Figure 7). This emphasis on discipline, obedience, and minute control are all features of total institutions and tends to produce particular kinds of dispositions among American football players. When Peyton Manning, one of the most famous players in American professional football, was asked how he felt about being removed from a game against his will, he said, "Until any player in here is the head coach, you follow orders and you follow them with all of your heart. That's what we've done as players. We follow orders."[8]

Moreover, even in societies with horizontal mass sport, the sports activities of specific groups can be steeply vertical. A clear example of this can be found in the students in publicly funded schools in Britain in the final decades of the nineteenth century (see Section 14.3). Students from upperclass families went to boarding schools where they played strongly horizontal sports, whereas students in publicly funded schools, who came almost exclusively from working-class families, were subjected to a strongly vertical program of physical activity that included military drill and regimented gymnastics. That program was constructed largely by individuals from the upper class who administered the publicly funded school system and who saw drill and gymnastics as a means of producing obedient students and reinforcing existing social hierarchies.

[6] Camp and Deland 1896, 228.
[7] R. Davies 2007, 67.
[8] See http://sportsillustrated.cnn.com/football/nfl/gameflash/2009/12/27/3602_recap.html.

MEMO TO: All Faculty and Staff

FROM: Paul Dietzel, Director of Athletics and Head Football Coach

SUBJECT: Faculty Football Breakfasts

DATE: September 3, 1971

The Department of Athletics would like for you to be our guest at breakfast on

Thursday morning, September 9, 1971, two days prior to our football season opener with

Georgia Tech. The football staff will brief you on the 1971 Gamecocks and give you a scouting

report on our opponent...

At each breakfast we will follow this schedule:

7:00 A.M.—Coach Bill Shalosky blows whistle and Coach Dietzel asks blessing.

7:05 A.M.—Breakfast

7:20 A.M.—Coach Dietzel introduces offensive coach to discuss Carolina offense.

7:25 A.M.—Coach Dietzel introduces defensive coach to discuss Carolina defense.

7:30 A.M.—Coach Dietzel introduces scout to discuss opponent.

7:40 A.M.—Coach Dietzel comments, questions and answers.

7:55 A.M.—Coach Shalosky blows whistle; breakfast adjourns.[1]

FIGURE 7. Text of 1971 Memo from the Football Coach at the University of South Carolina (From Harry Edwards, *Sociology of Sport*, p. 115)

Sport can thus take forms and be deployed in ways that push athletes beyond compliance and toward docility, a state that is more consonant with vertical than horizontal relationships and that inhibits democratization by deeply eroding self-efficacy and autonomy.

6.3. EXCLUSION

Much has been said to this point about the inclusionary power of sport, particularly in regard to sport's capacity to facilitate the formation of small, tightly bonded horizontal groups (Section 5.2). The same mechanisms that make it possible for sport to foster inclusion also simultaneously and inevitably create exclusion.[9] The emergence of horizontal relationships among

---

[9] The paradoxical power of sport to both unite and divide is insightfully discussed in Eitzen 2009, 19–39.

sport participants (and to a lesser extent among spectators and among volunteers organizing sport) rests in large part on strong in-group solidarity, which tends to be paired with a heightened perception of differentiation between in- and out-group members.

Moreover, sport is frequently an important component of shared lifestyles that enable group closure and thus exclusion. Groups achieve coherence in part through closure, the maintenance of boundaries that separate them from others, and hence through exclusion.[10] One of the more important forms those boundaries can take is a shared lifestyle that, on a daily basis, differentiates in-group from out-group members. Bourdieu has written extensively about how seemingly personal and minor distinctions such as taste in music are heavily influenced by social class and in turn play a major role in defining boundaries between social classes.[11] Bourdieu discusses sport as a source of distinction; individuals from specific kinds of socioeconomic backgrounds tend to play specific kinds of sport. This dimension of sport is nicely illustrated in the reminiscences of Caryl Rivers, who played high school basketball in the United States in the 1950s. She observed that:

> Basketball was sweaty and grubby – and rife with enough opportunity for body contact to be considered faintly seedy and lower-class. A girl who played tennis could lay claim to some panache; the very name of the sport rang with echoes of chic little dresses and long tanned legs and country club living.[12]

Membership in a tennis club may well link people together in a tight network of horizontal relationships that foster democratization, but it can also involve them in a lifestyle that separates them from their less well-off neighbors who are playing basketball. To say that sport is inclusionary is, therefore, also to say that sport is exclusionary.

The exclusionary power of sport may at first glance seem innocuous, but it is in fact thoroughly insidious. A benign view of exclusion in sport would be that it represents not positive harm but an absence of good, in that nonparticipants do not have access to the benefits associated with sport participation. That view, however, fails to take into account the ways in which exclusion in sport fosters vertical relationships and thus actively inhibits democratization. First, it leaves some individuals outside of the horizontal relationships fostered by sport, and that in turn tends to encourage the formation of vertical relationships between in-group and out-group members. This tendency is particularly noticeable in interactions between participants and nonparticipants because, although sport may generate hostility between opponents (see Section 6.4), meaningful competition requires relatively similar competencies and hence some degree of equality. Even in situations in

---

[10] Giddens 2006, 496.
[11] See Bourdieu 1984. See also the insightful analysis in Sugden and Tomlinson 2000.
[12] Rivers 1983, 309.

which individuals or groups do not compete directly against each other, participation in the same activity makes sport the basis for horizontal rather than vertical relationships. In interactions between participants and non-participants, however, sport can become a valorized activity that forms the basis for hierarchical relationships. A particularly clear example can be found in violent contact sports such as American football, in which there is a pattern of males playing and females cheering them on. That arrangement, the effects of which are thoroughly explored in the study by Douglas Foley discussed in Section 4.2, contributes significantly to the perpetuation of hierarchical gender relations in the form of hegemonic masculinity.

Second, exclusion produces groups of sport participants that tend to be relatively homogeneous, and that homogeneity makes it possible for sport to become a site for the reproduction of discourses that legitimize exclusion and verticality. Consider, for example, the American college rugby teams that were the focus of the study by Steven Schacht discussed in Section 4.2. The team members were exclusively male, and they consistently applied standards of judgment and used language that represented females as inherently inferior. (Put another way, the exclusion of women from these teams helped make them places where hegemonic masculinity could flourish.) This discourse was the foundation of hierarchical relationships that members of the team attempted to construct between themselves and the females with whom they came into contact at practice, at team-based social events, and elsewhere. Other forms of exclusion – on the basis of socioeconomic status, ethnicity, and so on – have the same potential. The inevitable element of exclusion in sport thus can easily foster verticality, and for that reason sport can act as an impediment to democratization.

6.4. HOSTILITY

Sport can generate hostility that makes the formation of trust and cooperative relationships more difficult; as George Orwell memorably put it, "sport is an unfailing cause of ill-will."[13] There was for a considerable period of time a strong belief that sport represents a "safety-valve" that reduces aggression by providing a controlled outlet for belligerent energies that would otherwise manifest themselves in other spheres.[14] More recent and more detailed research has shown that belief to be fallacious, and there is now strong evidence that sport frequently increases aggression. The competitive element in sport creates rivalrous situations that "breed hostility

---

[13] Orwell 1953, 192; the quote comes from an essay, "The Sporting Spirit," originally published in 1945.

[14] For a thorough examination of the relationship between sport and aggression, see Russell 2008.

among participants."[15] Moreover, the same effect extends to spectators of violent forms of sport. In a classic study, Jeffrey Goldstein and Robert Arms measured aggression among spectators at a college football game and at an intercollegiate gymnastics meet, both before and after the event in question. They found that, regardless of whether the team for which they were rooting won or lost, levels of aggression among football spectators were significantly higher after the game, whereas there was no change in the aggression level of the spectators at the gymnastics meet.[16] Insofar as the formation of cooperative relationships is a fundamental part of democratization, and insofar as cooperative relationships are founded on trust, the capacity of sport to engender aggression and hostility among both participants and spectators actively inhibits democratization.

6.5. INEQUALITIES SPRINGING FROM MERITOCRATIC COMPETITION

Democracy and meritocracy have, since the advent of democracy in sixth-century BCE Greece, frequently been associated with each other.[17] However, meritocratic competition can have the effect of undercutting the very egalitarianism that lies at the heart of democratization. The term "meritocracy" was in fact coined by Michael Young in 1958, in a satirical fictional account, set in the year 2033, of the establishment of a system of government in Britain based strictly on merit. Young depicted this rigorously meritocratic Britain as a society riven by inequalities; the narrator remarks that:

Now that people are classified by ability, the gap between the classes has inevitably become wider. The upper classes are…no longer weakened by self-doubt and self-criticism. Today the eminent know that success is just reward for their own capacity, their own efforts, and for their own undeniable achievement….Today, the elite know that…their social inferiors are inferiors in other ways as well….[18]

Subsequent thinkers have developed Young's ideas further and attacked meritocratic systems as deeply problematic in a variety of different ways. Kai Nielsen has, for instance, argued that, "A meritocratic society is also an anti-democratic, paternalistic, and elitist society."[19]

Meritocratic systems have the potential to inhibit democratization because they stress equality of opportunity rather than equality of outcome. A purely merit-based approach entails giving the largest possible number of

[15] Russell 2008, 94.
[16] Goldstein and Arms 1971; cf. Arms, Russell, and Sandilands 1979.
[17] See, for example, Thucydides, *The Peloponnesian War* 2.37.
[18] M. Young 1958, 85–86.
[19] Nielsen 1985, 162. Nielsen provides a detailed review of arguments for and against meritocracy on pp. 103–87. See also Longoria 2009.

individuals equal chances to compete to become unequal. The immediate rewards go to the winners of such competitions, although benefits may well also accrue to others, even the losers, because of the increased efficiency resulting from meritocratic selection processes. As a result, the more that merit-based competition is ramified, the more inequality is generated. Furthermore, perfect equality of opportunity is an unrealizable ideal, and merit-based competition can reproduce or extend extant social inequalities by assigning rewards based on the results of competitions in which some individuals have advantages accruing directly or indirectly from factors, such as inherited wealth, that have nothing to do with talent or motivation.[20]

Horizontal mass sport can impede democratization because it is an arena for meritocratic competition that invariably creates status differences between winners and losers. As John Hargreaves has noted, "sport approximates more to the ideal of a meritocratic social order than any other sphere of social life."[21] When sport participants compete against each other, the rewards of success are differentially distributed, which creates inequalities. That is problematic because democratization is built around horizontal, egalitarian relationships, which are undercut by the creation of status differentials in sport.[22]

---

[20] For a discussion of how skewed meritocratic competition can perpetuate existing social inequalities, in the specific case of education, see Bourdieu and Passeron 1990.

[21] Hargreaves 1986, 111.

[22] On meritocratic status competition in sport, see Section 10.2.

7

The Cumulative Effect of Horizontal
Mass Sport on Democratization

The preceding three chapters have examined in some detail three of the four possible views of the relationship between sport and democratization, and it is worth pausing briefly to consider the results.

Chapter 4 showed that the nature of sport reflects the society in which it is played and that democratization in society will generate democratization in sport. However, it also showed that sport has the capacity to shape the behavior of participants and spectators in other spheres of activity, and, as a result, mass sport not only reflects, but also shapes society as a whole. Chapter 5 identified four mechanisms by means of which sport fosters democratization at the societal level, Chapter 6 four mechanisms by means of which sport inhibits democratization at the societal level. These findings shift the focus of the inquiry to establishing the cumulative effect of those eight mechanisms, or, to put it another way, the question becomes whether horizontal mass sport, on balance, helps or hinders democratization at the societal level.

In an ideal world there would be quantitative data to measure the effect of each mechanism and on that basis reach a conclusion about the cumulative effect of all eight mechanisms. However, that data simply does not exist; as is typically the case in social analysis, particularly on a macro scale, it is much easier to identify relevant factors than it is to trace their immensely complicated, real-world interactions.

Nonetheless, it is possible to make a considerable amount of progress toward measuring the cumulative effect of horizontal mass sport on societal democratization. To begin with, one of those eight mechanisms, the capacity of horizontal mass sport to facilitate the formation of large numbers of small-scale, tightly bonded horizontal groups, exerts a particularly powerful democratizing effect on society as a whole. One key factor in this regard is the sheer quantity of sports teams and clubs in societies with horizontal mass sport; this is evident from the facts that roughly half of all American high school students, about 7.5 million individuals in all, play organized sports and that soccer clubs are by some margin the most common form of voluntary association in modern-day Italy.[1] Another key factor is the egalitarian, face-to-face interactions that take place between members of sports teams and clubs. As we saw at the outset of this text, the importance of such interactions for democratic societies was first emphasized by Tocqueville in his discussion of voluntary associations in the United States. In recent decades Tocqueville's insights have been intensively studied and extended, and, as Mark Warren pointed out in 2001, "within democratic theory a remarkable consensus is emerging around Tocqueville's view that the virtues and viability of a democracy depend on the robustness of associational life."[2] The small-scale, egalitarian groups generated by horizontal mass sport are precisely the sort of voluntary association that Tocqueville and his intellectual successors have shown to play a vital role in democratic societies. Horizontal mass sport thus produces a great deal of face-to-face interaction of a sort that has a proven, powerful capacity to exert a positive influence on societal democratization. Even in the absence of quantitative data, it is not evident that any of the mechanisms by means of which horizontal mass sport inhibits democratization produces effects of nearly the same magnitude.

Further progress is possible because four of the eight mechanisms explored in Chapters 5 and 6 function as antithetical pairs. The first antithetical pair consists of the cultivation of particularized and generalized trust on one hand and the generation of hostility among sport participants and spectators on the other. One of the ways in which horizontal mass sport fosters democratization is by building a sense of generalized trust that facilitates the formation of cooperative relationships. One of the ways in which horizontal mass sport inhibits democratization is by generating hostility that impedes the formation of cooperative relationships. It thus becomes possible to test the relative strength of these two mechanisms by asking the simple question of whether, on balance, horizontal mass sport creates trust or hostility.

The evidence, which is discussed in detail in Section 5.3, is quite clear that for participants horizontal mass sport on balance creates trust. There are three key studies that support this conclusion. First, Delaney and Keaney, in their analysis of the data from the European Social Survey, looked at both social trust, that is, trust in other people, and political/institutional trust, that is, trust in institutions of government. They found that at a national level "countries with high levels of sports participation also tend to have high levels of social and institutional trust and vice versa. In particular the correlations are substantial for the level of sports participation in a country

[1] See Sections 1.1 and 3.5.
[2] Warren 2001, 3.

and measures of social trust."[3] With regard to individuals rather than countries, "membership of sports clubs is associated with being more satisfied with life, more trusting, more sociable, healthier, and more positive toward state institutions."[4] In a study of members of sports clubs in Norway, Ørnulf Seippel found that "Being a member of a voluntary sport organization seems to contribute to generalized trust; less than for members of other organizations, but, nevertheless, with a significant positive effect."[5] Kevin Brown, using data from Sweden and Australia, found the same correlation between sport participation and generalized trust.[6] Delaney, Keaney, Seippel, and Brown did not explicitly test for the balance between trust and hostility, but their work leaves little doubt that, overall, trust outweighs hostility. For obvious reasons, if the reverse were true, there would be no data showing that horizontal mass sport fosters generalized trust.

There is no comparable evidence for the effect of horizontal mass sport on trust/hostility among spectators. We have already reviewed studies by Catherine Palmer and Kirrilly Thompson that showed that spectatorship can generate social capital (Section 5.2) and by Jeffrey Goldstein and Robert Arms that showed that spectatorship of violent contact sports can increase aggression (Section 6.4). There does not appear to be any evidence to directly test the relative strength of these contrary impulses among spectators. It is, however, significant that Palmer and Thompson studied spectators of Australian football, a notably violent contact sport, which indicates that even in such cases horizontal, trust-based relationships form. Moreover, Goldstein and Arms found no increase in aggression among spectators of nonviolent sports. The obvious, though very tentative conclusion, is that spectatorship, like participation, on balance probably builds trust.

A second antithetical pair is formed by the cultivation of a sense of political efficacy and the inculcation of docility. It is important here to make a clear distinction between a predisposition to obey rules and legally constituted authorities on one hand and docility on the other. These traits overlap to some extent in that they both lead individuals to adhere relatively closely to expectations expressed in norms and by authority figures, but docility involves an almost slavish adherence to expectations and a concomitant inability to take autonomous action. A predisposition to obey rules and legally constituted authorities is a useful trait in the citizens of a democratized society, because it helps them play both passive and active social roles, "to rule and be ruled." Docility is a threat to a democratized society because it deeply erodes individuals' capacity to play active social roles; it makes individuals ready to be ruled, but unable to rule. For that reason

---

[3] Delaney and Keaney 2005, 26.
[4] Ibid.
[5] Seippel 2006, 179.
[6] Brown 2008.

political efficacy and docility form an antithetical pair; political efficacy rests on a sense of individual empowerment, docility represents a near complete absence of that quality.

There is no data that makes it possible to test directly the balance between the political efficacy and the docility that are both generated by horizontal mass sport, but there is a proxy that indicates their relative strength. That proxy is delinquency, because if horizontal mass sport, on balance, inculcates docility rather than self-efficacy, then sport participants should show unusually low rates of delinquency, which entails purposeful action that involves an explicit violation of norms, not something one would expect from docile individuals. There have been literally dozens of studies of delinquency rates among athletes, and here again the evidence is quite clear: "Rates of off-the-field deviance among athletes are generally comparable with rates among peers in the general population."[7]

One important nuance is that at least some of the delinquency among sport participants comes as the result of what Jay Coakley has labeled "overconformity to the sports ethic," by which he means that athletes imbibe a series of norms associated with sport and pursue them even when that entails violating the official rules of the sports they play or other, more generalized norms. For example, athletes will use performance-enhancing drugs in order to pursue the goal of winning in sports competitions, even though the use of those drugs is illegal. Similarly, binge drinking by male athletes can be understood as overconformity to the norms of hegemonic masculinity that are reproduced in some forms of sport. One might argue that a considerable fraction of delinquency among athletes is thus the result of overconformity to norms specific to sport and that they are otherwise less likely than others to be delinquent.

It is probably true that athletes are, as a group, somewhat more likely than their peers who do not play sports to adhere to norms and expectations, but there is no evidence that athletes as a group are docile. Indeed, athletes score roughly the same or slightly higher than their nonathletic peers on measures of delinquency that are disconnected from sport, such as adherence to academic norms and to legal codes. In addition, overconformity to the sport ethic frequently requires a willingness and ability to violate rules and to take the actions necessary to circumvent enforcement mechanisms, such as drug-testing regimes, and that sort of proactive behavior is by no means consonant with docility.

With respect to both docility and other effects of sport, it is helpful to make one further distinction, and to separate elite sport from other forms of sports activity. Elite athletes represent a group of individuals who almost invariably build their lives around athletic training and competition. The

---

[7] Coakley and Pike 2009, 221. On delinquency and sport, see Coakley and Pike 2009, 172–223, as well as Miracle and Rees 1994, 101–25.

overriding importance they assign to sport can easily lead to overconformity to the sport ethic and can motivate them to place themselves in highly authoritarian training programs that are capable of producing, at least temporarily, something like docility. Numerous studies have found that as athletes spend more time competing at higher levels, their willingness to engage in behavior that violates written rules, but which frequently conforms to normative, "unwritten" rules specific to sport, increases.[8] Moreover, it is, for example, not coincidental that the Barker-Ruchti and Tinning's study of gymnasts whose training made them docile took place at a program that prepared athletes for international competition.[9] The tendency toward overconformity and docility is much less marked among nonelite athletes, for whom sport can be important but is rarely the central fact of their existence. And elite sport by definition represents a tiny minority of sport participants, so that studies documenting docility among elite athletes need to be taken seriously, but also need to be understood as by no means representative of the majority of sport participants.

There is, therefore, good reason to think that, with respect to four of the eight mechanisms by means of which sport affects democratization on a societal level, the capacity of sport to promote democratization outweighs its capacity to inhibit it.

7.2. OUTCOMES

Another approach to establishing the cumulative effect of the eight mechanisms by means of which horizontal mass sport shapes societal democratization is to focus on outcomes, which involves looking at democratization in societies with mass sport. There are two basic ways of studying outcomes with respect to horizontal mass sport and democratization.[10] First, one might look at societies with extant systems of horizontal mass sport, and examine whether rates of sport participation are positively or negatively correlated with democratization on a societal level. If the cumulative effect of horizontal mass sport is to foster democratization, rates of participation in horizontal sport should be positively correlated with societal democratization; if

---

[8] See, for instance, Shields, Bredemeier, Gardner, and Bostrom 1995 and Silva 1983. The factors that affect athletes' willingness to engage in rule-violating behavior are numerous, and include gender and the degree of contact in the sport the athletes in question play.

[9] Barker-Ruchti and Tinning 2010.

[10] It is also informative to consider societies with vertical mass sport, under the assumption that higher rates of participation in vertical sport should result in lower UDS. Here again the lack of quantified data for the horizontality/verticality of sport in individual countries is a problem. In addition, the number of countries with what appear *prima facie* to be systems of vertical mass sport dropped significantly with the collapse of Communist regimes in Eastern Europe and the Soviet Union. The particular cases of China, discussed in Section 4.1, and of Germany, discussed in Chapter 13, are both suggestive but no more than that.

TABLE 4. *Sport Participation Rates and Unified Democracy Scores for Thirty-Four Countries in the Years 2007–2008*

Country	Percentage of Population Regularly Participating in Sport	Unified Democracy Score	Country	Percentage of Population Regularly Participating in Sport	Unified Democracy Score
Argentina	34.1	0.74	Japan	34.1	1.17
Australia	54.3	1.40	Latvia	41.3	0.89
Austria	44.8	2.01	Mexico	31.5	0.67
Belgium	29.9	1.24	New Zealand	61.7	1.57
Britain	52.4	1.40	Norway	56.3	2.01
Bulgaria	13.3	0.96	Philippines	19.7	0.56
Chile	27.2	1.18	Poland	23.5	1.29
Croatia	37.0	0.89	Russia	20.4	-0.09
Cyprus	6.0	2.01	Slovak Republic	29.0	1.29
Czech Republic	37.9	1.11	Slovenia	50.9	1.40
Dominican Republic	25.2	0.67	South Africa	22.0	0.43
Finland	62.6	2.00	South Korea	55.6	0.83
France	47.3	1.12	Sweden	59.8	2.01
Germany	50.7	2.00	Switzerland	68.8	2.02
Hungary	34.3	1.40	Taiwan	47.8	1.17
Ireland	48.4	1.40	Uruguay	31.5	1.57
Israel	38.8	1.28	United States	54.0	1.57

the cumulative effect of horizontal mass sport is to inhibit democratization, rates of participation in horizontal mass sport should be negatively correlated with democratization. Table 4 shows rates of sport participation and Unified Democracy Scores for thirty-four countries.[11]

Sport participation rates and UDS for these thirty-four countries show a Pearson correlation of .53 on a scale of −1 to 1. (A score of −1 would

[11] The data on physical activity and sport participation come from the International Social Survey Programme (ISSP), which generated 49,730 survey responses from 34 countries. The definitions of sport and sport participation vary in different surveys, so the figures for sport participation rates from the ISSP are not identical with those based on other surveys. However, the ISSP used the same questionnaire for all 34 countries, so the figures on sport participation are internally consistent. The figures given here are taken from Humphreys, Maresova, and Ruseski 2010.

show that participation rates are perfectly negatively correlated with UDS, a score of 1 would show a perfect positive correlation.) There is, therefore, a good but not perfect positive correlation between sport participation and democratization. However, that calculation makes no allowance for whether or not mass sport is present or for the extent to which the sport systems of the various countries are horizontal or vertical.[12] There is no preexisting numerical data for the latter variable, but it is possible to suggest a geography-based proxy. There is good reason to think that the sport systems in European countries tend to be strongly horizontal, and participation rates are sufficiently high in all of them as to ensure the existence of mass sport. If correlation is calculated for the eighteen European countries included in the table, it jumps to .71.[13] High rates of sport participation are thus strongly positively correlated with high UDS in European countries in the present day.

This result is suggestive but not decisive because the data comes from a single point in time, which makes it difficult to draw any conclusions about causation. Democratization at a societal level is influenced by a range of factors other than sport, and it is theoretically possible, for example, that in some of these thirty-four countries UDS went down as sport participation rates went up, or that sport participation inhibited democratization but that other, positive factors counteracted that effect. Furthermore, there are significant similarities in the social structures of the European countries in the dataset, which in turn raises the possibility that, within the bounds of this dataset, there are one or more exogenous factors determining both sport participation rates and levels of societal democratization.

Another possibility is to look at societies in which there have been sharp changes in rates of participation in horizontal sport over time. In practice this means looking at societies with increases in sport participation rates, because those rates have climbed almost everywhere in the world over the past century. If horizontal mass sport promotes democratization, increased rates of participation in horizontal mass sport should be correlated with rising UDS; if horizontal mass sport inhibits democratization, increased rates of participation in horizontal mass sport should be correlated with falling UDS.

The number of societies with the requisite criteria is not infinite. Very recent programs to increase inclusiveness in sport that were launched in several countries in response to Putnam's work on social capital, although

---

[12] The potential democratizing effects of sport are more apparent when sport participation rates are relatively high, that is, when mass sport is present. This is clearly not the case for some countries in the table given above, most notably Cyprus.

[13] Those eighteen countries are: Austria, Belgium, Britain, Bulgaria, Croatia, the Czech Republic, Finland, France, Germany, Hungary, Ireland, Latvia, Norway, Poland, the Slovak Republic, Slovenia, Sweden, and Switzerland.

TABLE 5. *Changes in Sport Participation Rates and Unified Democracy Scores over Time in Denmark, Japan, and West Germany*

	Denmark		
	Percentage of Population Regularly Participating in Sport	UDS	Percentile Rank Among All Nations with UDS
1964	15	1.30	91.1
1998	51	2.00	94.2
	Japan		
	Percentage of Population Regularly Participating in Sport	UDS	Percentile Rank Among All Nations with UDS
1957	14	1.15	82.3
1979	68	1.29	90
	West Germany		
	Percentage of Population Regularly Participating in Sport	UDS	Percentile Rank Among All Nations with UDS
1958	8.7	.97	79.4
1986	32	1.29	87.3

thoroughly documented, are both too new and too small in scale to generate noticeable changes in democratization at the societal level. Better candidates are those nations that launched sport-for-all programs in the 1960s and 1970s. We have already seen that the institution of a sport-for-all program in Norway in 1967 and a resulting steep increase in rates of sport participation occurred at the same time that Norway's UDS was climbing sharply (Section 4.1). A number of other countries instituted sport-for-all programs at roughly the same time, and the same results are evident. Table 5 presents three examples that will give a sense of the larger pattern.[14]

There is much more data on sport participation in various countries at various dates, but an exhaustive listing of participation rates and UDS in different countries that instituted sport-for-all programs is unlikely to be helpful in examining the relationship between sport and democratization. To begin with, countries with strongly vertical systems of mass sport such as China are irrelevant, regardless of their sport participation rates. Another, equally important consideration is that the creation of governmental

---

[14] The data on participation rates are taken from DaCosta and Miragaya 2002, 314, 90, 526, respectively.

sport-for-all programs is a particularly clear case of the transference of institutions, practices, and norms from society to sport. If, as hypothesized here, sport and society are mutually determinative, in times and places in which governments explicitly seek to increase participation in horizontal sport, horizontal mass sport is plainly more effect than cause of democratization. Moreover, the nations that instituted horizontal sport-for-all programs had a strong, carefully thought out, institutionally based commitment to promoting democratization within their borders, as evidenced by their willingness to expend resources on horizontal sport-for-all programs. That commitment to democratization did not manifest itself solely in sport-related programs; for instance, many countries were also at the same time putting in place policies intended to socially and politically empower females. It is, as a result, difficult to draw a causal connection between sport-for-all programs and improvements in UDS. Multiplying the number of examples in which that process has unfolded does little to aid our understanding of sport's effect on society.

What we need are situations in which there have been significant upward shifts in participation in horizontal sport without government intervention. In those instances the effect of society on sport is much less direct and hence more muted, and other kinds of official programs to promote democratization are likely to be significantly fewer in number. To locate such situations we need to move backward in time, before the sport-for-all programs put in place in the 1960s and 1970s. The number of possible examples is quite limited because, as we have seen (Section 2.2), mass sport was until recently quite rare. There are three obvious instances that fit the requisite criteria: Greece in the sixth and fifth centuries BCE, Britain in the nineteenth century, and the United States in the early twentieth century. In all of those times and places, horizontal mass sport emerged spontaneously (i.e., without any government intervention) and sport participation rates climbed steeply. Greece and Britain are of particular interest because in both cases there was no preexisting model of horizontal mass sport, which meant that sport developed in the most organic fashion possible. The situation in the United States is somewhat more complicated, because people there could and did look to Britain as an example, and because the Progressives did implement programs, some private and some public, that were specifically intended to expand sport participation in the hope of furthering the democratization of society as a whole (Section 3.2 and Chapter 16). We will, therefore, examine in some detail the relationship between sport and democratization in Greece and Britain and, more briefly, in the United States.

7.3. THE USE OF HISTORICAL EVIDENCE

Most previous treatments of sport and democracy have worked within limited temporal horizons. The Progressives' interests centered on enacting political reform in the present, critical sport sociologists have habitually studied the sport of recent decades, and many newer studies of sport and democracy attempt to trace the results of recently enacted official policies of using sport to nurture social inclusion. This presentist bias, although understandable, is also problematic because the collective behavior of large groups of people tends to evolve slowly. Some of the most important effects of sport unfold over long periods of time, and one cannot draw any meaningful conclusions from a failure to find a strong statistical connection between sport and democratization as the result of the operation of a governmental program that has run for two years.

Another relevant consideration is that most recent scholarly work on the history of sport has avoided comparative approaches.[15] The complications involved in bringing together material from what are typically separate academic disciplines has been a nontrivial obstacle that has hindered such work. In addition, it has been close to an article of faith among sport historians for the past twenty-five years that modern-day sport has little or no connection with premodern sport.[16] That position was in part a reaction against earlier views, which heavily emphasized continuities between ancient and modern sport and which frequently stretched the relevant evidence to the breaking point.[17]

The relationship between premodern and modern sport and the extent to which they can and should be studied together are complex issues. The rarity of mass sport may tempt us to conclude that it was a custom that modern-day Europeans directly inherited from ancient Greece. That would be a mistake. It is certainly true that people involved in sport in the nineteenth century, many of whom spent years learning Greek and Latin, emphasized the similarities between their own athletic endeavors and those of what they saw as their Greek predecessors.[18] The problem is that mass sport disappeared in Europe in the sixth century CE and did not reappear for about 1,400 years, and sport underwent profound changes during that time. For example, team sports were virtually unknown in ancient Greece but were extremely popular in nineteenth-century Britain. Similarly, almost all of the sports that are widely popular today – such as soccer, basketball, volleyball, football, and baseball – were invented not in ancient Greece but in the nineteenth century in Britain or the United States.

The multiple divergences between premodern and modern sport are, however, less problematic than they might seem when analysis focuses not

---

[15] A large number of historical surveys, such as William Baker's *Sports in the Western World*, have been produced, but these typically focus on describing the development of sports, rather than exploring nuances of the relationship between sport and society.

[16] See, for example, Riess 1995.

[17] See, for instance, D. Young 1984 on the fabrication of classical roots for the concept of the amateur athlete.

[18] For example, when Pierre de Coubertin in the late nineteenth century founded recurring athletic contests in the hope of building international understanding, he named them after and modeled them on the ancient Greek Olympics.

on the specifics of individual sports, but on the relationship between sport and society. At that level of analysis, there are important uniformities and trends that persist in the face of major spatial and temporal variations.

Moreover, comparative approaches confer significant benefits, not the least of which is the opportunity to look at multiple examples of how the same process, in this case the interaction between sport and democratization, unfolds in different conditions. Max Weber pointed out that one of the problems with studying humans rather than the natural world is that experiments cannot be reproduced. If a scientist makes a claim about what happens when two chemicals are combined under certain conditions, that claim can be easily checked by running the experiment again. If a social scientist claims that a particular set of factors caused a group of people to act a certain way during a certain period, that claim is difficult to verify.[19] Comparative historical study of the relationship between sport and democratization is, in effect, a way of running a set of experiments. For obvious reasons it cannot produce absolute certainty, but it can produce clearer, stronger conclusions. When asked about how he would go about proving an assertion about the causes of differences in the way Basques on either side of the French-Spanish border play rugby, Orlando Patterson argued that "you prove it by looking at other cases, you test it by seeing if you can find other similar cases or challenging counter-cases."[20]

In the specific case of the relationship between sport and democratization, evidence from temporally diverse contexts is extremely valuable in that it makes it possible to test for the presence of a controlling exogenous factor. The correlation between increases in participation in horizontal sport and increased democratization at a societal level might be the product of a factor that determines both, which would mean that there is in reality no causal relationship between the two. Previous scholarship has made the case that changes in both modern sport and society were driven by one or more exogenous factors; the five standard candidates are capitalism, industrialization, urbanization, Protestantism, and modernization (in the Weberian sense of the term).[21] It is difficult to control for these factors in an analysis that focuses solely on horizontal mass sport and democratization in the past few decades, because the data comes from societies that are quite similar with respect to some or all of these factors.

This is where the Greek material becomes of considerable importance because none of the exogenous factors that have to date been identified as determinative of both sport and society were operative in ancient Greece. Economic activity in Greek communities centered on subsistence agriculture.

---

[19] Weber 1962, 36–39.
[20] Patterson, Tomlinson, and Young 2011, 556.
[21] See, for example, R. Davies 2007, 22 and *passim*; Dyreson 1998, 14 and *passim*; Guttmann 1978; Overman 1997; and Sage 2000.

The economies of those communities were, as a result, fundamentally different than the industrialized economies of recent centuries, so it would require an extremely loose use of the term to label ancient Greek economies as capitalist.[22] Urbanization was comparatively limited, and it is obviously impossible to talk of Protestantism or modernization in an ancient context.[23] These differences between ancient Greece and the other societies with horizontal mass sport are significant because they mean that, if the correlation between horizontal mass sport and democratization holds good in ancient Greece as well as in nineteenth-century Britain and present-day societies such as Norway, it is unlikely that a controlling exogenous factor is responsible.

With that in mind, we now turn our attention to an array of comparative evidence. Chapters 8–10 are devoted to a case study of sport and democratization in ancient Greece, Chapters 11–12 and 14–15 to a case study of sport and democratization in Britain. Chapters 13 and 16 provide more cursory explorations of sport and democratization in Germany and the United States, respectively. Germany is of some interest because it appears to represent the earliest known example of vertical mass sport and provides an instructive contrast to the situation in Greece, Britain, and the United States.

[22] On economic activity in the ancient Greek world, see the articles collected in Scheidel, Morris, and Saller 2007.

[23] This does not mean that the factors in question had no effect on sport or society, just that they did not play a determinative role in the growth of horizontal sport and democratization on a societal level.

8

Sport and Society in Early Iron Age Greece

8.1. INTRODUCTION

The approach pursued in this and the following chapters, up through the conclusion in Chapter 17, differs sharply from that pursued in previous sections of the text. The extant evidence is primarily qualitative rather than quantitative, and the discussion takes the shape of a standard, text-based historical account. No concerted attempt will be made to document the existence of the eight mechanisms by means of which sport promotes and inhibits democratization that were identified in Chapters 5 and 6, but contextually specific factors that enabled sport to contribute to democratization will be considered. Insofar as few readers are likely to be completely versed in the social and sport history of both Greece and Britain, basic background information is provided throughout. The citations in the footnotes are intended to offer guidance for the interested reader rather than a complete recitation of all relevant scholarship. The case study of sport and society in ancient Greece is divided into three chapters: sport and society in Early Iron Age Greece, sport and society in sixth- and fifth-century BCE Greece, and sport and democratization in sixth- and fifth-century BCE Greece.

Although Chapters 8–16 taken together provide a basic account of the early history of mass sport, it needs to be made unequivocally clear from the outset that they are not meant to provide exhaustive historical accounts or complete descriptions of sport in ancient Greece or nineteenth-century Britain, let alone Germany or the United States. For instance, relatively little will be said about the effects of industrialization on the nature of British sport in the nineteenth century, a topic that would necessarily feature prominently in any comprehensive survey of that subject. Instead, these studies are intended to provide only the background information necessary to examine the relationship between democratization and sport.

In regard to democratization, we will concentrate on changes in political institutions and practices, not because they represent the only or even

the most important form of democratization, but because they are, given
the available evidence, the most easily documented form of democratization and because they offer a useful proxy for democratization broadly construed. In regard to sport, we will concentrate on the extent to which sport
took the form of horizontal (or vertical) mass sport.

8.2. SOCIAL HISTORY

Ancient Greeks had political systems and played sports long before they had
anything resembling democratic governance or horizontal mass sport, and
when democratic governance and horizontal mass sport did come into being
in the sixth century BCE, they built upon preexisting traditions. For that
reason, we need to start our discussion of society and sport in sixth-century
Greece by looking back in time.[1]

A necessary preliminary is clarifying the meaning of the term "ancient
Greece." There is in the modern world a country named Greece with a single
government and a clearly defined territory. In the ancient world, Greeks emi-
grated in large numbers from their homeland in what is now more or less
the modern country of Greece and colonized much of the Mediterranean's
shoreline. They established literally hundreds of widely scattered communities, which were never united under a single government. The term "ancient
Greece" therefore typically refers not to a political or geographical entity,
but what might be called "the ancient Greek world" – the entire collection
of people who spoke Greek and lived around the Mediterranean basin. The
term will be used in that sense here. In cases in which the Greek homeland
as a geographical location is meant, the difference will be made clear.

Modern-day scholars usually divide the history of ancient Greece into the
following periods:

Bronze Age: c. 3000–c. 1100
Early Iron Age/Dark Ages: c. 1100–c. 700
Archaic Period: c. 700–480

---

[1] All dates in Chapters 8–10 are BCE unless otherwise specified. Greek words and names have
been transliterated in such a way as to be as faithful as possible to original spellings while
taking into account established usages for well-known individuals and places. The translator
of each cited passage from Greek and Latin sources is given at the end of the quote in question. In cases where no translator is indicated, the translation is my own. Some of the relevant
evidence comes from Greek authors whose work survives only in fragments. Fragments from
ancient Greek authors are normally identified by the number they have been given in a modern text that collects the extant fragments from one or more authors. The name following
the number is the name of the modern editor. The following abbreviations occur with some
frequency: *FGrH=Fragmente der griechischen Historiker*, by Felix Jacoby (a collection of
almost all of the known fragments from Greek historical writers), *IG=Inscriptiones Graecae*
(a collection of Greek inscriptions), *SEG=Supplementum Epigraphicum Graecum* (a journal
that each year publishes information on newly-discovered or newly-studied inscriptions).

Classical Period: 480–323
Hellenistic Period: 323–31
Roman Period: 31 BCE–476 CE

The Bronze Age in ancient Greece ended with a spectacular series of destructions that wiped out most of the large settlements and that contributed to a near-total societal collapse. Afterward the Greeks built a new society that was in many ways very different from what came before. It took a good deal of time for them to recover from the disasters that marked the end of the Bronze Age, which is why the period immediately afterward is known as both the Dark Ages and the Early Iron Age.[2]

The evidence for the social history of the Early Iron Age is not nearly as abundant as it is for the preceding and succeeding periods. The material remains from this time are relatively meager and have only recently received thorough attention from archaeologists. The vast majority of the surviving art produced during the Early Iron Age consists of pottery painted with geometric designs; this pottery is critical in providing dates for sites and buildings but is otherwise not as informative as some later forms of Greek art. The Greeks lost the use of writing at the end of the Bronze Age and did not produce substantial numbers of texts again until the seventh century.

We do, however, have invaluable sources in the poetry of Homer and Hesiod. It is generally thought that Homer lived in the second half of the eighth century and composed two poems, the *Iliad* and the *Odyssey*, both fictional stories set in what was at the time the distant past. The *Iliad* tells the story of a Greek army attacking the city of Troy; the *Odyssey* describes Odysseus' long and troubled trip from Troy back to his home in Greece after the end of the war. Hesiod's *Works and Days* was composed around 700 and offers advice on how to live an honest and prosperous life. The *Iliad*, *Odyssey*, and *Works and Days* seem to reflect the social realities of Greek life in the eighth century and can be taken as a reasonably good guide to Greek society in the Early Iron Age. All three of these poems were composed toward the end of the Early Iron Age, a long period during which important changes took place. There was, however, a considerable degree of continuity in social practices, and for our purposes it is possible to talk about the Early Iron Age as a whole on the basis of Homer's and Hesiod's work.[3]

If we think of societies as elaborate games with goals and rules that establish legitimate and nonlegitimate means of reaching those goals (Section 4.1), some of the more important questions we might ask about a society

---

[2] An overview of ancient Greek history can be found in Pomeroy, Burstein, Donlan, and Roberts 2007. For a more detailed account, see the relevant volumes in the *Cambridge Ancient History* series.

[3] On Homer, see the articles collected in Fowler 2004. On Hesiod, see the articles collected in Montanari, Rengakos, and Tsagalis 2009. On the use of the Homeric poems as sources for social history, see Morris 1986 and Raaflaub 1998.

are what sort of goals its members typically pursue and what are seen as legitimate means of achieving them. Many of the more important goals prevalent in Early Iron Age society, such as survival and the acquisition of wealth, are immediately familiar.

There was, however, another goal to which most others were to a large extent subordinated and that was winning *timê*. *Timê* can be defined as public recognition of one's skills and achievements in the form of esteem expressed by the members of one's community. There is no precisely equivalent term in English; it is frequently translated as "honor" but "respect" is closer to the mark. Some sense of the importance of *timê* can be had from the fact that it drives the plot of the *Iliad*. A vicious dispute arises between Agamemnon, the commander of the Greek army, and Achilles, the army's greatest warrior, over a matter of *timê*; Achilles, angered by being treated with disrespect, refuses to fight until his *timê* has been restored. In his absence, the Greek army suffers a series of devastating defeats that continue until Achilles returns to the battlefield.

There was an elaborate set of social rules about *timê*, and we need to have a firm grasp of them in order to understand the societal role of sport. *Timê* was inherently relative, which is to say that it was not measured in absolute terms but in relation to that of other members of one's community. The *timê* enjoyed by an individual gave him a place in a status hierarchy that might be pictured as a ladder, with each person occupying a rung on the ladder. Because *timê* was relative, any time anyone did something that increased his *timê*, he moved up the ladder – and other people necessarily moved down.[4]

The overriding importance attached to *timê* and its relative nature meant that people were intensely competitive. The competitive tendencies of ancient Greeks are nicely expressed by Hesiod, who claims that strife is good when it fosters competition that drives people to exert themselves to the utmost:

She (strife) stirs up even the shiftless to toil; for a man grows eager to work when he considers his neighbor, a rich man who hastens to plough and plant and put his house in good order; and neighbor vies with his neighbor as he hurries after wealth. This strife is wholesome for men. And potter is angry with potter, and craftsman with craftsman, and beggar is jealous of beggar, and poet of poet. (*Works and Days* ll. 20–6, trans. H. Evelyn-White, slightly modified)

Even a beggar, who clearly occupied one of the bottom rungs of the status hierarchy, competed with other beggars to prove that he was comparatively superior.

Notionally everyone had the chance to compete to prove their superiority and move up the status ladder, so that everyone, in effect, had equal

[4] On competition and *timê* in ancient Greece, see Burckhardt 1998 (1898–1902), 160–213; Gouldner 1969, 41–77; and Ulf 2011.

opportunity to compete to become unequal. In practice, however, the standing of members of various groups within a community was so different that there were in effect multiple status ladders in each town and functionally separate segments on individual ladders. For instance, women rarely competed with men but did compete with each other; they occupied two separate ladders. The same was true of other groups, such as children and adults, and free men and slaves.

Even people on the same status ladder whose social standing was poles apart rarely competed against each other. In the *Odyssey*, Odysseus returns home after having been gone for twenty years and being reckoned by almost everyone to be long dead. He adopts the disguise of a beggar because his house is occupied by a large group of powerful men competing to marry his wife Penelope, thought to be a rich widow. Penelope's suitors amuse themselves by arranging a boxing match between the newly arrived Odysseus-as-beggar and a local beggar named Iros; the two beggars are close enough in status to make the match reasonable. However, although Odysseus-as-beggar is a free adult male and notionally in a position to compete directly with them, the suitors have no interest whatsoever in doing so. Later in the story, Penelope, having recognized Odysseus and hatched a plan with him, proposes to marry whichever suitor wins an archery contest. The contestants will have to string a huge bow and use it to hit a difficult set of targets. None of the suitors can string the bow, and when Odysseus-as-beggar proposes to try, they are incensed, and one of them says:

Ah, wretched stranger, you have no sense, not even a little....I announce great trouble for you...if ever you string this bow; you will meet no kind of courtesy in our group, but we shall put you into a black ship and take you over to King Echetos, one who mutilates all men; there you will lose everything....(*Odyssey* 21.288–309)[5]

The idea of competing with someone so far below their standing outrages the suitors.[6]

To stay for the moment with the analogy that we have been using, the tallest status ladder in any given town was that for free adult men, and the people on the top of that ladder enjoyed more *timê* than anyone else. We will focus on that part of that ladder because, as we will see, its occupants were the ones who participated most actively in sport.

---

[5] Unless otherwise noted, all quotations from the *Iliad* and *Odyssey* provided in this chapter are taken from the translations of Richmond Lattimore, sometimes with minor changes to make the terminology in the original Greek more evident. Note that line numbers vary from translation to translation; the line numbers used here are those of Lattimore.

[6] The reading of the relevant scenes in the Homeric poems offered here is incomplete in that it does not take into account purely literary considerations that in part shape the content. For an insightful treatment of both the social historical and literary dimensions of sport scenes in the Homeric poems, see Perry 2012.

If one was a free adult male in a Greek community in the Early Iron Age and had any pretensions to being an important person in town, it was necessary to demonstrate *aretê* (excellence) in tasks that directly contributed to the well-being of one's community, and by far the most prestigious of such tasks was defending the community on the battlefield. The leading men in Greek communities in the Early Iron Age almost invariably had at some point distinguished themselves as soldiers, and it is no coincidence that the *Iliad* tells the story of Achilles, who is described as the greatest warrior in the Greek world.

There was in fact something that might be loosely described as a social contract: individuals who were willing and able to make sacrifices for the well-being of their communities, especially by putting themselves at risk in defending the community, were rewarded with an unusual degree of *timê*. This social contract represented an ideal, one that lasted for centuries. In order to understand how it worked in practice, we need some sense of how Early Iron Age Greek communities functioned.

Ancient Greece in the centuries immediately after 1100 had a very simple social system. People lived in small settlements – a town with a thousand people was an unusually large place – that had almost nothing in the way of formal political systems. To the limited extent that individual villages had governments, they consisted of loose, informal councils made up of powerful men and occasional assemblies of all the adult men in the town. The members of the council would meet in response to specific problems, such as an attack from outside or a conflict inside the village, and would decide upon a response. If the matter was sufficiently serious, they would present their plan to all the adult males in town for their approval.

The influential men within each community were called *basileis* (*basileus* in the singular) or chiefs. *Basileus* was an honorary title, not an elected office, that was bestowed on men whose *timê* set them apart from most other people in their communities. Being a *basileus* was closely connected to performance on the battlefield, as is evident in the following exchange between Glaukos and Sarpedon in the *Iliad*:

Glaukos, why do we two enjoy special *timê* in Lykia, with a seat of honor, and meats, and full cups and all the men look upon us as though we are gods?...Therefore we must now stand among the front ranks of the Lykians and do our part in raging battle so that someone of the armor-wearing Lykians might say "our *basileis* who rule in Lykia are not inglorious...their strength too is noble, since they fight among the front ranks of the Lykians." (12.310–21)

Basileis earned their *timê* the hard way, by demonstrating a willingness to "fight among the front ranks" and thus put themselves at considerable risk of dying.

 One crucial way of acquiring *timê* was thus to contribute to the well-being of the community by exhibiting *aretê* on the battlefield. Another means to the same end was to provide material support to other people, which we might call generosity, but which was a very particular form of open-handedness because it was driven not by moral considerations but by a desire for *timê*. In the absence of anything resembling a centralized government, violent attacks on other settlements were seen as completely legitimate and entirely normal, almost routine. Established and aspiring *basileis* would organize groups of men to go raiding in the hope of bringing back valuables such as livestock and women. The leaders of successful raids profited handsomely, but they also redistributed most of the proceeds to other people in order to win *timê*. Odysseus, for instance, during his journey home at one point brings back a number of sheep stolen from the Cyclops Polyphemos, and he immediately shares them out equally among his men, who give him back the largest ram as a mark of *timê* (*Odyssey* 9.543–57).[7]

Timê, power, and wealth were tightly bound together. People gave *timê* to and followed leaders who demonstrated military abilities and generosity. Individuals from households shattered by war or sickness joined stronger households in search of protection and sustenance. The power a *basileus* wielded spiraled upward as the number of men he could call on increased; Agamemnon's authority in the *Iliad* is grounded in the fact that he has more men under his command than anyone else, and when he threatens Achilles he says he will come against him "with many men behind me" (1.325). *Basileis* with manpower at their disposal could expand their agricultural production and launch raids at will, and they regularly received gifts from their followers. Odysseus' son Telemachos remarks that "It is not bad to be a *basileus*. Speedily his house grows prosperous, and he has more *timê* than others" (*Odyssey* 1.392–3). It is important, however, not to fall into the trap of thinking that *timê* was simply a means to other ends. People pursued *timê* as an end in itself even when it required voluntarily putting their lives at risk on the battlefield.

8.3. SPORT HISTORY

The Homeric poems, which include numerous scenes of athletic activity, are by far the most important source for sport in Early Iron Age Greece. We can also make some use of what is known about sport in later periods of Greek history and of the results of ongoing excavations at many sites. It is worth emphasizing that we are interested only in those aspects of sport that are directly relevant to understanding the role of sport in society. We will focus on four topics: occasions on which sport took place, the kind of sports that were played, who played sport, and the connection between sport and *timê*.[8]

---

[7] On the importance of *basileis* being generous, see Donlan 1998.

[8] On sport in ancient Greece, see Kyle 2007 and Miller 2004a. On sport in Early Iron Age Greece, see Laser 1987.

Sports were played on an informal basis as a casual pastime, as formally organized events on special occasions, and as part of initiation rites for boys and girls. Both the *Iliad* and the *Odyssey* show men entertaining themselves by casually playing sports. In the *Iliad*, Achilles pulls his forces out of battle during his quarrel with Agamemnon, and his men "amused themselves with discuses and with light spears for throwing and bows" (2.774–5). In the *Odyssey*, the men courting Penelope do much the same thing while waiting for dinner to be prepared (4.625–7).

More formally organized sport took place on special occasions, particularly at funerals for prominent men. In Book 23 of the *Iliad*, after his closest companion Patroklos is killed in battle, Achilles arranges an elaborate burial ceremony that includes athletic contests with valuable prizes. He sits the Greek army down to watch a program of events that includes a chariot race, boxing, wrestling, a footrace, armed combat (to the drawing of first blood), weight throwing, archery, and spear throwing.

Festivals were another kind of special occasion that might include sport. Homer makes passing reference to what seems to have been religious festivals that included the sacrifice of an animal and a footrace (*Iliad* 22.158–66); the winner in the footrace received parts of the animal as a prize. Sport was also associated with less religious gatherings. Odysseus' trip home includes a visit with the wondrous Phaiakians, who put on a display of their skill at running, wrestling, jumping, discus, boxing, and dancing (*Odyssey* 8.96–255). Although in the modern world sport and dance are typically separate undertakings, in ancient Greece they were deeply intertwined.

Group dancing was an essential element in Greek life starting well before the Early Iron Age and continuing for centuries afterward. A group of dancers was called a chorus and could include males and females of various ages, in various combinations, and in various numbers up to about fifty. Choral performances typically included singing and were accompanied by music from a small harp or a flute. A series of references in Homer show that choral dance was performed both casually and on many different kinds of special occasions. For example, Homer describes a group of girls performing a dance involving throwing a ball back and forth while waiting for their laundry to dry (*Odyssey* 6.100–9). The athletic contests held during Odysseus' visit to the Phaiakians are immediately followed by dancing; a poet-musician plays the harp and sings while a group of young men dance. Then two sons of the most important *basileis* in town put on a special performance in which they dance while tossing a ball back and forth (*Odyssey* 8.256–380).[9] Evidence from an inscription and from paintings on pottery

---

[9] On choral dance in ancient Greece, the best starting places are Calame 1997 (1977), Griffith 2001, and Lonsdale 1993.

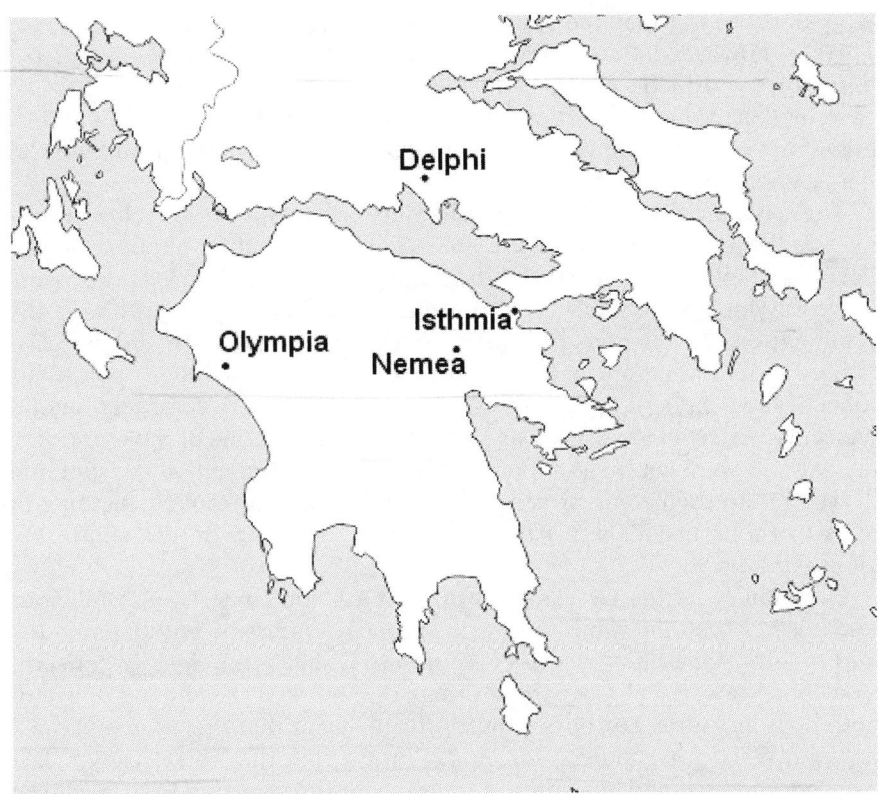

MAP 1. Map of Greece Showing Location of Olympia and Other Panhellenic Game Sites

from the eighth century show that competitions in both individual and choral dance were held.[10]

What would ultimately become perhaps the world's most famous sporting event, the Olympics, were probably founded at some point during the eighth century as part of a religious festival. Starting in the fifth century, when they became interested in such matters, Greeks were of the opinion that athletic contests had been intermittently held at Olympia (see Map 1) from very ancient times, but were unsure about the chronology of those contests. Most Greeks dated the beginning of a regular series of competitions at Olympia to 776, but some favored other possibilities, such as 884. Excavations at Olympia have shown that it became a religious sanctuary

[10] For the inscription, see Powell 1988. For the pottery, see, for example, Athens NM 874.

around 1000 and that the site was expanded and improved around 700. There is, however, no clear physical evidence that helps fix the date for the beginning of athletic contests there. Archaeologists working at Olympia have suggested that the improvements made around 700 show that contests began at that point, though it remains possible that events of purely local significance were held earlier.[11]

The Olympic Games were from the outset held as part of a religious festival dedicated to Zeus. We have no detailed information about what the Olympics looked like in the eighth century, but in later periods they were a five-day-long affair built around a huge sacrifice to Zeus. Although the combination of a religious rite and a sporting event may seem odd, we need to keep in mind that ancient Greek rites were not as consistently solemn as some of their modern counterparts. The single most important feature of a typical Greek religious ritual was a sacrifice, ideally of one or more animals; the animals were cut up and much of the meat was cooked on the spot and distributed to the people present. These rites had, as a result, something of the air of a barbeque. Seen from that perspective, sport fit nicely into religious festivals.[12]

How and why the Greeks came to link athletic contests with religious festivals has been the subject of much scholarly discussion without any definite result.[13] One thing that does seem clear is that from an early date athletic contests were held as part of rituals that marked the coming of age of both boys and girls. For boys coming of age meant that they were expected to begin serving as soldiers, for girls it meant that they were ready to get married. Boys seem to have gone through these rituals around age seventeen or eighteen, girls somewhere between twelve and fourteen. Rites of passage with athletic contests were held at least as early as the late Bronze Age and continued for literally centuries thereafter.[14]

The athletic contests associated with initiation rites were different from other Greek sport in a number of ways. Both males and females participated. Other than these rites, it was rare in most times and places in ancient Greece for girls to be permitted to participate in sports. (Married women were entirely excluded from sport.) The program of events was limited to a single, short footrace, as opposed to other occasions when multiple events

[11] On the dating of the first Olympics, see Christesen 2007a, 8–21. On the history of the sanctuary and the role of Zeus, see Morgan 1990, 26–105 and Moustaka 2002.

[12] On the ancient Olympics, see Spivey 2004.

[13] See the discussion in S. Murray 2012.

[14] There is no comprehensive work in English on initiation rites in ancient Greece. The best starting place is Graf 1996, in which the most important relevant bibliography is cited. Homer has nothing to say about athletic contests associated with initiation rites or about the Olympics. He does mention a chariot race in Elis, the area in which Olympia was located (*Iliad* 11.696–702). Some scholars have read this as a reference to the Olympics, but if so it is not an obvious one.

were held. Finally, the participants often wore a special outfit or went nude. During the Early Iron Age, Greek athletes typically wore a loincloth, and athletic nudity was limited to contests held as part of initiation rites.[15]

A good example of an athletic contest held as part of an initiation rite can be found in the Heraia Games at Olympia. Hera was among the numerous gods worshipped at Olympia beside the patron deity Zeus, and contests called the Heraia were held in her honor there. Other than using the same stadium, the Heraia Games had no known connection to the Olympics. The Heraia consisted of one event, a footrace for unmarried girls, with contestants running in three different age groups. Victors were rewarded with an olive wreath, part of an ox sacrificed to Hera, and the right to dedicate an image of themselves in the sanctuary. The girls ran wearing an unusual outfit, a short tunic that left their right breast bare. A marble statue now in the Vatican museum at Rome shows a girl running in just this outfit (see Figure 8); it is probably a copy of a bronze original from around 460 that served as a victory monument. This kind of tunic was normally worn not by girls, who dressed much more modestly, but by male laborers.[16]

The Heraia shares numerous features with initiation rites from all over the globe. Anthropologists have found that coming of age rituals typically consist of three parts: separating the boys or girls to be initiated from their community, a period of transition, and reintegration into the community but with a new status. During the transition period those going through the ritual frequently engage in physical tests and wear some form of unusual clothing or go nude to help mark it as something special and apart from everyday life.[17]

Having looked at the occasions on which people played sports and the sports that were played on those occasions, we can now turn our attention to who participated in sport. Although it is probable that men from all parts of the social spectrum participated in sport at least casually and occasionally, free adult men of high status – *basileis* – dominated athletics. (A note of caution is in order because our key source, Homer, was interested primarily in the lives of the rich and powerful and has relatively little to say about others.) The dominant role of *basileis* in Early Iron Age Greek sport was particularly noticeable when it came to participating in formally organized competitions.

Because participation in athletic contests was typically limited to *basileis*, participation was in and of itself a mark of status. We have already seen this in the reaction of Penelope's suitors when Odysseus disguised as a

[15] The evidence for athletic contests attached to initiation rites is discussed at length in Scanlon 2002. On the dress of Greek athletes in the Early Iron Age, see Christesen 2002.

[16] On the Heraia, see Scanlon 2002, 98–120 and Scanlon 2008 (though see also the skeptical comments in Kyle 2007, 220–21 and Langenfeld 2006).

[17] The classic anthropological study of initiation rites remains van Gennep 1960 (1906).

FIGURE 8. Marble Statue of a Girl Runner (Vatican Museum #2784) Roman-Era Copy of a Bronze Original from c. 460 BCE (From Wikimedia Commons, http://ca.wikipedia.org/wiki/Fixter:Atlanta_Vatican_Inv2784.jpg)

beggar proposes to compete in their archery contest. Another example can be found in the story of Odysseus' visit to the Phaiakians, during which the local *basileis* arrange for their sons to compete in athletic contests for Odysseus' entertainment. In the middle of these contests, two of the competitors, Laodamas and Euryalos, approach Odysseus and invite him to join them. Laodamas says:

It's fit and proper for you to know your sports. What greater glory attends a man, while he's alive, than what he wins with his racing feet and striving hands? Come and compete....(*Odyssey* 8.169–72)[18]

When Odysseus politely declines, Euryalos is enraged and verbally attacks Odysseus:

I never took you for someone skilled in games, the kind that real men play throughout the world. Not a chance. You're some skipper of profiteers, roving the high seas in his scudding craft, reckoning up his freight with a keen eye out for home-cargo, grabbing the gold he can! You're no athlete. I see that. (8.184–9)

Why is Euryalos so upset? The invitation to compete with the local elites marked Odysseus out as an elite himself, and Odysseus' refusal puts Laodamas and Euryalos in an awkward position. Either Odysseus thinks himself too good to compete with them, or they have greatly overestimated Odysseus' social standing and inadvertently issued an invitation to a man of low status who has no significant experience in sports competitions. Euryalos addresses the problem by in effect denying that he ever thought Odysseus was a man who enjoyed any prestige; he does this in part by accusing Odysseus of not being an athlete.

Euryalos' remarks arouse Odysseus' ire, and he retorts:

Your slander fans the anger in my heart! I'm no stranger to sports – for all your taunts – I've held my place in the front ranks, I tell you....I'll compete in your games, just watch. Your insults cut to the quick – you rouse my fighting blood! (8.206–15)

Odysseus then strips off his cloak, grabs a discus, and hurls it well beyond the longest throw of any of the Phaiakians. Odysseus goes on to boast about his skill in boxing, wrestling, archery, and spear throwing. The archery contest in Ithaka and the heated exchange between Euryalos and Odysseus in Phaiakia show that participation in athletic contests was not in practice open to everyone in any given community; rather, prominent men competed with other prominent men.

Perhaps the most important part of the practice of sport in Early Iron Age Greece, from the perspective of social history, is that it was an essential

---

[18] Quotations from Book 8 of the *Odyssey* here and below are taken from the translation of Robert Fagles, who does a better job than Lattimore of making evident in the English the sense of the original Greek in this part of Homer's work. The line numbers in these passages are those in Fagles' translation.

means for earning *timê*. As Laodamas says to Odysseus, "What greater glory attends a man, while he's alive, than what he wins with his racing feet and striving hands?" Skill in athletics was prized largely because sport was intimately linked to war, a link that is immediately apparent in the kinds of events in which Greeks competed. The standard array of contests included chariot racing, boxing, wrestling, running, armed combat, weight throwing, archery, spear throwing, and jumping. When Laodamas questions Odysseus' athletic credentials, Odysseus goes out of his way to make it clear not only that he is a superior athlete, but also that he is a great warrior. Recall that he says, "I'm no stranger to sports – for all your taunts – I've held my place in the front ranks." In boasting about his athletic skills, he states, "I'm no disgrace in the world of games where men compete. Well I know how to handle a fine polished bow, the first to hit my man in a mass of enemies" (*Odyssey* 8.245–7). For Odysseus the line between sport and war is virtually nonexistent.

8.4. SPORT AND SOCIETY IN EARLY IRON AGE GREECE

Early Iron Age Greece defies easy characterization with respect to democratization. From an institutionalist perspective, there was little in the way of formal government, and what government did exist was more oligarchic than democratic. There was a certain element of democracy, most notably in the assemblies in which all the adult male members of a community participated. In these assemblies all adult males could make their views known, and could, at least sometimes, decide on a course of action different from that favored by *basileis*. On a day-to-day basis, however, the political life of any given community in Greece in the Early Iron Age was dominated by a small number of *basileis* who collectively represented a dominant, oligarchic group.[19]

On the other hand, the distance between the top and bottom of the social pyramid was minimal. Odysseus, the richest and most powerful man on the island of Ithaka, boasts of his capacity for doing hard agricultural labor in the form of plowing and harvesting (*Odyssey*, 18.365–75), and archaeological evidence shows that, with a very few exceptions, *basileis* lived in homes that were not markedly more elaborate than those of other members of their communities.[20]

In addition, membership in the group of *basileis* in any given community was fluid over time because social status was to a considerable extent assigned on a meritocratic basis. *Basileis* had to prove their ability and willingness to serve the community in order to maintain a position on top of the local status hierarchy, and they could not automatically pass their position

[19] On the sociopolitical structure of Early Iron Age Greek communities, see Donlan 1999.
[20] On the material culture of Early Iron Age Greece, see Pedley 2012, 102–19.

down to their sons. On the other side of the coin, talented men could move up the status hierarchy. In the *Odyssey*, Odysseus disguises his identity at various points and makes up fictitious names and biographies; one of those biographies is of a man who is an illegitimate son of a *basileus*. He is treated badly by the legitimate sons after their father's death, but shows himself to be a great war leader and prospers accordingly. Odysseus claims that:

I was nine times a leader of men and went in fast-faring vessels against outland men, and much substance came my way, and from this I took out an abundance of things…and soon my house grew greater, and from that time on I went among the Cretans as one feared and respected. (14.229–34)

Ongoing, meritocratic status competition meant that the composition of the dominant group in a Greek community was not by any means fixed.

Meritocracy, however, only operated within certain limits. The sons of *basileis* enjoyed enormous advantages because they inherited their fathers' connections and to some extent their status, and in that way birth and wealth mattered a great deal. In addition, only *basileis* and their sons seem to have been given the opportunity to participate in important status-generating activities, including sport. It must in fact have been exceedingly rare for a boy born to a beggar to ascend to the top of the status ladder in his community. There was thus a considerable element of ascribed rank in Early Iron Age Greece.

Sport underpinned the operation of this semi-meritocratic system. Anyone who hoped to enjoy high social status and political influence had to demonstrate that he possessed the sort of physical prowess necessary to defend the community on the battlefield, and the best warrior in a town could expect to enjoy the most *timê*. However, the battlefield was a messy environment that was not ideally suited either to testing the relative talents of men from the same community (who fought on the same side) or to allowing the community to observe actions and outcomes. Athletic contests were ideal substitutes for the battlefield because they provided a venue in which men could compete on equal terms in activities that made their relative levels of physical prowess clear while performing in front of the assembled community. The expectation was that the great athlete would also be a great warrior, and great athletes were treated accordingly. Participation in sport, particularly in the form of formally organized competitions, was for all intents and purposes required of *basileis*.

The role that athletics played in status competition among powerful men is reflected in the absence of team sports and the importance of spectators. One of the striking characteristics of the list of events in which Early Iron Age Greeks competed is the complete absence of any team sports; all events pitted individuals against individuals. Athletics served to establish the relative physical prowess of current and future leaders, and individual sports were ideal for that purpose, whereas team competitions would have made it difficult to judge the performance of one individual versus that of another.

Insofar as athletics were to a great extent about *timê* and *timê* meant public recognition of one's achievements, Greeks understood athletic contests as requiring an audience. The idea of competing without spectators would have struck them as exceedingly odd, and this is reflected in the terminology Greeks used to describe contests. The basic term for an athletic competition was *agôn*, which was also used to describe a gathering of a group of people.[21] So, for instance, when Homer describes Achilles gathering the Greek army to watch Patroklos' funeral games, he says that Achilles "made them sit down in a broad *agôn*" (23.258). An *agôn* was both an athletic competition and a gathering of people because one presumed the other.

Sport also helped establish limits on the operation of meritocracy. Although there were no legal barriers preventing anyone from entering a formally organized athletic competition, in practice participation was limited to *basileis* and their sons. This is evident in the outraged reaction of the suitors when Odysseus-as-beggar announces his intention to enter the archery competition. Because only *basileis* participated in athletic competitions, just taking part immediately established someone as a distinguished member of the community, hence the virulent reaction of Laodamas and Euryalos when Odysseus declines their invitation to participate in athletic contests. By excluding most people from athletic competitions, *basileis* and their sons protected their standing against potential threats from other, lower-status members of their communities.

It is clear from all this that sport in Early Iron Age Greece was thoroughly horizontal, but mass sport was absent. Sports activity was organized by and for elite males, as is evident from the funeral games arranged by Achilles and the contests staged by the Phaiakians. The low degree of regimentation is apparent from the complete absence of team sports, though some element of synchronized activity was introduced by choral dance (a subject discussed at length in the next chapter). Sport was understood as an arena for elite display and meritocratic status competition that benefited individual athletes. The limitation on participation to elites meant that there was nothing approximating mass sport.

Thus, the political life of Early Iron Age Greece, with its mixture of horizontal and vertical elements, was democratized to a limited extent, while sport, although horizontal, was an activity restricted for the most part to elites.

[21] Scanlon 1983.

9

Sport and Society in Sixth- and Fifth-Century BCE Greece

9.1. SOCIAL HISTORY

During the Archaic (700–480) and Classical (480–323) periods, processes of change that were already evident in the Greek world in the eighth century continued and gathered strength. The basic social system in 800 was much like the one that came into being after the disasters at the end of the Bronze Age. By 700 a new system had begun to take shape, and in the sixth and fifth centuries there were fundamental shifts in almost every aspect of Greek life. A much larger percentage of the men in most Greek communities gained social and political privileges and participated regularly in sport, and, as a result, the earliest known systems of democratic governance came into being, as did the earliest known examples of mass sport.

The sources for the social history of the Archaic period present a certain number of peculiarities. The best evidence for the kinds of issues of interest to us comes from contemporary texts. Greeks produced a considerable amount of writing during the Archaic period, but very little of it survives, and what we do have comes down to us mostly in the form of short quotations of poetry in later authors. That is not as problematic as it might seem because for a long period of time Greek authors mostly composed poetry, much of which responded directly to contemporary events, and poetry from the Archaic period is, as a result, invaluable in reconstructing the history of the time. The sources for the Classical period are much richer and include the earliest historical accounts, which were written in the fifth century.

We begin once again with the issue of goals and legitimate means of achieving them. *Timê* continued to be a goal of overriding importance, but there was a long, running conflict in regard to two of the social rules pertaining to it: how it could be acquired and who could compete for the sort of high-level *timê* that made someone a *basileus* in the Early Iron Age. Elites sought to rewrite the social contract inherited from the Early Iron Age and to win *timê* not from the demonstration of *aretê* in support of the community, but rather from occupying official positions of power and from wealth and birth. Nonelites resisted attempts to rewrite the social contract and gradually came to claim the right to compete for *timê* on equal terms with elites.[1]

In considering the conflict between elites and nonelites in the Archaic and Classical periods, it will be helpful to have a clearer sense of the composition of both groups. Due to changes in political systems (discussed shortly), the term *basileus* went out of use. Starting in the seventh century Greeks seem to have divided the socioeconomic spectrum into three more or less distinct segments. *Plousioi* were people from households that were so wealthy and that had enough labor at their disposal from women, slaves, and hired dependents that their adult male members never had to work. Some adult men who were *plousioi* worked anyway, but Greek males placed a high value on having the leisure to pursue interests such as politics and less value on work as a good thing in and of itself. *Penêtes* were people from households that were prosperous but not rich enough that their adult males were entirely free from labor. The vast majority of households in all times and places in ancient Greece supported themselves through agriculture, and the climate and topography in most places where Greeks lived was such that farms required intense labor at some times of the year and relatively little at others. Adult men who were *penêtes* had to work hard on their farms for part of every year, but also had enough labor at their disposal from women, slaves, and dependents to enjoy a considerable amount of leisure during slack periods. *Ptôchoi* were people from households in which the adult male members had to work regularly, typically because they could not afford to buy slaves or hire laborers. The people in this category ranged from farmers who made a decent but not spectacular living to outright beggars. Members of the sort of wealthy and powerful families that tended to produce *basileis* in the Early Iron Age became known as *plousioi*. We might think of the *penêtes* as the rough equivalent of the upper middle class.[2]

The sociopolitical battles of the Archaic and Classical periods were fought largely between *plousioi* and *penêtes*. The *ptôchoi* were almost always largely excluded from social and political influence. What we would call elites were thus more or less the *plousioi*, and the nonelites were, for our purposes, mostly the *penêtes*. There was not, of course, perfect unanimity among the *plousioi* in any given community, but a community's elites did tend to act together with some frequency in order to defend their collective interests. The *penêtes* were initially even less unified than the *plousioi* but gradually developed a sense of being a group with similar priorities.

[1] The reader should be aware that there is among modern-day scholars a wide range of perspectives on the history of the Archaic and Classical periods. The perspective articulated here is based on Donlan 1999, Morris 2000, Raaflaub 1997, and Raaflaub and Wallace 2007.

[2] On the definition of rich and poor in ancient Greece, see Markle 1985 and Morris 2000, 109–54.

The *plousioi* had good reason to dislike the social contract inherited from the Early Iron Age. In order to maintain a position atop the status hierarchy, they had to take risks and expend hard-won resources for the benefit of others, and they could not automatically pass their position down to their sons. Moreover, new challenges appeared because of developments in Greek warfare. Warfare during the Early Iron Age had been relatively informal, and communities did not have unified, disciplined armies. Individual *basileis* led groups of followers on raids and, when a community was attacked, it fielded a loosely organized force made up of different bands of men attached to various leaders. In the course of fighting *basileis* took special risks by literally leading their men into battle. During the late eighth and early seventh centuries, Greek military forces became significantly more organized, and communities began to field a unified force of heavily armed infantrymen, called hoplites, who fought in a tight, rectangular formation called a phalanx.[3]

Phalanxes consisted primarily of *plousioi* and *penêtes* because Greek soldiers paid for their own arms and armor, and hoplite equipment was relatively expensive. Hoplites wore a helmet, a breastplate, and greaves and carried a shield, spear, and sword. Much of this equipment had to be either custom-made for the user or at least fitted for him; it cost in total about 75–100 *drachmai*, the equivalent of two or three months' pay for a skilled craftsman.[4] *Penêtes* could afford this expense, *ptôchoi* generally could not. *Ptôchoi* served in their community's army, but as lightly armed fighters who were only peripherally attached to the phalanx; in later periods, when some Greek communities developed fleets of oared warships, many *ptôchoi* served as rowers. The collective contribution of *ptôchoi* was in many cases significant, but it was always the phalanx and its members that received most of the credit for a community's military successes.

The phalanx changed relationships between *plousioi* and *penêtes* because it reduced the importance of any single person. No particular individual in the front few ranks was more valuable to the formation than any other. This tended to equalize all the soldiers in the phalanx and eroded the key means that Early Iron Age elites had had of distinguishing themselves and of winning *timê*.

The seventh century was, therefore, a period when preexisting and new challenges combined to make it increasingly difficult for *plousioi* to win the *timê* necessary to stay atop the status hierarchies in their communities. They responded by attempting to use control of emergent political systems, conspicuous consumption, and claims about lineage to stabilize their position.

---

[3] On the history of warfare in ancient Greece, see the articles in Sabin, van Wees, and Whitby 2007.

[4] On the cost of hoplite equipment, see Hanson 1995, 487 and van Wees 2004, 47–60.

Starting in the eighth century, the informal arrangements of the Early Iron Age gave way to more structured political systems built around the *polis* (plural *poleis*), which consisted of an urban center and the surrounding farmland. The formation of *poleis* affected the social rules regarding *timê* by making power an end in itself. As we have seen, *basileis* exercised power in part because they attracted followers by demonstrating military prowess and generosity. That situation changed markedly when *poleis* were established. A formal government by definition has considerable coercive powers, which on a day-to-day basis are exercised by the individuals who run the government, and this made it possible for someone to wield power in a *polis* simply by virtue of the fact that he held a magistracy. One result was that power could become completely separated from *timê* and a goal in its own right. Another, probably more important result was that power, which formerly was the result of *timê*, could increasingly become its cause. A person in a position of official authority, with the power of the state at his back, could compel respect from less eminent members of the community. In many places *plousioi* sought to control access to magistracies and by that means consolidate power, demand *timê*, and keep themselves atop the community's status hierarchy.

Plousioi also sought to make wealth in and of itself, particularly when displayed by means of conspicuous consumption, a source of *timê*. In the Early Iron Age, wealth could be used to win *timê*, when it was employed in providing support to other members of the community. *Basileis* were expected to be generous with the resources at their disposal and lived in a manner that was not much different from other members of their communities. During the Archaic period *plousioi* adopted habits that visibly set them apart from others and that flamboyantly displayed their wealth and their freedom from any need to labor. They began holding symposia, an elaborate style of group drinking and dining in which the participants laid on couches arranged in a rectangular room, and started dressing ostentatiously. The poet Asios of Samos, who wrote in the middle of the sixth century, described the appearance of the *plousioi* in his *polis*:

And so they would go, their locks carefully combed, into Hera's sanctuary, covered in their splendid cloaks, sweeping the ground with their snow-white robes, with golden grasshoppers [elaborate hair clips] adorning topknots. And their long-flowing hair, bound in golden ties, would swing in the breeze, and around their arms were fancy bracelets. (Fragment 13 Bernabé)

The *plousioi* also sought to establish birth as a source of *timê*, by claiming that they came from superior lineages and were worthy of respect on that basis alone. This shift is evident in the meanings assigned to the Greek words for "good" (*esthlos*) and "bad" (*kakos*). In the Homeric poems someone is *esthlos* because he is courageous on the battlefield and *kakos* because he is a coward. During the Archaic period, however, some poets began using these words to describe parentage.[5] The seventh-century poet Alcaeus, for instance, expresses his bitter opposition to Pittakos, a friend turned political rival, in the following terms:

Do you [Pittakos], sprung from such a lineage, have the reputation that free men born from *esthloi* parents possess? (Fragment 72 Lobel and Page, ll. 11–13)

They made the base-born [*kakopatris*] Pittakos tyrant of that...luckless *polis*. (Fragment 348 Lobel and Page)

The attempts of the *plousioi* to rewrite the social rules pertaining to the acquisition of *timê* met with active resistance from the *penêtes*. The *penêtes* probably initially had no aspirations to social or political dominance; it is unlikely, for instance, that they objected to *plousioi* holding most or all of the magistracies in the newly formed *poleis*.[6] The problem was one of incentives. In the Early Iron Age, elites derived *timê* from showing an active concern for the well-being of other members of the community and thus had a strong motivation to do so. If the *plousioi* were assured of prestige and power they had little motivation to concern themselves with the welfare of others. That would not have been to the benefit of the *penêtes* and was in any case a recipe for a dysfunctional community.

The *penêtes* responded by overtly rejecting the attempts of the *plousioi* to use wealth and birth to set themselves apart. This is evident in the following passage from the work of Xenophanes, who was active in the second half of the sixth century and who voices sentiments exactly the opposite of those we found expressed by his approximate contemporary Asios:

Having learned useless luxuries from the Lydians, so long as they were without grievous tyranny, they went to the marketplace dressed in clothes dyed purple, no less than a thousand in total, arrogantly rejoicing in their long, gold-adorned hair and sprinkling themselves with carefully applied scent. (Fragment 3 West)

The same idea appears prominently in the writings of the statesman Solon, who lived in Athens in the sixth century and wrote poetry to explain his political ideas. Solon argued that real wealth is having enough to eat and clothes to wear, not possessing large amounts of land or gold (Fragment 24 West).

The *penêtes* articulated an alternative set of goals and social rules that emphasized cooperation and sacrifice in the interests of the community and the importance of being an ordinary citizen of a well-ordered *polis*. They expressed those ideas in terms of the concepts of *mesos* (being in the middle,

---

[5] On changes in the usage of the terms *esthlos* and *kakos*, see Donlan 1999, 35–76.
[6] This speaks to the differentiation between the nomistic and kratistic views of power, outlined in Meier 1990 (1980).

literally and figuratively) and *eunomia* (good order). These ideas are nicely articulated in the work of the sixth-century poet Phocylides who wrote:

Many of the best things come to those who are in the *mesos*; I want to be *mesos* in the *polis*. (Fragment 12 Diehl)

A small, well-ordered *polis* on a rock is stronger than ridiculous Nineveh [a famously large and powerful city in Mesopotamia]. (Fragment 4 Diehl)

Some *penêtes* expressed disdain for sport because it was intensely competitive and did not contribute to the well-being of the community in any obvious way. This is apparent in the work of Xenophanes, who wrote:

If one of the people should be a skilled boxer or pentathlete or wrestler or even if one of them should be a swift runner, which is the most honored of deeds of strength in the contests of men, the *polis* would not possess more *eunomia* as a result. It would be but a small delight for a *polis* if some athlete won a victory alongside the banks of Pisa [i.e., at Olympia], for such things do not fatten the treasury of the *polis*. (Fragment 2 West, ll. 15–21)

The values championed by the *penêtes* had their roots in the social contract of the Early Iron Age, which linked *timê* to the act of contributing to the well-being of the community. However, there was also a good deal of innovation in that the *penêtes* made the case that it was perfectly acceptable to be an ordinary citizen and not seek to rise to the top of a community's status hierarchy.

The struggle between *plousioi* and *penêtes* was played out on these terms for much of the Archaic period in individual communities all over the Greek world. In some communities the *plousioi* won out for a time and established themselves as a hereditary aristocracy; only members of their families could hold magistracies, and they inherited fixed positions on top of their community's status hierarchy and all the *timê* that went with it.

Over the course of time, however, the *penêtes* gained the upper hand in most places, and a new and more democratized sociopolitical system gradually took shape in much of the Greek world. The *penêtes*, who do not seem to have had grand ambitions at the beginning of the Archaic period, came little by little to expect and demand equality with the *plousioi*. To understand what this meant in practice, it will be helpful to return to our analogy of status hierarchies as ladders (see Section 8.1). In the Early Iron Age, the status ladder for adult free men was divided into functionally separate segments – beggars competed with beggars for example. The top of the status ladder was occupied by *basileis* who typically competed for status only with each other. In the beginning of the Archaic period, *plousioi* occupied the top of the tallest status ladder in each town and competed with each other. By the sixth century, however, a new arrangement was emerging in many places in Greece, in which *penêtes* regularly competed with *plousioi* on equal terms and had the ability to win places on the highest rungs of the tallest status ladder in their *poleis*.

That new arrangement eventually had profound political and social consequences and resulted in a great deal of democratization in many Greek communities. The *plousioi* probably represented roughly 4–5% of the households in any given town, *penêtes* 30–50%.[7] The number of men in the dominant group in each town thus became roughly six to ten times larger than it had been. This process of democratization was evident all over the Greek world in the sixth and fifth centuries, but each *polis* was in a sense its own unique case, and the extant sources are such that we can follow it most closely in Sparta and in Athens.

Sparta was in many ways an unusual *polis*. By Greek standards it controlled a massive territory, c. 8500 square kilometers, about twenty times the size of that of a more typical *polis*. Its size was the result of a long campaign of conquest that first gave Sparta control of all of Laconia, the region in which the town of Sparta was located, and then all of Messenia, the region to the west (see Map 2).[8]

Before the seventh century the sociopolitical situation in Sparta seems to have been typical in that the *polis* was dominated by an influential group of *plousioi*. Change came as the result of a revolt among the conquered Messenians sometime around the middle of the seventh century. Suppressing the revolt required a long and costly war that put immense stress on Spartan society.

In the aftermath of that rebellion, Spartan society underwent major changes. Many, perhaps all, of the *penêtes* in Sparta were given large land grants in Messenia with attached serfs called helots, who produced enough food and income that the *penêtes* no longer needed to work to support themselves. Put another way, Sparta's *penêtes* were converted into *plousioi* by exploiting the land and labor of the conquered Messenians. Sparta's former *penêtes* were expected to use their new freedom from labor to undergo as youths long and arduous training to be citizens and soldiers and to serve the Spartan state in those capacities as adults.

Roughly contemporaneous changes in Sparta's sociopolitical system effected a good deal of democratization. The sovereign power in the Spartan *polis* was given to an assembly in which all Spartan male citizens, that is, *plousioi* and former *penêtes*, could vote. All male citizens also had the right to vote in elections by means of which magistrates were chosen, and could themselves stand for office. Sparta's *penêtes* were also given the opportunity to compete on relatively equal terms with *plousioi* in status-generating

---

[7] On the relative numbers in different segments of Greek *poleis*, see J. K. Davies 1967, J. K. Davies 1984, and Ober 1996. Estimates of the percentage of adult males in Greek communities that served as hoplites are also directly relevant. On that issue, see van Wees 2004, 47–60.

[8] A general introduction to ancient Sparta and its history can be found in Kennell 2010. For a more detailed account, see Cartledge 2002 and Cartledge and Spawforth 2002.

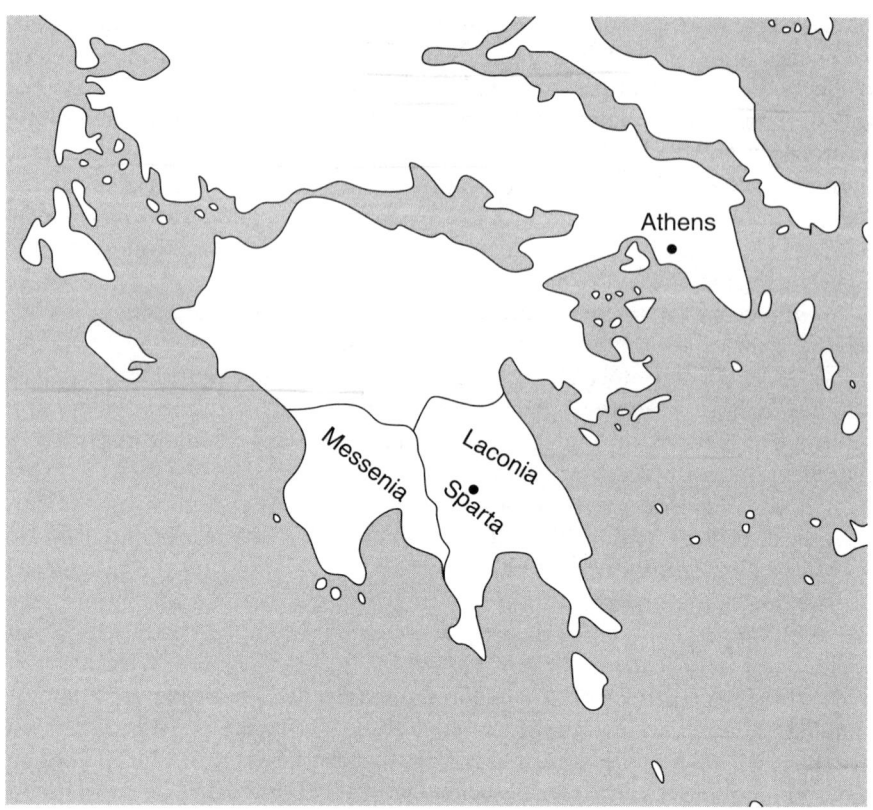

MAP 2. Map of Laconia and Sparta

activities of all kinds. Democratization and the concomitant expansion of horizontal relationships between what had been the *plousioi* and the *penêtes* of Sparta is reflected in the fact that all Spartan male citizens called each other *homoioi* (equals). The net result was that the number of men in Sparta who enjoyed full political and social privileges increased substantially. Precise figures are hard to come by, but there were probably about 8,000 *homoioi* in the Archaic period.

Despite the impact of the sociopolitical reforms enacted in Sparta, much inequality remained. Sparta had two hereditary kings who wielded considerable power. Families that had been among the *plousioi* before the middle of the seventh century continued to enjoy privileged social and political positions for a long period of time, so that some *homoioi* were, in practice, more equal than others.[9] A substantial fraction of the inhabitants of the Spartan

[9] On this point, see Hodkinson 2000, 399–445.

state consisted of people who were enslaved, and women had only limited social privileges and never had any political rights.[10]

Democratization unfolded at a slower pace but more fully in Athens. For much of the seventh century Athens was dominated by a small hereditary aristocracy called the *Eupatridai* (literally "descendants of good fathers") and was governed by nine magistrates selected by and from among the *Eupatridai*, and by a council of about 300 men consisting of former magistrates.[11] Over the course of the sixth century sociopolitical changes initiated a process of democratization. The landmarks in that process were two separate sets of reforms, one instituted by Solon sometime around 590, and a second by Kleisthenes in 508.

The *Eupatridai*, probably driven by fear of a violent revolution, empowered Solon to make whatever changes he believed necessary to quell unrest among the Athenian populace. Solon rearranged the terms of outstanding mortgages in such a way as to redistribute much of the land owned by the *Eupatridai* and assigned every family in Athens to one of four property classes based on how much their farm produced. He decreed that magistrates would be elected and made it possible for any man from a family in the top property class to run for office, regardless of whether or not he was one of the *Eupatridai*. Finally, he gave every male citizen of Athens the right to appeal a magistrate's decision to a jury drawn from men from all four property classes, a measure that represented a radical move toward democracy. Athenian juries as constituted by Solon consisted mostly of men from outside the ranks of the *plousioi* and wielded significant power, and in this way, not just the *penêtes* but also the *ptôchoi* were given a major share in the operation of Athens' government. Aristotle, or one of his students, wrote a history of the Athenian constitution in which he remarked that "the feature which is said to have contributed most to the strength of the democracy [is] the right of appeal to a jury, for when the people have the right to vote in the courts they control the state" (*Constitution of the Athenians* 9.1, trans. J. Moore, slightly modified).[12]

In 508 another round of reforms, this one overseen by Kleisthenes, made Athens into a full-fledged democracy in the institutionalist sense of the term. Kleisthenes began by creating ten new, identically structured political groupings called tribes, and every free adult male resident of the Athenian state was assigned to a tribe. All of these men, and their male descendants,

---

[10] Some ancient sources and much modern scholarship characterize Spartan women as enjoying considerable economic and social privileges, at least relative to other Greek women. This characterization is less well-founded than it might seem. For an up-to-date discussion of what is known about Spartan women, see Millender 2012.

[11] An overview of Athenian history can be found in Pomeroy, Burstein, Donlan, and Roberts 2007. For a more detailed account, see the relevant volumes in the *Cambridge Ancient History* series.

[12] An introduction to democracy in Athens can be found in Thorley 2004.

were citizens. (Women had some rights but never had a role in the Athenian political system.) Kleisthenes gave the sovereign power in the Athenian state to an assembly that met forty times a year and in which all citizens over the age of twenty had the right to vote.[13] On a day-to-day basis Athens was run by a new governing body called the Council of 500, which consisted of fifty men selected from each tribe. The Kleisthenic system represents the earliest known example of democratic governance.

The system of government established by Kleisthenes underwent a series of modifications in the next fifty years that made it into one of the most radically democratic states the world has ever seen. Citizens, who in c. 500 numbered about 25,000, were expected to participate actively in the governing of the Athenian state. All citizens were empowered to vote on all legislation, and many governmental positions were filled by lottery rather than by election, based on the principle that most if not all citizens should be ready, willing, and able to serve the state. For example, local governmental bodies within the Athenian state each year compiled lists of residents who were suitable potential members of the Council of 500, and fifty men from each tribe were then selected at random from those lists and served on the Council of 500 for a year. The Council of 500 had an executive officer, the very rough equivalent of the president in the United States, who was chosen by lottery and was changed every day.

Even in Athens, however, democratization occurred within circumscribed boundaries. *Ptôchoi*, who were disenfranchised in most *poleis*, were unusually influential in Athens, in no small part because in the early fifth century Athens built the largest navy in the Greek world, and *ptôchoi* manned the fleet. They thus became an irreplaceable part of the Athenian military and could make a good claim to social and political privileges on that basis. However, the property classes set up by Solon continued to operate, and many positions in the Athenian government were open only to wealthier citizens. In addition, established families that were wealthy and powerful before 508 continued for well over a century to occupy influential positions in the Athenian government out of all proportion to their actual numbers, and these families provided most of Athens' leading generals and statesmen. Women remained socially marginalized, and a considerable proportion of the population consisted of slaves who were denied even the most basic rights.[14]

Sparta and Athens were only two among literally hundreds of Greek *poleis*. The conflict between *plousioi* and *penêtes* played itself out in various ways in the hundreds of *poleis* in the Greek world, but the general trend was

---

[13] Athens was thus a direct rather than a representative democracy.

[14] On the influence of naval developments on the political history of Athens, see Raaflaub 2007. On the continuing influence of rich families, see J. K. Davies 1984 and Connor 1992 (1971). On groups that experienced social and political exclusion in democratic Athens, see Patterson 2007.

quite clear. During the sixth and fifth centuries more democratized sociopolitical systems in which both *plousioi* and *penêtes* shared equally became widespread.

Although the *penêtes* in most Greek communities had won their struggle with the *plousioi*, the social rules that shaped the behavior of the newly expanded dominant groups were something of a compromise. The *plousioi* had sought to impose a system in which *timê* remained a critical goal but in which it could be achieved primarily on the basis of wealth and birth, whereas the *penêtes* had articulated a more cooperative, less competitive alternative that stressed making sacrifices for the good of the community. The compromise adopted was an obvious choice – competition for *timê* continued to be essential and continued to be conducted in much the same way as before. That meant that high-status individuals needed to earn *timê* by taking risks defending the community on the battlefield and by being generous in supporting its members.

The continuing importance of the social contract that had taken shape in the Early Iron Age is apparent in the work of Tyrtaeus, who lived during the seventh century and who became one of Sparta's most famous poets. He wrote that:

The man who falls among the front ranks and loses his dear life bringing good reputation to city and people and fatherland, with many wounds having been driven through the front of his chest and through his breastplate and his bossed shield, he is mourned by young and old alike, and the entire city is troubled by a grievous pain. His tomb and his children and his descendants stand out among men, and his noble fame and name never perish…because he was proving his *aretê* and standing his ground and fighting for the sake of his fatherland and children when strong Ares destroyed him. But if he should escape the outstretched hand of death and, conquering with the point of his spear, should achieve his splendid object of prayer, all, both young and old alike, show him *time*, and he comes to Hades having experienced many delightful things, and as he grows old he remains conspicuous among his fellow citizens…and everyone in his homeland, young and old alike, cede their seats to him. (Fragment 12 West, ll. 23–42)

9.2. SPORT IN ATHENS

As was the case with regard to social history, the sources at our disposal for sport history are such that we are well informed about only two *poleis* – Athens and Sparta. We will begin with Athens, which was a more typical Greek *polis* when it came to sport, and will examine Athenian athletics by looking at how a boy from an affluent family would have been introduced to sport and how he might have pursued it as he got older.[15] In a few instances, where the material from Athens is spotty, we will make use of evidence from

[15] On athletics in Athens, see Kyle 1987.

other Greek *poleis*. Greek sport underwent a profound transformation over the course of the Archaic period, and it is important to bear in mind that the description provided here applies to Greek sport as it existed after the middle of the sixth century.

Formal schooling began in Greece (after the Bronze Age) at some point in the sixth century. During the Early Iron Age and for most or all of the seventh century, there was little in the way of formal education in Greece. Over the course of the sixth century a system of education came into being that took roughly the same form in most Greek communities.[16] Publicly funded schools were few and far between, and families that could afford to do so paid out of their own pockets to send their children, especially their sons, to private tutors. Between the ages of approximately seven and fourteen boys typically studied with three different teachers: one for basic reading, writing, and mathematical skills; one for music; and one for athletics.

Boys learned athletics from *paidotribai* (singular *paidotribês*), tutors who typically worked in *palaistrai* (singular *palaistra*), square structures with an inner courtyard.[17] *Paidotribai* trained their young charges in all the sports popular among Greeks during the Archaic and Classical periods. These sports included three different footraces, over the rough equivalents of 200 meters (*stadion*), 400 meters (*diaulos*), and 8 kilometers (*dolichos*). There was also a race in which the competitors ran about 400 meters wearing a helmet and carrying a shield but were otherwise nude (*hoplitês* or *hoplitodromos*). Pentathletes completed five separate events as part of a single contest: jumping, throwing the discus, throwing the javelin, wrestling, and a short sprint (the *stadion*). In addition to wrestling and boxing, there was a third combat sport, *pankration*, a combination of boxing and wrestling.[18]

Paidotribai taught not only technical skills, but also rules. During the Early Iron Age sports were played in accordance with informal customs, but by the second half of the sixth century formal, written rules had been created. For example, at Olympia sometime around 525 an inscription was put up in which the rules for the wrestling competition were laid out in great detail (*SEG* 48.541). The small fragments of the inscription that survive make it clear that it was against the rules for wrestlers to break each other's fingers and that infractions were punished by judges who struck offenders with a stick. *Paidotribai*, who are regularly depicted in art carrying a forked stick, made regular use of corporal punishment in training the boys under their tutelage.[19]

---

[16] On ancient Greek education, see Ducat 2006 and Joyal, McDougall, and Yardley 2009.
[17] For an overview of the history of Greek *palaistrai*, see Glass 1988. For a full-length treatment, see Delorme 1960.
[18] For details of how each of these events was practiced, see Miller 2004a.
[19] For a translation of the inscription from Olympia, see Miller 2004b, 73. On *paidotribai*, see König 2005, 305–15.

Children, both boys and girls, from well-to-do families were also introduced from an early age to another form of structured physical activity, choral dance. As we have seen (Section 8.2), Greeks during the Early Iron Age regularly participated in choruses in which groups of varying size and composition sang and danced together. Children learned choral dance primarily by participating in choruses organized for religious festivals and other special occasions. For the more important festivals, *polis* magistrates would assemble anywhere from a single to fifty or more choruses that performed in honor of a deity, and choruses also performed at private occasions such as weddings. A large percentage of choral performances were competitive, with judges at hand and prizes on offer. The members of a chorus preparing for competition rehearsed together for anywhere from a few days to six months or more, during which time they were supervised by at least one adult, and one chorus member was usually selected as a lead dancer. Choruses preparing for high-level competition typically had a trainer, a *didaskalos,* who in many cases was also responsible for producing original music and choreography. Much of this can be seen in a small vase painted around 580 in the *polis* of Corinth (Figures 9a and 9b). The vase shows a flute player and a chorus, consisting of a leaping lead dancer in front with three pairs of dancers behind him; all the dancers are shown without beards, which indicates that they are youths. The inscription on the vase says that it is a dedication to Pyrrhias, the lead dancer, and commemorates a victory in a choral dance contest.[20]

Children from well-to-do families, who regularly participated in choruses, were over the course of time thoroughly trained in singing and dancing as part of a group, and they expected to make good use of that training as both adolescents and adults. Athens certainly provided a suitable number of opportunities. By the end of the sixth century, a single Athenian religious festival, the Great Dionysia, included competitions in choral dance in which more than 1,000 males of all ages participated.[21] Competitions in choral dance were also held at other Athenian festivals such as the Panathenaia (discussed shortly).

Once boys were finished with their tutors at around age fourteen, they could continue to play sports without formal instruction, and many chose to do so. At least some of the time they continued to go to a *palaistra* owned by a *paidotribês*; in other cases they used publicly owned athletic training centers in the form of *gymnasia* (singular *gymnasium*). (The *gymnasium* was literally "the nude place," a space set aside for males to exercise in the nude. See section 10.4 for discussion of the social ramifications of athletic

[20] On this vase, see Roebuck and Roebuck 1955.
[21] On choral dance in ancient Greece, see Griffith 2001 and Lonsdale 1993. On choral dance in Athens, see Wilson 2000. On choral dancing by females in ancient Greece, see Calame 1997 (1977).

FIGURE 9a. Flute Player and Chorus from Vase Painted in Corinth c. 580 BCE (From Mary and Carl Roebuck. 1955. "A Prize Aryballos." *Hesperia* 24: 158–63, plate 63)

nudity.) The earliest known *gymnasia* are those at Athens; before the end of the sixth century, Athens had three *gymnasia*, the Academy, the Lyceum, and the Kynosarges.[22] The number of *gymnasia* in the Greek world multiplied quickly, and it rapidly became the case that every self-respecting Greek community had at least one. Pausanias, a travel-guide writer from the second century CE, comments that the small Greek town of Panopeus could hardly be described as a *polis* because it had "no government offices, no *gymnasium*, no theater, no market-place, no water conducted to a fountain..." (10.4.1, trans. J. Frazer).

Athenian boys and men who were talented and motivated athletes had a large and continually growing number of opportunities to participate in formally organized sports competitions. In the Early Iron Age, athletic competitions were held only intermittently, most typically at the funerals of prominent men; the only notable exception was the Olympics. During the sixth century communities all over the Greek world founded local athletic competitions that were held on a regular basis. These are sometimes called civic games by modern scholars to differentiate them from the contests held at major religious sanctuaries such as Olympia.

The best known of the civic games is the Panathenaia Games at Athens. These games were established in 566 when contests of various kinds were added to a preexisting religious festival that honored the city's patron deity, Athena. The Panathenaia was held every year and was celebrated with

[22] On the *gymnasia* in Athens, see Kyle 1987, 64–101.

FIGURE 9b. Drawing of the Entire Scene Painted on the Vase Pictured in Figure 9a (From Mary and Carl Roebuck. 1955. "A Prize Aryballos." *Hesperia* 24: 158–63, plate 64)

particular splendor every fourth year; the Athenians called the annual festival the Lesser Panathenaia and the special version held every fourth year the Greater Panathenaia. The Greater Panathenaia lasted for nine days and included competitions in musical performance, horse racing, athletics, and four special events: a male beauty contest, a boat race, a torch race (run by relay teams at night), and pyrrhic dancing. The last of these is of particular interest because it gives us some sense of what competitive choral dance could look like.

Each of the ten Athenian tribes entered three choruses, with each chorus consisting of male dancers from one of three different age groups (boys, youth, men), in the pyrrhic dance competition at the Panathenaia. The competitors wore helmets and shields but were otherwise nude and performed a dance that imitated warfare. Here is how Plato describes it:

> It consists of imitating, on the one hand, movements that evade all kinds of blows and missiles – by dodging, giving way completely, jumping up, humble crouching – and then again striving to imitate the opposites to these, aggressive postures involved in striking with missiles – arrows and javelins – and with all sorts of blows. (*Laws* 815a, trans. T. Pangle)

A number of surviving sculptured reliefs, typically put up by a winning chorus to celebrate its victory, show pyrrhic dancing (see Figure 10).[23]

The Panathenaia was only one of a substantial number of occasions on which athletic competitions were held in Athens. The *polis* of Athens organized other religious festivals such as the Eleusinia that included athletic

---

[23] The program of the Greater Panathenaia changed over the course of time, and its precise form in the sixth century is unknown. We are best informed about the Panathenaia as it existed in the fourth century. The discussion here draws on sources from different periods to provide a composite picture that gives a general sense of what the Panathenaia was like. For a thorough treatment of all the relevant evidence, see Neils 1992. On pyrrhic dance, see Ceccarelli 1998 and Delavaud-Roux 1993.

FIGURE 10. Chorus of Pyrrhic Dancers Shown on Marble Relief from Athens (Acropolis Museum #1338), 330–320 BCE (From Deutsches Archäologisches Institut-Athens, neg. no. 1972/3004, photo Gösta Hellner)

competitions. Outside of the city of Athens (but still within the territory of the Athenian state) there were dozens of villages of varying size, all of which held their own religious festivals for their residents, and at least some of these local festivals included athletic contests. Finally, later sources make it clear that *paidotribai* and the officials who ran *gymnasia* frequently organized competitions, some of which were held on a monthly basis, and the same is likely to have been true in Athens in the sixth and fifth centuries.[24] Most of the contests at the Panathenaia were open to people from all over the Greek world and offered substantial prizes, so the competition must have been fairly stiff. The array of other, less high profile competitions offered Athenian athletes who were not superstars a chance to compete. Modern parallels would include the thousands of running races held every year in towns throughout the United States, and annual tournaments organized by local tennis clubs.

The very best Athenian athletes went on to compete at the highest possible level, at the Panhellenic contests held at Olympia, Delphi, Isthmia, and Nemea. By the late seventh century the Olympics had become Panhellenic, which is to say that they attracted competitors from much of the Greek world. In the first quarter of the sixth century new Panhellenic athletic competitions were established at three other sanctuaries: the Pythian Games were founded in 586 at the sanctuary of Apollo at Delphi, the Isthmian Games were founded in 580 at the sanctuary of Poseidon at Isthmia, and the Nemean Games were founded in 573 at the sanctuary of Zeus at Nemea (see Map 1). The Greeks called these four games the *periodos* or circuit; the supreme athletic feat for an ancient Greek athlete was to win his event in all four *periodos* games.

---

[24] On Athenian festivals that included athletic or dance competitions, see Osborne 1993 and Fisher 2011. For an example of athletic contests held on a monthly basis at a *gymnasium*, see the extant regulations for the *gymnasium* at Beroia in Macedonia (published and discussed in Gauthier and Hatzopoulos 1993, English translation available at http://www.umich.edu/~classics/programs/class/cc/372/B015.html).

Panhellenic athletic competitions attracted large and growing crowds of spectators, and in the sixth century Greeks began to build special facilities for them. Before the sixth century, Greeks held athletic competitions in simple, open areas that in at least some cases had been specially leveled. The earliest extant Greek stadia have been excavated at Olympia and Isthmia and date to around 550; they have stone starting lines and provision for spectators in the form of earthen embankments (stone seating was always the exception rather than the rule in Greek stadia). The capacity of the earliest stadium at Olympia is unknown, but by the end of the sixth century it had room for about 25,000 spectators and by the middle of the fifth century it could hold more than 40,000.[25]

Successful Athenian athletes were richly rewarded with both wealth and *timê*. The prizes on offer at the Panathenaia had substantial cash value; the winner of the short footrace for boys, for instance, took home the equivalent of about $10,000. Sometime in the first half of the sixth century, the Athenian statesman Solon evidently instituted large cash payments to athletes who won at the Olympic and Isthmian Games. The amount given to an Olympic victor was about the same as the annual income of the wealthiest men in Athens. A surviving decree of the Athenian state (*IG* I³ 131) shows that by 430 Athenian athletes who won at any of the *periodos* games were given a free meal every day for life in the town hall and the right to a front row seat at all public events. The decree seems to be a restatement of existing privileges, which may have already been extant in the sixth century. Truly exceptional athletes might have a statue erected in their honor at state expense in Athens or at one of the Panhellenic sites such as Olympia.[26]

9.3. SPORT IN SPARTA

The situation in Sparta was sufficiently different and is sufficiently informative to merit separate consideration. The single most important source for sport in Sparta before the Roman period is the writing of Xenophon (c. 430–354), whose works include a short treatise, the *Constitution of the Spartans*, that provides a reasonably good sense of Spartan sport and its connection to the Spartan sociopolitical system in the fourth century. This treatise can also underpin a discussion of Sparta in the sixth century because a new sociopolitical system came into being in Sparta between roughly 650 and 550 and remained fairly stable down through the fourth century. We can, therefore, make cautious use of Xenophon's work to discuss sport and society in sixth- and fifth-century Sparta, while keeping in mind that many details no doubt changed over the course of time.[27]

[25] On Greek stadia, see Romano 1993.
[26] On the rewards offered to Athenian athletes, see D. Young 1984, 115–27.
[27] For an introduction to, English translation of, and commentary on Xenophon's *Constitution of the Spartans*, see Lipka 2002.

Spartan boys entered training to be citizens and soldiers at age seven and in some sense continued in it for the rest of their lives.[28] Whereas in Athens how much and what kind of education a boy received was entirely up to his family, in Sparta the sons of citizens could not themselves become citizens unless they successfully completed a course of instruction defined and supervised by the state. They were divided into three broad age groups, *paides* (from about 7 to 14 years of age), *paidiskoi* (ages 14 to 20), and *hêbôntes* (ages 20–30). A boy who had become one of the *hêbôntes* was in many ways an adult: he was officially one of the *homoioi* (equals), the group of Spartan male citizens, who were also called Spartiates to differentiate them from all the other residents of Sparta (such as women and slaves); he was enrolled in the Spartan army and could vote; and he was elected into a *syssition*, a group of fifteen to twenty men, which functioned as both a dining club (the members ate dinner together every night in their clubhouse) and a military unit. On the other hand, *hêbôntes* were subject to numerous restrictions and rarely married. Most Spartan men married shortly after turning thirty, but even then their *syssition* continued to be something of a surrogate family.

Sport and choral dance were key parts of the lifestyle of Spartiates from an early age. Families hired *paidotribai* who worked with *paides*, and during their time as *paidiskoi* and *hêbôntes* Spartan boys continued to train for and compete regularly in athletics and choral dance. Rigorous training in sport was part of a concerted effort to get Spartan *paides* used to enduring hardships; other measures intended to achieve the same end included restricting their diet so that they frequently went hungry and making them go barefoot at least some of the time.

Spartiates of all ages were expected and in some instances required to participate actively in sport. Xenophon makes it clear that Spartan men spent much of their time in the *gymnasium*. He writes that:

Once Lycurgus [a legendary lawgiver believed to have single-handedly designed the Spartan sociopolitical system] realized that those who keep in training develop good skin, firm flesh, and good health from their food, whereas the lazy look bloated, ugly, and weak, he did not overlook this matter either. But although he saw that anyone who trained hard of his own free will appeared to give his body sufficient exercise, he ordered that in the *gymnasium* the oldest man present should take care of everything, so that they never exercised less than the food they consumed required. (*Constitution of the Spartans* 5.8–9, trans. M. Lipka, slightly modified)

When discussing the regulations of the Spartan army, he points out that all Spartiates "are ordered by law to take exercise while they are on campaign" and that they do so in the morning and evening prior to eating (*Constitution*

---

[28] For detailed explorations of the Spartan educational system, see Cartledge 2001, 79–90; Ducat 2006; and Kennell 1995. For a review of what is known about the *realia* of Spartan sport, see Christesen 2012b. For a discussion of the sociopolitical dimensions of Spartan sport, see Christesen 2012a.

of the Spartans 12.5–7). Inscriptions erected by victors show that there was an array of local athletic contests held in and around Sparta in which Spartiates regularly competed. The most talented Spartan athletes went on to compete at Olympia.

The playwright Pratinas, writing about 500, characterized the Spartans as "eager for a chorus" (Fragment 4 Snell), one of the many indications of the seriousness with which choral dance was treated in Sparta. Choral dance was the centerpiece of one of the Spartans' most important religious festivals, the Gymnopaidiai. This festival was held annually and featured a multiday competition of choruses of males of different ages who danced in the nude while singing songs composed by famous Spartan poets.[29]

Females in Sparta were similar to their counterparts in other Greek communities in that they participated regularly in choruses and were dissimilar in that they also regularly took part in sport, an activity from which girls in most Greek communities were effectively debarred. Spartan girls, before they married but not after, regularly played sports and at least occasionally competed against each other (but not against boys). The range of events in which they took part is unclear, but they seem to have done mostly running and wrestling. Barring a few special ritual occasions, they, unlike the boys, did not go nude when playing sports but instead wore a short, revealing tunic. It was with some reason that Ibycus, a poet active in the mid-sixth century, called Spartan girls "thigh-flashers" (Fragment 339 Davies).

9.4. THE EMERGENCE OF MASS SPORT

In the sixth century Greece became the earliest known society to have mass sport. This conclusion is based not on detailed survey data, which does not exist for ancient Greece, but on a collection of qualitative evidence that is cumulatively persuasive.

It is clear that Greek sport underwent a fundamental transformation in the sixth century. During the seventh century, the Olympics was the only regularly scheduled athletic contest in Greece, and was just beginning to develop a Panhellenic profile.[30] Occasional, informal, local competitions were common but were largely restricted to elites.[31] Architectural spaces specifically dedicated to sport in the form of facilities for practice and competition could be found in neither sanctuaries nor cities. Athletic motifs

[29] On the Gymnopaidiai, see Ducat 2006, 265–74; Pettersson 1992, 42–56; and Richer 2005.

[30] On the geographic extent of participation in the early Olympic Games, see Morgan 1990, 57–105. The *Homeric Hymn to Apollo* (ll. 146–50) mentions boxing matches at the festival of Apollo on Delos, but the date of this hymn remains uncertain. The section that mentions boxing is typically dated to the early sixth century. See Kirk 1980–85.

[31] Irregularly scheduled funeral games were the predominant form of organized athletic contest before the sixth century. See Roller 1981.

appeared in art but with nowhere near the frequency that would later become the norm.[32]

All of this changed radically over the course of the sixth century.[33] New Panhellenic athletic contests were founded at Delphi (586), Isthmia (580), and Nemea (573). Communities began to found regularly scheduled athletic contests such as the Panathenaia in Athens (566), and the number of such games multiplied rapidly. The earliest stadia, the first Greek architectural form specifically intended for competitive athletics, were built starting around 550. The earliest *gymnasia*, places set aside for everyday athletic training, were founded at roughly the same time. Even venerable Olympia was not immune to change; sometime in the early sixth century it received its first permanent stone architecture in the form of a temple dedicated to Zeus and Hera. This edifice was the start of a major building program that in the succeeding decades brought the construction of numerous treasuries (small buildings for the storage and display of valuable dedications) and the first formal stadium.[34] Individuals began to pour resources into highlighting their participation in sport and their athletic successes. Athletic scenes became common on Greek pottery; the absolute number of surviving Athenian Black Figure vases with athletic scenes from the first half of the sixth century is dramatically higher than in the preceding half century, as is the percentage of surviving Athenian Black Figure vases with athletic scenes.[35] At the same time athletic victors began to pay sculptors to carve statues of themselves and to hire poets to write *epinikia*, odes that were specially commissioned to celebrate athletic triumphs.[36]

Since sport had been a basic part of the Greek social landscape long before the beginning of the sixth century, these changes are very difficult to explain unless they are understood as the result of an expansion of sport participation to a broader segment of the Greek populace than had been the case in the past. A broadening participation in sport is most immediately obvious in Sparta, where a program of sociopolitical reform produced a system in which all male citizens, both boys and men, were not just encouraged but required to participate in sport on a regular basis. However, Sparta was decidedly unusual because its conquest of Messenia enriched many of its *penêtes* so that they could behave like *plousioi*, and for that reason the situation in Athens is more instructive. The extent to which nonelites took part in sport and choral dance in sixth- and fifth-century Athens has been the

---

[32] The key evidence comes from pottery. See Legakis 1977, 370–88.

[33] On the changes in Greek athletics in the sixth century, see Christesen 2007b.

[34] On the architectural history of Olympia in the sixth century, see Drees 1968, 111–29; Mallwitz 1988; Moustaka 2002; and Schilbach 1992.

[35] On trends in the depiction of athletes in Greek vase painting, see Goossens and Thielemans 1996; Hollein 1988, 71–103; Legakis 1977.

[36] On athletic victor statues, see Kurke 1993, 141–49 and Lattimore 1988. See Golden 1998, 74–88 for a brief history of *epinikia*.

subject of considerable debate, so it is worth reviewing the relevant evidence in some detail.[37]

Abundant provision for both sport and choral dance was made in Athens, particularly after the democratization effected by the reforms of Kleisthenes in 508. At the end of the sixth century Athens had three separate public *gymnasia* in addition to an unknown number of privately owned *palaistrai*, at a time when there were probably about 1,000 adult male *plousioi* in the entire polity.[38] Both the state government of Athens and the local governments of its numerous constituent communities arranged an array of festivals that provided opportunities to participate in athletic and choral dance competitions. We have already seen that each year more than 1,000 male dancers took part in a single Athenian festival, the Great Dionysia. Most other Athenian festivals were significantly smaller but cumulatively formed an elaborate web of competitions that presumed and required widespread participation. Eric Csapo and Margaret Miller have recently argued that "the total annual requirement for choreuts [choral dancers] at Attic festivals was sufficiently high to suggest the participation of most citizen males in a choral...performance at some time in their lives."[39] It is particularly noteworthy that a number of athletic and dance contests were founded in Athens soon after it became a democracy. In an analysis of Athenian festivals that included competitions, Robin Osborne has observed that there was "perhaps a particularly high frequency of competitive innovations in the fifty years after 510," and Nick Fisher has shown that "In the years immediately following the establishment of the new tribes [as part of the Kleisthenic reforms] there was undoubtedly a massive expansion in numbers of singers, dancers, and athletes competing."[40] This high level of participation in sport and dance competitions speaks to an equally high level of participation in sport and dance in a noncompetitive fashion. More importantly, the fact that there was a major expansion in government-sponsored sport and choral dance competitions in the years immediately after Athens became institutionally democratic strongly suggests that participation in sport and choral dance was not limited to a small group of elites.

The textual sources from Athens also attest to regular participation in sport and choral dance on the part of boys and men from families that were not counted among the *plousioi*. The costs of mounting athletic and

---

[37] The idea that sport remained the preserve of a small elite has been repeatedly argued by David Pritchard. See, for instance, Pritchard 2003, Pritchard 2004, Pritchard 2009. The view adopted here, that participation in sport and choral dance was relatively widespread in Athens in the fifth century, has been well articulated before, most notably by Nick Fisher. See Fisher 1998, Fisher 2009, Fisher 2011.

[38] The population of ancient Athens at any given point in time can only be estimated within broad limits. See Hansen 2006 and Morris 2002.

[39] Csapo and Miller 2007, 5.

[40] Osborne 1993, 27; Fisher 2011, 187.

dance competitions at festivals were defrayed by having wealthy individuals, sometimes voluntarily and sometimes not, pay for part or all of them. This produced complaints, as is evident in a treatise called the *Constitution of the Athenians* written by an unknown author, typically called the Old Oligarch, around 430. The writer protests that:

> The people have spoiled the athletic and musical activities at Athens because they thought them unfitting (they know they can't do them). In the training of dramatic choruses and in providing for athletic contests…they know that it is the wealthy who lead the choruses, but the people who are led in them, and it is the wealthy who provide for athletic contests, but the people who are presided over…in the games. At least the people think themselves worthy of taking money for singing, running, dancing….(1.13, trans. C. Marchant)

The Old Oligarch's acerbic comments have an obvious satiric element, but they would have been incomprehensible to his contemporaries if participation in sport and choral dance were limited to *plousioi*.

Another helpful passage can be found in the writings of Xenophon, who recounts the violent *stasis* in Athens that resulted in the collapse of a short-lived oligarchic government imposed by the Spartans after the Athenians' defeat in the Peloponnesian War. Xenophon describes the herald Kleokritos attempting to reconcile two groups of Athenians about to come to blows:

> And Kleokritos, the herald…obtained silence and said: "Fellow citizens, why do you drive us out of the city? Why do you wish to kill us? For we never did you any harm, but we have shared with you in the most solemn rites and sacrifices and the most splendid festivals, we have been companions in the dance and schoolmates and comrades in arms, and we have braved many dangers with you both by land and by sea in defense of the common safety and freedom of us both." (*Hellenica* 2.4.20, trans. C. Brownson)

The fighting in Athens involved much of the free adult male population, and this appeal makes sense only if participation in dance, and presumably sport as well, was relatively widespread.

In a different work Xenophon crafts a fictional dialogue in which Socrates addresses Pericles' concerns about strife tearing Athens apart. Socrates takes an optimistic stance and says:

> No, no Pericles, don't think the wickedness of the Athenians so utterly past remedy. Don't you see what good discipline they maintain in their fleets, how well they obey the umpires in athletic contests, how they take orders from their chorus trainers as readily as any? (*Memorabilia* 3.5.18, trans. E. Marchant, slightly modified)

Here again the passage is built upon an unspoken assumption of widespread participation in sport and dance; good behavior in those activities on the part of a small minority of wealthy elites would hardly have been cause for optimism about the future of the Athenian democratic state.

If, as seems virtually certain, the sixth century saw sport participation expand to a broader segment of the populace than had been the case in the past, the identity of the new athletes becomes a question of considerable interest.[41] Broad swathes of the inhabitants of the Greek world can be immediately eliminated as potential candidates. There is no doubt that, leaving aside initiation rites and the special case of Sparta, Greek females were habitually excluded from sport.[42] Slaves of both genders represent another substantial group that was debarred from sport participation, not just by social but also by legal barriers; a number of *poleis* passed laws that overtly restricted access to *palaistrai* and *gymnasia* to free citizens. The Athenian orator Aeschines, for example, mentions such a law in a speech and explains its intended effects:

The law states that "a slave will not take exercise or rub himself with oil in the *palaistrai*." There is no addition stating that "the free man will anoint himself with oil and take exercise." For the lawgivers, observing the good that comes from physical training, forbade slaves to take part, and in so doing they thought that they were issuing an invitation to do so to the free. (1.138)

The Athenians believed that this law was written by Solon in the first half of the sixth century (Plutarch *Solon* 23.3), which is possible but not certain.[43]

Once women and slaves are removed from the equation, there are only two possible groups of any size left: free males from families of *penêtes* and of *ptôchoi*. The dividing line between these two groups was never sharp, and there must have been considerable variation spatially and temporally in regard to who participated in sport. For example, *ptôchoi* enjoyed significantly higher standing in Athens than in most other Greek communities, and that may well have been reflected to some degree in sport. That said, the evidence suggests that the sixth-century transformation of Greek sport was the result of sharply increased participation by *penêtes* and that *ptôchoi* did not take part in sport in large numbers with any regularity.

The changes in Greek sport that took place in the sixth century need to be read against the background of contemporary social and political changes. A prominent role in the defense of the community, social and political privileges, and playing sports had been closely linked together since the Early Iron Age. As *penêtes* became part of hoplite phalanxes and gained social

---

[41] There has been a great deal of inconclusive debate about the socioeconomic status of the families that produced elite athletes in ancient Greece; see, for instance, D. Young 1984, 107–70. The relevant evidence is insufficient to reach any firm conclusions, and the significance of those conclusions would in any case be quite limited. Even if most elite athletes came from very wealthy families, that would say little about the socioeconomic background of the vastly more numerous group of less accomplished athletes.

[42] On female participation in sport in the Greek world, see Kyle 2012.

[43] On the attribution of this law to Solon, see Kyle 1987, 21–22. Cf. Aristotle *Politics* 1264a17–23. On slaves and sport in the Greek world, see C. Mann 2012.

and political privileges, they increasingly enjoyed social standing and social power that made them similar to if not the precise equals of *plousioi*, and it would have been remarkable if the *penêtes* had, as part of that process, not eagerly taken up the practice of athletics, long the preserve of elites.[44] *Ptôchoi*, on the other hand, remained for the most part militarily and politically marginalized, and thus were in a very different position from *penêtes* when it came to sport participation.

Changes in military practice, sociopolitical arrangements, and sport thus all proceeded together. This is nicely illustrated in the case of Athens by the fact that in the fifth century (and quite possibly earlier) Athenian cavalrymen, hoplites, and archers (but not sailors in the navy) were required to make a yearly contribution toward the maintenance of the shrine of Apollo Lykeios at the Lyceum *gymnasium*.[45] The number of cavalrymen and archers in the Athenian army was relatively small, so most of the men making contributions were hoplites. The Lyceum was regularly used for military training exercises, and Apollo Lykeios was a patron deity for the Athenian army. The presence of both hoplites and athletes at a *gymnasium* was not coincidental. Three different groups of men – those who enjoyed social and political privileges, those who served in the hoplite phalanx, and those who regularly participated in sport – were largely identical in regard to their members. All three groups consisted largely of *plousioi* and *penêtes*.

Practical considerations relating to opportunity and means must also have played important roles in creating a de facto exclusion of *ptôchoi* from sport. Regular participation in sport required a considerable amount of free time, which boys and men from families of *plousioi* and *penêtes* had at their disposal for at least some parts of the year, but which was in much shorter supply among the *ptôchoi*.

Regular participation in sport was also founded on competence developed through formal training provided by *paidotribai*, whose fees were within the financial reach of *penêtes* but would have stretched the resources of most *ptôchoi*. *Paidotribai* seem to have charged roughly ten to fifteen *drachmai* per year per student. Some sense of the relative cost of hiring a *paidotribês* can be had from the facts that bare subsistence food for a family of four cost about half a *drachma* a day and that full equipment for a hoplite soldier cost 75–100 *drachmai*. Most *penêtes*, who by definition came from the upper half of the socioeconomic pyramid, would have had no great difficulty in paying for their sons' athletic training and, given the social importance of sport, would have seen such training as something approximating a necessity.[46] In one of his speeches in Plato's *Crito* (50d), Socrates suggests that

44 On the importance of status competition among non-elites in Athens, see Fisher 2001, 27, 34–36, 58–61 and Fisher 2008, 188–94.

45 This is known from an inscription, *IG* I³ 138, which is discussed in detail in Jameson 1980.

46 On the cost of hiring a *paidotribês*, see Athenaeus *Deiphnosophistae* 584c and Marrou 1956 (1948), 146. On the cost of living in ancient Athens, see Markle 1985. On the costs of hoplite equipment, see van Wees 2004, 47–60.

Athenian fathers saw giving their sons a proper training in sport and music as a powerful moral obligation. The same sums would have represented a much larger problem for *ptôchoi*. The relationship between wealth and athletic training is evident in Plato's *Protagoras*, in which the eponymous character discusses the practice of families sending their sons to tutors to learn reading and writing, music, and sport and observes that, "This is what people do who are most able; and the most able are the wealthiest. Their sons begin to go to tutors at the earliest age and stop going to them at the latest age" (326c, trans. W. Lamb, slightly modified).

One might also add that *penêtes* had a special incentive to participate regularly in sport in that they were expected to serve as hoplites, and that put a premium on maintaining a relatively high degree of physical fitness. Formal military training in Greek *poleis* other than Sparta was minimal at best, and hoplites used sport to help keep themselves fit. Because hoplites went into battle carrying roughly seventy pounds of weapons and armor, being in reasonably good physical condition was essential. (It is important to keep in mind that the average adult male in ancient Greece was perhaps 5'8" tall and weighed 150 pounds and that the hoplite shield alone weighed 18 pounds.) Plato's Protagoras points out that "people send their sons to a *paidotribês*...in order that they not be forced by bodily faults to play the coward in wars and other duties" (326b-c).[47]

It should come as no surprise, then, that Greek hoplites tended to show both familiarity with and interest in sport. For example, when a force of roughly 10,000 Greek hoplites serving as mercenaries was compelled to make a fighting withdrawal from the center of the Persian Empire in 401, an undertaking that consumed several months, they entertained themselves on numerous occasions by competing against each other in athletic contests (Xenophon *Anabasis* 1.2.10, 4.8.25, 5.5.6). Most of these men came from families with sufficient resources to pay for hoplite armor, but they were by no means elites in the sense that they came from the very wealthiest families in their respective communities; the sons of those families had little incentive to hire on as mercenaries in foreign campaigns. Most came from among the *penêtes* and had been exposed to sport from an early age.

It seems safe, therefore, to conclude that the sixth century saw the extension of the habit of regularly participating in sport to most if not all boys and men from families of *penêtes*. That in turn makes it possible to supply some rough numbers for levels of sport participation in the Greek world in the sixth and fifth centuries. *Plousioi* made up roughly 4–5% of the total number of households in any given Greek community, *penêtes* somewhere between 30–50%. The entry of *penêtes* into sport thus increased the number of regular sport participants from somewhere between six to ten times. In

---

[47] The relationship between athletics and warfare in ancient Greece has been the subject of extended controversy among modern-day scholars (see, for example, Poliakoff 1987, 94–103; Reed 1998; Spivey 2004, 1–29).

the specific case of Athens, there were probably something like 25,000 adult male citizens in 500 (out of a total population of around 175,000), which translates to roughly 1,000 *plousioi* and 10,000 *penêtes*. One can easily see how a shift from having 1,000 to 11,000 regular participants would fundamentally alter the practice of sport in Athens, and the same shift occurred all over the Greek world.

Did these shifts produce mass sport? In the modern world, roughly one-third of the total population in countries such as the United States and Norway actively participate in sport, whereas in ancient Greece somewhere between 5% and 10% did so. The numbers for Greece are, however, deceptively low. The social structure of ancient Greece was such that there were, relative to the modern world, fewer, larger households; slaves, for instance, which represented a substantial fraction of the population, almost invariably lived with their owners. The involvement of most *plousioi* and *penêtes* meant that boys and men from somewhere between a third and a half of a community's households participated regularly in sport. A substantial fraction of Greek households thus had at least some members at *palaistrai* or *gymnasia* with some regularity. Moreover, the 5–10% of the populace participating in sport represented most of those who enjoyed full social and political privileges. This greatly magnified the impact of sport, and its democratizing capacities. Furthermore, involvement in sport extended to much larger numbers in the form of spectatorship. There are no reliable figures pertaining to sport spectatorship in ancient Greece, though some sense of scale can be had from the fact that the stadium at Olympia seated about 40,000. People must have turned out in large numbers to watch sporting events.

Mass sport is defined here as a situation in which large numbers of people from a broad socioeconomic spectrum regularly engage in athletics as participants and spectators, and sport in Greece after the middle of the sixth century fits that definition. During the Archaic period, ancient Greece thus became the first known society to have mass sport.

9.5. HORIZONTALITY AND VERTICALITY IN GREEK SPORT

Greek sport as practiced in the Archaic and Classical periods was strongly horizontal. To return to the criteria articulated in Section 2.3, participants and organizers were typically one and the same or had similar social status and power. Participants were primarily males from families of either *plousioi* or *penêtes*, among whom there were not insignificant differences of wealth and status, but who enjoyed similar social and political privileges and were thus on the same social plane. Most sports activity was arranged on a voluntary basis by participants or their families. Many *poleis* provided publicly funded exercise facilities in the form of *gymnasia*, but the sport that took place in those places was arranged primarily by the participants themselves.

Starting in the fifth century, state-appointed officials called gymnasiarchs were common, but their primary role was to help defray the cost of the facilities' operation and to make sure something resembling good order was maintained.[48] Government intervention into how sport was played at *gymnasia* was, therefore, limited. *Palaistrai* were entirely private environments that operated under the supervision of the *paidotribai* who ran them. Formally organized competitions were run by political or religious officials, but they represented a small fraction of the total sports activity in any Greek community. As was the case in the Early Iron Age, organized sport was built around individual rather than team events and was only minimally regimented. The benefits of sport participation were understood as accruing to the individuals involved; we have, for instance, seen Plato's Protagoras claiming that training in sport helped boys acquit themselves honorably in war and other matters.

There was some limited verticality with respect to the enforcement of sport rules. *Paidotribai* made regular use of corporal punishment; indeed, the title itself means something like "boy grinder."[49] Furthermore, both boys and men participating in formal athletic competitions were flogged for rule violations. It was not unusual for boys to experience corporal punishment, but, starting in the Archaic period, free adult male citizens in most Greek communities were normally immune from such treatment. Flogging was in fact typically a punishment reserved for slaves.[50] Its use against boys being trained by *paidotribai* and against free men who broke rules in athletic competitions shows that elements of hierarchy were not entirely absent from Greek sport.

It is also necessary to bear in mind that Sparta represented an exception in that it was a place with a significantly more interventionist state. During their lengthy education, all of the activities of Spartan boys were closely supervised on a formal basis by state officials and on an informal basis by older citizens. A magistrate with the title of *paidonomos* had wide disciplinary powers over the boys, and punishments were carried out by his assistants, a group of young men carrying whips. If these officials were absent, any adult Spartiate who was at hand had authority over the boys and could discipline them if he wished (Xenophon *Constitution of the Spartans* 2.2). Presumably this oversight included the boys' sports activity, and in *gymnasia* the oldest man present acted in a supervisory capacity (*Constitution of the Spartans* 5.8–9). On the whole, then, sport in Sparta was more vertical than in most other Greek communities.

---

[48] On gymnasiarchs, see Golden 2004, 73–74. After the fourth century many *poleis* created formal systems of military training for the sons of particularly wealthy families, and gymnasiarchs sometimes were responsible for overseeing that training.

[49] The term *paidotribês* derives from the words *pais* (boy) and *tribô* (to wear down, grind, pound, trample). See the relevant entries in Liddell and Scott's *Greek-English Lexicon*.

[50] Crowther 2004, 141–60.

In both Sparta and elsewhere in the Greek world males encountered vertically oriented physical activity not so much in sport as in choral dance. We have already seen the strong connection between regimented forms of movement and hierarchical relationships in the context of military drill and mass calisthenics (Section 4.1), and choral dance was very much the same sort of activity. Choral dance in fact represented a prototypical Foucauldian disciplinary environment (Section 5.5).

The process of training for and then carrying out a choral performance involved all of Foucault's systematic arrangements for creating docile bodies. Space, time, and movement were all minutely controlled; the dancers were distributed in the tightly controlled physical space of the chorus, their activities were carefully organized, their mastery of music and choreography required seriated learning, and their efficient combination into a larger whole was the goal toward which they aimed. Choruses, especially those preparing for high-level competition, rehearsed under the strict supervision of a trainer and of the lead dancer, who exercised hierarchical observation and normalizing judgment. Choral dance was an intensely hierarchical experience that had clearly defined leadership positions and the expectation of prompt and unquestioned obedience to commands. The Athenian orator Demosthenes emphasizes the importance of the chorus leader (21.6), and Xenophon describes sailors struck into obedience by fear of a storm as waiting in silence for commands "just like choral dancers" (*Memorabilia* 3.5.6). The environments of both training and performance made examination and surveillance inevitable.

The coercive effects of choral dance were deepened because it was an intensely physical and highly regimented activity. Choral dancing was very much like drilling soldiers to march in formation in that it required immediate compliance with commands issued by authority figures and precise movement as part of a closely coordinated group. The similarity between choruses and marching soldiers was not lost on Xenophon. In a fictitious dialogue between a man and his wife, the *Oeconomicus*, Xenophon has the husband urge his wife to run the household in a highly organized fashion:

My dear, there is nothing so convenient or so good for human beings as order. Thus, a chorus is a combination of human beings; but when the members of it do as they choose, it becomes mere confusion, and there is no pleasure in watching it; but when they act and chant in an orderly fashion, then those same men at once seem worth seeing and worth hearing. Again, my dear, an army in disorder is a confused mass, an easy prey to enemies, a disgusting sight to friends, and utterly useless.... But an army in orderly array is a noble sight to friends, and an unwelcome spectacle to the enemy. What friend would not rejoice as he watches a strong body of troopers marching in order, would not admire cavalry riding in squadrons? And what enemy would not fear troopers, horsemen, light-armed, archers, slingers disposed in serried ranks and following their officers in orderly fashion? Nay, even on the march where order is kept, though they number tens of thousands, all move steadily forward as one man; for the line behind is continually filling up the gap. (8.3–7, trans. E. Marchant)

It is worth recalling that one form of choral dance, pyrrhic dance, was overtly martial in that it involved dancers imitating the use of weapons for attack and defense.

The physical activities of Greek males were thus a mixture of the horizontal and the vertical. Sport was strongly horizontal, choral dance strongly vertical.

Sport and Democratization in Sixth- and Fifth-Century BCE Greece

10.1. INTRODUCTION

The discussion in the preceding chapter showed that horizontal mass sport emerged for the first time in Greece during the sixth century, precisely the same period when a powerful wave of democratization swept through the Greek world and helped produce the earliest known systems of democratic governance.

Although the extant evidence is too exiguous to study the operation in ancient Greece of the eight previously identified mechanisms by means of which horizontal mass sport promotes and inhibits democratization, there is some evidence that the Greeks themselves recognized that sport could be connected to democratization.[1]

Consider, for example, the following comments, delivered by one of the characters in Plato's *Symposium*:

The Persian empire is absolute; that is why it condemns erotic attachments as well as philosophy and sport. It is no good for rulers if the people they rule cherish ambitions for themselves or form strong bonds of friendship with one another. That these are precisely the effects of philosophy, sport, and especially of erotic attachments is a lesson the tyrants of Athens learned directly from their own experience....(182b-c, trans. A. Nehamas and P. Woodruff, slightly modified)

Aristotle argues that the character of a state's citizens should be harmonized with the nature of its political system, one type of which is specified as being democratic, and that education, in which Aristotle includes sport, is an essential means to that end (*Politics* 1337a10–26). This presumes that sport can shape the character of citizens in such a way as to be suited for a democratic system of governance.

---

[1] For a discussion of the importance of generalized trust in ancient Greece, though without any explicit discussion of sport, see Johnstone 2011.

Of greater significance are Aristotle's comments on measures taken by *plousioi* intended to limit sport participation in the hope of gaining control over individual *poleis*. Although *penêtes* in most Greek communities won social and political privileges during the sixth and fifth centuries, *plousioi* were frequently dissatisfied with sharing power, and the struggle between these two groups for preeminence was repeatedly replayed throughout the Archaic and Classical periods. Aristotle, writing in the fourth century, argued that when the rich seek to push everyone else in their communities out of power, they strive to establish a predominance in five different spheres of activity:

The pretexts used...are five in number and concern the assembly, the magistracies, the courts, the bearing of arms, and sport.[2] (*Politics* 1297a14–17)

According to Aristotle, the rich set up a system in which they are given incentives to attend the assembly, hold magistracies, and participate actively in the legal system, whereas the less well-off receive no incentives to do any of these things. Aristotle then goes on to say:

The rich legislate in the same manner about both possessing arms and participating in sport [*gymnazein*]. For it is possible for the less well-off to not possess arms, but the rich not possessing arms are fined. And if the less well-off do not participate in sport [*gymnazein*], there is no fine, but there is a fine for the rich, so that the rich will, on account of the fine, take part in sport whereas the less well-off do not because they do not fear a fine. (*Politics* 1297a29–35)[3]

Aristotle's comments show that many *plousioi* believed that widespread participation in sport underpinned a more inclusive political system and that the gradual exclusion of the less wealthy from sport would contribute meaningfully to the ability of the *plousioi* to impose an oligarchic government. It is regrettable that Aristotle does not discuss the precise means by which exclusion from sport was believed to contribute to the establishment of an oligarchy. However, the fact that exclusion from participation from sport was put alongside exclusion from the assembly, magistracies, courts, and bearing arms indicates that sport participation was felt to have powerful political repercussions.[4]

---

[2] The Greek word *gymnasia* is here translated as "sport." During the Archaic period, when Greeks first began exercising in the nude on a regular basis (see Section 10.4), they coined a verb, *gymnazein*, to denote the act of regularly playing sports in the nude (*gymnos* in Greek). This verb referred only to sports activity that took place on a relatively informal basis in a *gymnasion* and was not used to describe the act of taking part in formally organized athletic competitions. The word *gymnasia* (not to be confused with the plural of *gymnasion*, denoting a place set aside for exercise) denotes performing the actions associated with the verb *gymnazein* and thus means something like "the act of regularly playing sports in the nude outside the context of formally organized competitions." On all of this terminology, see Christesen 2002.

[3] On these passages from the *Politics*, see Robinson 1995, 107–08.

[4] An opaque passage in Iamblichus' *Life of Pythagoras* (27.130) suggests that Pythagoras' disciples established in the city of Rhegion a *gymnasiarchê politeia*, a political system in which

Above and beyond the four transhistorically valid mechanisms by means of which sport promotes democratization, there were in addition in ancient Greece three further, contextually specific such mechanisms. All three were related to the fact that democratization resulted in the formation of new dominant groups in individual communities. These groups, made up of free adult males who enjoyed full social and political privileges, consisted of *plousioi* and *penêtes*. Democratization, both from a purely institutionalist perspective and in the broader sense, entailed the formation of effective horizontal relationships between *plousioi* and *penêtes* despite a long history of conflict and despite continuing heterogeneity springing, among other things, from enduring differences in wealth.

Within the bounds of that situation, sport fostered democratization by serving as an arena for meritocratic status competition between *plousioi* and *penêtes*, by serving as a model of and for emergent horizontal relationships between *plousioi* and *penêtes*, and by promoting closure within the newly formed dominant groups in individual Greek communities. Each of these three mechanisms will be examined in turn, primarily on the basis of evidence pertaining to Athens and to Sparta. We will focus our attention on the sixth and fifth centuries, because horizontal mass sport and democratic governance first manifested themselves in the sixth century and developed further in the fifth. Political and military changes in the fourth century, discussed in the concluding section to this chapter, changed the nature of both sport and society in the Greek world and to some extent reversed the processes of democratization that took place in the preceding two centuries.

10.2. SPORT AS AN ARENA OF MERITOCRATIC STATUS COMPETITION

The drawing of a connection between meritocratic status competition and democratization requires some justification, because meritocratic competition can have the effect of undercutting the very egalitarianism that lies at the heart of democratization (see Section 6.5). Meritocratic competition can, nonetheless, promote democratization, by undermining systems of ascribed rank and by hindering the development of steep differentials in social power. One of the ways sport contributed to democratization in ancient Greece was that it decreased inequality by offering a form of meritocratic competition that assigned status in ways that cut across and diminished the importance of distinctions based on lineage and wealth. During the Archaic period, *plousioi* had sought to tie *timê* to lineage and wealth, and those traits always remained important sources of status and power, even in the

---

sociopolitical privileges and access to the *gymnasium* were both tightly restricted. On this passage, see C. Mann 2001, 184.

most democratized communities. For example, in Athens for much of the fifth century political leaders tended to come from long-established, wealthy families.

Sport represented an alternative, nonheritable source of status and social power; athletic talent was a crucial source of *timê* in Early Iron Age Greece, and that continued to be true in the Greek world for well over a millennium. Recall the passage in the *Odyssey* in which one of the characters says:

It's fit and proper for you to know your sports. What greater glory attends a man, while he's alive, than what he wins with his racing feet and striving hands? Come and compete....(8.169–72)

The continuing importance of sport as a source of social status in later periods is perhaps most evident from the facts that in the fifth century a limited number of great athletes literally became objects of worship and that athletic success throughout Greek history could serve as a springboard to a political career.[5] On a more mundane basis, sport shaped everyday relationships between males from families of *plousioi* and *penêtes*; most of them played sports with some regularity, and it was an important means of determining relative standing.

The nature of the relationship between two individuals could be profoundly affected by the outcome of their competitive interaction on the playing field, regardless of their relative standing in other social spheres. The leveling potential of athletic competition is evident in the reaction of the suitors when Odysseus-as-beggar proposes to enter an archery contest with them (see Section 8.1), and in the comment of Alexander the Great to the effect that he would enter a footrace at the Olympic Games when he had other kings as competitors (Plutarch *Alexander* 4.10).

Meritocratic competition in sport promoted egalitarian relationships among the *plousioi* and *penêtes*, and hence democratization, because status hierarchies based on success in sports competitions did not align with those based on lineage and wealth, which in turn reduced net inequalities. Sport created a situation in which a fast runner who was undistinguished in terms of lineage and wealth and a slow runner who came from an unusually distinguished and wealthy family could meet on relatively equal terms. The effect of such cross-cutting sources of status was documented in a study by Thomas Bottomore from the early 1950s, in which he looked carefully at social interactions in 125 leisure groups in a small British town. He found that clubs built around a specific activity such as sport or music were more integrated than purely social groups because the status of members was determined by skill in performing the activity in question as well as wealth and occupation.[6]

---

[5] See Kurke 1993 and, for later periods, van Nijf 2001.
[6] Bottomore 1954.

The importance of the equalizing capacity of sport was amplified by the fact that it was impossible to transfer reliably athletic skill from one generation to the next, as opposed to lineage and wealth, which were entirely heritable. The relative stability of distinctions based on lineage and wealth made it feasible for families to accumulate on a gradual basis prestige and social power in amounts sufficient to create relatively steep social pyramids. The sharp differentials in athletic ability within and among generations of families pushed in the other direction, and, by introducing an element of instability, acted as a check on the formation of steep social pyramids.

It is important to note that the situations in the town studied by Bottomore and in ancient Greece were fundamentally similar in that in both cases there was significant social stratification outside of sport and hence meritocratic competition via sport participation had a leveling effect. The outcome would be different in situations in which the athletic competitors were functionally identical in social standing in all other spheres; in such instances meritocratic competition in sport could potentially increase inequality. In other words, the ramifications of meritocratic competition in sport with respect to democratization are contextually specific.

10.3. SPORT AS A MODEL OF AND FOR HORIZONTAL RELATIONSHIPS

The formation of horizontal relationships between the *plousioi* and *penêtes* in individual Greek communities, initially at least, had to overcome substantial obstacles. The more inclusive sociopolitical system that came into being in the sixth century, in which *plousioi* and *penêtes* were expected to relate to each other in a largely horizontal fashion, was the result of a long and difficult struggle. *Plousioi* had sought to create vertical relationships between themselves and all other members of their community, *penêtes* included, so the expectation of egalitarian interactions between members of the newly formed ruling groups in individual Greek communities was not necessarily easily realized. There was in addition a simple problem with numbers. The size of the group of men that enjoyed full social and political privileges in any given community became roughly six to ten times larger than it had been, and that in and of itself created difficulties in forming networks of horizontal relationships among the members of that group.

Sport participation helped promote the creation of the requisite horizontal relationships between *plousioi* and *penêtes*, and hence helped promote democratization, by serving as a model of and for such relationships. In order to understand how sport modeled horizontal relationships, it is helpful to think of sport as a ritualized activity. Use of the term "ritualized activity" typically carries the explicit or implicit assumption that almost any activity can potentially take on the qualities of a ritual to a greater or lesser extent. An extraordinarily wide range of activities has been characterized as ritualized, and numerous attempts have been made to find commonalities shared by all ritualized activities. Most theorists in recent decades have looked to the work of Victor Turner, Stanley Tambiah, and others in seeing a performative dimension as being an essential component of any activity that can be reasonably identified as being ritualized. Perhaps the most productive approach to establishing suitable parameters for separating ritualized from nonritualized activities is that outlined by Catherine Bell. She takes a performative element as a necessary but not sufficient condition and argues that ritualized activities are distinguished not so much by their content as by being contrasted with more mundane actions and by being framed as different and special ways of acting.[7]

It requires no great intuitive leap to see that sport can easily become a ritualized activity. Sport is inherently performative and is framed as being set apart and different. Johan Huizinga, in his famous *Homo Ludens*, characterized sport as a form of play and defined play as a "free activity standing quite consciously outside 'ordinary' life."[8] Huizinga pointed out that play is distinguished from everyday life by being autotelic and frequently carried out in spaces that are temporally and spatially apart. This "set-apart" quality of play is heightened in the case of sport, especially in regard to formally organized competitions. Bernard Suits, who has written extensively on the philosophy of sport, remarked that:

> to play a game is to engage in activity directed towards bringing about a specific state of affairs, using only means permitted by rules, where the rules prohibit the more efficient in favour of less efficient means, and where such rules are accepted just because they make possible such activity.[9]

In this sense, sport, a subcategory of games, is by definition overtly peculiar because it entails adhering to rules that establish arbitrary ends (e.g., drop your opponent to the ground three times to win a wrestling match) that must be achieved by specific, unnecessarily complex means (e.g., do not use an edged weapon to incapacitate your opponent). If other considerations, such as the provision of special playing fields and uniforms (or, in this case, nudity), are taken into account, the identification of sport as at least a potentially ritualized activity becomes almost an inevitability.[10] The ritualized dimension of sport is reflected in the regularity with which it is compared to religion; Michael Novak, for instance, wrote that "Sports is [*sic*], somehow, a religion."[11]

---

[7] Bell 1992, 37–168 and *passim*.
[8] Huizinga 1950 (1938), 13.
[9] Suits 1978, 34.
[10] There is a considerable body of scholarly literature that approaches sport as a ritualized activity or a secular ritual. See, for instance, MacAloon 1984 on the modern Olympic games.
[11] Novak 1988, ix. For detailed explorations of the overlaps between sport and religion see, in addition to Novak, the articles collected in Hoffman 1992 and Prebish 1993.

We have already seen that institutions, practices, and norms in society and sport tend toward congruence (Section 4.1). The identification of sport as a form of ritualized activity intersects with and extends this observation because ritualized activities are "flexible forms of symbolic activity that reaffirm cultural values and a sense of order."[12] As such, they can serve as models of and for certain kinds of social relationships. As models of society, ritualized activities have the capacity to present idealized and simplified visions of how society and relations between individuals could or should be.[13] Geertz famously described cockfights staged by the inhabitants of Bali as "a story they tell themselves about themselves."[14] The fact that ritualized activities are by definition set apart from everyday life is particularly significant, as they are for this reason immune to many of the mundane necessities of existence that otherwise can generate a divergence between the normative and normal. As a result, ritualized activities frequently, perhaps typically, reflect social norms with a degree of faithfulness that is otherwise difficult to achieve.[15]

Horizontal mass sport can be understood as presenting a paradigm of *plousioi* and *penêtes* interacting as equals. As John Hargreaves has observed, sport can offer "regular public occasions for discourse on some of the basic themes of social life – success and failure, good and bad behavior, ambition and achievement, discipline and effort and so on."[16] Sport was an activity set apart from everyday life and offered a figurative level playing field that strongly muted status differences based on factors such as lineage and wealth that were prominent in other contexts. To the extent that there were status differences among participants, they were largely the product of demonstrated competence at sport. Moreover, as had been the case in the Early Iron Age, the mere willingness of two men to compete against each other in sport was an implicit statement of their relative equality. Sport thus provided a particularly clear model of what horizontal relationships between *plousioi* and *penêtes* might look like.

The impact of the horizontal relationships embodied in sport was greatly amplified by the fact that they also served as a model *for* behavior in other social contexts. The power of ritualized activities to shape behavior is greatly enhanced by practice, particularly in the form of performance. The

---

[12] Bell 2005, 7849.

[13] This is a close paraphrase taken from the excellent discussion of ritual found at Kowalzig 2007, 34.

[14] Geertz 1973, 448.

[15] As Raymond Gram Swing put it in the introduction to Tunis 1941, "In sports, the problems of applying democratic truths is [sic] not complex, as in political and economic life" (viii). A good, brief introduction to ritual theory can be found in Bell 2005, 7849. For a longer, more detailed overview, see Bell 1997. The view of rituals as models of and for society is elucidated in Geertz 1973, 87–125.

[16] Hargreaves 1986, 12.

participants in ritualized activities do not simply hear about societal norms, they themselves enact those norms. As Geertz put it, "in a ritual, the world as lived and the world as imagined, fused under the agency of a single set of symbolic forms, turn out to be the same world."[17] Performance constitutes an essential bridge between ritual activities serving as models of social norms and serving as models for actual behavior because participants reproduce idealized forms of behavior they are expected to manifest in some form in their daily lives.[18]

The behavioral patterns enacted in ritualized activities inculcate habits of thought and dispositions that shape the actions of individuals in all settings and thus serve as models for activity outside the ritualized sphere. In that sense participation in ritualized activities is a powerful form of socialization, but it is probably more helpful to think of the effects of participation in ritualized activities in terms of Bourdieu's concept of *habitus*. Bourdieu sought to find a way to account for the influence of both social structure and individual agency in shaping behavior, and developed the argument that social structure strongly influences – without determining – actions via *habitus*, which he defined as "systems of durable, transposable *dispositions,* structured structures predisposed to function as structuring structures, that is, as principles of the generation and structuring of practices and representations."[19] One might think of *habitus* as a learned tendency to do things in a certain way. Because they are transposable, the dispositions acquired in one context manifest themselves in other areas as well.

Ritualized activities offer particularly clear models for how things ought to be done and so can be a particularly powerful means of shaping *habitus*. This dimension of ritualized activities has been explored by Catherine Bell, who built directly upon Bourdieu's ideas. She has argued that regular participation in ritualized activities physically inculcates the thought and behavioral patterns underpinning such activities and that "as bodies...absorb the logic of spaces and temporal events, they then project these structural schemes, reproducing liturgical arrangements out of their own 'sense' of the fitness of things."[20] This is an important insight because it makes clear how ritualized activities can shape behavior, without participants being aware that they are being socialized, potentially even against their conscious inclinations.

The influence of the model of horizontal relationships provided by sport on behavior in other contexts was particularly strong because of the identity of the participants. Democratization resulted in a sociopolitical system

[17] Geertz 1973, 112.
[18] The role of sport as a model of and for citizenship in a democratic society in the present-day United States is explored in Gillespie 2010.
[19] Bourdieu 1977 (1972), 72.
[20] Bell 2005, 7853. For a full discussion, see Bell 1992, 94–117.

in which *plousioi* and *penêtes* were expected to interact as relative equals. Most *plousioi* and *penêtes* participated in sport, and so the people involved in horizontal relationships in sport were exactly the same as those who were expected to form horizontal relationships in other contexts, an overlap that made the transfer of behavioral patterns from one to the other a much more straightforward proposition. Moreover, most Greek communities were much smaller than Athens or Sparta, and most if not all of the *plousioi* and *penêtes* in any given place had the opportunity to interact on a face-to-face basis, which also facilitated transference of behavioral patterns from sport to nonsport activities.[21]

Sport thus fostered democratization in ancient Greece in part by providing models of horizontal relationships between *plousioi* and *penêtes*, which served as models for horizontal relationships between *plousioi* and *penêtes* outside of sport, and by cultivating a predisposition among *plousioi* and *penêtes* to form egalitarian relationships with each other.[22] The importance of such models will vary widely; they were of considerable significance in ancient Greece because horizontal relationships between *plousioi* and *penêtes* were a new phenomenon. In societies in which horizontal relationships are a firmly established norm among a given segment of the population, those individuals' need for paradigms of egalitarian interactions in sport is likely to be limited. Here again, the effect of sport on democratization is contextually specific.

10.4. SPORT AND GROUP CLOSURE

The history of democratization can be seen as a story of exclusion retreating before successive waves of change that bring progressively greater levels of inclusion. As John Dunn put it, "Democracy's triumph has been the collapse of one exclusion after another, in ever-greater indignity, with the collapse of the exclusion of women, the most recent, hastiest and most abashed of all."[23]

The history of democratization could, however, also be told the other way around and treated as the story of the forms of exclusion that accompany and enable broadened inclusion. If inclusion is understood as involving membership in a group with some degree of coherence, inclusion and exclusion are inextricably linked. Groups achieve coherence in part through

---

[21] On the population of Greek communities other than Athens and Sparta, see the detailed studies in Hansen and Nielsen 2004.

[22] Sport was but one of a number of functionally similar institutions and practices that helped to sustain democratic governance in ancient Greece. For example, Strauss has argued that service as rowers in the fleet helped *ptôchoi* in Athens develop what is here called internal political efficacy and a sense of group solidarity. It is noteworthy that he asserts that serving as a rower imparted a "sense of belonging to the team" (1996, 317).

[23] Dunn 2005, 136.

closure, the maintenance of boundaries that separate them from others, and hence through exclusion.[24] The significant expansion of a group is likely to entail the construction of new boundaries, so that inclusion necessitates exclusion.

One of the more unusual aspects of the relationship between sport and democratization in ancient Greece is that horizontal mass sport promoted democratization by serving as a means of social exclusion that helped create a clear boundary around newly formed dominant groups consisting of *plousioi* and *penêtes*. That may seem a perverse argument given the understanding of democratization adopted here, but it is important to bear in mind that the sociopolitical system that emerged in the sixth century, which was significantly more democratized than what came before, was not some sort of historical inevitability. That sociopolitical system represented an innovation that came into being only after a struggle for preeminence between *plousioi* and *penêtes*. It could easily have collapsed, and in fact the expansion of Macedonian power in the second half of the fourth century contributed to the reemergence of more exclusive political systems that represented a step backward in terms of institutional democratization. One of the reasons why the more inclusive vision involving the sharing of social and political privileges between *plousioi* and *penêtes* persisted for the better part of two centuries was that the *plousioi* and *penêtes* in most communities came together to form a single, coherent group that maintained horizontal relationships among its members. That coherence was achieved in part through boundaries that separated males born into families of *plousioi* and *penêtes* from other members of their communities.

Sport contributed significantly to group closure among *plousioi* and *penêtes* in the Archaic and Classical periods. In some sense this can be understood in very simple terms, as part of the process of the formation of social capital, in which the creation of in-group loyalties can be accompanied by a sharpened sense of difference with out-groups (see Section 5.2). In addition, sport can be seen as part of a distinctive lifestyle that helps define a particular group (see Section 6.3); most *plousioi* and *penêtes* regularly participated in sport, most other people in their communities did not.

There was also one unusual feature of Greek sport that greatly magnified its ability to create boundaries, namely nudity. Sociologists and social psychologists who study group formation have found that membership is frequently linked to clothing. For example, Stephen Worchel and his colleagues argue that group formation is a cyclical process, the first stage of which they label "group identification" and describe as follows:

The group focuses on establishing clear boundaries, often seeking competition with other groups.... The group avoids accepting new members. There are strong

[24] Giddens 2006, 496.

pressures for conformity and members often adopt a group uniform. Groupthink…is common. Dissenters are punished and/or rejected. The norm of equality is adopted and little distinction is made between members.[25]

Although much of this is by now familiar, what is new is the role of clothing. In the case of ancient Greece, however, it was not clothing but its absence that was important.

The custom of athletic nudity was a relatively late arrival; Greeks did not begin exercising in the nude until the seventh century. Throughout the Bronze Age and Early Iron Age, Greeks played sports but always did so wearing at least some clothing. This is most evident in the Homeric poems, where men invariably compete wearing a loincloth. The only exceptions came in the context of footraces held as part of initiation rites, the participants in which sometimes wore an exotic outfit or went nude (see Section 8.2). Those occasions were, however, by definition unusual and very far from being something that happened every day. The relevant literary, artistic, and archaeological evidence shows that by the middle of the sixth century it had become standard practice for Greek men to do all their sports in the nude. The beginnings of athletic nudity cannot be dated more precisely than somewhere between roughly 700 and 575, and it is in any case likely that it took a good deal of time for this custom, which represented a radical innovation, to become widely accepted.[26]

The habit of stripping down completely for exercise rapidly became something that set the Greeks apart from all of the neighboring cultures in the Mediterranean basin, and it was seen as one of the defining elements that made Greek culture unique.[27] For instance, in Plato's *Republic*, one of the speakers proposes that women training for leadership roles in the ideal state should play sports and should do so in the nude. The speaker then adds:

We will ask the critics to drop their usual practice and to be serious for once, and remind them that it was not so long ago that the Greeks thought – as most non-Greeks still think – that it was shocking and ridiculous for men to be seen naked. (452c, trans. D. Lee, slightly modified)

Even among Greeks athletic nudity represented a distinctly anomalous practice, and throughout their history Greeks had a strong distaste for public nudity. Sport was the only exception to the general rule that to be nude in public was a form of humiliation. Spartans seem to have had an unusually relaxed attitude toward nudity, but as Ephraim David has pointed out, "for all its importance, the practice of nudity in Sparta should be kept in its proper perspective: this was not a nudist society. In most public contexts

---

[25] Worchel and Coutant 2001, 466.
[26] On the date of the appearance of athletic nudity in ancient Greece, see Christesen 2007a, 353–59 and McDonnell 1991.
[27] On athletic nudity as an ethnic marker, see Bonfante 1989.

the Spartans, like the other Greeks, were dressed and...they were extremely careful about their dress."[28] Furthermore, athletic nudity remained a source of some discomfort, as is evident from the design of *palaistrai* and *gymnasia*, both of which used walls to shield their users from outside view.

Strange as it may seem Greeks of later periods knew very little about why and how athletic nudity became a widespread custom. A key problem was that the practice of writing careful historical accounts was pioneered by the Greeks, but not until the fifth century, by which time the origins of athletic nudity were largely lost in the mists of time. There was some agreement that the Spartans had something to do with it, but that was about it. Greeks did, however, show notable ingenuity in inventing explanations for it. For example, some people speculated that a runner had tripped over his loincloth and died during a race, and that athletes thereafter took to nudity for safety reasons.[29] It is, as a result, difficult to reconstruct the origins of athletic nudity or to explain the reasons for its persistence, but it is possible to say something about its effects with respect to democratization, in part because Thucydides seems to have been exceptionally well informed about this matter.

Most of Thucydides' account of the Peloponnesian War (431–404) focuses on his own time, but he does provide a little background in order to prove that the war about which he was writing was the biggest one ever fought by Greeks. As part of that background he mentions Sparta and provides this information:

The Spartans were the first to adopt the moderate manner of dressing that is now the standard custom, and with respect to all other things the richer citizens conducted themselves in a fashion that as much as possible put them into an equal position with the general populace. The Spartans were the first to strip naked and to disrobe openly and anoint themselves with oil after playing sports in the nude [*gymnazein*]. Formerly, even in the Olympic Games, the athletes who contended wore loincloths; and it is but a few years since that practice ceased. And even now among non-Greeks, especially among those in Asia Minor, who hold contests in boxing and wrestling, the competitors still wear loincloths.[30] (*The Peloponnesian War* 1.6)

The account provided by Thucydides indicates that athletic nudity was connected to democratization in Sparta. Immediately after commenting that it was in Sparta that the rich first adopted a simple lifestyle that put them on an equal footing with the other members of their community, he observes

---

[28] David 2010, 152. David also points out that public nudity was typically humiliating in Sparta and was used as a form of social exclusion (149–52).

[29] This tradition is recorded in scholia B and T to *Iliad* 23.683, on which see Erbse 1969. Most of the ancient sources on the emergence of athletic nudity can be found in Sweet 1987, 124–33.

[30] Cf. Xenophon's observation that Spartiates "adorn themselves not with costly dress but with the fine condition of their bodies" (*Constitution of the Spartans* 7.3, trans. M. Lipka). See also Aristotle *Politics* 1294b24–29.

that the Spartans were the first to play sports in the nude. This implies that there was some connection between athletic nudity and democratization, but Thucydides did not make the nature of that connection explicit. In order to understand what he was getting at, we need to recall that during the Archaic period the *plousioi* had used conspicuous consumption, which included dressing elaborately, to try to create status differentials between themselves and others (see Section 9.1). Democratization in Sparta and elsewhere was accompanied by the imposition of social and in some cases legal constraints on conspicuous consumption.[31] Thucydides strongly implies, though he does not explicitly claim, that athletic nudity was part of the same process and that playing sports in the nude reduced social inequalities in Sparta.[32] His interpretive instincts were undoubtedly sound on this point; as modern-day sociologists have discovered, "the wearing of special clothing, or little clothing at all, tends to mask social differences and buttresses the impression of harmony and lack of social division."[33]

Although this subject is not addressed by Thucydides, the introduction of athletic nudity also promoted group closure by giving *plousioi* and *penêtes* an unusual uniform that set them apart from all other members of their communities. We have already seen that nudity was highly exceptional in ancient Greece, which meant that the men who adopted the practice of athletic nudity took up a custom that visibly distinguished them.

Athletic nudity also contributed to group closure by helping limit sport participation by free but not affluent men, the *ptôchoi*. The extent to which *ptôchoi* would participate in the process of democratization was an open question. Athens gradually moved toward a political system in which *ptôchoi* exercised a good deal of influence, but in most Greek communities they remained socially and politically marginalized straight through the Classical period. Although that clearly had a dampening effect on overall societal democratization, it did serve to consolidate the democratization effected by the extension of social and political privilege to *penêtes* by restricting the size and heterogeneity of the emergent dominant groups in individual Greek communities and thereby facilitating the formation of stable horizontal relationships between the members of those groups.

The extension of political and social privileges to the *ptôchoi* was in the interests of neither the *plousioi* nor the *penêtes*, and they took active, and largely effective, steps to prevent that from happening. In some communities *ptôchoi* were excluded from political rights through the imposition of

---

[31] On sumptuary laws in ancient Greece, with a particular focus on those applying to clothing, see Culham 1986 and H. Mills 1984. On the "democratization" of clothing in Athens, see Geddes 1987.

[32] For an argument that something similar happened in Athens after the establishment of a democratic form of government, see Miller 2000.

[33] Hargreaves 1986, 169.

property qualifications.[34] However, the effectiveness of legal restrictions of this sort was limited because the privileges at stake were as much social as political, and it was difficult to legislate lifestyles. The *plousioi* and *penêtes* needed means of excluding the *ptôchoi* socially.

Sport in general and athletic nudity in particular were important means by which *plousioi* and *penêtes* successfully marginalized *ptôchoi*. We have already seen that the combination of the practical necessities of free time and training and of the restricted resources at their disposal meant that it was difficult for *ptôchoi* to participate regularly in sport (Section 9.4). As Veblen noted in his acerbic comments on early twentieth-century CE America, leisure activities, because they are economically unproductive, can be an important form of conspicuous consumption.[35] This was certainly true in Greece, where sport was a form of conspicuous consumption that *plousioi* and *penêtes* could afford, and *ptôchoi* for the most part could not. Sport was, therefore, a very convenient means of social exclusion.

Athletic nudity reinforced the exclusionary capacity of sport because it made socioeconomic status apparent in bodily appearance. Regularly exercising in the nude gave athletes a smooth, all-over tan that was unique, because there were no other acceptable contexts for being fully nude on a regular basis. Men from poorer families typically spent much of their time outside working on farms while wearing a short tunic (very much like the one worn by Spartan girls when they exercised) and as a result had the ancient equivalent of a "farmer's tan." Alternatively they worked indoors, as craftsmen, and hence, were notably pale. These men could come to the *gymnasium* to exercise, but they had to strip down and in doing so immediately made their socioeconomic status evident to everyone present. That would have acted as a powerful deterrent that kept poorer men from participating in sport. It is probably not coincidental that there were specific Greek words for "white-rumped" (*leukopygos* or *leukoprôktos*) and "dark-bottomed" (*melampygos*) and that the first meant "cowardly and unmanly" and the second "brave like Herakles."

The multiple dimensions of athletic nudity all contributed meaningfully to the formation of horizontal relationships between *plousioi* and *penêtes*. It removed a status marker associated with wealth and thereby helped establish egalitarianism among athletes, and it also promoted group closure by marking out men from families of *plousioi* and *penêtes* and by helping to restrict sport participation by *ptôchoi*.

Sport thus facilitated democratization in Archaic and Classical Greece in part by promoting closure that stabilized newly formed, more inclusive ruling groups made up of *plousioi* and *penêtes*. It goes (almost) without saying that sport also inhibited democratization, by contributing to the social and

---

[34] See the discussion in Johnstone 2011, 99–102.
[35] Veblen 1912, 35–67.

political exclusion of *ptôchoi*. The extent to which sport's capacity to promote group closure does or does not foster democratization varies widely. In ancient Greece its role in solidifying innovative, democratizing sociopolitical arrangements probably outweighed its role in limiting the number of people who benefited from those arrangements. In other circumstances, particularly when it is not supporting ongoing processes of democratization, group closure founded in sport can have much less benign consequences.[36] Here again we have a contextually specific mechanism by means of which sport fosters democratization.

10.5. TRANSITION

The spatial and temporal correlation between the first known appearances of horizontal mass sport and democratic systems of governance, both of which emerged for the first time in Greece in the Archaic period, immediately raises the possibility that there is a causal relationship of some kind between sport and democratization. The tendency of sport and social systems to be congruent and the relatively greater strength of the transhistorically valid mechanisms by means of which sport promotes democratization, as against the mechanisms by means of which it inhibits democratization, both strongly suggest that the relationship between democratization in sport and society in ancient Greece was reciprocal: horizontal mass sport both resulted from and furthered democratization. That conclusion is reinforced by the existence of three contextually specific mechanisms by means of which sport fostered democratization.

The next task is to pursue horizontal mass sport forward in time and space, to its next major manifestation, in nineteenth-century CE Britain. Before doing so, however, it will be helpful to have some sense of the history of mass sport after the fifth century BCE.

The political dimensions of Greek sport diminished over time, and starting in the fourth century sport gradually became more of a means by which Greeks asserted their cultural identity than an arena in which contemporary struggles over social and political privileges were played out. This was the result of a number of changes, the first of which was that athletics, especially nude athletics, became one of the defining traits of Greek identity.[37]

The importance of reinforcing a sense of Greek identity grew markedly starting in the fourth century as the result of the conquests of Alexander the Great and the spread of Greek settlement into much of the Middle East.[38]

---

[36] See Section 6.3 for further discussion of this point.

[37] Bonfante 1989.

[38] For an introduction to Alexander's campaigns and their aftermath, see G. Shipley 2000. For a more in-depth exploration of the same subject, see the relevant volumes in the *Cambridge Ancient History* series.

Before Alexander's time there were very few Greeks in the territory that became the Ptolemaic and Seleucid kingdoms, and the rulers of these kingdoms made a concerted effort to encourage Greeks to emigrate east and serve as administrators and soldiers. For example, thousands of Greeks arrived in Egypt, where they became a distinct, elite minority of about 200,000 among roughly 4 million Egyptians.[39] The Greeks who settled in the Ptolemaic and Seleucid kingdoms were intent on maintaining their ethnic identity, not least because it marked them out as a privileged group.

Active participation in sport was one of the most important means by which these Greek emigrants asserted their ethnic identity. This is most apparent in Ptolemaic Egypt, where Greek settlers immediately built *gymnasia*, which were centers for schooling and physical training. Regular attendance at a *gymnasium* was so important that an officially recognized group of citizens, the "*gymnasium* class," eventually came into being, and some important magistracies were open only to members of this class.[40]

Alexander and his father Philip were also responsible for setting in motion a series of military and political changes that, in the long run, substantially reduced the political dimensions of athletics. Philip built a large army of professional soldiers that he used to expand his kingdom and gain control over most of mainland Greece. After Alexander's death the immense territory he ruled was divided into three large states, the Hellenistic kingdoms. At roughly the same time, the Romans were gradually taking over more and more of the Mediterranean basin. By the end of the third century they were in control of most of the Greek settlements in southern Italy and Sicily, and by the end of the first century they had taken over all of the kingdoms founded by Alexander's generals. Greek *poleis* lost most of their autonomy when they became part of these much larger political units, the rulers of which preferred that individual *poleis* be run by small groups of rich men. Over the course of time this became the standard political arrangement in most *poleis*.

The incorporation of *poleis* into the Hellenistic kingdoms and then the Roman state meant that local political and military activities lost much of their urgency. Political life in individual communities was frequently dominated by narrow groups of rich elites who were supported by the rulers of the larger states to which these communities belonged.[41] The process of institutional democratization that had begun in the sixth century was to a considerable extent reversed. Furthermore, the people running any individual

---

[39] For these figures, see Fischer-Bovet 2008, 78.

[40] On the importance of the *gymnasium* in the Ptolemaic and Seleucid kingdoms, see Brady 1936, Habermann 2007, and Mehl 1992. On the practice of sports in Ptolemaic Egypt, see Remijsen 2012.

[41] Democracy did not, however, disappear entirely; see the case studies and discussion in Carlsson 2010.

polis had relatively little freedom of action, and men from outside the dominant group had minimal opportunity to force their way into power and a reduced motivation to do so. In addition, the creation of large, professional armies meant that local forces consisting of citizen–soldiers became significantly less important.

These developments made athletics more a social than a political matter. Military service, social and political privileges, and participation in athletics had for centuries been closely connected. The men who played important roles in the defense of the community and who wielded political power tended to be athletes and vice-versa. The reconfiguration of the basic political and military situation fundamentally altered that equation. Military service at the local level became a much less pressing matter, and political arrangements were largely determined by forces outside of the control of individual communities. The ramifications of participation in athletics were thus reduced considerably. The rich men running individual *poleis* were better able to take the sort of steps described by Aristotle in the hope of keeping others out of sport (section 10.1), but there was much less urgency for them to do so because their position was relatively secure. Under these circumstances, participation in sport became largely a cultural issue, less an opportunity to stake a claim to share in political privileges and more of an opportunity to stake a claim to being a good Greek.

This trend was reinforced by the incorporation of the entire Greek world into the Roman Empire. After centuries of political autonomy followed by centuries of ruling over large swathes of the Mediterranean basin, Greeks as a group found themselves shorn of any real military or political power. One of the more important reactions to these new realities was that Greeks relied more than ever before on a sense of cultural uniqueness and superiority. Sport, performed in the nude, set Greeks apart from every other ethnic group in the Mediterranean and became a particular point of pride.[42]

Sport was as popular in the Greek world in the Hellenistic (323–31 BCE) and Roman (31 BCE-476 CE) periods as it had ever been. In part this was because Greeks had more reasons than ever before to concern themselves with asserting a unique cultural identity and claims to superiority. Another issue was that some of the inhabitants of the areas conquered by Alexander took up the practice of athletics. In most cases the motivation was seeking entry into the new power structure by adopting Greek customs. Many of the Greek kings who succeeded Alexander were happy to support the spread of Greek customs to indigenous peoples because they saw it as a way of building loyalty to their regimes. For example, in the second century the people of the non-Greek community of Tyriaon in Asia Minor wrote to the Seleucid King Eumenes II asking him to designate their city as an official *polis* (and thus entitled to certain privileges) and to allow them to construct a *gymnasium*.

---

[42] On this development, see König 2005.

Eumenes agreed to do so and offered to send specialists capable of building a *gymnasium* (*SEG* 47.1745). Similarly, the Jewish high priest Jason in the second century, when Palestine was part of the Seleucid kingdom, built a *gymnasium* in the heart of Jerusalem and actively encouraged people to take up Greek customs, including nude exercise (2 *Maccabees* 4.9–15, 18–19; Josephus *Antiquities of the Jews* 12.237–41).[43]

The process of Hellenization through sport was an ongoing one, and gained force in the first through third centuries CE, when the Romans brought groups of non-Greek peoples in the eastern Mediterranean more firmly under control than they had been when they were part of the Hellenistic kingdoms. Elites in many such groups made an effort to learn Greek and adopted some Greek customs, because Greek remained the basic language of government and the dominant culture in the eastern Mediterranean. This happened all over the Near East but most especially in Asia Minor. For example, the people of the town of Oinoanda in Asia Minor, who were not Greeks but Lykians, established no less than three separate athletic festivals starting in 125 CE. The result was that during the first through third centuries CE literally hundreds of new athletic contests came into being. By the end of the second century CE roughly 500 athletic contests were held each year in Asia Minor alone.[44]

These changes in the basic social, political, and military situation in the Greek world affected the actual practice of sport in a variety of different ways. First, they tended to reduce the importance of success in athletic competitions because what happened on the playing field did not translate into political power. Winning still mattered, but just participating was sufficient to validate claims to being a good Greek. A sign of this shift is the appearance in the first through third centuries CE of inscriptions for athletes who competed but did not win. For example, Valerius Hermaios' father erected an honorary statue for his son for taking part "with distinction" in the boys' wrestling contest in Oinoanda in 207 CE (*SEG* 44.1191). Valerius did not win the contest but his family commemorated his athletic activity. This would have been unthinkable in the sixth and fifth centuries BCE (cf., for example, Pindar *Pythian* 8.71–98).

A second effect was that spectatorship became more important than before because attending a Greek athletic contest was an obvious, and simple, way of displaying the appropriate cultural credentials. Alexander's conquest of the Middle East created a situation in which large numbers of non-Greeks necessarily developed a certain level of interest in Greek culture, and for many such people watching rather than participating in athletic contests was sufficient. That in turn created a need for itinerant athletes who

---

[43] On the *gymnasia* in Tyriaon and Jerusalem, see Kennell 2005.
[44] On athletic festivals in Asia Minor during the period of Roman rule, see Pleket 1998 and van Nijf 2001.

could be counted on to appear at annual athletic festivals, and that need was met by the appearance of professional athletes organized into guilds. Guilds of Greek actors and musicians had come into being in the third century in order to help ensure that performance schedules were properly organized and fulfilled; in the first century two separate guilds of Greek athletes came into being for the same reason. It is not coincidental that they seem to have been based not in the Greek homeland but further east, probably in Asia Minor.[45]

A third shift in Greek athletic practice was that the creation of hundreds of new athletic festivals and the appearance of highly organized professional athletes helped open up sport to talented boys from poorer families. The rapid expansion in the number of regularly scheduled athletic contests in the sixth century made it possible for particularly talented athletes to make their living solely from sport. However, for an extended period most athletes, even at the highest levels of competition, seem to have come primarily from relatively wealthy families. That changed in the third century, when cities and individuals began to pay the training costs of promising but impoverished young athletes. Cities did so in the hope that the athlete would go on to a successful athletic career that would glorify his hometown. Individuals did so in the hope of sharing in the resulting financial rewards. For example, documents from Egypt dated to 257 provide information about the situation of an athlete named Pyrrhos, who was evidently a slave. A wealthy man had offered to pay for Pyrrhos' athletic training if he showed promise, and the director of a *palaistra* in the city of Alexandria declared that Pyrrhos did indeed have the potential to be a successful professional athlete.[46] The fact that a slave could be considered a viable candidate for an athletic career is an indication of the diminished sociopolitical significance of sport.

None of these changes, however, had a profound effect on the everyday practice of Greek sport in that mass sport flourished straight through the Hellenistic and Roman periods. Participation in sport continued to be essential for boys and men from Greek upper-class families, and early and extended involvement in athletics remained a key component of their lives. They had less of a stranglehold on sport, but they did not by any means abandon sport to the professionals or to the poor.

What finally terminated mass sport in the Greek world was Christianity. Sport was problematic for Christians because Greek athletic contests had long been closely associated with festivals for pagan deities, and because Greek sport celebrated the nude body. The end of mass sport in the Greek world can be seen most clearly in the course of events at Olympia. In 391 and 392 CE the emperor Theodosius issued edicts forbidding participation

---

[45] On athletic guilds, see Kyle 2007, 335–37 and Pleket 1973. On the growing importance of athletics as a spectator sport after the Classical period, see Miller 2004a, 196–206.
[46] On Pyrrhos, see Golden 2008, 42–43.

in pagan cults. This should have ended the Olympic Games, which were part of a religious festival for Zeus. However, an important cultural tradition with roots reaching back more than a thousand years did not die easily, and it seems that the statue of Zeus was removed from his temple at Olympia but games continued to be held. In 435 the emperor Theodosius II ordered the destruction of all pagan temples, and if the Olympics did not end just then, they certainly did shortly thereafter. Even so, athletic contests in other parts of the Greek world persisted for some time. The city of Antioch in what is now southeastern Turkey continued to hold athletic contests until 520 CE, at which point the Emperor Justinus specifically and permanently banned them. By the middle of the sixth century CE mass sport in Europe was dead.[47]

---

[47] On the end of the Olympic Games, see Lennartz 1974 and Weiler 2004. On the date of the decree of Theodosius II, see D. Hunt 1993, 157.

Sport and Society in Britain from 1800 to 1840

11.1. INTRODUCTION

Mass sport disappeared from Europe in the sixth century CE and did not reemerge for over a millennium. In some times and places in Europe in the intervening centuries a limited number of elites played sport on a regular basis; nonelites played sport only occasionally and casually. When mass sport finally reappeared, it did so in Britain and Germany in the nineteenth century.[1]

The following case study of sport and democratization in Britain will take the same general form as that for Greece, but the material will be organized differently. The nineteenth century will be divided into three periods: 1800–40, 1840–70, and 1870–1900. (These three phases correspond roughly to what historians call the early, middle, and late Victorian periods.) For each period we will look at social history, education, and sport. This organization of the material is driven by the facts that society and sport evolved rapidly in Britain during the nineteenth century, schools played a critical role in the development of sport, and there is, compared to ancient Greece, a large amount of detailed evidence available. It is, therefore, both helpful and possible to work with shorter time periods and to integrate education more directly into the discussion. It is important to keep in mind

---

[1] An overview of the history of sport in Europe in the Medieval and Early Modern periods can be found in Guttmann 2004, 52–67. For lengthier treatments of the same subject, see Carter 1992 and the articles collected in McClelland and Merrilees 2010. The term "Britain" is here taken to mean the geographic and political totality made up by England, Scotland, and Wales. Ireland is not discussed because its social and sport history is related to but different from that of Britain. The focus here is primarily on England, with occasional glances at Wales and Scotland. There were significant variations in the social and sport history of different parts of Britain, but also enough basic similarity that, for our purposes, we can treat Britain as a whole.

TABLE 6. *Polity Project Democratization Scores for Nineteenth-Century Britain*

	Polity Democratization Score
1800–1836	-2
1837–1879	+3
1880–1900	+7

Polity scores are assigned for each year; the scores for Britain are identical for all of the years within each of these three periods. The score provided here is the Polity2 score. On the Polity Project, including all the relevant data, see http://www.systemicpeace.org/polity/polity4.htm. The only other widely used democratization index that extends back into the nineteenth century is that originally compiled by Tatu Vanhanen; there are, however, significant problems with Vanhanen's methodology, on which see Munck 2009, 13–37. For the most up-to-date version of the Vanhanen index, see http://www.prio.no/CSCW/Datasets/Governance/Vanhanens-index-of-democracy/.

that although there were landmark events, such as the Reform Acts of 1832 and 1867, there were no fundamental discontinuities in the development of society or of sport in Britain during this time period. Moreover, different but related societal processes unfolded at different paces over varying stretches of time.

The periods defined here are nonetheless useful because they reflect in a general way the overall trajectory of democratization in both society and sport in Britain over the course of the nineteenth century. This is evident in the democratization scores assigned by the Polity Project, which, although not having the breadth of Unified Democracy Scores and having a relatively strong institutionalist bias, have the advantage of going back to the year 1800 for many countries. Polity democratization scores range from −10 (hereditary monarchy) to 10 (consolidated democracy), with intermediate scores categorized in three groups: autocracies (−10 to −6), anocracies (−5 to +5), and democracies (+6 to +10). The Polity scores for Britian, shown in Table 6, suggest that major political shifts took place in the 1830s and 1870s. The tripartite division adopted here thus corresponds relatively closely with the progress of democratization in Britain, and, as we shall see, with the development of horizontal mass sport.

This chapter begins with some brief background information, and then explores social history, education, and sport in Britain from 1800 to 1840. During this time period important processes of democratization were under way, but there was no mass sport – serious and regular participation in sport was primarily the preserve of elites.

11.2. BACKGROUND

After a long period of monarchical and aristocratic dominance, revolutions in America and France in the late eighteenth century marked a fundamental shift toward more democratized forms of social and political life in Europe. Starting in the 1830s, political agitation with a strong democratic flavor spread to many parts of Europe, and a wave of revolutions swept through Europe in 1848 and 1849. Monarchs survived, but in some cases were forced to consent to the creation of constitutions that limited their powers and that gave an active political role to increasingly large percentages of the population.[2]

The course of events in nineteenth-century Britain was very much in line with what was happening in the rest of Europe. Britain was, however, unusual in that the process of democratization began relatively early and had, by the end of the nineteenth century, progressed farther than in most of the rest of Europe. In order to understand that process in more detail it is first necessary to delineate the major sociopolitical groups involved.

By the beginning of the nineteenth century there were three key groups in British society: the landed gentry, the middle class, and the working class.[3] The landed gentry, the male members of which were called "gentlemen," consisted of people who owned large amounts of land, from which they derived an income sufficient to free them from the need to work actively to support themselves.[4] Their land was typically held in the form of estates that were divided into farms run by rent-paying tenants. There were two distinct subgroups in the landed gentry: the peers and the gentry. Peers had hereditary titles (duke, marquess, earl, viscount, baron/lord) that were passed from a father to his eldest son; in the nineteenth century there were about 400–500

---

[2] An overview of the history of Europe can be found in Kerr 2009. For an overview of the history of Britain up through the 1840s, see Wasson 2010, 1–149. For a more thorough account, see the articles collected in F. M. L. Thompson 1990 as well as the volumes in the *New Oxford History of England* series.

[3] There are many other ways of grouping the various members of nineteenth-century British society. Daniel Defoe (1659–1731), for instance, identified seven categories of people: the very rich, the rich, the middle class, tradesmen, rural poor, the very poor, and the miserable (cited in Rudé 1971, 37). Thomas Wright suggested in 1868 that the working class should be understood as consisting of three distinct groups: educated working men, intelligent artisans, and working men (Wright 1868, 6). One could also focus more strongly on geography or religion as defining traits. Any and all such categories necessarily minimize a wide range of variation of beliefs and behavior within any given group. The approach taken here is regularly used by historians and is particularly helpful in understanding sport in Britain. On the importance of class in the study of nineteenth-century Britain, see Hewitt 2004.

[4] There are multiple possible definitions of the term "landed gentry." A narrow definition of the term would exclude peers. The broader definition adopted here is consonant with this book's focus on sport; the patterns of activity of peers and their untitled but still wealthy and landowning counterparts were not fundamentally different with regard to sport. The two groups can, therefore, for present purposes be placed under a single heading.

British peers at any given time. The gentry were major landowners who did not have a hereditary title. Because only the eldest son of a peer inherited a title, many members of the gentry were the children of a peer. Other members of the gentry came from families that had no claim to a hereditary title of any kind, but who had long resided on country estates. There were somewhere between 10,000 and 15,000 families of gentry in nineteenth-century Britain, less than 1% of the total population. The landed gentry as a group possessed immense wealth – collectively they owned roughly half of all the land in Britain. The yearly incomes of families among the landed gentry were rarely less than £400, and the property of the most well off among them brought in £50,000 or more annually.[5]

The British middle class consisted of people who were relatively prosperous and who owned property but who, unlike the gentry, had to work to support themselves. A British middle class appeared in substantial numbers starting in the second half of the seventeenth century, and by the mid-nineteenth century about 15–20% of the total population, about 4 million people in all, came from middle-class families. The incomes of these families varied widely, from roughly £150 to £5,000 per year, with the minimum being enough to employ at least one servant to perform household tasks. Middle-class men typically made their living as businessmen, doctors, lawyers, clergy, military officers, or government officials; in modern-day America, they would be called white-collar workers.[6]

The working class in Britain consisted of people who made their living from manual labor; in modern-day America, they would be called blue-collar workers. The British working class as a unified group took shape slowly over the course of the nineteenth century due in part to major shifts in occupation and residence generated by ongoing processes of industrialization and urbanization. It became common to differentiate between skilled workers, who typically made £80–90 per year, and unskilled workers, who typically made £40–50 annually. The number of families of skilled workers was about the same as that of the middle class and so represented about 15–20% of the total population, unskilled workers and their families about 60 or 70%.[7]

---

[5] All of the figures provided in this section, especially those pertaining to population and income, need to be understood as rough approximations. The sources in most cases do not permit a high degree of precision, there was a great deal of variation geographically within Britain and within social groups, and there was an equally great deal of change over the course of the nineteenth century. Brief discussions of social classes in nineteenth-century Britain can be found in Bédarida 1979 (1976), 36–72 and Rubinstein 1998, 279–97. On the British landed gentry, see Beckett 1986; Bush 1984, 17–84; and Harrison 1971, 87–121.

[6] On the middle class, see Davidoff and Hall 1987 and Harrison 1971, 87–121. It was possible for a wealthy middle-class family to make its way into the landed gentry by buying land and retiring from active work. Whole-hearted acceptance as a "legitimate" member of the gentry, however, usually took a generation or two.

[7] On the working class, see Harrison 1971, 19–54; Hobsbawm 1984, 176–213; E. P. Thompson 1963.

At the start of the nineteenth century the landed gentry played a dominant role in Britain's social and political life. Seventy-five years later they had ceded considerable privileges to the upper middle class, and the landed gentry and upper middle class came together to form a new ruling group. The working class gained some degree of influence, particularly in the latter decades of the nineteenth century, though it was not integrated into the power structure to nearly the same degree as the middle class.

11.3. SOCIAL HISTORY

In thinking about the social history of Britain in the early part of the nineteenth century, we will begin, as we did in the case study of ancient Greece, by thinking about society as a game, with goals and social rules. The focus for the moment will be on males from among the landed gentry and the middle class. It was not until later in the century that men from the working class and women of all backgrounds achieved some degree of social and political influence and began participating in sport in significant numbers.

At the start of the nineteenth century, the landed gentry and the middle class had very different sets of goals and rules, so each group needs to be looked at separately. The landed gentry placed an overriding emphasis on behaving like and being considered to be a gentleman. The basic means by which one established one's credentials as a gentleman, which had a long history, reaching back into the seventeenth century and beyond, included first and foremost birth; a man was a gentleman in large part because he came from a family of gentlemen. Daniel Defoe wrote in 1729 that, "Our modern acceptation of a Gentlemen...is this, A person BORN (for there lies the essence of Quality) of some known, or Ancient Family." An American observer noted in 1848 that "in England, a man has to be born a gentleman, to have his claim to the title acknowledged."[8]

However, a man born into a family of gentlemen also needed to play the part of a gentleman. Gentlemen were expected to display manliness and to live a particular lifestyle that featured relative freedom from work and a correspondingly large amount of leisure time devoted to public service, conspicuous consumption, education, and sport. Manliness, education, and sport were all tightly interconnected and will be considered together below. A gentleman owned land, derived much if not all of his income from that land, and had no need to work to support himself or his family. In 1626 Sir John Doderidge wrote that "he is a gentleman...who can live idly and without manuall labour." William Cavendish, the fifth Duke of Devonshire (1748–1811) observed of his cousin, the famous scientist Henry Cavendish, that "he is not a gentleman, he works."[9]

---

[8] Defoe 1890 (1729), 13; People 1848, 621.
[9] Quoted in Stone 1965, 49 and V. Murray 1998, 22, respectively.

The voluntary performance of public service was another mark of the gentleman. Public service for peers tended to take the form of filling major leadership roles in the armed forces and national government and of being a member of the House of Lords. Less prominent members of the landed gentry became high-ranking military officers, ran local governments, and were members of the House of Commons.

Gentlemen were, in addition, expected to lead a lavish lifestyle that involved a considerable amount of conspicuous consumption. When Sir George Selby died in 1625 he was given a tombstone with a long Latin inscription that began:

George Selby, knight, sprung from the ancient and illustrious family of the Selbys, of Selby, in the county of York, four times mayor of his town, sheriff of the county palatine of Durham, ennobled by his hospitality and service toward the most illustrious king James. Certainly everywhere most celebrated for his splendid and ever-abounding style of living, and the dispensing of a most liberal table.[10]

The British middle class, at the start of the nineteenth century, took as their overriding goal attaining what they called "respectability." The prominent British social critic John Ruskin, in a lecture delivered in 1864, commented that:

Indeed, among the ideas most prevalent and effective in the mind of this busiest of countries, I suppose the first – at least that which is confessed with the greatest frankness, and put forward as the fittest stimulus to youthful exertion – is this of "Advancement in life."...Practically...at present, "advancement in life" means, becoming conspicuous in life; obtaining a position which shall be acknowledged by others to be respectable or honourable.[11]

In 1850 the British writer Frederick Denison Maurice published, under a pseudonym, a pamphlet with the sarcastic title "Dialogue between Somebody (a person of respectability) and Nobody (the writer)."[12]

Leaving aside the issue of lineage, the goals of being a gentleman and of attaining respectability were not necessarily all that different, but the qualities that made someone respectable in the eyes of the middle class were, initially, very different from those that made someone a gentleman in the eyes of the landed gentry. Whereas gentlemen did not work for a living and were dedicated to public service and conspicuous consumption, members of the middle class championed hard work; a dedication to thrift, sobriety, and piety; and material success achieved through individual effort.[13]

The importance of all of these qualities is abundantly clear in the work of Samuel Smiles (1812–1904), a British writer who published a series

[10] Welford 1884–87, 3: 266.
[11] Ruskin 1891, 4–5.
[12] Maurice 1850.
[13] A brief discussion of "Victorian values" can be found in Briggs 1988.

of popular self-help books that preached the middle-class gospel. Smiles relentlessly drove home the idea that hard work was essential. In *Self-Help*, published in 1861, he wrote that:

Nothing that is of real worth can be achieved without courageous working. Man owes his growth chiefly to that active striving of the will, that encounter with difficulty, which we call effort; and it is astonishing to find how often results apparently impracticable are thus made possible.

Hard work needed to be accompanied by thrift, sobriety, and piety. Smiles quoted with approval a speech made by a Mr. Bright in 1847 in which the speaker praised hard work, frugality, and temperance and asked the rhetorical question, "What is it that has made, that has in fact created, the middle class in this country, but the virtues to which I have alluded?" These virtues were expected to eventuate in material success, which was critical because money represented "the means of physical comfort and social well being."[14]

The goals and social rules of the middle class also emphasized the importance of competitive, individualistic pursuit of self-interest which, it was felt, would produce a healthy meritocracy and ensure the general good of society. Smiles recognized that competition could produce social ills but nonetheless lavishly praised it:

All life is a struggle. Put a stop to competition, and you merely check the progress of individuals and classes. You preserve a dead uniform level....Stop competition, and you stop the struggle of individualism. You also stop the advancement of individualism, and, through that, of society at large.[15]

The clear expectation was that hard work and competition would make certain that each person's station in life reflected his or her demonstrated merits. Smiles claimed that:

Practical industry, wisely and vigorously applied, never fails of success. It carries a man onward and upward, brings out his individual character, and powerfully stimulates the action of others. All may not rise equally, yet each, on the whole, very much according to his deserts.

Smiles acknowledged the importance of contributing to the well-being of society as a whole, but unlike the landed gentry who pursued this end through public service, he echoed middle-class beliefs in arguing that the public good was best achieved through the self-interested efforts of individuals:

The spirit of self-help is the root of all genuine growth in the individual and, exhibited in the lives of many, it constitutes the true source of national vigor and strength. Help from without is often enfeebling in its effects, but help from within invariably invigorates....

[14] Smiles 1861, 205, 283, 279, respectively.
[15] Smiles 1876, 169.

National progress is the sum of individual industry, energy, and uprightness, as national decay is of individual idleness, selfishness, and vice.[16]

This belief in the value of individualistic, meritocratic competition was not shared by the landed gentry. They had every reason to be satisfied with the position into which they were born and had correspondingly little interest in a meritocracy based on individual competition. They were also conscious of being a small minority of the population and were ready to cooperate with other members of their class. A good example of that readiness can be found in the selection of members of the House of Commons. In theory all adult males who owned more than forty shillings worth of real estate (land and buildings) had, since 1430, the right to vote in elections for the House of Commons. In practice, however, the members of the landed gentry in each electoral district typically worked closely with each other and decided ahead of time who would run for office, and contested elections in which the votes of men from outside the landed gentry mattered were rare.[17]

The differing attitudes of the landed gentry and the middle class were in no small part grounded in differing approaches to religion. Most of the landed gentry belonged to the Church of England, but gentlemen were not as a group noteworthy for their dedication to religion or their high moral standards. Lord Byron (1788–1824) said that by the age of twenty four he had "gamed [gambled] and drank, and taken my degrees in most dissipations."[18] Perhaps the most notorious example of the landed gentry's relatively lax morals is provided by the fifth duke of Devonshire, whom we have already encountered. The duke, his wife, his mistress, and his children by both all lived together in the same house in London.[19]

The goals and rules of the middle class, on the other hand, were deeply influenced by Puritanism, a form of evangelical Christianity that flourished in Britain in the sixteenth and seventeenth centuries. Puritanism came into being as a protest against some of the practices of the dominant form of Christianity, the Church of England, and this brought the Puritans into conflict with much of the British power structure. The Puritans took advantage of political instability in the middle of the seventeenth century and briefly seized control of the British government. Puritans were known for their deep dedication to religion and for the great importance they attached to hard work, individualism, and to living simple, industrious, and moral lives. Many members of the British middle class, which emerged as a distinct group about the same time as Puritanism, became Puritans, and, although

---

[16] Smiles 1861, 15, 16, respectively.

[17] A good, albeit politically charged, survey of electoral systems in Britain can be found in Watt 2006.

[18] Cited in Margetson 1969, 21.

[19] On the Duke of Devonshire's unusually complicated living arrangements, see Foreman 1998.

Puritanism gradually faded out of existence in the eighteenth century, many of the ideas associated with it continued to be influential among the British middle class through the nineteenth century.[20]

There was thus, in the early years of the nineteenth century, a considerable degree of perceived incompatibility of values and even some antagonism between the landed gentry and the middle class. Some members of the middle class for instance, overtly disapproved of the landed gentry's avoidance of hard work. Samuel Smiles argued that "the rich man, inspired by a right spirit, will spurn idleness as unmanly; and if bethink him of the responsibilities which attach to the possession of wealth and property, he will feel even a higher call to work than men of poorer lot."[21]

11.4. EDUCATION

Through 1840 there was little in the way of publicly financed education in Britain, although some free or inexpensive schooling was provided by charitable organizations. Sunday schools, organized and run by churches and free to attend, taught mostly reading and had over a million children enrolled by the 1830s. Two different religious organizations were formed in 1811 and 1814 to found and run inexpensive though not free schools in places where the local populace could raise appropriate funding. Some larger towns had what were called grammar schools, which were created from an early period as charitable institutions that offered free education to boys who would later become clergymen.[22]

Families for the most part had to finance the education of their children out of their own pockets, with predictable results. Children from working-class families typically received little education. Middle-class families sent their sons either to grammar schools or to private schools, which were owned and run by individuals or groups as profit-making enterprises. Over the course of the eighteenth and nineteenth centuries an increasing percentage of grammar schools charged tuition. Private schools varied widely in size; some consisted of a single teacher working with a handful of students in his or her living room, whereas others were significantly larger. Both grammar and private schools were attended by boys from roughly age six to somewhere between thirteen and sixteen. Education was seen as a less pressing matter for girls than for boys, though middle-class families that had the funds and inclination sometimes sent their daughters to private schools run by women. The Taunton Commission, which studied British educational

---

[20] On the history of Puritanism in Britain, see Newton 1998.
[21] Smiles 1861, 305.
[22] On education in Britain in this period, see Lawson and Silver 1973, 164–266; Stephens 1998, 1–76; and Sutherland 1990.

institutions in the 1860s, found 572 grammar schools and about 10,000 private schools.[23]

Members of the landed gentry hired private tutors to teach their sons at home, or sent them either to grammar schools or to a special type of grammar school somewhat misleadingly called a public school. The term "public school" was based on the fact that these institutions came into existence as grammar schools that offered free instruction. However, over the course of time the institutions that became known as public schools began charging most of their students tuition and taking in boarders, and developed national reputations that drew in students from all over Britain. Public schools were relatively expensive and attracted boys primarily from families of landed gentry; Sydney Smith writing in the *Edinburgh Review* in 1810 stated that:

by a public school we mean an endowed place of education of old standing to which the sons of gentlemen resort in considerable numbers and where they continue to reside from eight or nine to eighteen years of age.[24]

In the early nineteenth century there were nine "canonical" public schools: Charterhouse School, Eton College, Harrow School, Merchant Taylors School, Rugby School, Shrewsbury School, St. Paul's School, Westminster School, and Winchester College.[25] Some boys went on to take a university degree from Oxford or Cambridge, though this was by no means felt to be necessary or even particularly important. The daughters of families of landed gentry typically received some education from either private tutors or local private schools.[26]

Public schools played a central role in the formation of modern-day sport, and the system of education used in those schools thus merits careful attention. The curriculum at these schools consisted largely of the study of Latin and Greek language and literature and Greek and Roman history, and gentlemen were expected to have at least some knowledge of the classical world. While at Eton in 1784, the future Lord Darnley wrote to his mother about studying Latin and the importance of acquiring "a refined Taste for the most elegant writings of the Classics, which is what no Gentleman should be without...."[27]

---

[23] The figures on the number of schools come from Mangan 1983, 314, drawing on Labouchere 1868–69.

[24] Quoted in McIntosh 1968, 16.

[25] Although the designation "college" is in the United States usually applied only to educational institutions for students that have completed twelfth grade, it can in Britain refer to something that corresponds very roughly to an American high school.

[26] On British public schools up through the nineteenth century, see Chandos 1984; Dunning and Sheard 2005, 40–49; Trevor May 2009; and the essays collected in Simon and Bradley 1975.

[27] Quoted in Wingfield-Stratford 1959, 269.

Students at public schools in the early nineteenth century were subjected to strict discipline in the classroom but otherwise had almost complete freedom. Each school was run by a headmaster with the help of teachers who were called masters. Students spent about fifteen or twenty hours per week in class, and during that time they were expected to obey the masters, who made heavy use of flogging. Most headmasters were clergymen, each school had a chapel, and students were required to go to chapel every morning and listen to the headmaster preach. Outside of the classroom and the chapel, students were at liberty to do largely as they pleased. Students typically came from much more privileged backgrounds than the masters and were not inclined to obey them except in the very specific contexts of the classroom and chapel. They lived in boarding houses that were privately owned and frequently run with minimal direct supervision by school officials. Edward Thring, later himself headmaster of a public school, recalled his experiences at Eton in the 1830s:

> Rough and ready was the life they led: cruel, at times, the suffering and the wrong; wild the profligacy. For after eight o'clock at night no prying eye came near till the following morning; no one lived in the same building; cries of joy and pain were equally unheard; and excepting a code of laws of their own, there was no help or redress for anyone.[28]

Unruly, sometimes outright violent, behavior by students was common. Drinking, gambling, consorting with prostitutes, and generally riotous behavior were all regular pastimes.

Intermittent attempts by headmasters and masters to control the boys' more outrageous conduct outside the classroom usually achieved nothing and sometimes ended in violent resistance. For example, in 1797, Dr. Ingles, the headmaster of Rugby, heard shots coming from one of the boarding houses in which students lived. He entered the house, saw a boy shooting out windows with a pistol loaded with cork pellets, and apprehended the culprit. The headmaster demanded to know who had sold him gunpowder. The boy gave the name of a local shopkeeper, who, fearful of trouble with the town's authorities, denied selling the boy gunpowder, whereupon the boy was flogged for lying. The boy and his friends retaliated by smashing the shopkeeper's windows, whereupon Dr. Ingles demanded that the boys pay for the damages. The boys responded by blowing the headmaster's office door open with explosives, smashing his windows, and burning desks, benches, and the headmaster's books. Soldiers and police were called in and restored order at sword-point. This was by no means a unique event. There were, for example, six major student rebellions at Winchester College between 1770 and 1818.[29]

---

[28] Quoted in Parkin 1900, 23.

[29] On the incident at the Rugby school, see Staunton 1869, 295–96. In some versions of the story, the boys contented themselves with nailing the headmaster's door shut instead of

There was, however, order of a sort imposed by the boys themselves, based largely on physical strength. Each school had a system of "fagging" in which older, stronger students compelled younger students to act as their personal servants. Informal assemblies were occasionally held in which the students as a whole, under the leadership of the oldest and strongest, discussed and decided upon matters that concerned them. Trials of strength between students were common. At Rugby "every new boy who entered the School, however young he might be...was invited to try his prowess with some other boy of the same size and age. There needed no quarrel, a boy's pluck must be shown, and if he declined to join the combat enjoined for him by bigger boys, he was taunted as a coward, and had to submit to be crowed over by the boy he declined to fight."[30]

The situation at public schools in the early 1800s may seem barbaric to modern-day sensibilities, but it needs to be seen in light of the strong importance the landed gentry attached to building and demonstrating manliness. Being a man was an essential part of being a gentleman, and a great deal of emphasis was placed on "manly character," which in practice meant possessing a strong, fit body and a high degree of mental and physical toughness. George Chapman, in his widely read *Treatise on Education* (first published in 1773), recommended that children be taught to "suffer pain with a manly spirit" and to that end suggested sports such as riding and fencing (with the cautionary note that "their exercises should be manly") as well as country air and cold baths.[31]

The education provided at public schools was much more focused on building character, particularly manliness, than on imparting knowledge. Boys who arrived at a public school at age eight were forced to fend for themselves in an environment that privileged physical toughness at all times, with the expectation that this would improve their character. The landed gentry certainly believed that the system worked; Sir John Moore, for example, wrote in 1786 that "I have perceived a certain hardihood and manliness of character in boys who have had a public education...."[32]

11.5. SPORT

In the early decades of the nineteenth century regular participation in sport in Britain was for the most part limited to the landed gentry. Boys from these families played sports from an early age, went on to public schools where sport was an essential component of their education, and

---

blowing it up. On rebellions at public schools, see Chandos 1984, 167–95; Dunning 1971, 135–36; and Dunning and Sheard 2005, 44–45.

[30] Bloxam 1889, 72–73.

[31] G. Chapman 1784, 135, 136, 131, respectively.

[32] Moore 1786, 1: 270.

continued playing sports as adults. People from the working class played sports occasionally. During this period a handful of sports attracted large numbers of spectators. The middle class tended to avoid sport, both as participants and spectators, because they saw it as a morally suspect activity.[33]

Sport was an important component of gentlemen's lifestyles. The landed gentry were notably fond of hunting, fishing, target shooting, and riding horses on their estates. John Chamberlayne in 1748 wrote in his *Magnae Britanniae Notitia, or the Present State of Great Britain* about "Hunting, Hawking, Setting, Horse-Racing, Fishing, Fowling, Coursing, Bowling, and Such Manly Sport, proper only to the Nobility, Gentry, and their Attendants."[34] An extreme example of the landed gentry's attachment to hunting can be found in George Robinson, the Marquess of Ripon (1827–1909), who calculated that he killed, over the course of thirty-three years of hunting: 142,343 pheasants; 97,579 partridges; 56,460 grouse; 29,858 rabbits; and 27,687 hares.[35] By the eighteenth century gentlemen had also picked up the habit of playing cricket. Games with a bat and ball had long been played informally in Britain, but it was not until the 1740s that the first set of formal rules for cricket were written and that gentlemen began playing the game regularly.[36]

Certain spectator sports, particularly horse racing, were also popular among the landed gentry. Horse racing had a long history in Britain and was closely associated with gentlemen, who raised horses and entered them in races. In the eighteenth century horse racing became more highly organized than before, due to the intervention of the landed gentry, who wrote formal rules and organized the Jockey Club to enforce them.[37] Much of the impetus for creating formal rules for cricket and horse racing was to provide a regularized environment that reduced gambling-related conflicts. About three-quarters of the contents of the earliest set of rules for horse racing, for example, had to do with betting.[38] Gentlemen were also known to watch, and in some cases sponsor, less reputable games in which both spectators and participants came largely from the working class. These games included

---

[33] On the history of sport in Britain in the eighteenth and early decades of the nineteenth centuries, good starting places can be found in N. Anderson 2010, 1–46; Brailsford 1999; and Holt 1992, 13–73, though see also Griffin 2005 and Malcolmson 1973, 34–51 (both of whom devote a great deal of attention to the use of space). On the social history of sport in nineteenth-century British public schools, see Mangan 1981. For details of how individual sports were played in nineteenth-century public schools, see Money 1997.

[34] Chamberlayne 1748, 415.

[35] These figures are given in Bédarida 1979 (1976), 132.

[36] On cricket, see Brookes 1978 and Williams 1989. On the particular subject of cricket in eighteenth-century Britain, see Underdown 2001.

[37] On horse racing in Britain, see Vamplew 1976 and Vamplew 1989.

[38] On betting and British sport during this period, see Brailsford 1992, 43–60.

boxing, wrestling, cock fighting, and bear and bull baiting (staged, bloody fights between dogs and a bear or a bull).[39]

The landed gentry played sports in part because they were a form of conspicuous consumption in that they absorbed considerable amounts of time without any obviously productive result. Moreover, members of the landed gentry were given to wagering large sums of money on a variety of different activities, such as card games and all kinds of sport, and looked upon sporting events as opportunities for a good party. Individual gentlemen were known to have wagered as much as £1,000, ten years salary for a skilled workman, on a single cricket match, and an article in the *Morning Chronicle* from 1774 reporting on a cricket match included a complaint about "excessive gambling and dissipation."[40]

Another and probably more important factor was that sport was seen as a key means of building and demonstrating manliness among the male members of the landed gentry. Sport was played by gentlemen from an early age and was a major component of life at public schools. Hunting, fishing, cricket, rowing, fives (a form of handball), cross-country running, and folk football were all popular with public school boys and were seen as healthy outdoor activities that built physical vigor and mental toughness. It is not coincidental that John Chamberlayne, quoted above, described hunting, horse racing, and fishing as "Manly Sport." However, it is in folk football that the sporting priorities of the landed gentry are perhaps most apparent.

A wide variety of informal games involving kicking a ball were played all over Europe from an early date. The details of those games, which had elements of the modern-day sports of soccer, rugby, and American football, varied from place to place; there were no written rules or limits on the number of participants or how long games could last. Historians, for want of a better term, put all of these games under the heading of "folk football." Folk football was played casually by boys from working-class families and, on major holidays, by both children and adults from the working class. It was also played on a regular basis by the students at public schools.[41]

The boys at each public school played their own version of folk football, all of which were, by modern-day standards, spectacularly violent. There were few if any restraints on what was permissible, and "hacking" – brutally kicking the shins of players on the opposing team – was customary. The students at Rugby wore special iron-tipped boots called "navvies" to heighten the damage they could do while hacking. Some sense of the chaotic violence of the folk football played at public schools during this

---

[39] On staged fights between animals in Britain in the late eighteenth and early nineteenth century, see Reid 1990.

[40] Quoted in Brailsford 1983, 36.

[41] On the origins of folk football and how it and its derivatives were played at British public schools, see Dunning and Sheard 2005, 1–68.

period can be had from Figure 3, an engraving with the title "Foot Ball at Rugby" dating from 1845; there is no sign of the ball, but many of the players seem intent on doing each other bodily harm. The Duke of Wellington, an Eton graduate from the late eighteenth century, is reputed to have said that "the battle of Waterloo was won on the playing fields of Eton."[42] It is unclear if Wellington ever actually made such a remark, but if he did there can be little doubt that what he had in mind were the qualities fostered by these types of games.

The violent games of folk football played at public schools were understood as a means of making the sons of the landed gentry into manly gentlemen. The classic account of sport in British public schools in the early decades of the nineteenth century can be found in Thomas Hughes' novel *Tom Brown's Schooldays*, which is based directly on Hughes' experiences at Rugby, where he was a student from 1834 to 1842. The hero of the story is Tom Brown, a boy from an old family of landed gentry, who is from the start an active, rugged individual who happily follows his father's advice to devote himself to sports such as cricket. He winds up at Rugby and immediately makes friends with a fellow student named East, who tells him about the version of folk football played at Rugby:

Why, you don't know the rules – you'll be a month learning them. And then it's no joke playing-up in a match, I can tell you.... Why, there's been two collar-bones broken this half, and a dozen fellows lamed. And last year a fellow had his leg broken.

The first game played after Tom's arrival consists of a two-hour long brawl between two teams, one with roughly 50 players and the other with 250, all of whom are on the field at the same time. At one point East defends his team's goal by charging head on into a much larger boy and succeeds, at some physical cost, in preventing the goal and demonstrating his manliness: "lame and half stunned...he hobbles back into goal, conscious of having played the man."[43]

After they left public school, gentlemen continued regularly playing most of the same sports that had occupied their attention as boys. The one sport that was played by gentlemen while at school but not afterward was folk football; despite its popularity at public schools, folk football's working-class origins made it problematic for a long time. Samuel Butler, the headmaster of Shrewsbury from 1798 to 1836, tried to prevent students from playing it on grounds that it was "more fit for farm boys and labourers than young gentlemen," and a former Eton student wrote in 1831 that, "I cannot consider the game of football at all gentlemanly. It is a game which the common people of Yorkshire are particularly partial to."[44]

---

[42] On this remark, see Boller and George 1989, 130–31.
[43] Hughes 1858 (1857), 2–3, 108, 123, respectively.
[44] Quoted in Dunning and Sheard 2005, 41, 36, respectively.

The sport-related activities of the working class were different and largely separate from those of the landed gentry. Until the early 1800s most of Britain's population lived in the countryside and made their living through agriculture. Working-class people in rural areas played sport informally on Sunday afternoons after church services and in a somewhat more formal way on special occasions that included local fairs and a half-dozen or so religious holidays each year. Informal sport was closely associated with pubs, which provided equipment and space for games such as cards and bowling. Special occasions featured events such as boxing and wrestling matches, cudgeling (fights with sticks), and bull and bear baiting. There was also a widespread tradition of villages competing against each other once a year in folk football. It would, therefore, be inaccurate to say that the working class suffered from a "leisure vacuum," but, at the same time, there was nothing resembling a system of organized sport that enabled and expected regular, avid participation and spectatorship by members of the working class.[45]

Some change in sport practice took place in the first half of the nineteenth century as large numbers of the working class moved to towns, where they took jobs in Britain's rapidly growing factories. The percentage of the population of Britain that lived in urban areas more than doubled from 1800 to 1850, from about 20% to about 50% of the total. Members of the working class living in cities and working in factories had less in the way of space and time to play sport, but more opportunities to spectate.[46]

Spectator sport emerged as a major pastime in the second half of the eighteenth century and continued to grow in popularity during the first half of the nineteenth century.[47] People in Britain had of course watched sport on an occasional basis from time immemorial. However, starting in the eighteenth century, it became much easier to bring large numbers of people together because improving transportation systems made it simpler to move around, and because urbanization meant that people lived in closer proximity to one another. The involvement of the landed gentry led to the growth of horse racing and cricket in the eighteenth century, and both sports attracted increasing numbers of spectators as time went on. In the eighteenth century, pedestrianism became a popular spectator sport. Pedestrianism included both competitive walking and running, and a pedestrian competition typically involved not a full slate of standard events but a specific challenge. For example, large crowds watched Barclay Allardice walk one mile every hour for a thousand hours in a row in June and July of 1809.[48] Boxing matches

---

45 On the sports played and watched by the British working class in the nineteenth century, see Cunningham 1980 and Jones 1988, 15–41.

46 On urbanization in Britain, see Gunn 2004 and the bibliography cited therein.

47 On the growth of commercialized sport in Britain in the late eighteenth and early nineteenth centuries, see A. Harvey 2004.

48 On pedestrianism, see Sears 2009, 40–56. On Barclay Allardice, see Thom 1813, 101–58.

attracted large audiences even though various acts of Parliament had made them illegal.[49] Other sports, such as rowing and cock fighting, were also popular with spectators.[50]

The participants in spectator sport other than cricket were primarily people from the working class seeking to earn money, and people from all levels of society came to watch them compete. Gentlemen showed a particular fondness for watching, and betting on, sport of all kinds. The reason why boxing matches could be regularly, if somewhat surreptitiously, held was that they were popular with gentlemen, which made enforcing the laws against them difficult.

Sport did not, however, do much to break down the barriers between social classes. At horse races members of the landed gentry typically sat in grandstands, separate from the rest of the crowd. Statutes in effect from the fourteenth century through the 1830s limited hunting, whether or not on one's own land, to those who owned estates.[51] Cricket was less socially exclusive, and teams, especially for relatively informal competitions held on local holidays, could include people from all social classes. However, the landed gentry dominated cricket played at a high level, because they devoted a great deal of time to becoming proficient. Moreover, individual gentlemen organized their own teams that could include a handful of professional players from the working class, who called their social betters "sir" and frequently used separate entrances and changing facilities.

Up through the 1840s the British middle class had a generally negative attitude toward sport and only limited involvement with it.[52] They inherited their negative attitude from the Puritans, who saw sport as a form of inexcusable idleness and who strongly objected to the gambling and drinking that took place at sporting events. The Puritans were particularly opposed to the habit, widespread in Britain from an early date, of playing sports informally on Sunday afternoons after the end of church services.

The Puritans' opposition to sport became one issue among many in their tense relationship with kings such as James I and Charles I. In 1618, James I reacted against Puritan attempts to curb sport on Sunday by issuing a "Declaration on Lawful Sports," which stated that "after the end of divine service our good people be not disturbed...or discouraged from any lawful recreation such as dancing, either men or women, archery for men, leaping,

---

[49] On boxing in Britain in the nineteenth century, see S. Shipley 1989.

[50] On spectator sport in early nineteenth-century Britain, see Guttmann 1985.

[51] On hunting laws in Britain in the nineteenth century, see Griffin 2007, 152–62.

[52] Many individual members of the middle class either participated in or watched sport, but sport was not at this point in time an activity that met with general approbation among the British middle class as a whole.

vaulting, or any other such harmless recreation."[53] James' successor Charles I reissued this declaration in 1633.[54]

When the Puritans gained control of the state in the 1640s, they launched an attack on sport. In 1643 they ordered all copies of the "Declaration on Lawful Sports" burnt, and in 1644 they banned sport on Sundays in a statute that read in part:

No person or persons shall hereafter upon the Lords-day use, exercise, keep, maintain, or be present at any wrestlings, Shooting, Bowling, Ringing of Bells for Pleasure or Pastime, Masque, Wake, otherwise called Feasts, Church-Ale, Dancing, Games, Sport, or Pastime whatsoever.[55]

In 1654 the Puritans banned entirely a range of sports such as hunting and horse racing.

The Puritans' bans on sport were overturned when they were driven from power, but their attitude toward sport persisted among the middle class. As Richard Holt has pointed out, in the early years of the nineteenth century, sport was an important element "in a festive culture that...had a high customary tolerance for violent behavior of all kinds along with a good deal of gambling, eating, and drinking."[56] All of these dimensions of sport provoked strongly negative reactions from most members of the middle class, and they typically did not play sports, and attended sporting events only with some hesitation. They had particularly strong objections to blood sports such as boxing and bear and bull baiting and sought to have them banned. William and Robert Chambers, for example, who came from a solidly middle-class family that made its money in textile manufacturing, wrote in 1842 that:

Horse-racing, with all its train of evils, may certainly be considered a disgrace of the age; and as one of the relics of barbarism, along with cock-fighting, bull-baiting, and prize-fighting, we should rejoice to see it for ever abandoned.[57]

Sport in Britain from 1800 to 1840, especially among the landed gentry, was profoundly horizontal; organizers and participants were for the most part one and the same, there was minimal regimentation, and the emphasis was squarely on benefits to participants. In regard to scale, there was more than a little sports activity in Britain from 1800 to 1840 but nothing that could be called mass sport. As Mike Huggins put it, "sport was not central to early Victorian life. It operated more on the margins, being irregular but not rare...."[58]

[53] Cheyney 1922, 422.
[54] On the British Puritans' attitudes toward sport and the social and political complications that resulted from those attitudes (including the reactions from James I and Charles I), see Birley 1993, 75–94.
[55] Quoted in Durston 1996, 214.
[56] Holt 1992, 28.
[57] Chambers and Chambers 1842, 419.
[58] Huggins 2004, 1.

12

Sport and Society in Britain from 1840 to 1870

12.1. SOCIAL HISTORY

A key moment in the democratization of Britain came in 1832 with the passage of the Representation of the People Act (typically known as the Reform Act of 1832 or the Great Reform Act). The early decades of the nineteenth century saw growing pressure to solve two problems: the right to vote was restricted to adult males who owned a certain amount of property, and the districts that sent representatives to the House of Commons were based on long out-of-date population distributions that favored rural areas and the landed gentry, so that many newer, large towns, where a substantial fraction of the middle class lived, were left without any representation at all. The landed gentry, which dominated both houses of Parliament, resisted calls for change for an extended period but finally gave way and passed the Reform Act of 1832, which reorganized many voting districts and provided for parliamentary representation for urban areas that had been previously unrepresented. It also changed the property requirements for voting in such a way as to increase the number of men eligible by 50% with the result that roughly 20% of all adult men in Britain, including all of the adult males in the landed gentry and most of those in the middle class, could vote.[1]

The erosion of the privileges formerly enjoyed by the landed gentry extended well beyond the electoral system. Up through the middle of the nineteenth century civil service jobs, which in many cases were prestigious and well-paid positions, were handed out primarily on the basis of family and political connections and tended to go to men from the landed gentry. Starting in 1853, however, many posts began to be filled on the basis of a

---

[1] For an overview of the history of Britain in this period, see Wasson 2010, 150–80. For a more thorough account, see the articles collected in F. M. L. Thompson 1990 as well as the volumes in the *New Oxford History of England* series. On the Reform Act of 1832, see Wicks 2006, 65–82.

competitive exam. A government decree of 1868 stated that "promotion by merit is the established rule in the Civil Service and to every young man who becomes the servant of the Crown in the CS [Civil Service], a way is opened to independence and even eminence."[2]

Much the same thing happened in the British army. Starting in the seventeenth century, most army officers had to purchase their commissions. Whereas Lord Cardigan set a record of sorts in 1836 when he paid £40,000 for a colonelcy that gave him command of the 11th Hussars, lower-ranking positions in less stylish units could be had for sums starting around £500. For obvious reasons these positions, which were felt to be well suited to gentlemen, were held almost entirely by men from among the landed gentry and from very wealthy middle-class families. The substandard performance of the British army during the Crimean War was blamed in part upon the incompetence of officers (Cardigan was the commander of the ill-fated charge of the Light Brigade in 1854), and in 1871 the sale of commissions as officers in infantry and cavalry regiments was abolished. A system of promotion based on merit was installed, over the objections of some senior army officers and members of Parliament, who felt that it would create a situation in which many officers would come from the lower classes, such men being suspected of harboring revolutionary tendencies.[3]

A similar shift took place at the same time in regard to education, and an array of different kinds of entrance and scholarship examinations came into being. For example, during the 1850s, Oxford and Cambridge Universities began offering standardized tests, the Oxford and Cambridge Local Exams, at sites all over Britain. They were intended for boys between sixteen and eighteen years of age, particularly those who had not gone to a public school, and scores on these exams were used to determine eligibility for entrance to many engineering, military, and medical schools and for civil service and teaching jobs. It is significant that they were frequently called "the middle class exams."[4]

The same process unfolded throughout British society, which, as a result, underwent a wave of democratization that was fueled in large part by meritocratic competition. Frances Cobbe, writing in 1864, observed that "life among all classes in the last generation seems to have been much less of a struggle than it is with us....As the classes were more marked, and there was very little possibility of rising from one into the other, so there was very little effort to do so...."[5]

That is not to say that Britain in 1870 was a completely democratized society. The landed gentry and the middle class reached a compromise that

[2] On meritocracy in the British civil service, see J. Davis 2006. The quote supplied here comes from page 29 of Davis' work.

[3] On the purchase of army commissions, see Bruce 1980 and Raugh 2004, 79–83.

[4] Lawson and Silver 1973, 314–63; Mitchell 2009, 181.

[5] Cobbe 1864, 482.

gave the middle class power and influence while excluding the working class. This is evident in the parliamentary debates that took place before the passage of the Reform Act of 1832. In speaking in favor of this act, Lord Brougham stated that the goal of the bill was, "to admit the middle class to a large and direct share in the representation, without any violent shock to the institutions of our country." He argued that:

the end of government is the happiness of the people; and I do not conceive that, in a country like this, the happiness of the people can be promoted by a form of government in which the middle classes place no confidence.

However, he also overtly rejected the idea that the vote should be extended to all adult men. He spoke in favor of giving the vote only to those people whose wealth put them solidly among the middle class and concluded that:

For the sake, therefore, of the whole society, for the sake of the labouring-classes themselves, I hold it to be clearly expedient that, in a country like this, the right of suffrage should depend on a pecuniary qualification....I oppose universal suffrage because I think it would produce a destructive revolution.[6]

The middle class thus gained power and privileges without evincing much concern for the working class. A new dominant group, composed of both the landed gentry and the more successful members of the middle class, took shape in the middle of the nineteenth century. For the purposes of simplicity we will call that group the "new dominant group" or simply "the upper class."[7]

The upper class adopted a set of goals and values that reflected the ideas of both the landed gentry and the middle class and that were enshrined in the ideal of the "Christian gentleman."[8] The Christian gentleman valued meritocracy based on competitive, individual effort and was devoted to achieving success through hard work and to living a sober, pious life. However, the Christian gentleman also necessarily came from a respectable family, was well educated and concerned about his manliness, saw public service as an important goal, and was ready to work cooperatively with others. The Christian gentleman thus pursued goals and social rules that came as much from the landed gentry as from the middle class.[9]

---

[6] MacAulay 1853, 1:12, 21, 13, respectively.

[7] On the social classes in Britain in the middle of the nineteenth century, see Hoppen 1998, 31–90.

[8] The term "Christian gentleman" had a long history in Britain. During the nineteenth century it was redefined and became significantly more popular. See Nicolson 1955, 184–204.

[9] It is important to bear in mind that the landed gentry and the middle class continued in some ways to exist as separate groups for an extended period of time. Issues such as geography and occupation continued to set them apart from each other, and less well-off members of the middle class were not in a position to mingle freely with the landed gentry.

12.2. EDUCATION

The ideal of the new Christian gentleman was to a large extent shaped in Britain's public schools and was embodied in their graduates. In the public schools the sons of the landed gentry and the middle class mixed together and created a new elite with a hybridized set of goals and social rules. As Martin Wiener put it, there was:

a new upper stratum...produced by the coming together of businessmen, the rapidly expanding professional and bureaucratic classes, and the older gentry and aristocracy. The central institution of the consolidation [was] the public school ....[10]

As members of the middle class gained social and political privileges in the first half of the nineteenth century, they increasingly saw it as critical that their children receive the sort of education given at the public schools. An important reason for this shift was that these schools were believed to provide an education particularly well suited to training boys for positions of responsibility.

When the Reform Act of 1832 was nearing passage, Thomas Arnold, a prominent educator and headmaster at Rugby School from 1828 to 1841, wrote two letters to the *Sheffield Courant* with the title "Education of the Middle Classes." Arnold began by pointing to the ongoing political shifts in British society:

We are all aware of the growing power of the middling classes of society, and we know that the Reform Bill will at once increase this power, and consolidate it. But power, like every other gift bestowed upon us by God's Providence, is not a mere gratuity, but a trust ....

He went on to argue that giving the vote to the middle class required that they have a suitable education and expressed concern that the schools that children from middle-class families typically attended did not prepare them for the exercise of power, because they received a practical rather than a liberal (i.e., one suited to a free man) education. He called for government intervention "to provide for the middling classes something analogous to the advantages afforded to the richer classes by our great public schools...."[11]

Arnold's opinion was shared by many members of the middle class, who began looking for ways to give their sons something like a public school education. The wealthiest middle-class families managed to get their sons into the established nine public schools, but these schools had neither the ability nor desire to accommodate large numbers of middle-class students.

---

[10] Wiener 2004, 11. On education in Britain in this period, see Lawson and Silver 1973, 267–313; Stephens 1998, 1–76; and Sutherland 1990.

[11] Arnold 1858, 226 and 230, respectively.

The solution was found in the creation of significant numbers of new schools modeled closely on the established public schools and in the restructuring of some extant schools. These new schools, typically private institutions that charged tuition and at which students boarded, were squarely aimed at the middle class. Nathaniel Woodward, who founded what became a chain of seventeen such schools, wrote that his goal was to offer "a good and complete education for the middle Classes at such a charge as will make it available to most of them."[12] The term "public school" was gradually expanded to include both the original nine public schools and the other schools that imitated them.

Middle-class families, however, deeply disapproved of many aspects of the system of education at public schools, and the same became true of many members of the landed gentry as they began to adopt the middle class belief in the importance of hard work, sobriety, and piety. William Roberts, an Eton graduate whose *Portraiture of a Christian Gentleman* (1829) proved to be very popular, asked, "Can it be affirmed of any of our public schools, that any system exists in them for placing virtue, reason, and religion, above force, and tyranny, and passion?"[13] He supplied a litany of reasons to answer that question in the negative.

A movement to reform the established public schools took shape, and the measures put in place at Rugby by Thomas Arnold were widely imitated elsewhere. Arnold sought to curb the prevailing anarchy and moral laxity by establishing some control over the fagging system, reforming the boarding houses, ruthlessly expelling boys who refused to conform to his expectations, and preaching passionately. He did not want to eliminate so much as to put some checks on the boys' traditional liberty to do as they wished outside the classroom. To that end, he left the fagging system largely intact but himself appointed a group of boys, called praepostors, who oversaw its daily operation, and he sought to appoint praepostors who would make certain that all students behaved morally. The running of the boarding houses in which the students lived was supervised more closely than before, and Arnold, unlike most prior headmasters, was unafraid to expel misbehaving students regardless of their family connections. Finally, Arnold, who was renowned for the ardent sermons he preached to his students in chapel, was deeply dedicated to making Rugby into a school that produced Christian gentlemen. After expelling several boys for misbehavior, he told the students that "It is *not* necessary that this should be a school of three hundred, or one hundred, or of fifty boys; but it *is* necessary that it should be a school of Christian gentlemen."[14]

---

[12] Quoted in Dixon, McIntosh, Munrow, and Willetts 1960, 179.

[13] Roberts 1831, 105.

[14] Stanley 1845, 77. On Arnold's reforms at Rugby and on those subsequently enacted at other public schools, see Chandos 1984, 247–351. Influential early biographical treatments of

The reforms instituted by Arnold and by other headmasters made the public schools into institutions that socialized boys into the new system of goals and social rules that were coming to characterize the merged ruling group of landed gentry and the middle class. This involved not just the establishment of order and a higher moral tone, but also a strong meritocratic ethos. A nineteenth-century history of the Rugby School praised Arnold's system of choosing praepostors as one that ensured "that power shall be in the hands of those who are not only fitted by bodily strength for the mastery, but are, on the whole, an 'aristocracy selected by merit.'"[15] A biographer of Samuel Butler, headmaster of Shrewsbury from 1798 to 1836, wrote that "his crowning merit was the establishment of an emulative [i.e., competitive] system, in which talent and industry always gained their just recognition and reward in good examinations."[16]

The reformed public schools were seen as playing a critical role in turning boys from the landed gentry and from wealthy, middle-class families into men suited to occupy positions of power and influence. The Clarendon Commission, which investigated the state of the nine canonical public schools in the 1860s, issued a report that read in part:

Among the services which [these schools] have rendered is...the creation of a system of government and discipline for boys...which is admitted to have been most important in its effects on national character and social life. It is not easy to estimate the degree to which the English people are indebted to these schools for the qualities on which they pique themselves most – for their capacity to govern others and control themselves, their aptitude for combining freedom with order, their public spirit, their vigour and manliness of character...their love of healthy sports and exercise. These schools have been the chief nurseries of our statesmen; in them, and in schools modeled after them, men of all the various social classes that make up English society...have been brought up on a footing of social equality...and they have had perhaps the largest share in moulding the character of the English gentleman.[17]

12.3. SPORT

Between 1840 and 1870, sport in Britain was reshaped and formalized in accordance with the goals and social rules of the new upper class, and men from wealthier middle-class families became regular and avid athletes. Both of these changes had their roots in the new and old public schools, which in many ways were the cradles of modern-day sport in the Western world.[18]

Arnold can be found in Stanley 1845 and Strachey 1918, 205–42. For a more up-to-date consideration of his life, see Copley 2002.

[15] Rouse 1898, 337.

[16] Butler 1896, 1:252.

[17] Clarendon 1864, 1: 56.

[18] On the history of sport in Britain in the middle of the nineteenth century, see N. Anderson 2010, 23–86; Holt 1992, 57–202; Holt 2008; Huggins 2006; and Tranter 1998, 1–51. On sport in nineteenth-century British public schools, see Mangan 1981.

The sports played at public schools in the middle of the nineteenth century were largely the same as those played in the preceding generation. The most prestigious sports were football, cricket, and rowing. Hunting and fishing became less important at the old public schools and did not take hold at the new ones. Cross-country running was gradually regularized into the sport that became track-and-field (which was called "athletics" in Britain) and became increasingly popular with time.

The changing tone of the lives of students at public schools was almost immediately reflected in their sport. This is most evident in folk football, and here again Rugby School led the way. The local version of folk football at Rugby became progressively more organized and less violent starting around 1840. In 1839 or 1840, football matches with equal numbers of boys on each team began to be played. In 1845 Rugby students drew up the first set of written rules for their version of folk football, and those rules limited the degree of permissible violence in the game. Rules XXV and XVIII, for example, were "No hacking with the heel or above the knee is fair" and "No player may wear projecting nails or iron plates on the soles or heels of his shoes or boots." The other established public schools followed suit, with the result that widely varying sets of written rules for playing folk football came into being.[19]

Thomas Arnold had almost no interest in sport, but headmasters at other public schools rapidly seized upon sports such as football and cricket as a means of establishing a greater degree of order in the lives of their students. At the most basic level this was because playing these sports kept boys on the grounds of the school, where they were less likely to get into trouble and where it was easier to supervise them. To this end, Arnold actively sought to prevent his students from going hunting and fishing, which seems to have had the unintended effect of making football and cricket more popular. He did not, however, do anything to encourage his students' interests in sport.

G. E. L. Cotton, who had worked as a master under Arnold at Rugby, took the next logical step when he became headmaster of a newly founded public school, Marlborough College, in 1852. He made a conscious decision to use sport to help control students' behavior. Upon his arrival at Marlborough he sent a letter to the parents of his students in which he wrote that:

The mass of the school are not trained up to cricket and football at all, which, as healthy and manly games, are certainly deserving of general encouragement. Instead of this, the money [from fees paid by the boys] which should be devoted to the

---

[19] On the transformation of folk football in nineteenth-century British public schools, see Dunning and Sheard 2005, 17–86. The Rugby School rules of 1845 are discussed on pages 81–83. For a critique of Dunning and Sheard's work, in which it is argued that members of the working class played a key role in the formation of modern football, see Goulstone 2000.

legitimate games of the school, is spent on other amusements, often of a questionable character in themselves, or at least liable to considerable abuse, and which have no effect in providing constant and wholesome recreation for the boys.[20]

Cyril Norwood, who was headmaster at Marlborough in the early twentieth century, observed that Cotton created "a school out of mutineers, and he consciously developed organised games as one of the methods by which the school should be brought into order."[21]

Cotton broke new ground by encouraging the regular playing of sports by his students and by imposing a much higher level of organization. He divided the students into "houses," each of which had about fifty members and each of which was run by masters who were chosen for their enthusiasm for sport and who spent as much time playing sports with their students and serving as athletic coaches as they did teaching. When choosing praepostors, Cotton showed a marked preference for talented athletes. He also introduced competitions between houses in order to heighten students' interests in sport and raised money to buy land for sports fields; Marlborough had two acres of sports fields in 1845, sixty-eight acres in 1900.[22]

Boys from middle-class families who attended public schools became enthusiastic supporters of playing sports in a regular and serious fashion. This is most apparent from the fact that it was the new public schools, places like Marlborough, that took a leading role in promoting the importance of sport. These schools were specifically created for and largely populated by the sons of the middle class.

This major shift in attitudes of the middle class toward sport was the result of a number of factors. The imposition of formal, written rules and regular adult supervision curbed many of the violent excesses that had characterized public school sports in earlier periods, and this made sport more respectable and acceptable. As upward social mobility became more possible, members of the middle class became eager to show that they belonged in polite society, and participation in sport was an important way to do that. Public health became something of an obsession in Victorian England, and sport was seen as helpful in producing *mens sana in corpore sano*.

Sport was also a way for boys from middle-class families to prove their manliness. Middle-class families tended to come from urban areas and frequently did not have backgrounds in which everyday life included regular, vigorous physical activity of the sort common among the landed gentry, who typically lived in the countryside. Time spent on sports fields was portrayed as an essential means of toughening boys up, and for the many

---

[20] Quoted in McIntosh 1968, 38–39.
[21] Quoted in Mangan 1981, 28. On G. E. L. Cotton, see Mangan 1981, 22–28, 32–34, 66–67, 74–75 and McIntosh 1968, 38–39.
[22] The figures on the area devoted to sports fields at Marlborough come from Mangan 1981, 71.

public-school graduates who went on to become military officers and who served in Britain's army all over the globe, sport was understood as preparation for the battlefield.[23] Henry Newbolt's poem *Vitai Lampada*, published in 1897, clearly articulates the perceived connection between playing sports and battlefield bravery:

> There's a breathless hush in the Close tonight
> Ten to make and the match to win-
> A bumping pitch and a blinding light,
> An hour to play and the last man in.
> And it's not for the sake of a ribboned coat,
> Or the selfish hope of a season's fame
> But his captain's hand on his shoulder smote
> Play up! Play up! and play the game.
> The sand of the desert is sodden and red
> Red with the wreck of a square that broke
> The Gatling's jammed and the Colonel dead,
> And the regiment blind with dust and smoke.
> The river of death has brimmed his banks
> And England's far and Honour a name,
> But the voice of a schoolboy rallies the ranks;
> Play up! Play up! and play the game.[24]

Finally, and perhaps most significantly, playing sports became closely linked to Christian piety through what was typically called Muscular Christianity, the most basic element of which was the belief that Christians had a duty to keep their bodies fit. Moses Coit Tyler wrote in 1869 that:

The creed of Muscular Christianity is as brief as it is just, comprehensive, and sublime:
ALL ATTAINABLE HEALTH IS A DUTY.
ALL AVOIDABLE SICKNESS IS A SIN.[25]

This ran directly counter to a deeply engrained habit among Christian thinkers that took the body as a source of sin and something to be suppressed rather than celebrated. However, Muscular Christians frequently went further and asserted that playing sports helped shape physically and spiritually sound individuals who were equipped to go out in the world and do

---

[23] On concerns about masculinity in middle-class families in Britain in the nineteenth century and how those concerns were reflected in sport, see the articles collected in Mangan and Walvin 1987.

[24] Newbolt 1897, 21. The fascinating connections between the emergent obsession with sport and British imperialism have been the subject of much good scholarship. See, for instance, Holt 1992, 203–79; Holt 1996; and Mangan 1998. An overview of many of the key themes in that scholarship can be found in N. Anderson 2010, 155–77.

[25] Tyler 1869, 164.

good. Charles Kingsley, who was among the earliest advocates of Muscular Christianity, wrote that:

Games conduce, not merely to physical, but to moral health…in the playing-field boys acquire virtues which no books can give them; not merely daring and endurance, but better still, temper, self-restraint, fairness, honour, unenvious approbation of another's success, and that "give and take" of life which stand a man in such good stead when he goes forth into the world ….[26]

There was of course nothing particularly new in Britons looking to sport to build character. What was new was that the character traits fostered by sport were now seen as extending well beyond physical and mental toughness and being specifically linked to what were understood as Christian values.[27]

The ideas associated with Muscular Christianity are clearly articulated in the work of Thomas Hughes, who published *Tom Brown's Schooldays* in 1857 and *Tom Brown at Oxford* in 1861. In *Schooldays*, Tom Brown is a star athlete who undergoes a religious conversion while at Rugby; his dual interests are nicely symbolized when a friend gives him two gifts, a fishing rod and a Bible.[28] However, when *Schooldays* was written the belief that sport fostered piety had not yet coalesced. That had changed by the time Hughes wrote *Tom Brown at Oxford*, which contains a chapter with the title "Muscular Christianity," in which Hughes writes:

Our hero on his first appearance in public some years since [i.e., in *Schooldays*], was…at once…enrolled for better or worse in the brotherhood of muscular Christians, who at that time were beginning to be recognized as an actual and lusty portion of general British life….I cannot see where he could in those times have fallen under a nobler brotherhood.

Hughes goes on to differentiate between the "muscleman" who has "no belief whatever as to the purposes for which his body has been given him" and Muscular Christians:

The least of the muscular Christians has hold of the old chivalrous and Christian belief, that a man's body is given him to be trained and brought into subjection, and then used for the protection of the weak, the advancement of all righteous causes, and the subduing of the earth which God has given to the children of men.[29]

Proponents of Muscular Christianity thus argued that sport produced gentlemen who were prepared to go out in the world and be good Christians.

[26] Kingsley 1893, 86.
[27] On the early history of Muscular Christianity, see N. Anderson 2010, 67–86 and Putney 2001, 11–18.
[28] Hughes 1858 (1857), 357.
[29] Hughes 1895 (1861), 112 and 113, respectively.

That, in turn, made sport much more acceptable than it had been in the past, when it was associated with vices such as drinking and gambling.

By 1870 regular participation in sport was compulsory in most public schools, and sport grew to be so important that in many cases intellectual training became almost an afterthought. Edward Thring, headmaster of Uppingham School from 1853 to 1887, rearranged teaching schedules so that boys were done with the classroom by noon and could devote entire afternoons to sport. Oscar Browning, a master at Eton in the 1860s, complained that:

> It is the most difficult thing at a public school to create a proper appreciation of intellectual distinction....The most influential boys in the school are the captains of the boats, and of the eleven [the cricket team], and those who chiefly support them. These, though admirable for regularity and good conduct, are scarcely ever distinguished for scholarship or mathematics.[30]

There were also complaints that star athletes did little in the way of academic work, which was mostly done for them. Arnold Lunn, who attended Harrow in the 1870s, recalled that:

> The Homeric heroes who led our cohorts into battle on the playing fields of Harrow disported themselves at ease during the hours set aside for homework, while the local intelligentsia did their homework for them.[31]

This development is not entirely surprising given that students were expected to spend two to three hours a day on sport, and captains and the best athletes typically spent five hours a day on the playing fields.

The entrance of the sons of middle-class families into public schools, the rapid expansion of the number of public schools, and the escalating importance of sport at those schools all combined to produce an unprecedented number of British men who were dedicated athletes. Starting in the 1840s there was a large and growing number of public school graduates – called "old boys"[32] – who were in the habit of playing sports and who wished to continue doing so after they left their various schools.

Some of the earliest effects of this phenomenon were felt at Cambridge and Oxford, which were populated largely by public school graduates. Sports had been played at these universities from an early date; at Cambridge, for example, the vice-chancellor had decreed in 1555 that "the unscholarlike exercise of football and meetings tending to that end [must] henceforth utterly cease."[33] However, up through the early decades of the nineteenth century the students at both universities played sports intermittently and informally. Oxford, for example, had but a single cricket field in 1800, and

[30] Clarendon 1864, 2: 147.
[31] Lunn 1940, 29.
[32] The term is a shortened version of "old school boy," where "old" means "former" and school refers to a public school. The complete phrase in contemporary American English would be something like "former public school student."
[33] Quoted in Baker 1988, 75.

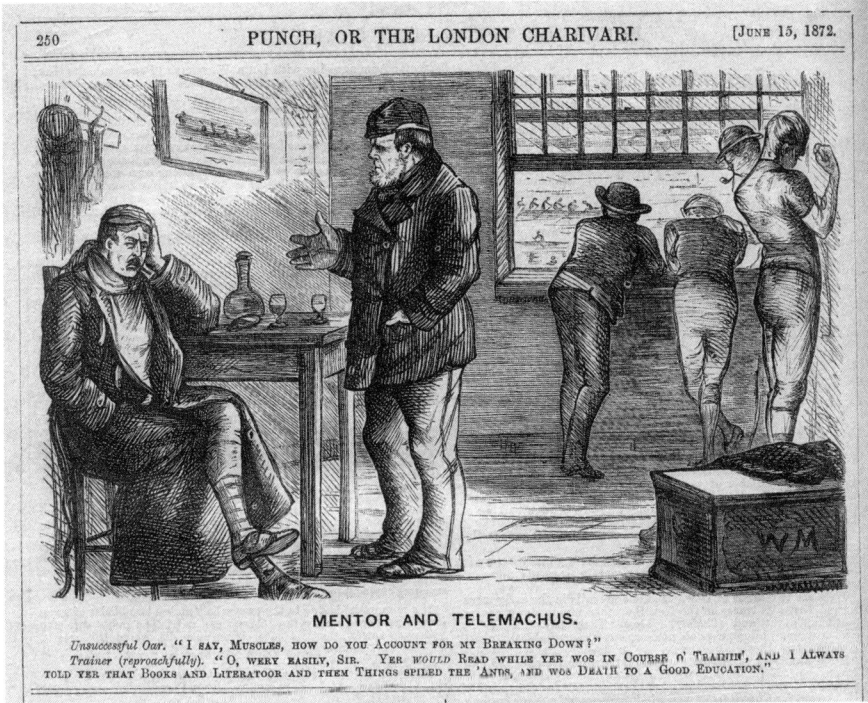

FIGURE 11. Cartoon from the June 15, 1872, Edition of *Punch* Showing Unsuccessful Rower and Coach

to the extent that students got regular exercise, it mostly came in the form of walking in the countryside around campus. The situation changed suddenly as a wave of public school graduates arrived with a near-fanatical interest in sport. Signs of things to come were already evident in the late 1820s, when the earliest sports competitions between Cambridge and Oxford were held: in 1827 they played their first cricket match against each other, and two years later they squared off against each other in rowing for the first time. It is striking that these universities existed in relatively close proximity for over six centuries (Oxford was founded in 1096, Cambridge in 1209), before they competed against each other in sports.[34]

The student–athlete who was more athlete than student rapidly became as common at Oxford and Cambridge as he was at the public schools. A cartoon that reflects this situation, showing what is probably an Oxford or Cambridge rower speaking to his trainer after losing a race, appeared in the British humor magazine *Punch* in 1872 (Figure 11).

As the number of old boys accustomed to playing sports rose sharply, they needed to build new organizations and facilities and to create standardized

[34] On sport at Oxford and Cambridge Universities in the nineteenth century, see Chandler 1988.

sets of rules. This process was particularly evident in regard to folk football, which changed so much in the 1840s as to make it virtually a new sport. In the 1830s and 1840s old boys at Oxford and Cambridge began playing football with some regularity, which caused immediate difficulties because different public schools played different versions of the game. Almost from the outset the versions played at Eton and Rugby established themselves as the primary alternatives; the Eton game prohibited carrying the ball and hacking (intentionally kicking other players in the shins), whereas the Rugby game permitted both. A group of old boys at Cambridge in 1848 agreed on a set of rules that were based largely on the Eton game. In the 1850s old boys who were finished with school began forming clubs to play football, and, as the number of clubs multiplied and clubs began playing each other, it became imperative to establish standardized rules. In 1863, representatives of some of the leading clubs formed the Football Association to serve as a governing body for the sport and settled on a set of rules that was based directly on those drawn up at Cambridge in 1848. This enraged the representatives of several clubs, who played the Rugby version of football; they saw the prohibition on hacking as "unmanly" and refused to join the Football Association. The clubs that played the Rugby game eventually formed their own association, the Rugby Football Union, and wrote their own set of rules in 1871. The Football Association version of the game picked up a nickname by the shortening of its official name, Association Football, first to "socca" or "socker" and then to "soccer."[35]

Similar changes took place in other sports, new and old. A couple of examples will suffice to give a sense of the nature and scale of these changes. Track-and-field, drawing on the earlier traditions of cross-country running and pedestrianism, became a clearly defined sport around 1840. The first purpose-built tracks were constructed in the late 1830s, starting with a narrow cinder track, designed for two-man races, around Lord's cricket ground in London in 1837. Shrewsbury held one of the earliest recorded track meets in 1840, and regular meets were held at Oxford beginning in 1850. In 1861, the West London Rowing Club, a highly respectable group, held what proved to be a popular track meet for its members. In 1864 Oxford and Cambridge competed against each other in track-and-field for the first time. In 1866, the Amateur Athletic Club was founded to arrange track-and-field competitions for its members and was an immediate success.[36]

Formalization and growth also occurred in long-established sports such as rowing. Professional boatmen working on the Thames had organized

---

[35] On the history of Association football, see Taylor 2008. On the history of rugby, see Collins 1998. For revisionist accounts of the early history of soccer, accounts that diverge from the version given above, which is influenced by the work of Dunning and Sheard, see Collins 2005 and Goulstone 2000.

[36] On the early history of track-and-field in Britain, see Crump 1989 and Lovesey 1979.

races in the early part of the eighteenth century, and by the end of that century, boys at public schools were racing oared boats. For a long time, however, there was little in the way of formal rules, there was no standardization of the boats used in races in regard to such issues as the number of rowers, and the boats used were the same as those employed on an everyday basis for practical purposes of getting about. Starting in the 1820s rowing competitions became more common at public schools and at Oxford and Cambridge (the first Oxford-Cambridge boat race was held in 1829). Not long thereafter competitions for individuals who were rowing enthusiasts but not professional boatmen, a group in which old boys figured prominently, began to be founded in growing numbers. (The Henley Regatta, currently the most prestigious rowing competition in the world, was established in 1839.) During the same period the sport was rapidly systematized, specific types of boats became standard, and specially designed racing boats began to be built. Outriggers, which made narrower and faster boats possible, were first used in 1828 and were perfected in 1841. The first completely functional racing shell – a boat with a thin, smooth hull and without a keel – was built in 1856. Sliding seats began to be used around 1870.[37]

These examples could be multiplied further, but the basic point is already clear: British sport underwent a profound transformation between 1840 and 1870. New sports such as Association football and rugby were invented, and old sports such as rowing were updated and systematized. Sport became seen as a critical element in the education and lifestyle of the new upper class. Most importantly, there was a fundamental upward shift in participation. Members of the middle class, due in large part to their experiences in the public schools, began playing sports in large numbers both at school and afterward. This made Britain unique among its contemporaries, with the result that "Visitors to Victorian Britain were often surprised by the amount of time devoted to sport amongst the middle and upper classes."[38]

The changes that took place between 1840 and 1870 introduced to British sport more of a vertical element than had been the case before, but sport in Britain nonetheless remained fundamentally horizontal, as is clear from the fashion in which it was organized, the absence of regimentation, and the stress on the benefits to participants.

Did Britain have mass sport in 1870? The best answer is: almost. A comparison with the situation in ancient Greece may be helpful in establishing some basic parameters. By the sixth century BCE, boys and men from 40% or 50% of the families in any given Greek community were expected to play sports regularly. The equivalent figure for Britain in 1870 would be 15–20%, and even that figure is probably too high. Many if not most of the

---

[37] On the development of the sport of rowing in the nineteenth century, see Dodd 1989 and Lehmann 1908, 1–23.
[38] Holt 1992, 74.

male members of middle-class families who became avid athletes between 1840 and 1870 picked up the habit at a public school. The costs of attending such schools ranged from as much as £200 per year for a high-brow institution such as Eton to as low as £50 for more modest schools. This put them within reach of wealthier middle-class families, and the social and economic benefits of attending a public school were so obvious that families that could afford to send their sons to one tended to do so. However, public schools were out of reach for many less well-off middle-class families, which had incomes of £150–200 annually.[39] This meant that it was mostly the wealthier members of the middle class who took up the practice of sport between 1840 and 1870. On the other hand, sport participation by even that section of the middle class produced an exponential increase in the number of regular athletes, who had previously come primarily from the landed gentry, which represented less than 1% of the total population of Britain. Moreover, the social structure of nineteenth-century Britain was such that households were relatively smaller than those in ancient Greece, so that the 15–20% of families that had male members actively involved in sport represented a larger percentage of the total population than it would have in Greece. If Britain did not have mass sport by 1870, it was certainly on the verge of it.

Before moving on to look at social history, education, and sport in Britain from 1870 to 1900, we will pause briefly to consider the situation in nineteenth-century Germany.

[39] Detailed evidence on the cost of attending a public school can be found in the testimony recorded in Clarendon 1864.

13

Sport in Nineteenth- and Early
Twentieth-Century Germany

This chapter provides background information on the development of German gymnastics and a brief sketch of the history of mass sport in Germany up to the outbreak of World War II. Some knowledge of the origins of gymnastics is necessary to understand sport in late nineteenth-century Britain, and Germany seems to have been the first known example of a society that had vertical mass sport. The history of sport in Germany thus warrants a certain amount of attention but not, in the context of a study of the relationship between horizontal mass sport and democratization, a full-blown case study along the lines of those of Greece and Britain undertaken in other chapters.

13.1. HISTORICAL OVERVIEW

Prior to 1870, the territory that became Germany was divided into a number of independent states, most of which were relatively small. The two big states to the west and south, France and Austro-Hungary, did not want these independent states to coalesce into a large nation that would be a threat to them and did everything they could to keep them apart. However, by the early nineteenth century, many people in the various German states had begun to argue for unification. The biggest of the German states, Prussia, gradually built a united Germany under its leadership, a process that culminated in 1870.[1]

The structure of German society throughout the nineteenth century bore some resemblance to that in Britain at the start of the nineteenth century in that there was a small hereditary aristocracy, a sizeable middle class that was divided into an upper (the *Bürgertum*) and lower (the *Mittelstand*) stratum, and a large working class. The middle class subscribed to a set of

---

[1] For a concise introduction to German history, see Fulbrook 1990 or Kitchen 1996. For more detailed accounts, see Kitchen 2006 and G. Mann 1968.

values that stressed "the principles of achievement and education, work, thrift, and self-reliance" and many of its members "supported the emerging vision of a modern, secularized, postcorporate, self-regulating, enlightened order."[2]

The waves of democratization that swept through Europe starting in the late eighteenth century affected Germany in a variety of ways, but throughout the nineteenth century German society was less democratized than its British counterpart. The national legislative body formed as part of unification, the *Reichstag*, was elected through universal male suffrage, and a strong strain of radical socialism developed in Germany at a relatively early date. However, a monarchy and an aristocracy, along with a bureaucracy and army led by aristocrats, wielded a great deal of influence. Post-unification Germany "was an authoritarian state and its parliament…had limited powers. The power of the monarchy was untouched, the nobility retained their privileged position, and the army was further strengthened."[3] Full parliamentary government did not arrive until after Germany's defeat in World War I, and even then met with stiff resistance and lasted less than twenty years before being dissolved by the Nazis. When Hitler took power he told a group of generals that he would deliver "strict authoritarian rule that would rid Germany of the 'cancer' of democracy."[4]

The relative lack of democratization in Prussia and later a united Germany is evident from a comparison of the democratization scores assigned by the Polity Project to Britain and Prussia/Germany, as shown in Figure 12. The scholars who generate the Polity Project democratization scores suggest that a democratic regime is represented by a score of plus six or higher, which Britain achieved in 1880 and maintained thereafter, but which Germany did not achieve until 1919 and maintained only until 1932, before collapsing into autocracy.[5]

One of the reasons why democratization made less progress in Germany than elsewhere in Europe was a deeply rooted attachment to a set of ideas that included a valorization of tradition, a Romanticized view of the history of the German *Volk*, and a chauvinistic belief in the superiority of the German *Volk* and in the need for racial purity. Those ideas were popular among the aristocracy and found increasing support among a middle class reacting against growing political radicalism among workers. The popularity of such ideas played an important role in enabling unification, but also nurtured a considerable degree of social and political conservatism and acquiescence in if not active support for authoritarianism.

[2] Kocka 2010, 12.
[3] Kitchen 1996, 203.
[4] Kitchen 2006, 258.
[5] On the Polity Project democratization scores, see Section 11.1.

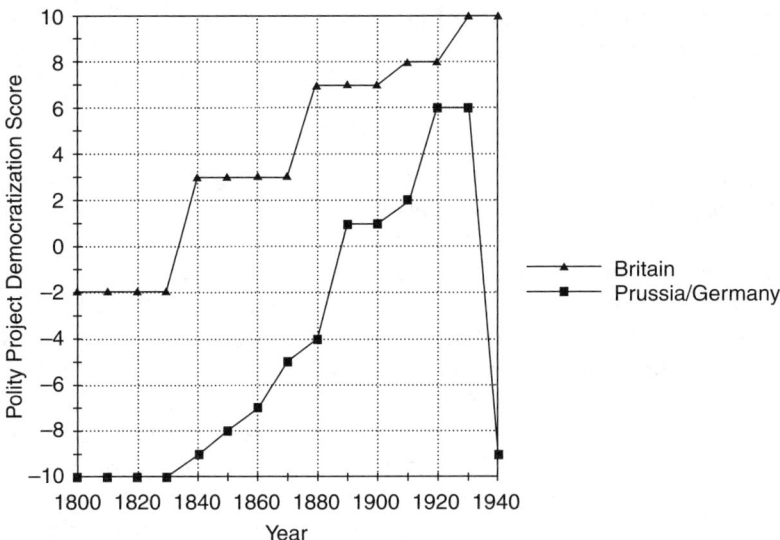

FIGURE 12. Polity Project Democratization Scores for Britain and Germany, 1800–1940, by Decade

13.2. EDUCATION

In the eighteenth century, Prussia initiated the construction of one of Europe's first publicly funded education systems. State inspection of religious and private educational institutions began in 1715, compulsory attendance laws for children five to thirteen years of age were instituted in 1763, and by the 1830s there was a nationwide system of tax-financed public schools attended by the majority of children up to the age of fourteen. Further education in secondary schools and universities was available to much smaller numbers.[6]

The Prussian education system was noteworthy for the degree to which it was subject to direct state control and for the discipline it demanded from teachers and students. "Prussian education developed under rigid central control with a disciplined and hierarchical organizational structure and a level of political policing over the curriculum which was scarcely matched in any other country."[7] The French philosopher and educational reformer Victor Cousin, who visited and wrote about Prussia's schools in the early part of the nineteenth century, commented that, "When we enter one of the great normal schools of Saxony, or of Brandenburg, we cannot help being

---

[6] On the Prussian education system, see Cousin 1834 (1831); Green 1990, 116–30; and Pollard 1956, 85–99.
[7] Green 1990, 120.

struck with the perfect order and austere discipline which prevail there, as in a Prussian barrack."[8]

13.3. GYMNASTICS

During the nineteenth century what was then called "gymnastics" became one of the most important forms of sport in much of Europe. In the present day, gymnastics involves exercises that display strength, balance, and agility in movement, either on a mat or on apparatus such as a vaulting horse or parallel bars. In the nineteenth century, however, gymnastics could be something very different and frequently had a strong element of regimented group movement that was similar in many ways to military drill.

Gymnastics developed first in Germany, starting in the late eighteenth century. This was a period when there was a considerable amount of experimentation with new and different forms of education. Many people in Germany were influenced by Rousseau, who argued that education should include time spent exercising outdoors, and German educators set up a small number of experimental schools where boys were required to go outdoors regularly and jump over ditches, balance on beams, climb ropes, and so on. One of the leading figures in designing and promoting these exercises, Johann Christoph Friedrich GutsMuths, called them *Gymnastik*, based on the ancient Greek terminology for sport.[9]

In the early nineteenth century, German gymnastics underwent something akin to a rebirth due to the efforts of Friedrich Ludwig Jahn, who redesigned the exercises inherited from GutsMuths and set up a small outdoor training ground in Berlin, the capital of Prussia. Gymnastics rapidly became a popular sport and spread to other places in Prussia and to other German states.

Jahn's gymnastics was constructed around a philosophy that included both an emphasis on German racial superiority and purity and an almost socialist combination of democracy, egalitarianism, and collectivism. In 1810, Jahn published *Deutsches Volkstum*, in which he appealed for unity among all German-speaking peoples. He portrayed the German *Volk* as a superior, chosen people who needed to rediscover their heritage in order to claim their rightful place in the world, and argued that a prerequisite for doing so was an unswerving dedication to racial purity. Jahn also articulated a Rousseauian vision of a future Germany, in which democracy and egalitarianism were realized through collectivism. He wrote that "the citizen will feel, think, and act with the state, through it, for it, and in it; he will be one with it and the people in life, woe, and love."[10]

---

[8] Cousin 1834 (1831), 206.

[9] For an overview of the history of German gymnastics, see Guttmann 1994, 141–56. For much more detailed accounts, see F. Leonard and McKenzie 1927 and Neuendorff 1934. See also Hofmann and Pfister 2004; Mack 2000, 34–46; and Naul 2002.

[10] Quoted in Mack 2000, 39.

Jahn saw gymnastics as a means of educating the German people and preparing them for military service against the Germans' enemies (the French foremost among them) and of furthering the creation of a unified, democratic, egalitarian, collectivist Germany. Gymnastics were portrayed as a means by which boys and men could rediscover a German racial inheritance of physical vigor, while liberating body and soul. Participants wore a costume invented by Jahn, consisting of long trousers and a short jacket in a simple fabric, in order to eliminate status distinctions, and addressed each other with the informal *Du*. Jahn replaced the term *Gymnastik* with *Turnen* because it sounded more German. (People doing gymnastics were called *Turner* (both singular and plural), and the place where *Turnen* were performed was called a *Turnplatz*.) The desire to actively reshape *Turner* into individuals better suited to serve the collectivity is evident in the etymology of the term Jahn chose to describe his training program. *Turnen* was derived from the Latin verb *tornare*, which means "to make round by turning on a lathe." The idea of a craftsman refining raw material thus underlies Jahn's gymnastics.[11] *Turnen* frequently became occasions for patriotic speeches and rallies; when war broke out between Prussia and France in 1813, Jahn and most of the *Turner* who were old enough joined the Prussian army. The *Turner* rapidly developed into a large, influential group that actively promoted German unity and democracy.

The Prussian government had a difficult time deciding on a policy toward the *Turner* because it was in favor of German unification but opposed to democracy. In 1819 the Prussian government began to explore the possibility of incorporating gymnastics into the national school curriculum, something that Jahn resisted because "the ideal of social attitudes developed by gymnastic exercises did not fit into the frame of the rigorously controlled hierarchical Prussian education system."[12]

In the 1840s the Prussian state finally committed itself to promoting gymnastics, but the gymnastics it sponsored was very different from that invented by Jahn. In 1842 physical education became part of the prescribed educational program for boys in German schools, and in practice physical education meant gymnastics. Adolf Spiess was tasked with designing an appropriate curriculum, and Spiess' version of gymnastics differed sharply from that of Jahn in a variety of ways, not the least of which was that he stressed hierarchy, order, discipline, and obedience. Spiess published a number of books about gymnastics, which included the following admonitions:

The gymnastic art is really made the one branch of instruction in school-life which teaches how to practice and display discipline....

---

[11] On the etymology of *Turnen*, see the relevant entries in *Wahrig Deustsches Wörterbuch* and the *Oxford Latin Dictionary*. Compare the meaning of the Greek word for athletic tutor, *paidotribês*, discussed in Section 9.5.

[12] Naul 2002, 16.

Here, as everywhere else, the pupil must first learn what it is to obey, before he is allowed to do as he pleases.

Wherever gymnastics are taught they must be taught earnestly and treated strictly as a branch of study, which before all educates the scholar to prompt obedience and willingness to be of use to others. All pupils, and especially the older ones, must learn to obey promptly and implicitly....[13]

Spiess' gymnastics had a strong military element. The exercises were directed by a leader who first described what the students were to do and then issued a command for the students to do the exercise in unison. The combination of Prussian attitudes toward education and Spiess' gymnastics created a situation in which "schools, where rows and columns of children moved in synchronized response to barked commands, became a means for the authorities to inculcate the political virtues of discipline and unquestioning obedience to authority."[14]

With the weight of the Prussian and later the German state behind it, gymnastics became immensely popular in Germany. By 1864 there were 834 public *Turnplätze* and 121 *Turnhallen* (covered spaces for performing gymnastics).[15] Clubs were formed so that people who had done gymnastics in school could continue to do them as adults. A union of German gymnastics clubs was formed in 1863; by 1914 there were two such organizations: the *Deutscher Turnerschaft*, which was ostensibly nonpolitical but nonetheless clearly supportive of the prevailing sociopolitical system, with nearly 2 million members, and the *Arbeiter Turnerbund*, which had a leftist political orientation, with 190,000 members.[16]

Despite the changes in gymnastics that occurred over the course of the nineteenth century, there was a continuing emphasis on racial purity and collectivism. This is evident from the code of the *Deutscher Turnerbund*, founded in 1919 as an umbrella organization for German and Austrian gymnastics clubs. That code included the following provisions:

(1) The aim of the *Deutscher Turnerbund* and its clubs is the creation and strengthening of the spiritual and physical ability and the consciousness of Germanness in the German people. The basis for such a...racially based education is in the three wisdoms of *Turnvater* Friedrich Ludwig Jahn, i.e., *purity of the race, purity of the people,* and *liberty of the spirit.* Each member shall pursue these ends on the sports field and in his private life. ...

(6) In all competition rules of the organization the following has to be included: Testing of the knowledge about the racial foundations of our people has to be included in all events. The events to be part of the gymnastic competitions are

---

[13] These quotes come from pp. 6, 7, and 9, respectively of Spiess 1860, an English translation of select passages from a number of Spiess' books.
[14] Guttmann 1994, 143–44.
[15] Eisenberg 1999, 122.
[16] These numbers come from Hofmann and Pfister 2004, 16–17.

FIGURE 13. *Turnfest* in Cologne, Germany, 1928 (From Deutsches Bundesarchiv Bild 102–06313B/photo Georg Pahl)

not to be announced in advance so that there will be no undue specialization. Military gymnastics are always to be included.…There will be no competitions for prizes.[17]

Competition was opposed on the grounds that it ran counter to the ideal of collectivism and because it was linked to British sport (see below).

Turner organizations arranged gatherings, called *Turnfest*, for the public performance of gymnastics. The opposition to competition meant that "mass displays of cadenced movement…were the centerpiece of every gymnastics festival" (see Figures 13 and 14).[18]

13.4. OTHER FORMS OF SPORT

The growing popularity of sport in Britain in the first half of the nineteenth century inspired similar activity in some communities in the German states, particularly those with close commercial links with Britain. For instance, British merchants living in Hamburg organized the English Rowing Club there in 1836, and local residents organized the Mathilde Rowing Club in the same year.[19] Many of the early enthusiasts of British-style sport in Germany were individuals who had spent stretches of time in Britain and

---

[17] Quoted in Krammer 1996, 83.
[18] Guttmann 1994, 145.
[19] Mack 2000, 33.

FIGURE 14. *Turnfest* in Frankfurt, Germany, 1930 (From Deutsches Bundesarchiv Bild 102–10066/photo Georg Pahl)

who had picked up the practice of sport there. A German translation of *Tom Brown's Schooldays* appeared in 1859.[20]

Sport other than gymnastics did not, however, become popular in Germany until the early part of the twentieth century.[21] This is in some ways surprising because the ideals that were attached to British sport, especially after the mid-nineteenth century, were very much in line with the values of the German middle class, which believed in the importance of individual achievement and self-reliance.

A major obstacle to the spread of sport was the deeply embedded tradition of gymnastics, the organizing principles of which were in many ways incompatible with British-style sport. The *Turner* emphasized German racial purity and superiority, collectivism, and discipline, whereas the sport arriving from Britain was foreign, individualistic, and oriented toward autonomy. Proponents of *Turnen* argued that British sport was "alien to German behavior" and a sign of "rabid anglomania that is now horribly infecting a part of our people," that it encouraged pride and egoism, and that it destroyed "what the *Turner* have dedicated themselves to creating: a national community (*Volkgemeinschaft*)."[22]

---

[20] On sport in Germany in the nineteenth century, Eisenberg 1999 is fundamental, though see also Mack 2000, 1–46 and *passim* and Naul 2002.

[21] Eisenberg (1999, 11) points out that as late as the 1880s there was no precise equivalent in German for the English term "sport."

[22] All these quotes from contemporary German sources (including Edmund Neuendorff, national leader of the *Deutscher Turnerschaft*) are taken from Guttmann 1994, 144. Eisenberg (1999, 250–61) argues that gymnastics was favored and staunchly defended by

Resistance from *Turner* was gradually overcome and in the last two decades of the nineteenth century sports other than gymnastics gained numbers of new adherents, but it was not until after World War I that British-style sport became popular on a wide scale. This is evident in the history of Association football, which turned into the most popular form of sport in Weimar Germany, attracting large numbers of participants and spectators. "Until 1914, football in Germany was a minority sport in a society that, to a considerable extent, regarded sport with contempt." A national governing body, the *Deutscher Fußball-Bund*, was founded in 1900, but had only 82,300 members in 1910. By 1921, however, membership had increased to 780,500.[23] The emergence in the early twentieth century of the Olympics as a prominent forum for international athletic competition and nationalistic displays also helped promote interest in sport.

It was, not coincidentally, precisely during this period that democratization in Germany was sufficiently advanced as to make it, by the measures of the Polity Project, a democratic state. British-style sport was much more in harmony with the movement toward democratization than gymnastics. As Erik Jensen has observed, "Because competitive sports rewarded merit alone and made a claim to democratic openness, they seemed perfectly suited to Germany's new postwar republic."[24] Walter Schönbrunn, writing in 1930, criticized the hierarchy and political conservatism enshrined in gymnastics and dismissed *Turnen* as an activity best suited for "the subjects of a monarchical government," not for the citizens of the new republic.[25]

Even so, gymnastics remained a fundamental part of German sport straight through the outbreak of World War II, and suspicion of other forms of sport remained strong. Gymnastics continued to be a required part of the state-dictated school curriculum, gymnastics clubs had roughly 2 million members in 1914, and *Turnfeste* such as the one held in Munich in 1923 attracted hundreds of thousands of participants.

Moreover, during the Weimar Republic there was a strong trend toward the militarization of sport, in part as a response to restrictions on military training imposed by the Treaty of Versailles. For instance, the *Deutscher Turnerschaft* created what it called *Wehrturnen* (military gymnastics), and the German Swimming Federation (the *Deutscher Schwimm-Verband*) introduced *Wehrsportschwimmen* (military sport swimming).[26]

---

members of the established German middle class, whereas sport was popular among an emergent middle class that included people such as bankers, engineers, and managers.

[23] Quote taken from Pyta 2006, 3. Information on membership in the *Deutscher Fußball-Bund* taken from Eisenberg 1999, 180 and 330.

[24] Jensen 2011, 184.

[25] Quoted in Jensen 2011, 185.

[26] On the militarization of sport during the Weimar Republic, and changes in German sport practice under the Nazis, see Bernett 1992.

Hitler was a strong advocate of sport, which he saw as an indispensable means of preparing Germans to succeed in military and political struggles, and the Nazis' rise to power in the 1930s was accompanied by increasingly strict state control over sport. Hitler wrote in *Mein Kampf* that:

If the German nation were presented with a body of young men who had been perfectly trained in athletic sports, who were imbued with an ardent love for their country and a readiness to take the initiative in a fight, then the national State could make an army out of that body within less than two years if it were necessary....[27]

1934 saw the foundation of a new national sport governing body, the German League of the Reich for Physical Activities (*Deutscher Reichsbund für Leibesübungen*, later renamed the *Nationalsozialistischer Reichsbund für Leibesübungen* (National Socialist League of the Reich for Physical Activities)), and all national sport organizations, such as the umbrella groups for local gymnastics and Association football clubs, were subordinated to it. Sports organizations linked to political parties other than the Nazis, such as the *Arbeiter-Turn-und-Sportbund*, were disbanded, and a series of regulations effectively excluded Jews from organized sport of all kinds.

Sports activities increasingly took place under the aegis of paramilitary organizations such as the Hitler Youth (*Hitler-Jugend*) and Stormtroopers (*Sturmabteilung*). For example, the Hitler Youth, which more than half of all German children joined during its heyday, was an organization in which "discipline, hierarchy, physical training, and indoctrination were strictly observed."[28] Members of the Hitler Youth regularly participated in gymnastics, boxing, various team sports, sailing, diving, and swimming, and ten-year-old boys were given a *Pimpfenprobe* in which they had to run 60 meters in 12 seconds, swim 300 meters in less than 10 minutes, throw a ball 25 meters, perform a long jump of 2.75 meters, take part in a multiday hike, and demonstrate knowledge of Hitler youth songs and slogans. The girls' wing of the Hitler Youth, the League of German Girls (*Bund Deutscher Mädel*), devoted one of two weekly meetings to physical training that included gymnastics and track-and-field. From the perspective of the officials running the Hitler Youth:

Sport was not an end in itself, but a means of training the youth of the future in accordance with National Socialist ideals. Its goal was inner discipline. Consequently no free movement or spontaneous sport or dance was allowed. Any expression of individualistic movement that went against the National Socialist sense of order was proscribed. Instead, regulation and discipline were emphasised.[29]

---

[27] Hitler 1939 (1925–26), 418.
[28] Lepage 2008, 84. On the Hitler Youth, see the just-cited work of Lepage as well as Kater 2004.
[29] Pine 1997, 51.

Nazi educational policy made physical education the most important part of the curriculum and increased the amount of time dedicated to sport. Physical education programs in school were run by a newly founded department of the Ministry of Public Education. Male students were trained in a series of sports: swimming for grades five to seven, Association football for grades eight to ten, and boxing for grades eleven to twelve. Female students pursued gymnastics, track-and-field, and field hockey. Nazi officials believed that the purpose of physical education was:

to develop a "hygienic Aryan race," to foster the "mentality of a good soldier," and to build strong "leadership qualities."...The role to be aspired to was a strong fellow who disregarded risk of physical injury as a challenge for the individual body, who did not fear man-to-man combat as an integral part of the "national body," and who would pursue whatever his leader, Adolf Hitler, wanted him to do.[30]

The summer Olympics in 1936, which had been promised to Berlin two years before Hitler came to power, became an opportunity for the Nazi Party to put on a display of German strength. A major push was made to build spectacular facilities and to locate and prepare German athletes capable of competing at a high level in events that had in previous Olympics been dominated by countries such as the United States in which British-style sports had long enjoyed widespread popularity. Leni Riefenstahl, who had directed *Triumph of the Will*, a renowned film about the Nazi Party congress at Nuremberg in 1934, and *Day of Freedom: Our Army*, a short film that glorified the German military, was commissioned by Hitler to make a film documenting and celebrating the 1936 summer Olympics. The result, *Olympia*, remains perhaps the single most well-known film about the Olympic Games.[31]

The Nazis thus initiated changes that increased the already significant vertical and collectivist dimensions of German sport. Buichi Otani, a Japanese observer at the 1936 Olympics, noted that:

In Germany sport is for the development of the discipline of the mind and body, that is for physical education and even more for the fatherland. On the other hand, in England sport is for sport's sake, and it has no higher use. This is the difference between the two countries' sporting ability.[32]

---

[30] Naul 2002, 25.

[31] On the 1936 Berlin Olympics, see Large 2007. On Leni Riefenstahl, see Sontag 1980, 73–105 and Trimborn 2007.

[32] Quoted in Nakamura 2003, 137. After the 1936 Olympics Nazi sport officials, with active participation by Hitler, planned a new set of national games, the *Nationalsozialistischen Kampfspiele*. These games, which had a strong military element (e.g., they included contests in pistol shooting), were held in 1937 and 1939. Construction of a vast stadium in Nuremberg to house the *Kampfspiele* was begun but never completed. (See Bernett 1987.) These games were in a sense a continuation of the *Deutschen Kampfspiele* held from 1922 to 1930, originally as a substitute for the Olympics, from which Germany was temporarily excluded after World War I.

This is in many ways a neat summary of the difference between vertical and horizontal sport.

13.5. CONCLUSION

Sport in nineteenth-century Germany consisted almost entirely of gymnastics, which was taught to children throughout the national network of publicly funded schools and which was also widely popular among adults who formed literally hundreds of gymnastics clubs. One might well, therefore, speak of something approximating mass sport. It need hardly be said at this point that gymnastics as practiced in Germany after the 1840s was a strongly vertical form of sport. The existence of a system of vertical mass sport in nineteenth-century Germany – what appears to be the earliest example of that phenomenon – was very much in line with the strongly authoritarian tenor of the German sociopolitical system.

Democratization, though muted, was not entirely absent, and became a more prominent part of the German social landscape with the coming of the Weimar Republic. British-style sport gained an increasing number of German adherents starting at the end of the nineteenth century, but gymnastics continued to be a popular and important activity. Mass sport in Germany was to some extent democratized, but it remained significantly more vertical than its counterpart in Britain. The Nazis made German sport much more vertical than it had been previously.

It would be absurd to attribute the ephemerality of the Weimar Republic to the absence of horizontal mass sport, but it is worth pointing out that the absence of horizontal mass sport reflects the relative weakness of horizontal institutions, practices, and norms in German society. That weakness undoubtedly contributed to the collapse of the Weimar Republic less than two decades after it came into being. Furthermore, the presence of vertical mass sport for much of the nineteenth century was virtually certainly one of many factors that inhibited democratization and the growth of horizontality of all kinds in German society, and there can be little doubt that vertical mass sport reinforced authoritarian rule in Nazi Germany.

14

Sport and Society in Britain from 1870 to 1900

14.1. SOCIAL HISTORY

The period from 1870 to 1900 in Britain was marked by both the growth of the power and privileges enjoyed by members of the working class and by attempts, in large part successful, to limit the extent and effects of the working class's influence. This same period saw the first significant stirrings of a women's rights movement and the granting of some limited social and political rights to women.[1]

It was only in the latter decades of the nineteenth century that members of the British working class developed a clear sense of being part of a unified group with a shared set of goals and social rules. Before, roughly, 1870 there was a great deal of local and regional variation in the habits and customs of members of the working class from different parts of Britain, but in the decades that followed, as Eric Hobsbawn has noted, there was a "growing sense of a single working class, bound together in a community of fate irrespective of its internal differences."[2] Members of the British working class adopted a shared lifestyle, which included elements such as men wearing a particular kind of flat cap and playing and watching Association football.[3]

The goals and social rules of the British working class placed heavy emphasis on a "powerful moral code based on solidarity, 'fairness,' mutual aid, and cooperation" and on being ready, willing, and able to fight for just treatment, particularly in the workplace.[4] In 1867 Thomas Wright published a book with the title *Some Habits and Customs of the Working*

---

[1] For an overview of the history of Britain in this period, see Wasson 2010, 150–210. For a more thorough account, see the articles collected in F. M. L. Thompson 1990 as well as the volumes in the *New Oxford History of England* series.

[2] Hobsbawm 1984, 207.

[3] On the British working class in the closing decades of the nineteenth century, see Harrison 1990, 67–92 and Hobsbawm 1984, 176–213.

[4] Hobsbawm 1984, 191.

Classes in which he characterized the average British working man in the following way: "He will maintain a battle for what he conceives to be his rights, 'and never count the cost;' he will stand by his friend in cloud as well as sunshine."[5]

The belief in the importance of piety and in the inherent moral value of work that characterized the middle class, and by this point in time much of the landed gentry, was not as influential among members of the working class. Wright noted that, "Numbers of working men regularly attend some place of worship on Sundays...but the greater bulk of the working classes do not attend places of worship," though he added that the working class was not "actively or avowedly irreligious."[6] He also discussed at some length a habit, relatively widespread among men from the working class, of frequently taking part or all of Monday off from work.

In the same vein, the working class in the latter decades of the nineteenth century continued to show tolerance and even a taste for the sort of drinking and riotous behavior that had earlier been popular with the landed gentry. Although Wright stoutly claimed that the working man was "an infinitely better man, and a more useful and creditable member of society, than the snobby-genteel kind of person," he also admitted that, "in him human nature has not yet attained the maximum of perfectibility....He is often drunken, and not always ashamed thereof; and sometimes his love of drink leads to his being guilty of conduct which – to put it mildly – is not all that may become a man."[7] Monday "holidays," for example, were spent in excursions, watching and betting on sporting events such as wrestling and boxing matches, drinking, or just loafing.[8] Continuing attempts by the upper class to control what they saw as objectionable behavior, through means such as temperance movements, the use of the police, and providing alternative forms of recreation, were at best only partially successful.

One of the earliest significant and sustained bursts of political activism by the British working class took shape in the form of the Chartist movement in the 1830s and 1840s. The Chartists produced a list of demands, the People's Charter, which included the extension of the rights to vote and to run for the House of Commons to all adult men and the granting of salaries to members of Parliament so that both poor and rich could afford to hold high office. In 1839 the People's Charter was sent to the House of Commons with well over a million signatures attached, and mass meetings were held in support of it in the 1840s. However, the landed gentry and the newly empowered middle class closed ranks and successfully resisted attempts to make it into law.[9]

---

[5] Wright 1867, vii.
[6] Wright 1867, 244.
[7] Wright 1867, vii.
[8] Wright 1867, 108–30.
[9] On Chartism, see M. Chase 2007.

Men from British working-class families were nonetheless fully enfranchised by 1918. The Representation of the People Act of 1867, sometimes called the Second Reform Act, gave the franchise to the wealthier members of the working class, primarily skilled workers and thereby doubled yet again the percentage of adult men able to vote. The Representation of the People Act of 1884, the Third Reform Act, gave the vote to most working men living in urban areas and removed property qualifications so that any adult male could run for high office. The final major step came with the Representation of the People Act of 1918, the Fourth Reform Act, which established something close to universal male suffrage.[10]

British women too made some, though far from complete, progress toward winning full political and social rights. The first significant women's rights movements in Britain took shape in the 1840s. John Stuart Mill led an attempt, which failed badly, to give women the right to vote as part of the Representation of the People Act of 1867. Signs of change were evident by 1870 with the passage of the Married Women's Property Act, which gave married women a certain degree of control over their incomes. By 1900 women had gained the right to vote in most local elections and to be elected to school boards and to some lower governmental positions. The Representation of the People Act of 1918 gave women who were over thirty years old and who owned a minimum amount of property the right to vote in national elections. All women over the age of twenty were enfranchised by the Representation of the People Act of 1928, the Fifth Reform Act.[11]

The relationship between the upper and working classes in the closing decades of the nineteenth century was complex and frequently tense. As ongoing processes of democratization began to have positive effects on the relative standing of the working class, it became notionally possible that its members would adopt the goals and values of the upper class and that the members of both groups would interact and compete on equal terms. In practice that did not happen. Many members of the working class aspired to "respectability" and upward social mobility, but others viewed the upper class with a mixture of antagonism and contempt. The goals and social rules that came to characterize the working class were in no small part conceived in opposition to those that characterized the upper class and hence in many ways diverged sharply from them.

Looking at matters from the other direction, some members of the upper class sought to literally and figuratively evangelize members of the working class and to persuade or compel them to behave in what they believed to be an appropriate fashion. Some of these social evangelists simply wished members of the working class to be quiescent and obedient, whereas others believed in at least some degree of mixing of people from the upper and

[10] A good, albeit politically charged, survey of electoral systems in Britain can be found in Watt 2006.
[11] On the history of women's suffrage in Britain, see van Wingerden 1999.

working classes on something like an equal basis.[12] Other members of the upper class were more than happy with the existence of strong social boundaries and were content to leave the working class largely to its own devices.

Moreover, the male members of the landed gentry and the middle class took active and in large part successful steps to maintain their positions of power and privilege. For example, though civil service positions were notionally open to all on a meritocratic basis, the working class was effectively excluded from many such posts because applicants had to take written examinations that stressed knowledge of esoteric subjects that were taught primarily in public schools and universities. The civil service examinations for 1898, for instance, included subjects such as Sanskrit, Greek, Latin, Greek history, Roman history, and Roman law. The sort of education available to the less well-off members of British society made it difficult if not impossible for them to succeed on these exams.[13]

The complex relationship between the upper and working classes in Britain found no neat resolution in the period under consideration here, but in general terms they remained largely separate groups. That said, the extent and degree of the separation should not be exaggerated. The goals and social rules of the two groups diverged but were not completely different, and people in both classes interacted with each other on a daily basis.

14.2. EDUCATION

The education of the landed gentry and members of the middle class did not change radically between 1870 and 1900. The basic patterns that came into being between 1840 and 1870 continued. Radical change did, however, take place in regard to the education of members of the working class.[14]

Britain did not have anything approximating a publicly funded national system that made basic education available to everyone until 1870. In 1833, Parliament began supplying funds to charitable organizations that operated schools. However, many areas of Britain had either no schools that working-class families could afford or too few to meet the existing demand. Moreover, the limited amount of such schooling on offer and the need to work to provide their families income meant that most working-class children received the equivalent of only two or three years of education. Class sizes were large, discipline was strict, and the actual level of education attained was typically rather minimal.

---

[12] On the upper class in Britain in the closing decades of the nineteenth century, see Harrison 1990, 29–66.

[13] Civil Service 1897, 161.

[14] On education in Britain in this period, see Lawson and Silver 1973, 314–63; Stephens 1998, 77–124; and Sutherland 1990.

Parliament sought to remedy these problems with the Elementary Education Act of 1870. This bill made it possible for taxpayers in any area where there was a shortage of schools to create a local school board, establish a school, and impose taxes to fund its operation. These newly founded schools were empowered to provide a basic education for both boys and girls from ages five to twelve. Students had to pay fees to attend, but those fees were waived for anyone who could not afford them. By the 1890s over 2,000 new schools had been founded using the provisions of the Elementary Education Act. Starting in 1880 all children who came from working-class families and who were between the ages of five and ten were required to attend school, and attendance rates climbed sharply thereafter.

14.3. SPORT

Between 1870 and 1900 the habit of regularly playing sports spread to the lower middle class, a substantial portion of the working class, and many women from affluent families. During the same period, mass spectatorship came into being. By 1900 Britain definitively had mass sport.[15]

Clubs, particularly those associated with churches, were among the most important contexts in which members of the lower middle class picked up the habit of regularly playing sports. We have seen that the British middle class at the beginning of the nineteenth century had a deep-seated belief in the overriding importance of continuous hard work; they suspected that free time of any sort was nothing more than an opportunity for misbehavior and immorality. However, as the result of legal restrictions (especially on child labor), advocacy by unions, and general societal change, members of both the middle and working classes had increasing amounts of leisure time as the nineteenth century progressed. The question of what people might do with their nonwork hours caused considerable anxiety among many members of the middle class, and that anxiety led to the creation of a vast array of highly engineered, "rational" forms of recreation in order to make it possible for people to spend their leisure time in what were considered to be wholesome ways. Public parks and libraries were built, regular series of classes and lectures were organized, and clubs that arranged suitable activities for their members were founded.[16]

As sport became, in the eyes of the middle class, a respectable form of activity, many religious organizations founded sports clubs. The influence of Muscular Christianity was critical here, since it made sport into an overtly

---

[15] On the history of sport in Britain in the closing decades of the nineteenth century, see N. Anderson 2010, 47–177; Holt 1992, 57–202; and Tranter 1998, 13–93. On sport in nineteenth-century British public schools, see Mangan 1981.

[16] For an overview of the Rational Recreation movement, see Holt 1992, 136–48. For a full-length treatment, see Bailey 1978.

Christian activity. Proponents of Muscular Christianity, many of whom were public-school graduates, were eager to spread the gospel of sport, and clubs linked to churches were an ideal means of doing so. How this worked in practice can be seen from a detailed study of the formation of Association football clubs in the English city of Birmingham. Of the 354 Association football clubs that were in existence in Birmingham in 1880, 24% were connected to a church, chapel, or religious organization.[17]

Schools were the other important venue where members of the lower middle class became athletes. Public schools, either old or new, were too expensive for many lower middle-class families, which typically sent their sons to local grammar or private schools. Prior to 1850 the education offered by these schools was purely intellectual because the people who ran them did not have the time, facilities, or interest in organizing sports for their students. That began to change as sport became an increasingly important element in public-school education and in the lifestyle of the middle class. In the closing decades of the nineteenth century many grammar and private schools, a considerable fraction of them under the leadership of headmasters who had attended a public school, acquired or rented fields and started organizing sports activities for their students.[18]

Gymnastics arrived in Britain at an early date, but it never became a major rival to other forms of sport. German gymnastics became popular in much of Europe during the nineteenth century. A variant, developed in Sweden, was less overtly nationalistic and militaristic and included more free movement. German and Swedish gymnastics were taken up to a certain extent by the British military for the training of recruits, individuals set up gymnastics centers here and there in Britain, and gymnastics was introduced at some public schools, where it received a lukewarm reception. A British government report from 1868 noted that:

Nothing however will make an ex-schoolboy of one of the great English schools regard the gymnastics of a foreign school without a slight feeling of wonder and compassion, so much more animating and interesting do the games of his remembrance seem to him.[19]

Despite the fact that students in public schools were much more interested in British-style sports such as cricket than in the more regimented forms of sport developed in Germany, the latter rather than the former formed the basis of the physical education programs in publicly funded British schools in the nineteenth century. The Elementary Education Act of 1870 suggested that students in schools funded in part or whole by government money

---

[17] McIntosh 1987, 72.

[18] On the integration of sport into the curriculum of these schools in the late nineteenth century, see Leinster-Mackay 1981 and Mangan 1983.

[19] Quoted in McIntosh 1987, 68.

should give boys up to two hours a week of military drill. The instructors were drill sergeants who took exercises from the War Office's *Field Exercise Book,* and drill sessions were immensely monotonous and not at all popular with students. Physical education for girls typically took the form of Swedish gymnastics (see Section 2.3 and Figure 4). There was no official effort until the early twentieth century to make other sports available in schools attended by working-class children, though some teachers on their own organized teams to play Association football, cricket, and so on.[20]

It is not coincidental that horizontal forms of sport were felt to be appropriate in public schools and vertical forms of sport were prescribed for publicly funded schools. Members of the upper class arranged their own sport and pursued sports that were organized and carried out in a fundamentally horizontal fashion. When the officials in charge of publicly funded schools that were populated almost entirely by the working class, officials who were rarely from the working class themselves, established programs of physical education, they imposed vertical sport with the overt expectation that it would make the students more compliant and would reinforce existing social hierarchies. We have already seen (Section 2.3) that Lord Elcho announced in Parliament in 1862 that drill programs in school made boys from poor families "obedient, orderly, and respectable."[21]

Members of the working class came to sport through clubs affiliated with churches and companies, through after-school activities, and, probably most importantly, on their own. Here again Muscular Christianity was important. Charles Kingsley and Thomas Hughes, for example, helped found the Working Men's College in 1854 to provide adult education to skilled artisans, and Hughes taught boxing and organized cricket and rowing clubs there. Undertakings of that sort helped produce a considerable enthusiasm for playing sports among the working class. Thomas Wright, in a description written in 1867 of a section of London inhabited mostly by skilled workmen, noted that:

[They] are, almost to a man, admirers of muscular Christianity, much of their leisure during the summer months is occupied in practising or promoting boat-racing, foot-racing, and other athletic sports.[22]

Some sports were picked up more eagerly by the working class than others. Association football, which could be played almost anywhere with little more than a ball, rapidly achieved immense popularity among the

---

[20] On the history of physical education in schools in nineteenth-century Britain, see McIntosh 1968, 11–142. On gymnastics in British schools, see McIntosh 1968, 77–142. On the specific subject of drill and its use in British schools in the closing decades of the nineteenth century, see also Mangan and Hickey 2006 and Penn 1999.

[21] Parliament 1862, 26.

[22] Wright 1867, 256. On the spread of sport among the British working class in the late nineteenth century, see Holt 1992, 135–202.

working class. The shift in the social background of Association football players between 1870 and 1900 is evident in the teams that won the annual championship sponsored by the Football Association starting in 1871. Between 1871 and 1882 the F.A. Cup was won each year by teams made up of public school graduates. In 1883, however, Blackburn Olympic beat the Old Etonians in overtime; the Blackburn Olympic squad was captained by a master plumber and his team included three weavers, a spinner, a dental assistant, a picture framer, and a foundry worker.[23]

The changes in the social background of F.A. Cup players reflected a fundamental shift in British sport as a whole during the closing decades of the nineteenth century, as members of the working class began playing and watching sports much more regularly and seriously than before. Indeed, "by 1900 the scale of working-class involvement in organized sports was astounding."[24]

Opportunities for girls and women from better-off families to play sports gradually expanded over the course of the nineteenth century, though they never came close to being equal to those available to boys and men. Women from families of landed gentry had long spent a good deal of time riding and walking, and starting in the 1860s they also hunted with increasing frequency. In the second half of the nineteenth century many girls from wealthy families spent five or six years in their teens at boarding schools, modeled on public schools for boys, that encouraged girls to play what were felt to be appropriate sports, such as field hockey. Another shift that took place after the middle of the century was that a certain number of sports were created, such as croquet and lawn tennis, which were played in mixed male-female groups on the grounds of houses belonging to well-off families. A final important development came at the end of the century, when bicycling became very popular with women.[25] Little effort was invested in introducing girls from the working class to sports, though some publicly funded schools, particularly those in London, offered them Swedish gymnastics.

The significant broadening of the range of Britons who participated in sport produced something of a sports boom in the latter decades of the nineteenth century. This is reflected in the number of governing organizations for different sports that were founded between 1870 and 1900, as shown in Table 7.

Sports that had long had considerable followings became more popular than ever before. For example, the number of cricket clubs increased sharply, and matches were played with much greater frequency. The members of the

---

[23] Baker 1988, 124.

[24] Holt 1992, 135.

[25] On women and sport in nineteenth-century Britain, see McCrone 1987; McCrone 1988; McCrone 2006; and Tranter 1998, 78–93. On the history of lawn tennis, see H. Walker 1989.

TABLE 7. *Dates of the Creation of Sports Governing Bodies in Nineteenth-Century Britain*

Sport	Earliest National Organization	Date
Horse racing	Jockey Club	c. 1750
Golf	Royal and Ancient Golf Club	1754
Cricket	Marylebone Cricket Club	1788
Mountaineering	Alpine Club	1857
Association football	Football Association	1863
Track and field	Amateur Athletic Club, Amateur Athletic Association	1866, 1880
Swimming	Amateur Metropolitan Swimming Association	1869
Rugby football	Rugby Football Union	1871
Sailing	Yacht Racing Association	1875
Cycling	Bicyclists' Union	1878
Skating	National Skating Association	1879
Rowing	Metropolitan Rowing Association	1879
Boxing	Amateur Boxing Association	1884
Hockey	Hockey Association	1886
Lawn tennis	Lawn Tennis Association	1888
Badminton	Badminton Association	1895
Fencing	Amateur Fencing Association	1898

Information in this chart is taken from McIntosh 1987, 63.

Marylebone Cricket Club, the epicenter of cricket since its foundation in 1787, played only a handful of matches every year up through the early 1860s, but by 1869 they were playing 46 matches a year, a number which increased to 196 by 1900.[26] Existing sports that had not previously been particularly prominent, such as bowling, curling, and golf, suddenly enjoyed greatly enhanced popularity. By World War I there were more than 600,000 bowlers in northern England alone.[27]

New sports, including badminton, croquet, cycling, field hockey, and lawn tennis, were invented and attracted substantial followings, but it was Association football and rugby that experienced the most explosive growth. There were less than fifty Association football clubs in all of Britain in 1860. By 1899, Sheffield, a medium-sized city, had 880 clubs, and there were over 10,000 in Britain as a whole.[28]

[26] On the sharp growth in the number of athletes and spectators in Britain in the latter part of the nineteenth century, see Huggins 2004, 1–18 and Tranter 1998, 13–31. On the specific subject of the growth of cricket, see Sandiford 1994, 53–79.

[27] Tranter 1998, 16.

[28] Huggins 2004, 8; Baker 1988, 124–26.

Spectatorship also increased sharply between 1870 and 1900. The ever-growing number of athletes, along with continued improvements in transportation networks and urbanization, helped make sporting events more popular and easier to attend. At the same time, the popularity of sporting events with audiences made it increasingly possible to make substantial sums from selling tickets, which in turn made it possible to field professional teams that became focal points for local identity. Sports old and new drew larger audiences than ever before. The number of spectators at high-level cricket matches increased from an average of 2,000–3,000 in the 1840s to between 8,000 and 24,000 in the early 1900s. In the 1890s premier horse races drew crowds of 70,000–80,000. It was Association football, however, that became the prime sports attraction. This is evident from the audience at F.A. Cup finals, which rose from 2,000 in 1871 to 110,000 in 1901. By the early 1900s total paid admissions at Association football matches throughout Britain on any given weekend was around 1 million.[29]

Throughout the nineteenth century, British sport remained predominantly horizontal. Some vertical elements were introduced, most notably in the form of written rules, frequently enforced by officials; sport governing bodies that organized events; and the imposition of drill and gymnastics on children from working-class families who attended publicly funded schools. However, most sport continued to be organized by participants or by those with similar social status or social power, the sports played were relatively nonregimented, and emphasis was always on the benefits to participants.

Neil Tranter summarized the changes in British sport that took place during the second half of the nineteenth century as follows: "In less than fifty years the number of sports and the numbers playing and watching sport increased dramatically [and] the social composition of participants and the spatial parameters of the sports they practised substantially widened...."[30] By the close of the nineteenth century Britain became the second known example of a society with horizontal mass sport.

[29] All these figures come from Tranter 1998, 17. For a brief discussion of the appearance of professional sports teams in late nineteenth-century England, see N. Anderson 2010, 137–54. For a much more thorough treatment of the same subject, see Vamplew 1988.
[30] Tranter 1998, 15–16.

15

Sport and Democratization in Nineteenth-Century Britain

15.1. INTRODUCTION

Democratization and the emergence of horizontal mass sport were deeply intertwined in nineteenth-century Britain. Starting in the 1830s members of the middle class gained social and political privileges and began playing sports regularly and in large numbers. In the latter decades of the century members of the working class gained many social and political privileges and began playing sports regularly and in large numbers. In those same decades women gained a limited range of social and political privileges and began playing sports in a limited way.

The relationship between sport and democratization in Britain was in all probability the same as in the other times and places examined to this point, which is to say that the relationship was reciprocal. The four mechanisms by means of which sport fosters societal democratization (see Chapter 5) virtually certainly played a role in Britain's sociopolitical transformation. Quantitative data to document the functioning of those mechanisms in nineteenth-century Britain is lacking, but there is a good deal of anecdotal evidence that suggests that they were indeed operative. Some examples will give a sense of what is a substantial collection of textual material.

Two of the four mechanisms in question are the facilitation of the formation of small-scale, tightly bonded horizontal groups that literally enact democratization and the cultivation of particularized and generalized trust. The functioning of these mechanisms in nineteenth-century Britain is reflected in the following statement by Edmund Warre, headmaster of Eton from 1884 to 1905:

What good fellowship, what trusting friendships, are cemented by social athletics! They test a man's real nature, they reveal his temper, and along with his faults, his good qualities are not hidden. And, accordingly, they knit together men, not only in the bond of common pursuits and common memories of pleasant days and hard-fought struggles, but by the tie of mutual confidence which a mutual knowledge gives to friends who have long played, or rowed together in the course of an athletic career.[1]

Warre in this passage in many ways anticipates the research on social capital and sport carried out in recent decades. He not only speaks to sport's capacity to build social networks, but also highlights the fact that sport offered opportunities to observe others' behavioral propensities and hence promoted the growth of trust. This is quite a subtle reading of the effects of sport participation.

The cultivation of trust is important because it facilitates the growth of cooperative, horizontal relationships, and many British athletes of the nineteenth century eulogized team sports as a method for teaching cooperation. For example, in *Tom Brown's Schooldays* Tom and an unnamed school master discuss the importance of cricket in the following terms:

"The discipline and reliance on one another which it teaches is so valuable, I think," went on the master, "it ought to be such an unselfish game. It merges the individual in the eleven; he doesn't play that he may win, but that his side may." "That's very true," said Tom, "and that's why foot-ball and cricket, now one comes to think of it, are such much better games than fives [handball] or hare-and-hounds [cross-country running] or any others where the object is to come in first or to win for oneself, and not that one's side may win."[2]

F. Gale, writing in 1885, approached the same subject from the opposite direction in claiming that "Goodwill and hearty co-operation *must* make good cricket in the end."[3] These and other writers of like mind may not have clearly grasped the precise means by which sport facilitated cooperative relationships, but their intuition was sound.

A third mechanism by means of which sport fosters societal democratization is the cultivation of self-disciplined individuals with a predisposition to obey rules and legally constituted authorities. The functioning of this mechanism is evident from the writings of Edward Lyttelton, headmaster at Haileybury College from 1890 to 1905 and of Eton from 1905 to 1916, who argued that:

A boy is disciplined by athletics in two ways: by being forced to put the welfare of the common cause before selfish interests, to obey implicitly the word of command and act in concert with the heterogeneous elements of the company he belongs to; and secondly, should it so turn out, he is disciplined by being raised to a post of command, where he feels the gravity of the responsible office and the difficulty of making prompt decisions and securing obedience. Good moral results of this sort may be

[1] Warre 1884, 6.
[2] Hughes 1858 (1857), 394.
[3] Gale 1885, 182.

expected from games wherever they have spontaneously developed, and where all, even to the youngest, eagerly engaging, choose their own commanders....[4]

Lyttelton implicitly and no doubt unconsciously echoes the ancient Greek notion that democratic citizenship requires the capacity "to rule and be ruled in turn" (Aristotle *Politics* 1317b2, see Section 5.4).

15.2. MERITOCRATIC STATUS COMPETITION, HORIZONTAL RELATIONSHIPS, AND GROUP CLOSURE

The case study of sport and democratization in ancient Greece presented in Chapters 8–10 found that there were three other, contextually specific mechanisms by means of which sport fostered democratization: by serving as an arena for meritocratic status competition, by serving as a model of and for horizontal relationships, and by promoting closure within newly formed dominant groups. All three of these mechanisms seem to have been operative in some form in nineteenth-century Britain as well.

The first two mechanisms require relatively little discussion because they functioned in Britain much as they did in Greece. In the beginning of the nineteenth century Britain had a system of ascribed rank that supported steep differentials in social status and social power, and sport contributed to democratization in part because it decreased inequality by offering a form of meritocratic competition that assigned status in ways that cut across and diminished the importance of distinctions based on lineage and wealth. There is no need to rehearse here the discussion of how this worked in practice (see Section 10.2), and it is sufficient to point out that at least some Britons were aware that sport could have this effect. An anonymous student, writing in the *Oxford Magazine* in 1888 noted that:

At school boys learn their own worth in athletic contests, and differences of rank and wealth are happily sunk in the common emulation [i.e., competition] to gain honours in sports in which everybody takes his share.[5]

Another important similarity between Greece and Britain is that in both cases democratization entailed the formation of a new dominant group through the merging of an elite, which had sought to create vertical relationships between itself and all other members of its community, with the class immediately below it. In both cases the expectation of egalitarian interactions between members of the newly formed ruling groups was not necessarily easily realized, and sport fostered democratization by providing a model of and for horizontal relationships practiced in other social contexts. Here again, there is no need to review arguments that have already been

---

[4] Lyttelton 1880, 44.
[5] Anonymous 1888.

articulated in some detail (see Section 10.3). One need only point out that the merging of gentry and middle class was effected in large part in public schools, where sport played an important, sometimes predominant role in students' lives, and hence offered an obvious model of and for egalitarian relationships between boys from these two groups.

The role of sport in promoting group closure requires considerably more discussion because the course of events was in this regard significantly more complex in Britain than in Greece. In both cases sport promoted democratization by aiding in the formation of coherent groups that maintained horizontal relationships among their members. In Greece there was a single group within each community that played sports and that enjoyed full social and political privileges, and in most communities that group was small enough that its members related through face-to-face interactions. In Britain there were multiple groups that played sports, and those groups were more national than local in character. It is, therefore, necessary to look carefully at the relationship between sport and class in nineteenth-century Britain and at how sport promoted closure in much larger groups.

The relationship between sport and social class in nineteenth-century Britain can be studied at widely varying levels of resolution; Mike Huggins, for example, has argued that there was considerable diversity of opinion about sport within the British middle class in the second half of the nineteenth century.[6] For our purposes it is feasible to operate at a relatively high level of abstraction and to divide the British population into two large groups, the upper class (formed from the merging of the landed gentry and the wealthier section of the middle class) and the working class.[7]

The social status of sport participants became a significant issue starting around 1870. Before that time serious athletes with working-class backgrounds tended to be professionals who made a living from coaching and playing; they were hired to offer expert instruction or were paid to be a small but highly competent component of cricket teams and rowing crews that otherwise consisted of upper-class men. Gentlemen-athletes mixed with these professionals regularly and without much in the way of social complications.

The problems began when many members of the working class started playing sports with some regularity. This change gave rise to situations in which men from different social classes mixed in significant numbers while playing sports and competed directly with each other on relatively equal terms. For some people, these situations were invaluable opportunities to

---

[6] Huggins 2006.

[7] The social realities of sport in Britain in the nineteenth century were obviously quite complex, and the approach outlined here does not, for example, account for the actions of the lower middle class. That said, it remains true that two large, class-based patterns of sports activity did take shape. The relative absence of nuance in the discussion that follows would be problematic in a detailed survey of British sport history, but it is well-suited to the issues treated here in that it simplifies and clarifies without introducing major distortions.

bring the social classes together. The president of the Football Association, J. C. Shaw, wrote approvingly in 1877 that the Sheffield team in the F.A. Cup final:

> was a mixed one of gentlemen of the middle classes and working men. Such meetings broke down prejudice and had a beneficial effect in cementing good feeling between all classes.[8]

However, views of this sort were the exception rather than the rule. It was more commonly perceived, probably rightly, that sporting events with participants from both the upper and working classes had the potential to destabilize relationships between these two groups.

Starting in the 1870s many members of the upper class took active steps to ensure that they did not play sports with people they saw as their social, if not physical, inferiors. There were three important means of achieving this end. First, they formed clubs that charged membership fees that were beyond the reach of men from the working class. Opportunities for adult males to play sports came largely via clubs that rented or purchased appropriate facilities and that organized games between their members and with other clubs. It took no great effort for men from the upper class to raise the cost of belonging to a club to the point of excluding working men. An editorial published in 1885 in a Scottish newspaper, the *Stirling Observer*, noted that:

> No doubt the Stirling County Cricket Club *is* open to anyone. But what artisan can afford the heavy annual subscription and last season take three or four trips, to Perth, Dundee, Cupar, etcetera, thereby losing a day's work and wages, not to mention the 2s (shillings)-6d (pennies) luncheon with which these matches generally open and the cost of the dress? Artisans may be equal on the field, but they are not made to feel equal in the pavilion ....[9]

Second, members of the upper class gravitated toward sports that were relatively expensive to play, which, for obvious reasons, kept the number of competitors from the working class to a minimum. This is most evident in regard to golf, a sport that required access to large stretches of carefully maintained grounds and that was, as a result, a costly habit. An early form of golf was played in Scotland in the twelfth century, but it remained a relatively exotic sport in the rest of Britain for a long period of time, and even in Scotland it was far from being wildly popular. In the middle of the nineteenth century there was but a single golf club (i.e., a group that owned or leased land with one or more golf courses on it) in England, and in 1879 there were still only fifty-two golf clubs in Scotland and twenty in England and

---

[8] Quoted in Tranter 1998, 37.
[9] Quoted in Tranter 1998, 42. On attempts by the upper class to exclude the working class from their sports activity, see Tranter 1998, 32–51.

Wales. A radical shift came in the 1890s when the popularity of golf suddenly increased sharply. In the space of less than fifteen years, 704 new golf clubs were founded, and by 1912 there were 1,200 golf clubs in England alone.[10]

Finally, members of the upper class invented a distinction between amateur and professional athletes that excluded working men from many sporting events. Since the eighteenth century a distinction had been made in sports such as rowing and cricket between people who made their living practicing the requisite skill and those who participated more casually. For instance, in the 1830s a professional rower was someone who rowed for a living, typically ferrying passengers in small boats across or along rivers such as the Thames. These men were felt to have a distinct advantage in contests over people, called amateurs, who rowed competitively but not for a living.[11]

By the early 1860s, however, the definitions of professional and amateur athletes were evolving so that they became more and more based on social class. The *Rowing Almanack* for 1861 defined amateurs by listing the schools and universities from which they were expected to have graduated and included the provision that amateurs were, without exception, not "tradesmen, labourers, artisans, or working mechanics."[12] When the Amateur Athletic Club, one of the earliest track-and-field clubs, was founded in London in the late 1860s its members had an extended debate about who was eligible to join. They settled on the following rules:

An amateur is any gentleman who has never competed in an open competition, or for public money, or for admission money, and who has never at any period of his life taught or assisted in the pursuit of athletic exercises as a means of livelihood, or is a mechanic, artisan, or labourer.[13]

Working-class men, who could rarely afford to take time off from their jobs to train and compete without some form of recompense, were thus excluded both by specifying unacceptable occupations and by prohibiting amateurs from accepting money for playing sports.

In an interesting reflection of the effects of democratization that was proceeding at the societal level, rules that overtly excluded working men rapidly became politically unacceptable and were dropped, but the requirement that amateurs not accept money for playing sports was maintained, and the end result was largely the same. Working-class men were effectively excluded from clubs and competitions run by the upper class. As Allen Guttmann put it, "The amateur rule was an instrument of class warfare."[14]

---

[10] On the history of golf in Britain in the nineteenth and early twentieth centuries, see Lowerson 1989. The figures supplied here come from Tranter 1998, 22–23.

[11] On the history of amateurism in Britain, see Holt 1992, 74–134. On rowing in particular, see Halladay 2006.

[12] Quoted and discussed in Vamplew 1988, 186.

[13] Quoted and discussed in Lovesey 1979, 19–23.

[14] Guttmann 1978, 31.

Although there were no doubt some working-class men who would have liked to have played sports with members of the upper class, many others were more than happy to play largely with others of similar social standing. Association football, and to a lesser extent, rugby, rapidly became the favorite sports of working-class men, and in the latter decades of the nineteenth century, playing and watching Association football became more and more a working-class pastime. A modern-day study of the social background of people who regularly played sports in the region of Stirling in Scotland in the second half of the nineteenth century found that nine out of every ten Association football players came from the working class.[15]

The working class rapidly developed its own approach to Association football that differed in many ways from the emphasis on amateurism that was common among the upper class, because members of the working class were much more open to the idea that athletes should be paid for playing their sport. In the 1880s a number of Association football clubs became entirely professional and began playing regularly scheduled matches against each other. The players on these clubs were mostly working-class men, and clubs rapidly developed immense followings among members of the working class. Powerful attachments were formed between individual clubs and people residing around their home field.[16]

Members of the upper and working classes thus played sports largely with people whose social standing was similar to their own, and sport helped draw boundaries around each group, in three different ways. First, sport brought large numbers of people together as participants and spectators. The mere fact of being in the same place and same time for the same experience gave people the sense of belonging to a group.[17] As a recent analysis of the psychology of spectatorship in ancient Rome has pointed out:

Since crowds usually comprise large numbers of likeminded people who have assembled in subgroups of mutual friends and acquaintances for a pre-determined reason, deeply consequential sensations of connectedness, validation, purposefulness, agency, and empowerment come to the fore and bind the crowd together in its social identity. The liberating expression of this shared identity in the crowd...generates excitement and sensations of belonging and solidarity.[18]

---

[15] Tranter 1998, 40.
[16] On the history of Association football, see Taylor 2008. Taylor (pp. 90–101) provides a nuanced discussion of the role of social class in playing and watching Association football. He points out that "football was certainly a people's game in the sense that the majority of those who played and watched were working class" (91), but also goes on to discuss the important role played by members of the upper class at the organizational level and significant cleavages among working-class football supporters along lines of gender and religion.
[17] This insight goes back to Durkheim, see Durkheim 1965 (1912), 474–75 and *passim*.
[18] Fagan 2011, 279. See also Lever's analysis of the social role of soccer in modern-day Brazil, in which the author argues that "Spectator sport is one mechanism that builds people's consciousness of togetherness" (Lever 1983, 3).

Because the upper and working classes frequently played and watched different sports, the people playing or watching sport on any given occasion tended to be largely from one class or the other, and that in turn reinforced distinctions between the two groups and individuals' sense of belonging to one group or the other.

Second, because members of the upper and working classes tended to play different sports, sport contributed to the formation of distinctive, class-based lifestyles. We have already had occasion to remark on Bourdieu's research on the correlation between socioeconomic status and individual choices about what sports to play and the resulting capacity of sport to create social distinctions (see Section 6.3).

Third, both the upper and working classes crafted sport experiences that enacted and hence reinforced their respective, quite different goals and social rules. In the second half of the nineteenth century the goals and social rules of the upper class were very much a work in progress, because the merging of the landed gentry and the middle class resulted in the emergence of a new set of goals and social rules embodied in the ideal of the Christian gentleman. An emphasis on competition, individual effort, and on achieving success through hard work, sobriety, and piety represented something new and different for the landed gentry, whereas an emphasis on manliness, public service, working cooperatively as a member of a larger group, and playing sports was something new and different for the middle class. This new set of goals and social rules was not created in the course of a single, magical day; it took shape by means of a slow, complex process that was not planned in advance and the workings of which were beyond the conscious grasp or control of the people involved in it.

Sport was a ritualized activity that offered the upper class models of and for the emergent ideal of the Christian gentleman and hence helped solidify a sense of belonging to a single, unified group. As John Hargeaves put it, "Games were a medium whereby common understandings among the dominant classes about the nature of social existence could be developed and stated in a condensed, striking form...."[19] Meritocratic competition among people considered to be equals, orderly behavior in conformity with rules, an ability to cooperate with others, concern for the common good, and manliness were all essential traits of the Christian gentleman that were enacted in sport. Sport taught participants and spectators what was now expected of them both on the playing field and in life, and the great value placed on sport ensured that there were rich rewards in terms of social standing for those who displayed the appropriate traits. Sport helped define what it meant to be a Christian gentleman, shaped men from the upper class accordingly, and conferred on them a strong sense of a shared identity.

---

[19] Hargreaves 1986, 43. On sport as a ritualized activity, see the discussion in Section 10.3.

Sport did much the same for the working class, but it enacted a very different set of goals and social rules. For example, individualistic, meritocratic competition was a matter of more pressing concern to the upper than the working class. In part this was because the goals and social rules of the upper class stressed individual striving to get ahead, whereas members of the working class put a higher value on mutual aid and cooperation. In addition, members of the upper class had ample opportunity to advance themselves through demonstrated competence, whereas genuine opportunities for social mobility were much less available to members of the working class. The son of a factory worker probably had few illusions that he could pass a civil service exam that required extensive knowledge of Latin and Greek.

The difference in how the two classes approached sport is perhaps most evident in Association football. As the sport gained popularity in the last quarter of the nineteenth century, games played by local Association football teams became major events that were attended by literally thousands of people from the working class and frequently included what were, from the perspective of the upper class, unrestrained forms of behavior on the part of spectators. Ernest Ensor, a prominent cricket player, wrote an essay in 1898 with the title "Football Madness" in which he compared the two sports in the following terms:

The influence of cricket upon the spectators makes undoubtedly for good....There is an air of courtesy and self-restraint about the game itself which has its due effect. There are very few important cricket grounds on which the behavior of the crowd is anything but irreproachable. Generally the spirit of fair play is present....The effect of [Football] League matches and cup ties is thoroughly evil....Rough play, so long as it escapes punishment from the referee...delights the crowd. Nothing but the firmest action by the Association prevents assaults on referees and players. The passions are excited to the highest pitch of human feeling....The excitement during the match is epidemic, and twenty thousand people, torn by emotions of rage and pleasure roaring condemnation and applause, make an alarming spectacle....That the tendency of it all is toward brutality cannot be doubted....Groans and hoots make pandemonium; the foulest curses of an artisan's vocabulary are shouted...murder and sudden death seem to be abroad.[20]

Ensor clearly displays his class prejudices, but his concerns were not groundless. What is currently called soccer hooliganism was common in the late nineteenth and early twentieth centuries. A modern-day study found 159 incidents of turbulent and openly unruly behavior among spectators at Association football matches in the town of Leicester alone between 1894 and 1914.[21]

---

[20] Ensor 1898, 757–58.
[21] On crowd behavior at football matches in nineteenth-century Britain, see Dunning, Murphy, Williams, and Maguire 1984 and Vamplew 1980.

Association football matches in Britain in the late-nineteenth century were in many ways a clear expression of working-class culture past and present. Association football came from a long-established tradition of folk football, which included annual matches in which a substantial fraction of the residents of two neighboring villages played a violent and unrestrained game as part of a raucous festival (see Section 11.5). In addition, as compared to the norms of the upper class, working-class culture in the late nineteenth century put much less stress on sobriety and piety and more emphasis on group solidarity. In Association football of the late nineteenth century, players and their fans were in a real sense all part of the same team. An Association football match in Britain in the late 1800s thus shared many traits with earlier folk football and was an occasion for the members of a working-class community to come together and enact their unity. John Hargreaves summed up the situation nicely:

Working-class people stamped sports like Association football and rugby league with their own character and transformed them in some ways into a means of expression for values opposed to the bourgeois athleticist tradition: vociferous partisanship, a premium on victory, a suspicion of and often a disdain for, constituted authority, a lack of veneration for official rules, mutual solidarity as the basis of team-work, a preference for tangible monetary rewards for effort, and a hedonistic "vulgar" festive element, were all brought to sports.[22]

By bringing together class-specific groups of people as participants and spectators, by forming an important part of distinctive, class-specific lifestyles, and by enacting two divergent, class-specific sets of goals and social rules, sport helped create boundaries around the upper class and working class and thereby contributed to group closure.

The ability of sport to create boundaries around large, national groups was a function of widespread, almost mandatory participation in sport among the upper class and widespread spectatorship among the working class. There was a strong expectation that upper-class families would send their sons to public schools, and once they arrived there boys had little choice but to dedicate a good deal of their time to sport. In the latter decades of the nineteenth century, boys in many British public schools were required, not encouraged, to play sports. Peter McIntosh in his work on the history of sport in Britain has in fact referred to the "tyranny of organised games."[23] Immense pressures were brought to bear on boys who would have preferred to not dedicate much of their time to sport, a reality which is highlighted in the following observations of Percy Lubbock, who attended Eton toward the end of the nineteenth century:

---

[22] Hargreaves 1986, 67. The strong elements of continuity in British sports over the entire course of the nineteenth century, especially sports as played by and among the working class, have been rightly emphasized by Richard Holt (Holt 1992, 135–94 and *passim*).

[23] McIntosh 1968, 68.

This huge unpausing roundabout of pastime doesn't maintain its pace without infinite care and forethought, as we know; there is nothing unpremeditated in these revels. Do you suppose that the boys come tumbling out of school, rejoicing in their release, to disperse to their games on the inclination of the moment – to fly to the field or the river, the court or the wicket, as fancy dictates? No such freedom is theirs. The great machine is prepared for the ordering of their sports, as of their lessons in school; it catches and despatches them to their pleasure prescribed. Do they make their own compulsion, do they themselves invent that immense particularity in the scheming and ordaining of their delights? They simply don't know; so it is, and so they accept it. Certainly they are firm in enforcing it, as utterly as they may, on any young rebel or fugitive in their midst, they aren't tender to eccentricity, they hold the rods of discipline, and they do not neglect them.[24]

A notice posted on a bulletin board at Eton during this period read, "Any lower boy in this house who does not play football once a day and twice on half holiday will be fined half a crown and kicked."[25]

Required participation in sport was something that had also been true of Sparta, something which was not lost on public school boys who were well versed in the ancient Greek sources. An essay written by a Harrow student in the second half of the nineteenth century opened with the observation that "the education of a Spartan and of an English boy were very much the same." The author concluded that "on the whole, a Spartan boy was rather the best off, because in their history there is no mention of Greek verb card punishments, reps, compulsory football, going to bathe only once a day, bills [roll-call], cricket fagging [younger boys being forced to chase down cricket balls for older players], several other things, and extra school."[26] It is note-worthy that the Harrow boy's complaints include "compulsory football."

Boys from upper-class families were sent to schools with similar educational programs that gave a privileged place to sport, and, as a result, sport had the capacity to help create a shared lifestyle that united the upper class as a whole. As Eric Hobsbawn put it:

The institution of old boys, which developed from the 1870s on, demonstrated that the products of an educational establishment formed a network which might be national or international, but it also bonded younger generations to older. In short, it gave social cohesion to a heterogeneous body of recruits. Here...sport provided much of the formal cement.[27]

The situation was somewhat different with the working class, in part because the number of people involved was so much larger and in part because education was not the unifying force that it was among the upper

---

[24] Lubbock 1932, 118–19, quoted in McIntosh 1968, 68.
[25] Quoted in Holt 1992, 76.
[26] The essay is preserved among the papers of R. H. Quick, a master at Harrow in the 1870s. It is quoted in Storr 1899, 505–06.
[27] Hobsbawm 1987, 179.

class. In this case, the key was spectatorship, and it is important to recall here that by the early 1900s total paid admissions at Association football matches throughout Britain on any given weekend was around 1 million.[28] A passionate attachment to Association football and regular attendance at matches was a custom that bonded and bounded the working class.[29]

Sport thus contributed meaningfully to the closure of the upper and working classes in Britain in the second half of the nineteenth century, but it remains to explain how that contributed to democratization. Indeed, one might argue that democratization would have been better served if sport had not helped solidify class boundaries. The relevant considerations are in some ways very similar to those that came into play in ancient Greece. There was nothing inevitable about the expansion of social and political privilege to include the middle class, and group closure of the newly formed upper class helped stabilize and consolidate a significant phase of democratization. In regard to the working class, closure helped develop a sense of being a unified group with common interests. That was important because the members of the upper class showed every sign of being ready, willing, and able to leverage the extensive social, political, and economic resources at their disposal in order to hold tightly onto their power and privileges. The major advantage the working class had was numbers – they made up the majority of the population of Britain – but that advantage could not be brought to bear unless a significant fraction of the members of the working class acted in unison. Playing and watching Association football helped pull the working class together. Even bitter rivalries between competing teams and their fans were productive in that they created a shared experience that ultimately did more to unite than divide. The British working class did in due course find a united political voice, most clearly by means of the formation of the Labor Party in 1900.

In the best of all possible democratic worlds it would have been preferable that all Britons had been given equal rights and opportunities in the nineteenth century, but that may well have been beyond what was at the time feasible. The emergence of the working class as a unified group was in many ways a second-best solution because it helped give working men and their families a powerful political voice. Insofar as sports helped unify both the upper and working classes, they contributed meaningfully to democratization in Britain in the nineteenth century.

---

[28] This figure comes from Tranter 1998, 17.

[29] On the importance of Association football in the formation of a bounded working class, see Hobsbawm 1984, 176–213.

16

Mass Sport in the United States

We end our exploration of mass sport where we began, with the United States. The goal here is not to provide a full case study but rather a rapid sketch that connects the material covered to this point with the specific context most familiar to many readers, while also completing the outline of the early history of mass sport.[1]

Sport did not typically enjoy a wholesome reputation in the United States in the first half of the nineteenth century. As was the case in Britain, it tended to be associated with gambling, drinking, and generally riotous behavior. In 1840 the editor of the *Christian Index* in Georgia wrote that:

We think the injunction of the Apostle quite sufficient – Abstain from all appearance of evil. Now can it be a compliance with this requisition to be seen playing ball, marbles, backgammon, or any such thing? Surely no. The parties say indeed, "We don't bet anything, we intend no harm, it is only pastime." Very well, and the card player and horse-racer may say the same – But how would it look for Baptists or Methodists to be seen playing cards and running horses?

Washington Gladden, writing in 1885, recalled that as a youth he wished to join his family's church in upstate New York but that would have entailed "giving up all my boyish sports – ball playing, coasting, fishing."[2]

The reputation of sport began to improve around the middle of the nineteenth century, due in part to the emergence of baseball as a sport played by respectable people in a respectable fashion. A variety of casual games with bats and balls were played in Europe from a very early period, and these games were brought to America. A particularly popular bat-and-ball game was variously known as rounders, base, base ball, or goal ball and

---

[1] On the history of sport in the United States, see R. Davies 2007, Guttmann 2004, and Rader 2008a.

[2] Quoted in Gorn and Goldstein 1993 at 62, 61, respectively. On the early history of sport in the United States, see R. Davies 2007, 1–41.

was played according to informal rules that differed markedly from place to place. In 1845 Alexander Cartwright helped form a club in New York City with the goal of arranging base ball games among its members and wrote a new set of rules that resulted in something that closely resembled the present-day game of baseball.[3]

From the outset baseball was seen as a sport for reputable men who could be expected to behave properly. Cartwright's club, the Knickerbocker Base Ball Club, set the tone by instituting fines against any member who swore or disobeyed a team captain during a game. When baseball became a professional sport in the 1870s and began to be associated with many of the same vices as other sports, players and coaches made a concerted effort to keep the sport "clean." When the National League of Professional Ball Clubs (now known as the National League) was established in 1876, its founders wrote a constitution that began by listing the objects of the league, which included:

1st.   To encourage, foster, and elevate the game of base ball.
2nd.   To enact and enforce proper rules for the exhibition and conduct of the game.
3rd.   To make base ball playing respectable and honorable.[4]

National League teams banned gambling and selling beer at baseball games and did not play on Sunday.

Muscular Christianity, which arrived in the United States from Britain, also helped make sport into an acceptable pastime. Among the leading American advocates for Muscular Christianity were Thomas Wentworth Higginson and Oliver Wendell Holmes. In 1858, Higginson published a widely read article, "Saints and Their Bodies," in which he lamented what he described as a long-standing Christian distaste for all things physical and then praised developments in Britain:

But, happily, times change, and saints with them. Our moral conceptions are expanding to take in that "athletic virtue" of the Greeks, *aretê gymnastikê*, which Dr. Arnold, by precept and practice, defended. The modern English "Broad Church" aims at breadth of shoulders, as well as of doctrines.[5]

The foundations of mass sport in the United States were laid in the period between the end of the Civil War and the beginning of the twentieth century. During this period the YMCA began spreading the gospel of physical activity; gymnastics became popular; baseball developed into a national sport

---

[3] On the history of baseball, see Rader 2008b. On the early history of baseball, see Martin 2009.
[4] Quoted in Spalding 1911, 211.
[5] Higginson 1858, 584. On Muscular Christianity and sport in the United States in the nineteenth century, see Putney 2001.

played by large numbers of men from all walks of life; sport became an increasingly important part of the curriculum at schools; and football, basketball, and volleyball were all invented.

Starting in the 1860s the YMCA became a powerful proponent of Muscular Christianity in the United States and played a significant role in encouraging sport participation. The Young Men Christian's Association, founded in Britain in 1844 as an evangelical organization that arranged prayer meetings, came to the United States in the 1850s, and in the 1860s the people running American YMCAs became enthusiastic supporters of Muscular Christianity. They began providing facilities for and opportunities to participate in sport, and founded a college in Springfield, Massachusetts that helped train people who oversaw YMCA-sponsored physical activities. The YMCA also built more than 400 gymnasia, spaces intended primarily for gymnastics, by 1890.[6]

The YMCA's sponsorship of gymnastics highlights an important difference between Britain and the United States: gymnastics established itself as an important form of sport in the United States in a way that it never did in Britain. Gymnastics instructors arrived in the United States from Germany in the 1820s and started running sessions at Harvard and a number of other schools in the Northeast. In addition, German immigrants to the United States continued performing gymnastics in their new homeland, and a massive wave of arrivals from Germany in the middle of the century helped make gymnastics quite popular. Groups of *Turner* were established, and national gymnastics festivals were held starting in 1851.[7]

In the years after the Civil War large numbers of men from a broad socioeconomic spectrum began playing baseball. Cartwright's version of base ball, which was spread all over the United States by soldiers during the Civil War, had by the 1870s become something like a national sport. The editor of the popular magazine *Spirit of the Times* observed in 1873 that:

The game is truly a national one. In every little town and hamlet throughout the country we find a ball club, generally two, bitter rivals, at it with hammer and tongs, ding-dong the entire summer, as though all creation depended on the defeat of the other crowd, and then away goes a challenge – to the next town, and from there to the next, and so on.[8]

The growing popularity and respectability of sport in the second half of the nineteenth century helped give it an important place in American educational institutions. Schoolchildren in the United States had long played sports informally, but the people running schools did nothing to encourage

---

[6] On the YMCA and sport, see Baker 1994.
[7] On the early history of gymnastics in the United States, see Hofmann and Pfister 2004 and Welch 2004, 96–134.
[8] Quoted in Baker 1988, 145.

such activities and in some cases actively discouraged them. The code of conduct at Dartmouth College in the eighteenth century suggested that students forget about sport and devote themselves to productive activities such as gardening.[9]

Starting in the 1850s, American students began playing sports in a more serious and organized fashion. Physical education programs run by schools focused almost entirely on gymnastics, in large part because American *Turner* clubs, many members of which had encountered gymnastics during their school years in Prussia, effectively advocated for the introduction of gymnastics into public elementary and secondary schools. By 1900 gymnastics was part of the curriculum in the school systems of more than fifty of the larger cities, and many universities, especially in the Northeastern United States, built gymnasia as spaces for gymnastics. In 1875, when given the choice between two electives, ancient Greek language and gymnastics, virtually the entire undergraduate population of Yale, including William Howard Taft, a future president of the United States, opted for gymnastics.[10] Physical education programs in the United States continued to center around gymnastics until the early twentieth century.

Other forms of sport became a major activity on many American university campuses starting in the 1860s, almost entirely as the result of student-led initiatives. "Throughout the nineteenth century sports and athletics...had no place in...official school or college programs. They were recognized only as the students' own after-school projects."[11] The first intercollegiate sports contest in the United States was a rowing match between Yale and Harvard held in 1852, 1859 saw the first intercollegiate baseball game, and 1869 the first intercollegiate football game.[12]

During this same period, the years between 1865 and 1900, American-style football came into being and developed into a major sport. Folk football had been played in North America virtually from the moment Europeans arrived there, and students at Northeastern universities began playing the sport with some regularity in the early nineteenth century. As was the case in Britain, a different version of the game was played at each school, and high levels of violence were common. Harvard students had a tradition of playing folk football on the first day of the fall semester each year, a day that became known as "Bloody Monday." In 1860 Cornelius Felton, the president of Harvard, wrote that the annual folk football game had become "a struggle of brute force" and "dangerous to life and limb" and noted that many incoming students took boxing lessons to prepare for it.[13]

[9] Quint 1914, 246. On the history of physical education programs in the United States, see Lee 1983 and Welch 2004.
[10] Lee 1983, 87 n. 10.
[11] Lee 1983, 82.
[12] On the early history of intercollegiate sports in the United States, see Rader 2008a, 81–97.
[13] Felton 1860, 32.

A major change came in 1874 after students from McGill University in Canada introduced their counterparts at Harvard to the official rules for Rugby football, rules that had been crafted three years earlier in Britain. Rugby football was an immediate hit at other Northeastern universities, particularly Ivy League institutions. American students had no deep attachment to the rules they inherited from Britain and almost immediately began changing them in ways that rapidly produced a new and different game, American football. Many innovations were devised at Yale University, whose team compiled a record of 231 wins, 10 losses, and 11 ties between 1876 and 1900. The 1888 Yale football team set a probably unbeatable record in going 13–0 and outscoring its opponents 698–0.[14] Football quickly became widely popular in much of the United States, as is evident from the fact that more than 5,000 football games were played on Thanksgiving Day in 1896.[15]

By the 1890s, sports had grown to such a point that university administrators felt obliged to exert some degree of institutional control over them. Football in particular was played with near fanatical competitiveness in front of increasingly large crowds. The Yale-Princeton game in 1888, for example, attracted 40,000 spectators. There were concerns about the amount of time students were spending training for and playing football, about alumni recruiting star athletes and supplying them with financial assistance, and about managing the rapidly growing revenues and expenses associated with football programs. Some attempts were made to curb football and other sports, but the popularity of athletics with students and alumni, and the revenues they produced, made that a functional impossibility. Most universities settled for establishing committees made up of students, faculty members, and administrators that were charged with overseeing athletic programs and with trying to put a stop to some of the more obvious abuses.[16]

Universities were quick to realize and seize upon the revenue-generating capacity of sport. The course of events at Harvard gives a good sense of the general trend. Harvard President Charles Eliot wrote in 1874 that he felt it was necessary to take steps to prevent "students from making athletic sports the main business, instead of one of the incidental pleasures, of their college lives."[17] An attempt to ban football in the mid-1880s rapidly failed. By 1904, Harvard had built the first major football stadium in the United

---

[14] On the history of football in America, see D. Anderson 1997 and Guttmann 2004, 142–54. On football at Harvard and Yale, see Corbett 2002 and Rubin 2006, respectively.

[15] Betts 1974, 124.

[16] On college football during the late nineteenth century, see R. Davies 2007, 74–82 and Rader 2008a, 83–97. On Princeton football, see Bernstein 2009. Possibly the best single source for college sports in America up through the 1930s is *American College Athletics* (Savage 1929), a comprehensive report issued in 1929 by a committee assembled by the Carnegie Foundation for the Advancement of Teaching.

[17] Eliot 1875, 23.

States and by the early twentieth century the football coach at Harvard was being paid substantially more than the highest paid professor.[18] Football games enriched institutions both through ticket sales and providing valuable fund-raising opportunities. When the University of Chicago was founded in 1892, its first president immediately set about building a winning football program, and Amos Alonzo Stagg, an instructor at the YMCA training college in Springfield, Massachusetts, was brought in as coach. When Stagg arranged a game between the new school and the University of Michigan on Thanksgiving Day in 1893, President Harper took the opportunity to invite potential donors to attend the game as his guests.[19]

Football was not the only significant new sport to come into being in the United States in the later decades of the nineteenth century; basketball and volleyball were also invented in this period. In 1891 the director of the YMCA training college asked one of the instructors, James Naismith, to come up with a game that could be played indoors because the people in charge of organizing sports activities at YMCAs throughout the country had made it known that there was a need for a game that could be played in gymnasia during cold weather. Naismith tried various experiments before inventing basketball, which became widely popular almost overnight. One of Naismith's students, William Morgan, became director of physical education at the YMCA in Holyoke, Massachusetts and invented volleyball in 1895 to cater to older businessmen who found basketball too strenuous.[20]

As the practice of sport became more common, concerns arose about people from different parts of the socioeconomic spectrum mixing together, just as was the case in Britain. Caspar Whitney, an American author who wrote regularly about sports for magazines such as *Harpers* and *Outing*, suggested in 1895 that:

The laboring classes are all right in their way; let them go their way in peace, and have their athletics in whatsoever manner best suits their inclinations....Let us have our own sport among the more refined elements....[21]

The situation in the United States was somewhat different from that in Britain because of the identity of the groups involved. In Britain it was a matter of an upper class and a working class, both defined by wealth, occupation, and education, consciously separating themselves from each other. In the United States the lines of division were drawn more on the basis of wealth, ethnicity, and how recently one's family had immigrated.

---

[18] Lee 1983, 154.

[19] R. Davies 2007, 73. On the history of football at the University of Chicago, see Lester 1995.

[20] On the invention of basketball, see Guttmann 2004, 159–62 and Peterson 1990. On volleyball, see Shewman 1995.

[21] Whitney 1895, 167.

Nonetheless, just as was the case in Britain, many wealthy people in the United States sought to play sports only with people from similar socioeconomic backgrounds. To that end, they turned to sports such as golf that were expensive to play and built exclusive clubs, including the first country clubs, which were established in and around Boston between 1870 and 1882.[22] With the same end in mind the distinction between amateur and professional athletes was imported from Britain and rigorously applied.[23]

However, attempts to impose socioeconomic barriers on sport were not nearly as successful in the United States as they were in Britain. During the first half of the twentieth century athletics became increasingly democratized in the United States as more and more people from throughout the socioeconomic spectrum took up the habit of regularly playing and watching sports. This was in part the result of the efforts of the Progressives, who founded a number of well-organized and funded groups that actively and successfully promoted sport participation across a broad socioeconomic spectrum. For example, the Public School Athletic League, founded in New York in 1903 and widely imitated elsewhere in the United States, collected funds from wealthy donors and aimed at making opportunities to play sports available outside of school hours to both boys and girls who were enrolled in public schools. The Playground Association of America, founded in 1906, established an immensely successful program to create public playgrounds, many with hired staff to organize sports activities. In 1906 there were 87 playgrounds in 24 American cities. By 1916 there were 3,940 playgrounds in 481 cities.[24]

Perhaps the biggest factors in the continuing democratization of sport in the United States in the first half of the twentieth century were the expansion of publicly funded schooling and the incorporation of sport programs into school curricula. In his work on sports in America, George Sage points out that "American youth and school sports were popularized in the first half of the 20th century when educational programs were increasingly directed at lower- and middle-class youth."[25] Starting in the late nineteenth century, free education was made available to all children, who were compelled to attend school for an increasing number of years. Between 1890 and 1930, for instance, the percentage of children aged five through seventeen in some type of public school increased from 50% to 81%.[26] At the same time, physical education became a central element in the curriculum of American

[22] On the history of country clubs in the United States, see Mayo 1998.
[23] On amateurism in the United States in the late-nineteenth and early-twentieth centuries, see Pope 1996 and Rader 2008a, 72–79.
[24] On children's sports and playgrounds in the United States in the early years of the twentieth century, see Guttmann 1988, 82–100 and Wood 1913. The figures on playgrounds come from Guttmann 2004, 156–57.
[25] Sage 1998, 262.
[26] Snyder 1993, 25–27.

educational institutions at all levels. In addition, it rapidly became standard practice for high schools to follow the lead of universities and field a wide array of sports teams.[27]

When educators running middle and elementary schools balked at introducing sports teams, due to fears about the effects of competitive athletics on young children, parents established youth sports leagues. Pop Warner football, which organizes teams for boys aged five through sixteen, was founded in 1929. Little League baseball was founded in 1939. Similar organizations for other sports followed.[28]

The process of democratization in American sport continued through the second half of the twentieth century as largely successful efforts were made to open athletics up to groups, particularly women and African Americans, who had been previously largely excluded. Landmark moments in that process included the integration of professional baseball in 1947 and the enactment of Title IX of the Education Amendments of 1972, which required that high schools and universities make equal provisions for sports for male and female students.[29]

Although there were not insignificant elements of verticality, most notably in the form of the gymnastics imported from Germany, American sport was very much like British sport in being largely horizontal. Here again the key factors are organizational structure, degree of regimentation, and stated goals, in all of which dimensions American sport was markedly on the horizontal end of the spectrum.

The date of the arrival of horizontal mass sport in the United States is a matter of judgment. It could be argued that the growing popularity of baseball and the incorporation of various sports including gymnastics into school curricula meant that there was mass sport in the United States in the last quarter of the nineteenth century. However, it is probably safer to point to the early decades of the twentieth century, when programs such as the Public School Athletic League, which were closely associated with the Progressives and their fervent belief in the democratizing powers of sport, were established.

It should come as no great revelation at this point that the appearance of a system of horizontal mass sport in the United States occurred at the same time as a process of democratization was unfolding on the societal level. This is particularly evident in regard to the Civil Rights Movement and the integration of baseball. Two landmarks in the extension of full civil rights to African Americans are the integration of military units ordered by President Truman in 1948 and the decision made by the Supreme Court in 1954 in

---

[27] On sports programs in American elementary and secondary schools in the first half of the twentieth century, see Lee 1983, 133–91.

[28] On early youth sports programs in the United States, see Berryman 1988; Coakley 2006; Rader 2008a, 98–116; and Wiggins 1987.

[29] On Title IX, see the discussion in Section 4.2.

FIGURE 15. Jackie Robinson Integrates Baseball, Opening Day, April 15, 1947 (From Associated Press Photos)

the case of Brown vs. the Topeka Board of Education, which resulted in the integration of public schools.[30] The stage had been set for both these events in 1947, when Jackie Robinson became the first African American to play major league baseball since the 1890s (see Figure 15). Correlation is not causation, but the idea that integration in sport served as an important model of and for integration in American society as a whole has a long history, starting with the players involved in the process.[31] As Roy Campanella, one of the earliest African Americans to follow Jackie Robinson into major league baseball, pointed out, "All I know is, we were the first ones on the trains, we were the first ones down South not to go around the back of the restaurant, first ones in the hotels....We were like the teachers of the whole integration thing."[32]

---

[30] On the history of civil rights in the United States, see Klarman 2007.

[31] On the sociopolitical ramifications of the integration of baseball, see Malec and Beckles 1999 and Zirin 2005, 37–52.

[32] Quoted in Zirin 2005, 33. Cf. A. S. D. Young 1963, an article that appeared in *Ebony* magazine in 1963, under the title "How Sports Helped Break the Color Line."

17

Conclusion

Our exploration of the relationship between democratization in sport and society has taken us on a long, winding journey, and it will be useful at this juncture to summarize the key points that have developed along the way. We began by observing that a clear correlation exists between democratization in sport and in society. That correlation raised the question of whether democratization in sport is an effect or a cause of democratization in society.

In order to find a satisfactory answer to that question, it was first necessary to define carefully the term "democratization" and to differentiate between situations in which a small fraction of a society's populace is actively involved with sport and situations in which sport is played and watched on a mass scale. It was also necessary to differentiate between sport that embodies egalitarian relationships, horizontal sport, and sport that embodies hierarchical relationships, vertical sport.[1] To the extent that sport has the power to foster horizontal rather than vertical relationships outside of sport, that is, to the extent that it has the capacity to democratize society, that power is most clearly vested in horizontal mass sport.

There are four possible views of the relationship between sport and society with respect to democratization:

(1) democratization in both society as a whole and in sport are determined by one or more exogenous factors;
(2) democratization in society is cause, democratization in sport effect, or, to put it differently, the nature of sport reflects and is determined by the nature of the society in which it is played, whereas the nature of sport has little or no effect on the nature of society;
(3) democratization in sport contributes meaningfully to the democratization of society;

---

[1] See Chapter 2.

(4) democratization in both society and in sport is more apparent than real, and society and sport function primarily as mutually reinforcing systems of domination and oppression; sport, to the extent that it acts on society in this regard, typically inhibits democratization.

The first view runs up against the difficulty that the correlation between democratization in sport and society holds good across diverse societies that do not share any exogenous factor that has the apparent capacity to generate the correlation in question. Previous scholarship has made the case that changes in both sport and society are driven by one or more of five factors: capitalism, industrialization, urbanization, Protestantism, and modernization. However, democratization in sport and society were strongly correlated in ancient Greece, where none of these factors was operative.[2] It is, therefore, unlikely that there is an exogenous factor that is determinative of the level of democratization in both sport and society.

A special case of the exogenous-factor view of sport and democratization merits brief mention. One might argue that increased wealth generates societal democratization while also creating leisure time that makes horizontal mass sport possible. Wealth would thus be an exogenous factor that directly causes democratization in society and indirectly causes democratization in sport. It is, however, unlikely that wealth in and of itself determines levels of societal democratization, as is evident from the divergent trajectories of democratization in Britain and Germany between 1800 and 1945, during which time industrialization made the residents of both countries noticeably wealthier.[3] In addition, increased leisure time, even when it is devoted to sport instead of other activities, does not necessarily eventuate in horizontal sport, as is evident in the growth of vertical mass sport in Germany in the nineteenth century.

One might also argue that wealth makes mass sport possible while also contributing to societal democratization, which in turn determines the nature of sport. This is, however, a special case of the second possible view of the relationship between sport and democratization, namely that the nature of sport is determined by the nature of the society in which it is played. This view is partially sound insofar as the nature of sport undoubtedly reflects the nature of the society in which it is played, and democratization in society will be reflected in democratization in sport. However, it is also true that sport has the capacity to shape the behavior of participants and spectators

---

[2] See Section 7.3. This list does not include factors that may have affected only societal democratization, because those factors are incapable of accounting for the correlation between democratization in society and sport. For instance, the growth of a middle class may well have a positive effect on societal democratization, but it has no evident necessary effect on sport. This is evident from the fact that a sizeable middle class existed in Britain for well over a century before mass sport came into being.

[3] See also the discussion in Grugel 2002, 46–51.

in other spheres of activity and that mass sport can shape society as a whole. Democratization in sport is, therefore, unlikely to be solely a dependent variable.[4]

The third view is sound in that there are four distinct mechanisms by means of which democratization in horizontal mass sport fosters democratization on a societal level. Those four mechanisms are:

- the facilitation of the formation of small-scale, tightly bonded horizontal groups that literally enact democratization;
- the inculcation of particularized and generalized trust;
- the cultivation of a sense of political efficacy;
- the cultivation of self-disciplined individuals with a predisposition to obey rules and legally constituted authorities.[5]

The fourth view also has some validity, because there are four additional mechanisms by means of which horizontal mass sport inhibits democratization on a societal level. Those four mechanisms are:

- the inculcation of docility,
- the creation of boundaries that heighten exclusion,
- the generation of hostility among sport participants and spectators,
- the generation of inequality via meritocratic competition.[6]

Horizontal mass sport thus has the capacity to both foster and inhibit democratization in society as a whole. As a result, exploring the relationship between democratization in sport and society becomes a matter of establishing the cumulative effect of the mechanisms by means of which horizontal mass sport simultaneously promotes and impedes societal democratization.

Although there is no quantitative data that would make it possible to specify the magnitude of the positive or negative effect of each of these mechanisms with respect to democratization, there are various ways to assess their relative efficacy. There can be little doubt that the capacity of horizontal mass sport to facilitate the formation of large numbers of tightly bonded, horizontal groups in and of itself exerts a powerful democratizing effect on society as a whole. That effect is sufficiently significant as to be overcome by countervailing factors only with considerable difficulty. The democratizing effects of half of American high school students being members of sports teams, for instance, are not easily erased.

Moreover, four of the eight mechanisms form antithetical pairs: the inculcation of particularized and generalized trust on one hand and the generation of hostility among sport participants and spectators on the other make

---

[4] See Chapter 4.
[5] See Chapter 5.
[6] See Chapter 6.

one pair, the cultivation of a sense of political efficacy and the inculcation of docility another. The relative strength of the mechanisms within these pairs can be established with some confidence, and in both cases the positive effects of sport on societal democratization outweigh the negative effects.[7]

Furthermore, historical case studies of sport and society in Greece and Britain show that the two remaining mechanisms by means of which sport can inhibit democratization are capable, under certain circumstances, of fostering it as well. Exclusion can promote closure, which aids in the formation of large, relatively egalitarian groups. Meritocratic status competition can promote egalitarianism, by undermining systems of ascribed rank and by hindering the development of steep differentials in social power.[8]

The mechanisms by means of which sport fosters societal democratization thus appear to be considerably more efficacious than those by means of which sport inhibits democratization. This conclusion is reinforced by the observable outcomes of participation in horizontal mass sport.

One approach to studying outcomes is to examine whether rates of sport participation are positively or negatively correlated with democratization on a societal level in present-day societies with horizontal mass sport. Data from a wide array of countries shows a strong positive correlation between rates of participation in horizontal mass sport and societal democratization. This finding suggests that the cumulative effect of horizontal mass sport is to foster democratization, but it leaves some room for doubt, because the data cannot support any conclusions about how the correlation in question came into being. Democratization at a societal level is influenced by a range of factors other than sport, and it is theoretically possible, for example, that sport participation inhibits democratization but that other factors counteract that effect. Moreover, the lack of temporal depth in the data means that there are significant structural similarities in all of the countries studied, which in turn raises the possibility that, within the bounds of this dataset, there are one or more exogenous factors determining both sport participation rates and levels of societal democratization.

Another approach is to consider societies in which rates of participation in horizontal sport have increased sharply over time and observe the effect of increased sport participation on societal democratization. Sport-for-all programs instituted in many countries in the 1960s and 1970s resulted in steep increases in sport participation, and data from Denmark, Japan, Norway, West Germany, and elsewhere show that increasing participation in horizontal sport was correlated with increasing societal democratization. However, countries with government-sponsored sport-for-all programs represent a situation in which the nature of sport is unusually heavily influenced by society, rather than vice-versa. In addition, countries that instituted

---

[7] See Chapter 7.

[8] See the discussion in Chapters 10 and 15.

sport-for-all programs were in many cases also simultaneously instituting other initiatives intended to increase democratization. Both of these factors make it difficult to ascribe changes in societal democratization to increased levels of participation in horizontal sport.[9]

A better alternative is to focus on societies in which there were sharp increases in the level of participation in horizontal sport without any government intervention. In those instances the effect of society on sport is significantly less pronounced, and governments are less likely to be investing in other kinds of social programs specifically designed to increase democratization. Societies that fit these criteria are few in number because mass sport is a relatively recent phenomenon. They are limited to sixth- and fifth-century BCE Greece, nineteenth-century Britain, and early twentieth-century America.

Careful study of sport and society in those three historical contexts shows a strong and consistent correlation between participation in horizontal sport and societal democratization. In all three instances horizontal mass sport emerged at the same time that strong trends toward societal democratization manifested themselves. Moreover, in addition to the four transhistorically operative mechanisms by means of which horizontal mass sport fosters democratization, in both Greece and Britain horizontal mass sport promoted democratization at a societal level by means of three further, contextually specific mechanisms: by serving as an arena for meritocratic status competition that undermined systems of ascribed rank, by serving as a model of and for emergent horizontal relationships, and by enabling group closure.[10]

The relevant data from present-day European countries, from countries that instituted sport-for-all programs in the 1960s and 1970s, and from historical case studies of Greece, Britain, and the United States thus all show a strong positive correlation between participation in horizontal sport and societal democratization. Insofar as the existence of the eleven mechanisms specified earlier leaves little doubt that mass sport can affect democratization on a societal level, there are three ways to interpret the consistent, strong, positive correlation between horizontal mass sport and societal democratization:

(a) the various mechanisms by means of which horizontal mass sport affects societal democratization more or less cancel each other out, with the result that horizontal mass sport has no significant effect on

---

[9] This and the preceding paragraph summarize the discussion found in Chapter 7.

[10] On sport and society in Greece, see Chapters 8–10. On sport and society in Britain, see Chapters 11–12 and 14–15. Chapter 13, an excursus on the practice of sport in Germany up through World War II, shows that the creation of a system of vertical mass sport in the nineteenth century reflected and reinforced an authoritarian sociopolitical structure and likely contributed in some fashion to the collapse of democratic government in Germany in the 1930s. On sport and society in the United States, see Chapter 16.

societal democratization; the correlation between democratization in sport and society is thus primarily the result of the effect of society on sport;

(b) horizontal mass sport inhibits democratization at a societal level; the correlation between horizontal mass sport and democratization exists *in spite* of the effects of horizontal mass sport and as the result of the effect of society on sport;

(c) horizontal mass sport fosters democratization at a societal level; the correlation between horizontal mass sport and democratization exists partly as a result.

The first two interpretations cannot be entirely ruled out, because horizontal mass sport is by no means the only influence on the level of societal democratization and because the nature of sport is to some extent determined by the nature of the society in which it is played. It does, however, appear to be the case that those two interpretations are significantly less likely than the third. The first two interpretations run up against the difficulty that there are strong indications that the mechanisms by means of which horizontal sport fosters societal democratization are considerably more efficacious than those by means of which it impedes it. The second interpretation has the additional difficulty that, in order to explain the utter consistency of the positive correlation between participation in horizontal mass sport and societal democratization across a range of different societal and historical contexts, it must assume that the effect of sport on societal democratization is outweighed by other, countervailing factors that are always present and always sufficiently powerful to overwhelm the negative effects of sport. It is impossible to assess the probability of that assumption, but *prima facie* it seems low if only because the presumed disinhibiting factors need to be consistently present in times and places as diverse as ancient Greece and present-day Norway.

The third interpretation, that the cumulative effect of horizontal mass sport is to foster democratization on a societal level, is considerably more economical and persuasive. It aligns with the evidence for the relative importance of the mechanisms by means of which sport promotes and impedes democratization, and it easily accounts for the consistent positive correlation between upward shifts in participation in horizontal sport and societal democratization, without requiring any further assumptions. Moreover, this understanding of the relationship between democratization in sport and society is consonant with the foundational assumption of functionalism, namely that the various spheres of activity within individual societies are at least to some degree interdependent. It also meshes perfectly with well-established understandings, which go back to Tocqueville, of the importance of voluntary associations in democratic societies. As was pointed out earlier, the conclusion that horizontal mass sport does *not* have a positive effect on societal democratization would be significantly more surprising and difficult to defend than the conclusion that it promotes democratization on a societal level.

Certainty is impossible here, and the study of the relationship between democratization in sport and society is fairly typical of social analysis in presenting a situation in which the best that can be hoped for is "a particularly plausible hypothesis."[11] That said, there is a considerable body of evidence that strongly supports the argument that horizontal mass sport is, in and of itself, an important form of democratization and that horizontal mass sport both springs from and reinforces democratization on a societal level. Sport, in other words, shows every sign of being a school for democracy.

An important nuance to bear in mind is that one's views on the effect of sport on democratization are to some extent dependent upon the specific dimension of democratization on which one focuses. It is entirely possible that overall democratization within a society can be increasing while democratization within specific spheres of that society is static or decreasing. Moreover, as Merton pointed out, the functional effect of a given social institution or practice can vary for different groups and individuals. For instance, the establishment of a radically egalitarian political system in Athens in the fifth century BCE seems to have generated genuine democratization for males across the entire socioeconomic spectrum, while simultaneously lowering the status of women.[12] It is thus possible that sport can have an overall positive democratizing effect while having a negative effect for specific groups or individuals. For example, there is some reason to think that, despite all the changes that have taken place in recent decades, sport continues to perpetuate hierarchical gender relations. Analyses that concentrate on the relationship between sport and gender relations are, therefore, likely to reach the conclusion that sport inhibits democratization, whereas analyses with different loci of interest may well reach divergent conclusions.

Furthermore, the nature of the relationship between horizontal mass sport and democratization in any given time and place may depend on the extent to which the society in question is democratized. It may well be that horizontal mass sport promotes democratization until a certain threshold is reached, after which point it is either irrelevant or counterproductive. The evidence from Norway would suggest that if this is indeed the case, the level of democratization at which sport ceases to promote democratization is quite high.

A final consideration is that assessments of the relationship between sport and democratization are to some extent conditioned by one's perspective on the ideal level of democratization. The knowledge that horizontal mass sport has helped make possible the current levels of democratization

---

[11] Weber 1962, 37.
[12] See the discussion in Jameson 1997.

in Western liberal democracies, and that sport contributes to maintaining those levels of democratization is, for those satisfied with the current levels of democratization, likely to be cause for seeing sport in a positive light. Those who are dissatisfied with current levels of democratization and are driven by a strongly-felt commitment to achieving more egalitarian social relations are likely to see sport in a negative light, because, at least in its present form, it has not demonstrated the capacity to enable the sort of social change they desire.

The preceding discussion has suggested that horizontal mass sport promotes democratization on a societal level. In the case of liberal democracies in Europe, North America, Australasia, and elsewhere what this typically means in practice is that horizontal mass sport contributes to ongoing processes necessary to maintain current, relatively high levels of democratization. Although the democratizing effects of horizontal mass sport are most easily traced when rates of sport participation increase sharply, they are no less operative in seemingly static situations in which sport participation rates and levels of societal democratization are relatively stable. Unceasing social change, and the birth and death of individuals involved in the horizontal relationships that constitute the substance of democratization, mean that democratization is a condition that requires constant renewal. Regular involvement of significant fractions of a populace in horizontal sport from an early age plays a profoundly important role in holding onto hard-won gains in societal democratization. Moreover, there is every indication that increased participation in horizontal mass sport would, as it has consistently in the past, help further democratize society.

Public spending on sport can, therefore, be seen as an investment in democratization, but it is not obvious that current levels of public spending on sport will continue. This book has been written during a period of unusually severe economic distress in the United States and in much of Europe, as a result of which governments in many places, both at the local and national levels, have been forced to make drastic cuts in spending. In the United States, physical education classes and sports teams funded by public schools have been high on the list of programs to reduce or eliminate. The National Football League has felt obliged to launch a national "Keep Gym in School" campaign in response to a sharp and continuing decline in the number of schools that offer physical education classes on a regular basis.[13] High schools and universities all over the United States are dissolving sports teams that they can no longer afford, and many teams that were once funded by their schools now rely on fees paid by participants and donations by parents. Cuts of this sort fall more heavily on less well-off institutions and families and inevitably reduce participation in sports.

[13] http://www.keepgyminschool.com/

It is already noteworthy that in most countries those who come from wealthy families are much more likely to participate in sports as both children and adults than those from less fortunate circumstances.[14] One can see this as nothing more than an issue of money: people from wealthy families can better afford the direct and indirect costs of playing sports. However, the differing rates of sport participation among the wealthy and the less well-off can also be seen as a reflection and source of social and political inequalities. If participation in sport increasingly becomes the preserve of the wealthy, there is every reason to think that, sooner or later, the exclusion of the less wealthy from sport will result in higher levels of inequality in society as a whole, and that current levels of democratization will accordingly fall.

We might recall in this regard Aristotle's observation that in some ancient Greek communities, the rich sought to exclude others from participation in sport as part of a concerted program intended to exclude all but the rich from wielding significant social and political influence.[15] By cutting public funding and thereby making it more difficult for the less well-off to participate in sport, local and national governments in the United States and elsewhere are unintentionally doing exactly the same thing as oligarchically inclined members of some ancient Greek communities did intentionally, almost certainly with the same result.

If we take democratization seriously, we should, therefore, take sport seriously. Taking sport seriously does not mean putting on rose-colored glasses and endlessly singing its praises. It does mean recognizing and acknowledging both the positive and negative effects of sport and managing sport in such a way as to maximize the former and minimize the latter. This is not the place to launch into a series of detailed public policy prescriptions, but it is possible to suggest a few simple guidelines. Societies with horizontal sport that wish to maintain or increase prevailing levels of democratization should take steps to:

- maximize sport participation and the diversity of sport participants, which requires the expenditure of public funds to underwrite participation by individuals who would otherwise be unable or unlikely to take part in sport;
- maximize the horizontal elements in sport while minimizing the vertical elements, which requires a consistent dedication to giving sport participants the largest possible role in organizing and determining their own sports activity;

[14] There is a mass of data which proves this to be true beyond doubt. See, for example, Spreitzer 1994.

[15] See Section 10.1.

- curb competitive excesses, which requires a consistent dedication to framing sport with a discourse that privileges cooperation and participation rather than competition and winning.

Members of societies that support democratization should care about providing ample opportunities for everyone, regardless of their socioeconomic status, ethnicity, gender, or any other distinguishing quality, to play horizontal sport. When participation is maximized, participants have control over their own activity, and competitive excesses are curbed, sport can realize its potential to be a school for democracy.

Bibliography

Abercrombie, Nicholas, Stephen Hill, and Bryan S. Turner. 1980. *The Dominant Ideology Thesis*. London: G. Allen and Unwin.

Abrams, Philip. 1980. "History, Sociology, Historical Sociology." *Past and Present* 87: 3–16.

Abramson, Lyn, Martin Seligman, and John Teasdale. 1978. "Learned Helplessness in Humans." *Journal of Abnormal Psychology* 87: 49–74.

Adler, Paul and Seok-Woo Kwon. 2002. "Social Capital: Prospects for a New Concept." *Academy of Management Review* 27: 17–40.

Almond, Gabriel. 1980. "The Intellectual History of the Civic Culture Concept." In *The Civic Culture Revisited*, edited by Gabriel Almond and Sidney Verba, 1–36. Boston: Little, Brown, and Company.

Almond, Gabriel and Sidney Verba. 1963. *The Civic Culture: Political Attitudes and Democracy in Five Nations*. Princeton, NJ: Princeton University Press.

   eds. 1980. *The Civic Culture Revisited: An Analytic Study*. Boston: Little, Brown.

Anderson, Dave. 1997. *The Story of Football*. 2nd ed. New York: W. Morrow.

Anderson, Nancy. 2010. *The Sporting Life: Victorian Sports and Games*. Santa Barbara, CA: Praeger.

Anonymous. 1888, February 8. "Mr. Goschen and the Universities." *The Oxford Magazine*, 6.12, 208.

Arms, Robert, Gordon Russell, and Mark Sandilands. 1979. "Effects on the Hostility of Spectators of Viewing Aggressive Sports." *Sociometry* 42: 275–79.

Arnold, Thomas. 1858. *The Miscellaneous Works of Thomas Arnold*. 2nd ed. London: T. Fellowes.

Atherley, Kim. 2006. "Sport, Localism, and Social Capital in Rural Western Australia." *Geographical Research* 44: 348–60.

Augestad, Pål and Nils Asle Bergsgard. 2008. "Norway." In *Comparative Elite Sport Development: Systems, Structures, and Public Policy*, edited by Barrie Houlihan and Mick Green, 194–217. Oxford: Butterworth-Heinemann.

Bailey, Peter. 1978. *Leisure and Class in Victorian England: Rational Recreation and the Contest for Control, 1830–1885*. London: Routledge and Kegan Paul.

Baker, William. 1988. *Sports in the Western World*. 2nd ed. Urbana: University of Illinois Press.

1994. "To Pray or to Play? The YMCA Question in the United Kingdom and the United States, 1850–1900." *International Journal of the History of Sport* 11: 42–62.

Bales, Robert. 1950. *Interaction Process Analysis: A Method for the Study of Small Groups*. Cambridge, MA: Addison-Wesley Press.

Bandura, Albert. 1986. *Social Foundations of Thought and Action: A Social Cognitive Theory*. Englewood Cliffs, NJ: Prentice-Hall.

1995. "Exercise of Personal and Collective Efficacy in Changing Societies." In *Self-Efficacy in Changing Societies*, edited by Albert Bandura, 1–45. Cambridge: Cambridge University Press.

1997. *Self-Efficacy: The Exercise of Control*. New York: W. H. Freeman.

Bandy, Susan and Anne Darden. 1999. "Prelude." In *Crossing Boundaries: An International Anthology of Women's Experiences in Sport*, edited by Susan Bandy and Anne Darden, ix–xiv. Champaign, IL: Human Kinetics.

Barker-Ruchti, Natalie and Richard Tinning. 2010. "Foucault in Leotards: Corporeal Discipline in Women's Artistic Gymnastics." *Sociology of Sport Journal* 27: 229–50.

Barnes, Barry. 1995. *The Elements of Social Theory*. Princeton, NJ: Princeton University Press.

Beaumont, Elizabeth. 2010. "Political Agency and Empowerment Pathways for Developing a Sense of Political Efficacy in Young Adults." In *Handbook of Research on Civic Engagement in Youth*, edited by Lonnie Sherrod, Judith Torney-Purta, and Constance Flanagan, 525–58. Hoboken, NJ: John Wiley and Sons.

Beckett, J. V. 1986. *The Aristocracy in England, 1660–1914*. Oxford: Blackwell.

Bédarida, François. 1979 (1976). *A Social History of England, 1851–1975*. Translated by A. S. Forster. London: Methuen.

Beetham, David. 1992. "Liberal Democracy and the Limits of Democratization." *Political Studies* 40: 40–53.

Bell, Catherine. 1992. *Ritual Theory, Ritual Practice*. New York: Oxford University Press.

1997. *Ritual: Perspectives and Dimensions*. New York: Oxford University Press.

2005. "Ritual, Further Considerations." In *Encyclopedia of Religion*, edited by Lindsay Jones, 11: 7848–56. 2nd ed. 15 vols. Detroit: Macmillan.

Bergsgard, Nils Asle, Barrie Houlihan, Per Mangset, Svein Inge Nødland, and Hilmar Rommetvedt, eds. 2007. *Sport Policy: A Comparative Analysis of Stability and Change*. Amsterdam: Elsevier.

Bergsgard, Nils Asle and Jan Ove Tangen. 2011. "Norway." In *Participation in Sport: International Policy Perspectives*, edited by Matthew Nicholson, Russell Hoye, and Barrie Houlihan, 59–75. London: Routledge.

Berkowitz, Steve and Jodi Upton. 2011, June 16. "Money Flows to College Sports." *USA Today*. Retrieved from http://www.usatoday.com/NEWS/usaedition/2011-06-16-berko-copyART_ST_U.htm.

Bernett, Hajo. 1987. "Zur Grundsteinlegung vor 50 Jahren: Das 'Deutsche Stadion' in Nürnberg – ein Phantom nationalsozialistischen Grössenwahns." *Sozial- und Zeitgeschichte des Sports* 1: 14–40.

1992. "Sport and National Socialism: A Focus of Contemporary History." In *Sport Science in Germany: An Interdisciplinary Anthology*, edited by Herbert Haag, Ommo Grupe, and August Kirsch, 439–61. Berlin: Springer.

Bernstein, Mark. 2009. *Princeton Football*. Mount Pleasant, SC: Arcadia Publishing.

Berryman, Jack. 1988. "The Rise of Highly Organized Sports for Preadolescent Boys." In *Children in Sport*, edited by Frank Smoll, Richard Magill, and Michael Ash, 3–16. 3rd ed. Champaign, IL: Human Kinetics Books.

Betts, John. 1974. *America's Sporting Heritage: 1850–1950*. Reading, MA: Addison-Wesley Publishing.

Birley, Derek. 1993. *Sport and the Making of Britain*. Manchester: Manchester University Press.

Blinde, Elaine, Diane Taub, and Lingling Han. 1993. "Sport Participation and Women's Personal Empowerment: Experiences of the College Athlete." *Journal of Sport and Social Issues* 17: 47–60.

Bloxam, Matthew. 1889. *Rugby, the School, and the Neighbourhood*. London: Whittaker and Company.

Boller, Paul and John George. 1989. *They Never Said It: A Book of Fake Quotes, Misquotes, and Misleading Attributions*. Oxford: Oxford University Press.

Bonfante, Larissa. 1989. "Nudity as a Costume in Classical Art." *American Journal of Archaeology* 93: 543–70.

Bottomore, Thomas. 1954. "Social Stratification in Voluntary Organizations." In *Social Mobility in Britain*, edited by D. V. Glass, 349–82. London: Routledge and Kegan Paul.

Bourdieu, Pierre. 1977 (1972). *Outline of a Theory of Practice*. Translated by Richard Nice. Cambridge: Cambridge University Press.

1984. *Distinction: A Social Critique of the Judgement of Taste*. Translated by Richard Nice. Cambridge, MA: Harvard University Press.

1988. "Program for a Sociology of Sport." *Sociology of Sport Journal* 5: 153–61.

Bourdieu, Pierre and Jean-Claude Passeron. 1990. *Reproduction in Education, Society, and Culture*. Translated by Richard Nice. London: Sage Publications.

Bradbury, Steven and Tess Kay. 2008. "Stepping into Community? The Impact of Youth Sport Volunteering on Young People's Social Capital." In *Sport and Social Capital*, edited by Matthew Nicholson and Russell Hoye, 285–316. Oxford: Butterworth-Heinemann.

Brady, Thomas. 1936. "The Gymnasium in Ptolemaic Egypt." *University of Missouri Studies* 11: 9–20.

Brailsford, Dennis. 1983. "The Locations of Eighteenth-Century Sport." In *Geographical Perspectives on Sport*, edited by John Bale and Charles Jenkins, 26–60. Keele: Department of Education, University of Keele.

1992. *British Sport: A Social History*. Cambridge: Lutterworth Press.

1999. *A Taste for Diversions: Sport in Georgian England*. Cambridge: Lutterworth Press.

Branigan, Tania. 2010, August 10. "Beijing Workers Shape Up for Return of Compulsory Exercises." *The Guardian*. Retrieved from http://www.guardian.co.uk/world/2010/aug/10/beijing-workers-compulsory-exercises?intcmp=239.

Briggs, Asa. 1988. "Victorian Values." In *In Search of Victorian Values: Aspects of Nineteenth-Century Thought and Society*, edited by Eric Sigsworth, 10–26. Manchester: Manchester University Press.

Brohm, Jean-Marie. 1981. "Theses Toward a Political Sociology of Sport." In *Sport in the Sociocultural Process*, edited by Mabel Hart and Susan Birrell, 107–13. Dubuque, IA: W. C. Brown.

Bronner, Stephen. 2011. *Critical Theory: A Very Short Introduction*. New York: Oxford University Press.

Brookes, Christopher. 1978. *English Cricket: The Game and Its Players through the Ages*. London: Weidenfeld and Nicolson.

Brown, Kevin. 2008. "Community Sport/Recreation Members and Social Capital Measures in Sweden and Australia." In *Sport and Social Capital*, edited by Matthew Nicholson and Russell Hoye, 165–86. Oxford: Butterworth-Heinemann.

Brownell, Susan. 1995. *Training the Body for China: Sports in the Moral Order of the People's Republic*. Chicago: University of Chicago Press.

2000. "Why Should an Anthropologist Study Sports in China?" In *Games, Sports, and Cultures*, edited by Noel Dyck, 43–63. Oxford: Berg.

Bruce, A. P. C. 1980. *The Purchase System in the British Army, 1660–1871*. London: Royal Historical Society.

Burckhardt, Jacob. 1998 (1898–1902). *The Greeks and Greek Civilization*. Translated by Sheila Stern. New York: St. Martin's.

Burdsey, Daniel and Robert Chappell. 2003. "Soldiers, Sashes, and Shamrocks: Football and Social Identity in Scotland and Northern Ireland." *Sociology of Sport Online 6*.

Burnett, Cora. 2006. "Building Social Capital Through an 'Active Community Club.'" *International Review for the Sociology of Sport* 41: 283–94.

Burt, Ronald. 2005. *Brokerage and Closure: An Introduction to Social Capital*. Oxford: Oxford University Press.

Bush, M. L. 1984. *The English Aristocracy*. Manchester: Manchester University Press.

Butler, Samuel. 1896. *The Life and Letters of Dr. Samuel Butler*. 2 vols. London: John Murray.

Calame, Claude. 1997 (1977). *Choruses of Young Women in Ancient Greece: Their Morphology, Religious Role, and Social Functions*. Translated by Derek Collins and Jane Orion. Lanham, MD: Rowman and Littlefield.

Camp, Walter and Lorin Fuller Deland. 1896. *Football*. Boston: Houghton, Mifflin and Company.

Campbell, Angus, Gerald Gurin, and Warren Miller. 1954. *The Voter Decides*. Evanston, IL: Row.

Caprara, Gian Vittorio. 2008. "Will Democracy Win?" *Journal of Social Issues* 64: 639–59.

Caprara, Gian Vittorio, Michele Vecchione, Cristina Capanna, and Minou Mebane. 2009. "Perceived Political Self-Efficacy: Theory, Assessment, and Applications." *European Journal of Social Psychology* 39: 1002–20.

Carlsson, Susanne. 2010. *Hellenistic Democracies: Freedom, Independence, and Political Procedure in Some East Greek City-States*. Stuttgart: Franz Steiner Verlag.

Carter, John Marshall. 1992. *Medieval Games: Sport and Recreations in Feudal Society*. New York: Greenwood Press.

Cartledge, Paul. 2001. *Spartan Reflections*. Berkeley: University of California Press.

2002. *Sparta and Lakonia: A Regional History 1300–362 B.C.* 2nd ed. London: Routledge.

Cartledge, Paul and Anthony Spawforth. 2002. *Hellenistic and Roman Sparta: A Tale of Two Cities.* 2nd ed. London: Routledge.

Ceccarelli, Paola. 1998. *La pirrica nell' antichità greco romana: Studi sulla danza armata.* Pisa: Istituti Editoriali e Poligrafici Internazionali.

Chamberlayne, John. 1748. *Magnae Britanniae Notitia, or the Present State of Great Britain.* London: S. Birt.

Chambers, William and Robert Chambers. 1842. "The Horse." *Chambers's Information for the People* 77: 417–32.

Chandler, Timothy. 1988. "The Development of a Sporting Tradition at Oxbridge, 1800–1860." *Canadian Journal of the History of Sport* 19: 1–29.

Chandos, John. 1984. *Boys Together: English Public Schools, 1800–1864.* New Haven, CT: Yale University Press.

Chapman, George. 1784. *A Treatise on Education.* 3rd ed. London: T. Cadell.

Chapman, Gwen E. 1997. "Making Weight: Lightweight Rowing, Technologies of Power, and Technologies of Self." *Sociology of Sport Journal* 14: 205–23.

Chase, Laura. 2006. "(Un)Disciplined Bodies: A Foucauldian Analysis of Women's Rugby." *Sociology of Sport Journal* 23: 229–47.

Chase, Malcolm. 2007. *Chartism: A New History.* Manchester: Manchester University Press.

Cheyney, Edward, ed. 1922. *Readings in English History Drawn from the Original Sources.* Boston: Ginn and Company.

Christesen, Paul. 2002. "On the Meaning of Gymnazo." *Nikephoros* 15: 7–37.

2007a. *Olympic Victor Lists and Ancient Greek History.* Cambridge: Cambridge University Press.

2007b. "The Transformation of Athletics in Sixth-Century Greece." In *Onward to the Olympics,* edited by Gerald Schaus and S. R. Wenn, 59–68. Waterloo, ON: Wilfred Laurier University Press.

2012a. "Athletics and Social Order in Sparta in the Classical Period." Forthcoming in *Classical Antiquity.*

2012b. "Athletics and Sparta." In *A Companion to Sparta,* edited by Anton Powell, Malden, MA: Blackwell.

Civil Service Commission. 1897. *Rules and Regulations Respecting Examinations for the Home Civil Service, the Army, the Navy, the Civil Service of India, &c.* London: Eyre and Spottiswoode.

Clarendon Commission, ed. 1864. *The Clarendon Report: English Public Schools in the Nineteenth Century.* 4 vols. London: G. E. Eyre and W. Spottiswoode.

Clark, Jon, Celia Modgil, **and** Sohan Modgil, eds. 1990. *Robert K. Merton: Consensus and Controversy.* London: Falmer Press.

Cleary, Matthew and Susan Stokes. 2009. "Trust and Democracy in Comparative Perspective." In *Whom Can We Trust? How Groups, Networks, and Institutions Make Trust Possible,* edited by Karen Cook, Margaret Levi, and Russell Hardin, 308–38. New York: Russell Sage Foundation.

Clumpner, Roy and Brian Pendleton. 1978. "The People's Republic of China." In *Sport under Communism,* edited by James Riordan, 103–40. Montreal: McGill-Queen's University Press.

Coakley, Jay. 1987. "Children and the Sport Socialization Process." In *Advances in Pediatric Sport Sciences: Volume 2: Behavioral Issues*, edited by Daniel Gould and Maureen Weiss, 43–60. Champaign, IL: Human Kinetics.

    2006. "Organized Sports for Young People: A 20th-Century Invention." In *Learning Culture through Sports: Exploring the Role of Sports in Society*, edited by Sandra Spickard Prettyman and Brian Lampman, 3–14. Lanham, MD: Rowman and Littlefield.

Coakley, Jay and Eric Dunning. 2000a. "General Introduction." In *Handbook of Sports Studies*, edited by Jay Coakley and Eric Dunning, xxi-xxxviii. London: Sage Publications.

    eds. 2000b. *Handbook of Sports Studies*. Los Angeles: Sage.

Coakley, Jay and Elizabeth Pike. 2009. *Sports in Society: Issues and Controversies*. 9th ed. London: McGraw-Hill.

Coalter, Fred. 2007. *A Wider Social Role for Sport: Who's Keeping the Score?* London: Routledge.

Cobbe, Francis Power. 1864, April. "The Nineteenth Century." *Fraser's Magazine for Town and Country* 481–94.

Coffë, Hilde and Benny Geys. 2007. "Toward an Empirical Characterization of Bridging and Bonding Social Capital." *Nonprofit and Voluntary Sector Quarterly* 36: 121–39.

Cohen, Percy. 1968. *Modern Social Theory*. New York: Basic Books.

Coleman, James. 1988. "Social Capital in the Creation of Human Capital." *American Journal of Sociology* 94: 95–120.

Collins, Tony. 1998. *Rugby's Great Split: Class, Culture, and the Origins of Rugby League Football*. London: Frank Cass and Company.

    2005. "History, Theory, and the 'Civilizing Process'." *Sport in History* 25: 289–306.

Connell, R. W. 1983. *Which Way Is Up? Essays on Sex, Class, and Culture*. Sydney: George Allen and Unwin.

    1990. "An Iron Man: The Body and Some Contradictions of Hegemonic Masculinity." In *Sport, Men, and the Gender Order: Critical Feminist Perspectives*, edited by Michael A. Messner and Donald F. Sabo, 83–95. Champaign, IL: Human Kinetics.

Connor, W. R. 1992 (1971). *The New Politicians of Fifth-Century Athens*. Indianapolis, IN: Hackett.

Coolidge, Calvin. 1926. *Foundations of the Republic*. New York: C. Scribner's Sons.

Copley, Terence. 2002. *Black Tom: Arnold of Rugby: The Myth and the Man*. London: Continuum.

Corbett, Bernard. 2002. *Harvard Football*. Mount Pleasant, SC: Arcadia Publishing.

Cousin, Victor. 1834 (1831). *Report on the State of Public Instruction in Prussia*. Translated by Sarah Austin. London: Effingham Wilson.

Cromartie, Warren and Robert Whiting. 1992. *Slugging It Out in Japan*. New York: Signet Books.

Crowther, Nigel. 2004. *Athletika: Studies on the Olympic Games and Greek Athletics*. Hildesheim: Weidmann.

Crump, Jeremy. 1989. "Athletics." In *Sport in Britain: A Social History*, edited by Tony Mason, 44–77. Cambridge: Cambridge University Press.

Csapo, Eric and Margaret Christina Miller. 2007. *The Origins of Theater in Ancient Greece and Beyond: From Ritual to Drama*. Cambridge: Cambridge University Press.

Culham, Phyllis. 1986. "Again, What Meaning Lies in Colour!" *Zeitschrift für Papyrologie und Epigraphik* 64: 235–45.

Cunningham, Hugh. 1980. *Leisure in the Industrial Revolution*. New York: St. Martin's Press.

Cuskelly, Graham. 2008. "Volunteering in Community Sport Organizations: Implications for Social Capital." In *Sport and Social Capital*, edited by Matthew Nicholson and Russell Hoye, 187–204. Oxford: Butterworth-Heinemann.

Cuzzort, R. P. 1989. *Using Social Thought: The Nuclear Issue and Other Concerns*. Mountain View, CA: Mayfield Publishing.

d'Aquili, Eugene and Charles Laughlin Jr. 1979. "The Neurobiology of Myth and Ritual." In *The Spectrum of Ritual: A Biogenetic Structural Analysis*, edited by Eugene d'Aquili, Charles Laughlin Jr., and John McManus, 152–82. New York: Columbia University Press.

DaCosta, Lamartine and Ana Miragaya, eds. 2002. *Worldwide Experiences and Trends in Sport for All*. Oxford: Meyer and Meyer Sport.

Dahl, Robert. 1971. *Polyarchy: Participation and Opposition*. New Haven, CT: Yale University Press.

1989. *Democracy and Its Critics*. New Haven, CT: Yale University Press.

David, Ephraim. 2010. "Sparta and the Politics of Nudity." In *Sparta: The Body Politic*, edited by Anton Powell and Stephen Hodkinson, 137–63. Swansea: Classical Press of Wales.

Davidoff, Leonore and Catherine Hall. 1987. *Family Fortunes: Men and Women of the English Middle Class, 1780–1850*. London: Hutchinson.

Davies, John Kenyon. 1967. "Demosthenes on Liturgies: A Note." *Journal of Hellenic Studies* 87: 33–40.

1984. *Wealth and the Power of Wealth in Classical Athens*. Reprint ed. Salem, NH: Ayer Co.

Davies, Richard. 2007. *Sports in American Life*. Malden, MA: Blackwell.

Davis, Jon. 2006. "Meritocracy in the Civil Service, 1853–1970." *The Political Quarterly* 77: 27–35.

Davis, Kingsley. 1980 (1936). *A Structural Analysis of Kinship*. New York: Arno Press.

de Tocqueville, Alexis. 2000 (1835–40). *Democracy in America*. Translated by Harvey Mansfield and Delba Winthrop. Chicago: University of Chicago Press.

Defoe, Daniel. 1890 (1729). *The Compleat English Gentleman*. London: D. Nutt.

Delaney, Liam and Emily Keaney. 2005. *Sport and Social Capital in the United Kingdom: Statistical Evidence from National and International Survey Data*. Department of Culture, Media and Sport. Retrieved from http://www.ippr. org/uploadedFiles/research/projects/Arts_and_Culture/sport%20and%20 social%20capital.pdf.

Delavaud-Roux, Marie-Hélène. 1993. *Les danses armées en Grèce antique*. Aix-en-Provence: Publications de l'Université de Provence.

Delorme, Jean. 1960. *Gymnasion*. Paris: de Boccard.

Department of Culture, Media and Sport Strategy Unit. 2002. *Game Plan: A Strategy for Delivering Government's Sport and Physical Activity Objectives.* Retrieved from http://www.gamesmonitor.org.uk/files/game_plan_report.pdf.

Department of the Army, Headquarters. 2003. *Drill and Ceremony (Field Manual 3–21.5).* Retrieved from http://www.gasdf.com/regs/FM_3–21–5_Drill_Ceremonies.pdf.

Diem, Carl. 1948. "Development and Aims of Physical Education in Germany." *The Journal of Health and Physical Education* 19: 390–92, 430–31.

Dixon, J. G., P. C. McIntosh, A. D. Munrow, and R. F. Willetts. 1960. *Landmarks in the History of Physical Education.* 2nd ed. London: Routledge and Kegan Paul.

Dodd, Christopher. 1989. "Rowing." In *Sport in Britain: A Social History*, edited by Tony Mason, 276–307. Cambridge: Cambridge University Press.

Donlan, Walter. 1998. "Political Reciprocity in Dark Age Greece: Odysseus and His *Hetairoi*." In *Reciprocity in Ancient Greece*, edited by Christopher Gill, Norman Postlethwaite, and Richard Seaford, 51–71. Oxford: Oxford University Press.

   1999. *The Aristocratic Ideal and Selected Papers.* Wauconda, IL: Bolchazy-Carducci.

Downing, Lisa. 2008. *The Cambridge Introduction to Michel Foucault.* Cambridge: Cambridge University Press.

Drees, Ludwig. 1968. *Olympia: Gods, Artists, and Athletes.* Translated by Gerald Onn. New York: Praeger.

Dreyfus, Hubert, Paul Rabinow, and Michel Foucault. 1983. *Michel Foucault: Beyond Structuralism and Hermeneutics.* 2nd ed. Chicago: University of Chicago Press.

Ducat, Jean. 2006. *Spartan Education.* Translated by Emma Stafford, P.-J. Shaw, and Anton Powell. Swansea: Classical Press of Wales.

Dunn, John, ed. 1992. *Democracy: The Unfinished Journey, 508 BC to AD 1993.* Oxford: Oxford University Press.

   2005. *Setting the People Free: The Story of Democracy.* London: Atlantic.

Dunning, Eric. 1971. "The Development of Modern Football." In *The Sociology of Sport*, edited by Eric Dunning, 133–51. London: Frank Cass and Company.

Dunning, Eric, Patrick Murphy, John Williams, and Joseph Maguire. 1984. "Football Hooliganism in Britain before the First World War." *International Review for the Sociology of Sport* 19: 215–40.

Dunning, Eric and Kenneth Sheard. 2005. *Barbarians, Gentlemen, and Players.* 2nd ed. London: Routledge.

Durkheim, Émile. 1949 (1893). *The Division of Labor in Society.* Translated by George Simpson. Glencoe, IL: Free Press.

   1965 (1912). *The Elementary Forms of the Religious Life.* Translated by Joseph Swain. New York: The Free Press.

Durston, Christopher. 1996. "Puritan Rule and the Failure of Cultural Revolution, 1645–1660." In *The Culture of English Puritanism, 1560–1700*, edited by Christopher Durston and Jacqueline Eales, 210–33. Hampshire: Palgrave MacMillan.

Dworkin, Gerald. 1988. *The Theory and Practice of Autonomy.* Cambridge: Cambridge University Press.

Dyreson, Mark. 1998. *Making the American Team: Sport, Culture, and the Olympic Experience.* Urbana: University of Illinois Press.

2001. "Maybe It's Better to Bowl Alone: Sport, Community, and Democracy in American Thought." *Culture, Sport, Society* 4: 19–30.

Edwards, Harry. 1973. *Sociology of Sport*. Homewood, IL: Dorsey Press.

Eisenberg, Christiane. 1999. *"English Sports" und deutsche Bürger*. Paderborn: Schöningh.

Eitzen, D. Stanley. 2000. "Social Control and Sport." In *Handbook of Sports Studies*, edited by Jay Coakley and Eric Dunning, 370–81. London: Sage Publications.

2009. *Fair and Foul: Beyond the Myths and Paradoxes of Sport*. 4th ed. Lanham, MD: Rowman and Littlefield.

Eliot, Charles. 1875. *49th Annual Report of the President of Harvard College*. Cambridge, MA: John Wilson and Son.

Elwell, Frank. 2009. *Macrosociology: The Study of Sociocultural Systems*. Lewiston, ME: Edwin Mellen Press.

Ensor, Ernest. 1898. "Football Madness." *The Contemporary Review* 74: 751–60.

Erbse, Hartmut. 1969. *Scholia Graeca in Homeri Iliadem (Scholia Vetera)*. 7 vols. Berlin: Walter de Gruyter.

Europe, Council of, ed. 1970. *Sport for All*. Strasbourg: Council for Cultural Cooperation.

Fagan, Garrett. 2011. *The Lure of the Arena: Social Psychology and the Crowd at the Roman Games*. Cambridge: Cambridge University Press.

Farr, James. 2004. "Social Capital: A Conceptual History." *Political Theory* 32: 6–33.

Farrar, Cynthia. 1988. *The Origins of Democratic Thinking: The Invention of Politics in Classical Athens*. Cambridge: Cambridge University Press.

Felton, Cornelius. 1860. *34th Annual Report of the President of Harvard College to the Overseers*. Cambridge, MA: Welch, Bigelow, and Company.

Feltz, Deborah. 1992. "Understanding Motivation in Sport: A Self-Efficacy Perspective." In *Motivation in Sport and Exercise*, edited by G. C. Roberts, 93–105. Champaign, IL: Human Kinetics.

Feltz, Deborah, Sandra Short, and Philip Sullivan. 2008. *Self-Efficacy in Sport: Research and Strategies for Working with Athletes, Teams, and Coaches*. Champaign, IL: Human Kinetics.

Field, John. 2008. *Social Capital*. 2nd ed. London: Routledge.

Fine, Gary Alan and Brooke Harrington. 2004. "Tiny Publics: Small Groups and Civil Society." *Sociological Theory* 22: 341–56.

Finkel, Steven, Edward Muller, and Karl-Dieter Opp. 1989. "Personal Influence, Collective Rationality, and Mass Political Action." *American Political Science Review* 83: 885–903.

Fischer-Bovet, Christelle. 2008. "Army and Society in Ptolemaic Egypt." Ph.D. diss., Stanford University.

Fisher, Nick. 1998. "Gymnasia and the Democratic Values of Leisure." In *Kosmos: Essays in Order, Conflict, and Community in Classical Athens*, edited by Paul Cartledge, Paul Millett, and Sitta von Reden, 84–104. Cambridge: Cambridge University Press.

ed. 2001. *Against Timarchos: Introduction, Translation, and Commentary*. Oxford: Oxford University Press.

2008. "The Bad Boyfriend, the Flatterer, and the Sycophant: Related Forms of 'Kakos' in Democratic Athens." In *KAKOS: Badness and Anti-Value in Classical Antiquity*, edited by I. Sluiter and R. M. Rosen, 185–232. Leiden: Brill.

2009. "The Culture of Competition." In *A Companion to Archaic Greece*, edited by Kurt Raaflaub and Hans van Wees, 524–41. Malden, MA: Wiley Blackwell.

2011. "Competitive Delights: The Social Effects of the Expanded Programme of Contests in Post-Kleisthenic Athens." In *Competition in the Ancient World*, edited by Nick Fisher and Hans van Wees, 175–219. Swansea: Classical Press of Wales.

Foddy, Margaret and Toshio Yamagishi. 2009. "Group-Based Trust." In *Whom Can We Trust? How Groups, Networks, and Institutions Make Trust Possible*, edited by Karen Cook, Margaret Levi, and Russell Hardin, 17–41. New York: Russell Sage Foundation.

Foley, Douglas. 1990. "The Great American Football Ritual: Reproducing Race, Class, and Gender Inequality." *Sociology of Sport Journal* 7: 111–35.

Forbes, George. 1911, December 2. "Buttressing the Foundations of Democracy." *The Reform Advocate*, 589–95.

Foreman, Amanda. 1998. *Georgiana: Duchess of Devonshire*. London: Harper Collins.

Foucault, Michel. 1977 (1975). *Discipline and Punish: The Birth of the Prison*. Translated by Alan Sheridan. New York: Vintage Books.

1980. *Power/Knowledge: Selected Interviews and Other Writings, 1972–1977*. Translated by Colin Gordon, Leo Marshall, John Mepham, and Kate Soper. New York: Pantheon Books.

1994 (1966). *The Order of Things: An Archaeology of the Human Sciences*. New York: Vintage Books.

Fowler, Robert, ed. 2004. *The Cambridge Companion to Homer*. Cambridge: Cambridge University Press.

Fulbrook, Mary. 1990. *A Concise History of Germany*. Cambridge: Cambridge University Press.

Fullinwider, Robert. 2006. *Sports, Youth, and Character: A Critical Survey (CIRCLE Working Paper 44)*. The Center for Information and Research on Civic Learning and Engagement. Retrieved from http://www.civicyouth.org/PopUps/WorkingPapers/WP44Fullinwider.pdf.

Gale, F. 1885. "Cricket: About the 'National' Cricket of Last Season." *The Year's Sport: A Review of British Sports and Pasttimes for the Year, 1885*: 113–99.

Gambetta, Diego. 1988. "Can We Trust Trust?" In *Trust: Making and Breaking Cooperative Relations*, edited by Diego Gambetta, 213–37. New York: Blackwell.

Gardiner, E. Norman. 1910. *Greek Athletic Sports and Festivals*. London: The Macmillan Company.

Gatz, Margaret, Michael Messner, and Sandra Ball-Rokeach. 2002. "Introduction: Framing Social Issues through Sport." In *Paradoxes of Youth and Sport*, edited by Margaret Gatz, Michael Messner, and Sandra Ball-Rokeach, 1–8. Albany: State University of New York Press.

Gauthier, Philippe and M. B. Hatzopoulos. 1993. *La loi gymnasiarchique de Beroia*. Athens: Centre de recherches de l'antiquité grecque et romaine.

Gecas, Viktor. 1989. "The Social Psychology of Self-Efficacy." *Annual Review of Sociology* 15: 291–316.

Geddes, A. 1987. "Rags and Riches: The Costume of Athenian Men in the Fifth Century." *Classical Quarterly* 37: 307–31.

Geertz, Clifford. 1973. *The Interpretation of Cultures*. New York: Basic Books.

　1983. *Local Knowledge: Further Essays in Interpretive Anthropology*. New York: Basic Books.

Gerdy, John. 2002. *Sports, the All-American Addiction*. Jackson: University Press of Mississippi.

Giddens, Anthony. 1990. "R. K. Merton on Structural Analysis." In *Robert K. Merton: Consensus and Controversy*, edited by Jon Clark, Celia Modgil, and Sohan Modgil, 97–110. London: Falmer Press.

　2006. *Sociology*. 5th ed. Cambridge: Polity Press.

Gillespie, Michael Allen. 2010. "Players and Spectators: Sports and Ethical Training in the American University." In *Debating Moral Education: Rethinking the Role of the Modern University*, edited by Elizabeth Kiss and J. Peter Euben, 296–316. Durham, NC: Duke University Press.

Glanville, Jennifer and Pamela Paxton. 2007. "How Do We Learn to Trust? A Confirmatory Tetrad Analysis of the Sources of Generalized Trust." *Social Psychology Quarterly* 70: 230–42.

Glass, Stephen. 1988. "The Greek Gymnasium." In *The Archaeology of the Olympics*, edited by Wendy Raschke, 155–73. Madison: University of Wisconsin Press.

Goffman, Erving. 1961. *Asylums: Essays on the Social Situation of Mental Patients and Other Inmates*. Garden City, NY: Anchor Books.

Golden, Mark. 1998. *Sport and Society in Ancient Greece*. Cambridge: Cambridge University Press.

　2004. *Sport in the Ancient World from A to Z*. London: Routledge.

　2008. *Greek Sport and Social Status*. Austin: University of Texas Press.

Goldstein, Jeffrey and Robert Arms. 1971. "Effects of Observing Athletic Contests on Hostility." *Sociometry* 34: 83–90.

Goossens, E. and S. Thielemans. 1996. "The Popularity of Painting Sports Scenes on Attic Black and Red Figure Vases." *Bulletin Antike Beschaving* 71: 59–94.

Gorn, Elliott and Warren Goldstein. 1993. *A Brief History of American Sports*. New York: Hill and Wang.

Gouldner, Alvin. 1969. *The Hellenic World: A Sociological Analysis*. New York: Harper and Row.

Goulstone, John. 2000. "The Working-Class Origins of Modern Football." *International Journal of the History of Sport* 17: 135–43.

Graf, Fritz. 1996. "Initiation." In *Der neue Pauly: Enzyklopädie der Antike*, edited by Hubert Cancik, Helmuth Schneider, August Friedrich von Pauly, and Georg Wissowa, 6: 811–13. 15 vols. Stuttgart: J. B. Metzler.

Granovetter, Mark. 1973. "The Strength of Weak Ties." *American Journal of Sociology* 78: 1360–80.

　1982. "The Strength of Weak Ties: A Network Theory Revisited." In *Social Structure and Network Analysis*, edited by Peter Marsden and Nan Lin, 105–30. Beverly Hills, CA: Sage Publications.

　1985. "Economic Action and Social Structure: The Problem of Embeddedness." *American Journal of Sociology* 91: 481–510.

　2002. "A Theoretical Agenda for Economic Sociology." In *The New Economic Sociology: Developments in an Emerging Field*, edited by Mauro Guillén, Randall Collins, Paula England, and Marshall Meyer, 35–60. New York: Russell Sage Foundation.

Green, Andy. 1990. *Education and State Formation: The Rise of Education Systems in England, France, and the USA.* New York: St. Martin's Press.

Griffin, Emma. 2005. *England's Revelry: A History of Popular Sports and Pastimes, 1660–1830.* Oxford: Oxford University Press for the British Academy.

2007. *Blood Sport: Hunting in Britain since 1066.* New Haven, CT: Yale University Press.

Griffith, Mark. 2001. "Public and Private in Early Greek Institutions of Education." In *Education in Greek and Roman Antiquity*, edited by Yun Lee Too, 23–84. Leiden: Brill.

Grugel, Jean. 2002. *Democratization: A Critical Introduction.* London: Palgrave.

Gruneau, Richard. 1999. *Class, Sports, and Social Development.* 2nd ed. Champaign, IL: Human Kinetics.

Gunn, Simon. 2004. "Urbanization." In *A Companion to Nineteenth-Century Britain*, edited by Chris Williams, 238–52. Malden, MA: Blackwell.

Guttmann, Allen. 1978. *From Ritual to Record: The Nature of Modern Sports.* New York: Columbia University Press.

1979. "Who's on First? or, Books on the History of American Sports." *The Journal of American History* 66: 348–54.

1985. "English Sports Spectators: The Restoration to the Early Nineteenth Century." *Journal of Sport History* 12: 103–25.

1988. *A Whole New Ball Game: An Interpretation of American Sports.* Chapel Hill: University of North Carolina Press.

1994. *Games and Empires: Modern Sports and Cultural Imperialism.* New York: Columbia University Press.

2004. *Sports: The First Five Millennia.* Amherst, MA: University of Massachusetts Press.

Guttmann, Allen and Lee Thompson. 2001. *Japanese Sports: A History.* Honolulu: University of Hawaii Press.

Habermann, Wolfgang. 2007. "Gymnasien im ptolemäischen Ägypten: Eine Skizze." In *Das hellenistische Gymnasion*, edited by Daniel Kah and Peter Scholz, 335–48. Berlin: Akademie Verlag.

Halladay, Eric. 2006. "Of Pride and Prejudice: The Amateur Question in English Nineteenth-Century Rowing." In *A Sport-Loving Society: Victorian and Edwardian Middle-Class England at Play*, edited by J. A. Mangan, 239–54. London: Routledge.

Hansen, Mogens Herman. 2006. *The Shotgun Method: The Demography of the Ancient Greek City-State Culture.* Columbia: University of Missouri Press.

Hansen, Mogens Herman and Thomas Heine Nielsen, eds. 2004. *An Inventory of Archaic and Classical Poleis.* Oxford: Oxford University Press.

Hanson, Victor Davis. 1995. *The Other Greeks: The Family Farm and the Agrarian Roots of Western Civilization.* New York: Free Press.

Hargreaves, John. 1986. *Sport, Power, and Culture.* New York: St. Martin's Press.

1992. "Revisiting the Hegemony Thesis." In *Leisure in the 1990s: Rolling Back the Welfare State*, edited by John Sugden and Colin Knox, 263–80. Eastbourne: Chelsea School Research Centre.

Harrison, J. F. C. 1971. *The Early Victorians, 1832–1851.* London: Weidenfeld and Nicolson.

1990. *Late Victorian Britain, 1875–1901*. London: Fontana Press.

Harvey, Adrian. 2004. *The Beginnings of a Commercial Sporting Culture in Britain, 1793–1850*. Aldershot: Ashgate.

Harvey, Jean and Maurice Lévesque. 2007. "Sport Volunteerism and Social Capital." *Sociology of Sport Journal* 24: 206–23.

Hechter, Michael **and** Christine Horne, eds. 2009. *Theories of Social Order: A Reader*. 2nd ed. Stanford, CA: Stanford Social Sciences.

Heikkala, J. 1993. "Discipline and Excel: Techniques of the Self and Body and the Logic of Competing." *Sociology of Sport Journal* 10: 397–412.

Heine, Patricke Johns. 2008 (1971). *Personality in Social Theory*. Chicago: Aldine Publishing.

Heinemann, Klaus. 1992. "Sport Sociology: Fundamental Aspects." In *Sport Science in Germany: An Interdisciplinary Anthology*, edited by Herbert Haag, Ommo Grupe, and August Kirsch, 379–402. Berlin: Springer.

Henry, Ian. 2006. "Sport and Social Capital: Using Sport to Build Integration." *TAFISA Magazine*: 27–40.

Hewitt, Martin. 2004. "Class and Classes." In *A Companion to Nineteenth-Century Britain*, edited by Chris Williams, 305–20. Malden, MA: Blackwell.

Higginson, Thomas Wentworth. 1858. "Saints and Their Bodies." *Atlantic Monthly* 5.1: 582–95.

Hitler, Adolf. 1939 (1925–26). *Mein Kampf*. Translated by James Murphy. London: Hurst and Blackett.

Hobsbawm, E. J. 1984. *Workers: Worlds of Labor*. New York: Pantheon Books.
1987. *The Age of Empire, 1875–1914*. New York: Pantheon Books.

Hoch, Paul. 1972. *Rip Off the Big Game*. New York: Anchor Books.

Hodkinson, Stephen. 2000. *Property and Wealth in Classical Sparta*. London: Duckworth.

Hoffman, Shirl, ed. 1992. *Sport and Religion*. Champaign, IL: Human Kinetics.

Hofmann, Annette and Gertrud Pfister. 2004. "*Turnen* – A Forgotten Movement Culture: Its Beginnings in Germany and Diffusion in the United States." In *Turnen and Sport: Transatlantic Transfers*, edited by Annette Hoffman, 11–24. New York: Waxmann Münster.

Hogan, P. I. and J. P. Santomier. 1984. "Effect of Mastering Swim Skills on Older Adults' Self-Efficacy." *Research Quarterly for Exercise and Sport* 55: 294–96.

Hogg, Michael. 1996. "Intragroup Processes, Group Structure, and Social Identity." In *Social Groups and Identities: Developing the Legacy of Henri Tajfel*, edited by W. Peter Robinson, 65–93. Oxford: Butterworth-Heinemann.

Hollein, Heinz-Günter. 1988. *Bürgerbild und Bildwelt der attischen Demokratie auf den rotfiguren Vasen des 6.-4. Jahrhunderts v. Chr.* Frankfurt am Main: Peter Lang.

Holloway, Jean Barret, Anne Beuter, and Joan Duda. 1988. "Self-Efficacy and Training for Strength in Adolescent Girls." *Journal of Applied Social Psychology* 18: 699–719.

Holmwood, John. 2005. "Functionalism and Its Critics." In *Modern Social Theory: An Introduction*, edited by Austin Harrington, 87–110. Oxford: Oxford University Press.

Holowchak, M. Andrew, ed. 2002. *Philosophy of Sport: Critical Readings, Crucial Issues*. Upper Saddle River, NJ: Prentice-Hall.

Holt, Richard. 1992. *Sport and the British: A Modern History*. Oxford: Clarendon Press.

    1996. "Contrasting Nationalisms: Sport, Militarism, and the Unitary State in Britain and France before 1914." In *Tribal Identities: Nationalism, Europe, Sport*, edited by J. A. Mangan, 39–54. London: Frank Cass and Company.

    2008. "The Amateur Body and the Middle-Class Man: Work, Health, and Style in Victorian Britain." In *Amateurism in British Sport*, edited by Dilwyn Porter and Stephen Wagg, 8–25. London: Routledge.

Hong, Fan and Lu Zhouxiang. 2011. "China." In *Participation in Sport: International Policy Perspectives*, edited by Matthew Nicholson, Russell Hoye, and Barrie Houlihan, 160–82. London: Routledge.

Hooghe, Marc. 2003. "Voluntary Associations and Democratic Attitudes: Value Congruence as a Causal Mechanism." In *Generating Social Capital: Civil Society and Institutions in Comparative Perspective*, edited by Marc Hooghe and Dietlind Stolle, 89–111. New York: Palgrave Macmillan.

Hoppen, K. Theodore. 1998. *The Mid-Victorian Generation, 1846–1886*. New York: Clarendon Press.

Huggins, Mike. 2004. *The Victorians and Sport*. London: Hambledon and London.

    2006. "Prologue: Setting the Scene: Second-Class Citizens? English Middle-Class Culture and Sport, 1850–1910: A Reconsideration." In *A Sport-Loving Society: Victorian and Edwardian Middle-Class England at Play*, edited by J. A. Mangan, 11–42. London: Routledge.

Hughes, Thomas. 1858 (1857). *Tom Brown's School Days*. Cambridge: Macmillan and Co.

    1895 (1861). *Tom Brown at Oxford*. New York: MacMillan and Co.

Huizinga, Johan. 1950 (1938). *Homo Ludens: A Study of the Play Element in Culture*. New York: Roy Publishers.

Humphreys, Brad, Katerina Maresova, and Jane Ruseski. 2010. *National Sport Policy, Sporting Success, and Individual Sport Participation: An International Comparison*. Public Choice Society. Retrieved from http://www.pubchoicesoc.org/papers_2011/RuseskI_Humphreys_Maresova.pdf.

Hunt, David. 1993. "Christianising the Roman Empire." In *The Theodosian Code: Studies in the Imperial Law of Late Antiquity*, edited by Jill Harries and Ian Wood, 143–58. London: Duckworth.

Hunt, Lynn. 1986. "French History in the Last Twenty Years: The Rise and Fall of the Annales Paradigm." *Journal of Contemporary History* 21: 209–24.

Hurt, J. S. 1977. "Drill, Discipline, and the Elementary School Ethos." In *Popular Education and Socialization in the Nineteenth Century*, edited by Phillip McCann, 167–91. London: Methuen and Company.

Inglehart, Ronald. 1997. *Modernization and Postmodernization: Cultural, Economic, and Political Change in 43 Societies*. Princeton, NJ: Princeton University Press.

Jameson, Michael. 1980. "Apollo Lykeios in Athens." *Archaiognosia* 1: 213–36.

    1997. "Women and Democracy in Fourth-Century Athens." In *Esclavage, guerre, économie en Grèce ancienne: Hommages à Yvon Garlan*, edited by Pierre Brulé and Jacques Oulhen, 95–107. Rennes: Presses Universitaires de Rennes.

Jensen, Erik. 2011. "Sweat Equity: Sports and the Self-Made German." In *Weimar Culture Revisited*, edited by John Alexander Williams, 183–98. New York: Palgrave Macmillan.

Johnstone, Steven. 2011. *A History of Trust in Ancient Greece*. Chicago: University of Chicago Press.

Jones, Stephen. 1988. *Sports, Politics, and the Working Class*. Manchester: Manchester University Press.

Joyal, Mark, Iain McDougall, and John Yardley. 2009. *Greek and Roman Education: A Sourcebook*. New York: Routledge.

Kater, Michael. 2004. *Hitler Youth*. Cambridge, MA: Harvard University Press.

Kennell, Nigel. 1995. *The Gymnasium of Virtue*. Chapel Hill: University of North Carolina Press.

2005. "New Light on 2 Maccabees 4:7–15." *Journal of Jewish Studies* 56: 10–24.

2010. *Spartans: A New History*. Chichester: Wiley-Blackwell.

Kerr, Gordon. 2009. *A Short History of Europe*. Harpenden: Pocket Essentials.

Kincaid, Harold. 1996. *Philosophical Foundations of the Social Sciences: Analyzing Controversies in Social Research*. Cambridge: Cambridge University Press.

Kingsley, Charles. 1893. *Health and Education*. New York: D. Appleton.

Kirk, G. S. 1980–1985. "The Homeric Hymns." In *The Cambridge History of Classical Literature*, edited by P. E. Easterling and B. M. W. Knox, 1: 110–16. 2 vols. Cambridge: Cambridge University Press.

Kitchen, Martin. 1996. *The Cambridge Illustrated History of Germany*. Cambridge: Cambridge University Press.

2006. *A History of Modern Germany, 1800–2000*. Malden, MA: Blackwell.

Klarman, Michael J. 2007. *Unfinished Business: Racial Equality in American History*. Oxford: Oxford University Press.

Kocka, Jürgen. 2010. *Civil Society and Dictatorship in Modern German History*. Hanover, NH: University Press of New England.

König, Jason. 2005. *Athletics and Literature in the Roman Empire*. Cambridge: Cambridge University Press.

Kowalzig, Barbara. 2007. *Singing for the Gods: Performances of Myth and Ritual in Archaic and Classical Greece*. Oxford: Oxford University Press.

Krammer, Reinhard. 1996. "Austria: 'New Times are With Us'." In *The Story of Worker Sport*, edited by Arnd Krüger and James Riordan, 81–95. Champaign, IL: Human Kinetics.

Kurke, Leslie. 1993. "The Economy of *Kudos*." In *Cultural Poetics in Archaic Greece*, edited by Carol Dougherty and Leslie Kurke, 131–64. New York: Oxford University Press.

Kyle, Donald. 1987. *Athletics in Ancient Athens*. Leiden: Brill.

2007. *Sport and Spectacle in the Ancient World*. Malden, MA: Blackwell.

2012. "Females and Greek Sport and Spectacles." In *Companion to Sport and Spectacle in Greek and Roman Antiquity*, edited by Paul Christesen and Donald Kyle, Malden, MA: Wiley-Blackwell.

Laberge, Suzanne and Joanne Kay. 2002. "Pierre Bourdieu's Sociocultural Theory and Sport Practice." In *Theory, Sport, and Society*, edited by Joseph Maguire and Kevin Young, 239–66. Amsterdam: JAI.

Labouchere, Henry, Baron Taunton. 1868–69. *Report of the Schools Inquiry Commission*. 21 vols. London: Her Majesty's Stationery Office.

Langenfeld, Hans. 2006. "Olympia-Zentrum des Frauensports in der Antike? Die Mädchen-Wettläufe beim Hera-Fest in Olympia." *Nikephoros* 19: 153–85.

Large, David Clay. 2007. *Nazi Games: The Olympics of 1936.* New York: W. W. Norton.

Laser, Siegfried. 1987. *Sport und Spiel.* Göttingen: Vandenhoeck & Ruprecht.

Lash, Scott. 1991. "Genealogy and the Body: Foucault/Deleuze/Nietzsche." In *The Body: Social Process and Cultural Theory*, edited by Mike Featherstone, Mike Hepworth, and Bryan S. Turner, 256–80. London: Sage.

Lattimore, Steven. 1988. "The Nature of Early Greek Victor Statues." In *Coroebus Triumphs*, edited by Susan Bandy, 245–56. San Diego: San Diego State University Press.

Lawler, Jennifer. 2002. *Punch: Why Women Participate in Violent Sports.* Terre Haute, IN: Wish Publishing.

Lawson, John and Harold Silver. 1973. *A Social History of Education in England.* London: Methuen.

Lebow, David and Richard Ned Lebow. Forthcoming. *Changing Narratives of Self-Interest and American Foreign Policy.*

Lee, Mabel. 1983. *A History of Physical Education and Sports in the U.S.A.* New York: John Wiley and Sons.

Legakis, Brian. 1977. "Athletic Contests in Archaic Greek Art." Ph.D. diss., University of Chicago.

Lehmann, R. C. 1908. *The Complete Oarsman.* London: Methuen & Co.

Leinster-Mackay, D. 1981. "Victorian Quasi-Public Schools: A Question of Appearance and Reality or an Application of the Principle of the Survival of the Fittest?" *British Journal of Educational Studies* 29: 54–68.

Lennartz, Karl. 1974. *Kenntnisse und Vorstellungen von Olympia und den Olympischen Spielen in der Zeit von 393–1896.* Schorndorf: Karl Hofmann.

Leonard, Fred and R. Tait McKenzie. 1927. *A Guide to the History of Physical Education.* 2nd ed. Philadelphia: Lea and Febiger.

Leonard, Madeleine. 2004. "Bonding and Bridging Capital: Reflections from Belfast." *Sociology* 38: 927–44.

Lepage, Jean-Denis. 2008. *Hitler Youth, 1922–1945: An Illustrated History.* Jefferson, NC: McFarland.

Lester, Robin. 1995. *Stagg's University: The Rise, Decline, and Fall of Big-Time Football at Chicago.* Urbana: University of Illinois Press.

Lever, Janet. 1983. *Soccer Madness.* Chicago: University of Chicago Press.

Lipka, Michael. 2002. *Xenophon's Spartan Constitution: Introduction, Text, Commentary.* Berlin: Walter de Gruyter.

Longoria, Richard. 2009. *Meritocracy and Americans' Views on Distributive Justice.* Lanham, MD: Lexington Books.

Lonsdale, Steven. 1993. *Dance and Ritual Play in Greek Religion.* Baltimore, MD: Johns Hopkins University Press.

Lopez, Mark Hugo and Kimberlee Moore. 2006. *Participation in Sports and Civic Engagement.* The Center for Information and Research on Civic Learning and Engagement. Retrieved from http://www.civicyouth.org/PopUps/FactSheets/FS_06_Sports_and_Civic_Engagement.pdf.

Lovesey, Peter. 1979. *The Official Centenary History of the Amateur Athletic Association.* London: Guinness Superlatives Limited.

Lowerson, John. 1989. "Golf." In *Sport in Britain: A Social History*, edited by Tony Mason, 187–214. Cambridge: Cambridge University Press.

Loy, John and Douglas Booth. 2000. "Functionalism, Sport, and Society." In *Handbook of Sports Studies*, edited by Jay Coakley and Eric Dunning, 8–27. London: Sage Publications.

2004. "Social Structure and Social Theory: The Intellectual Insights of Robert K. Merton." In *Sport and Modern Social Theorists*, edited by Richard Giulianotti, 33–47. New York: Palgrave Macmillan.

Lubbock, Percy. 1932. *Shades of Eton*. London: J. Cape.

Lunn, Arnold Henry Moore. 1940. *Come What May, An Autobiography*. London: Eyre and Spottiswoode.

Lyttelton, Edward. 1880. "Athletics in Public Schools." *The Nineteenth Century* 7: 43–57.

MacAloon, John. 1984. "Olympic Games and the Theory of Spectacle in Modern Societies." In *Rite, Drama, Festival, Spectacle: Rehearsals Toward a Theory of Cultural Performance*, edited by John MacAloon, 241–80. Philadelphia: Institute for the Study of Human Issues.

MacAulay, Thomas, ed. 1853. *Speeches, Parliamentary and Miscellaneous*. 2 vols. London: Henry Vizetelly.

Mack, Christopher. 2000. "The Idea of Sports in Germany, 1880–1936." Ph.D. diss., City University of New York.

Malcolm, Dominic. 2012. *Sport and Sociology*. London: Routledge.

Malcolmson, Robert. 1973. *Popular Recreations in English Society, 1700–1850*. Cambridge: Cambridge University Press.

Malec, Michael and Hilary McD. Beckles. 1999. "Baseball, Cricket, and Social Change: Jackie Robinson and Frank Worell." In *Anthropology, Sport, and Culture*, edited by Robert Sands, 137–44. Westport, CT: Bergin and Garvey.

Mallery, Otto. 1910. "The Social Significance of Play." *Annals of the American Academy of Political and Social Science* 35: 152–57.

Mallwitz, Alfred. 1988. "Cult and Competition Locations at Olympia." In *The Archaeology of the Olympics*, edited by Wendy Raschke, 79–109. Madison: University of Wisconsin Press.

Mangan, J. A. 1981. *Athleticism in the Victorian and Edwardian Public School: The Emergence and Consolidation of an Educational Ideology*. Cambridge: Cambridge University Press.

1983. "Grammar Schools and the Games Ethic in the Victorian and Edwardian Eras." *Albion* 15: 313–35.

1998. *The Games Ethic and Imperialism: Aspects of the Diffusion of an Ideal*. 2nd ed. Portland: Frank Cass and Company.

Mangan, J. A. and Colm Hickey. 2006. "English Elementary Education Revisited and Revised: Drill and Athleticism in Tandem." In *A Sport-Loving Society: Victorian and Edwardian Middle-Class England at Play*, edited by J. A. Mangan, 65–89. London: Routledge.

Mangan, J. A. and J. Walvin, eds. 1987. *Manliness and Morality: Middle-Class Masculinity in Britain and America, 1800–1940*. New York: St. Martin's Press.

Mann, Christian. 2001. *Athlet und polis im archaischen und frühklassischen Griechenland*. Göttingen: Vandenhoeck & Ruprecht.

2012. "People on the Margins of Greek Sport." In *Companion to Sport and Spectacle in Greek and Roman Antiquity*, edited by Paul Christesen and Donald Kyle, Malden, MA: Wiley-Blackwell.

Mann, Golo. 1968. *The History of Germany Since 1789*. Translated by Marian Jackson. New York: Praeger.

Margetson, Stella. 1969. *Leisure and Pleasure in the Nineteenth Century*. New York: Coward-McCann.

Markle, M. M. 1985. "Jury Pay and Assembly Pay at Athens." In *Crux: Essays in Greek History Presented to G. E. M. de Ste. Croix on His 75th Birthday*, edited by Paul Cartledge and F. David Harvey, 265–97. London: Duckworth.

Markula, Pirkko and Richard Pringle. 2006. *Foucault, Sport, and Exercise: Power, Knowledge, and Transforming the Self*. London: Routledge.

Marrou, H. I. 1956 (1948). *A History of Education in Antiquity*. Translated by George Lamb. New York: Sheed and Ward.

Marsh, Herbert and Sabina Kleitman. 2003. "School Athletic Participation: Mostly Gain with Little Pain." *Journal of Sport and Exercise Psychology* 25: 205–28.

Martin, Jay. 2009. *Live All You Can: Alexander Joy Cartwright and the Invention of Modern Baseball*. New York: Columbia University Press.

Maurice, John Frederick. 1850. *Dialogue between Somebody (a person of respectability) and Nobody (the writer)*. London: G. Bell.

May, Thomas. 1994. "The Concept of Autonomy." *American Philosophical Quarterly* 31: 133–44.

May, Trevor. 2009. *The Victorian Public School*. Oxford: Shire.

Mayo, James. 1998. *The American Country Club: Its Origins and Development*. New Brunswick, NJ: Rutgers University Press.

McClelland, John and Brian Merrilees, eds. 2010. *Sport and Culture in Early Modern Europe*. Toronto: Centre for Reformation and Renaissance Studies.

McCrone, Kathleen. 1987. "Play Up! Play Up! And Play the Game! Sport at the Late Victorian Girls' Public Schools." In *From 'Fair Sex' to Feminism: Sport and the Socialization of Women in the Industrial and Post-Industrial Eras*, edited by J. A. Mangan and R. J. Park, 97–129. London: Frank Cass and Company.

1988. *Sport and the Physical Emancipation of English Women, 1870–1914*. London: Routledge.

2006. "The 'Lady Blue': Sport at the Oxbridge Women's Colleges from Their Foundation to 1914." In *A Sport-Loving Society: Victorian and Edwardian Middle-Class England at Play*, edited by J. A. Mangan, 153–76. London: Routledge.

McDonnell, Myles. 1991. "The Introduction of Athletic Nudity." *Journal of Hellenic Studies* 111: 182–93.

McGerr, Michael. 2003. *A Fierce Discontent: The Rise and Fall of the Progressive Movement in America, 1870–1920*. New York: Free Press.

McHoul, Alec and Wendy Grace. 1997. *A Foucault Primer: Discourse, Power, and the Subject*. New York: New York University Press.

McIntosh, Peter. 1968. *Physical Education in England Since 1800*. 2nd ed. London: G. Bell and Sons.

1987. *Sport in Society*. 2nd ed. Twickenham: West London Press.

McNay, Lois. 1999. "Gender, Habitus, and the Field: Pierre Bourdieu and the Limits of Reflexivity." *Theory, Culture and Society* 16: 95–117.

Mehl, Andreas. 1992. "Erziehung zum Hellenen – Erziehung zum Weltbürger: Bemerkungen zum Gymnasion im hellenistischen Osten." *Nikephoros* 5: 43–73.

Meier, Christian. 1990 (1980). *The Greek Discovery of Politics*. Translated by David McLintock. Cambridge, MA: Harvard University Press.

Mélio, George. 1889. *Manual of Swedish Drill Based on Ling's System*. New York: Excelsior Publishing House.

Merton, Robert King. 1957. *Social Theory and Social Structure*. Rev. and enl. ed. Glencoe, IL: Free Press.

    1975. "Structural Analysis in Sociology." In *Approaches to the Study of Social Structure*, edited by Peter Blau, 21–52. New York: Free Press.

    1996. *On Social Structure and Science*. Chicago: University of Chicago Press.

Millender, Ellen. 2012. "Spartan Women." In *A Companion to Sparta*, edited by Anton Powell, Malden, MA: Wiley-Blackwell.

Miller, Stephen. 2000. "Naked Democracy." In *Polis and Politics: Studies in Ancient Greek History Presented to Mogens Herman Hansen on His Sixtieth Birthday*, edited by Pernille Flensted-Jensen, Thomas Heine Nielsen, and Lene Rubinstein, 277–96. Copenhagen: Museum Tusculanum Press.

    2004a. *Ancient Greek Athletics*. New Haven, CT: Yale University Press.

    2004b. *Arete: Greek Sports from Ancient Sources*. 3rd ed. Berkeley: University of California Press.

Mills, C. Wright. 1959. *The Sociological Imagination*. London: Oxford University Press.

Mills, Harrianne. 1984. "Greek Clothing Regulations: Sacred and Profane." *Zeitschrift für Papyrologie und Epigraphik* 55: 255–65.

Miracle, Andrew Jr. and C. Roger Rees. 1994. *Lessons of the Locker Room: The Myth of School Sports*. Amherst, NY: Prometheus Books.

Mitchell, Sally. 2009. *Daily Life in Victorian England*. 2nd ed. Westport, CT: Greenwood Press.

Money, Tony. 1997. *Manly & Muscular Diversions: Public Schools and the Nineteenth-Century Sporting Revival*. London: Duckworth.

Montanari, Franco, Antonios Rengakos, and Christos Tsagalis, eds. 2009. *Brill's Companion to Hesiod*. Leiden: Brill.

Moore, John. 1786. *A View of Society and Manners in France, Switzerland, and Germany*. 6th corrected ed. 2 vols. London.

Morgan, Catherine. 1990. *Athletes and Oracles*. Cambridge: Cambridge University Press.

Moritz, Sandra, Deborah Feltz, Kyle Fahrbach, and Diane Mack. 2000. "The Relation of Self-Efficacy Measures to Sport Performance: A Meta-Analytic Review." *Research Quarterly for Exercise and Sport* 71: 280–94.

Morris, Ian. 1986. "The Use and Abuse of Homer." *Classical Antiquity* 5: 81–138.

    2000. *Archaeology as Cultural History*. Oxford: Basil Blackwell.

    2002. "Hard Surfaces." In *Money, Labour, and Land: Approaches to the Economies of Ancient Greece*, edited by Paul Cartledge, Edward Cohen, and Lin Foxhall, 8–43. London: Routledge.

Moustaka, Aliki. 2002. "Zeus und Hera im Heiligtum von Olympia." In *Olympia 1875–2000: 125 Jahre Deutsche Ausgrabungen*, edited by Helmut Kyrieleis, 301–15. Mainz: Philipp von Zabern.

Mouzelis, Nicos. 1995. *Sociological Theory: What Went Wrong? Diagnosis and Remedies*. London: Routledge.

Munck, Gerardo. 2009. *Measuring Democracy: A Bridge between Scholarship and Politics*. Baltimore, MD: Johns Hopkins University Press.

Murray, Sarah. 2012. "The Role of Religion in Greek Sport and Spectacle." In *Companion to Sport and Spectacle in Greek and Roman Antiquity*, edited by Paul Christesen and Donald Kyle, Malden, MA: Wiley-Blackwell.

Murray, Venetia. 1998. *High Society: A Social History of the Regency Period, 1788–1830*. London: Viking.

Nakamura, Tetsuo. 2003. "Japan: The Future in the Past." In *The Nazi Olympics: Sport, Politics, and Appeasement in the 1930s*, edited by Arnd Krüger and William Murray, 127–44. Urbana: University of Illinois Press.

Nannestad, Peter. 2008. "What Have We Learned about Generalized Trust, If Anything?" *Annual Review of Political Science* 11: 413–36.

Naul, Roland. 2002. "History of Sport and Physical Education in Germany, 1800–1945." In *Sport and Physical Education in Germany*, edited by Roland Naul and Ken Hardman, 15–27. London: Routledge.

Neils, Jenifer, ed. 1992. *Goddess and Polis: The Panathenaic Festival in Ancient Athens*. Princeton, NJ: Princeton University Press.

Neuendorff, Edmund. 1934. *Geschichte der neueren deutschen Leibesübungen vom Beginn des 18. Jahrhunderts bis zur Gegenwart*. 4 vols. Dresden: Limpert Verlag.

Newbolt, Henry. 1897. *Admirals, and All Other Verses*. London: Elkin Matthews.

Newton, Diana. 1998. *Papists, Protestants, and Puritans, 1559–1714*. Cambridge: Cambridge University Press.

Nicolson, Harold. 1955. *Good Behaviour; Being a Study of Certain Types of Civility*. London: Constable.

Nicholson, Matthew and Russell Hoye, eds. 2008. *Sport and Social Capital*. Oxford: Butterworth-Heinemann.

Nicholson, Matthew, Russell Hoye, and Barrie Houlihan, eds. 2011. *Participation in Sport: International Policy Perspectives*. London: Routledge.

Nielsen, Kai. 1985. *Equality and Liberty: A Defense of Radical Egalitarianism*. Totowa, NJ: Rowman and Allanheld.

Novak, Michael. 1988. *The Joy of Sports: End Zones, Bases, Baskets, Balls, and the Consecration of the American Spirit*. 2nd ed. Lanham, MD: Hamilton Press.

Ober, Josiah. 1996. *The Athenian Revolution: Essays on Ancient Greek Democracy and Political Theory*. Princeton, NJ: Princeton University Press.

Orwell, George. 1953. *Shooting an Elephant and Other Essays*. London: Sacker and Warburg.

Osborne, Robin. 1993. "Competitive Festivals and the *Polis*: A Context for Dramatic Festivals at Athens." In *Tragedy, Comedy, and the Polis*, edited by Alan Sommerstein, Stephen Halliwell, Jeffrey Henderson, and Bernhard Zimmerman, 21–37. Bari: Levante Editori.

Overman, Steven. 1997. *The Influence of the Protestant Ethic on Sport and Recreation*. Aldershot: Avebury.

Ozer, Elizabeth and Albert Bandura. 1990. "Mechanisms Governing Empowerment Effects: A Self-Efficacy Analysis." *Journal of Personality and Social Psychology* 58: 472–86.

Paden, Roger. 1987. "Foucault's Anti-Humanism." *Human Studies* 10: 123–41.

Palmer, Catherine and Kirrilly Thompson. 2007. "The Paradoxes of Football Spectatorship: On-Field and Online Expressions of Social Capital Among the 'Grog Squad'." *Sociology of Sport Journal* 24: 187–205.

Parkin, George Robert. 1900. *Edward Thring, Headmaster of Uppingham School: Life, Diary, and Letters*. London: Macmillan and Co.

Parliament, of Great Britain, ed. 1862. *Hansard's Parliamentary Debates*. London: Cornelius Buck.

Pateman, Carole. 1970. *Participation and Democratic Theory*. Cambridge: Cambridge University Press.

Patterson, Cynthia. 2007. "Other Sorts: Slaves, Foreigners, and Women." In *The Cambridge Companion to the Age of Pericles*, edited by Loren Samons, 153–78. Cambridge: Cambridge University Press.

Patterson, Orlando, Alan Tomlinson, and Christopher Young. 2011. "The Culture of Sports." *Journal of Historical Sociology* 24: 549–63.

Paxton, Pamela. 2002. "Social Capital and Democracy: An Interdependent Relationship." *American Sociological Review* 67: 254–77.

    2007. "Association Memberships and Generalized Trust: A Multilevel Model Across 31 Countries." *Social Forces* 86: 47–76.

Pedley, John Griffiths. 2012. *Greek Art and Archaeology*. 5th ed. Boston: Prentice Hall.

Pemstein, Daniel, Stephen Meserve, and James Melton. 2010. "Democratic Compromise: A Latent Variable Analysis of Ten Measures of Regime Type." *Political Analysis* 18: 426–49.

Penn, Alan. 1999. *Targeting Schools: Drill, Militarism, and Imperialism*. London: Woburn Press.

People, One of the. 1848. "Gentlemen Born or, Englishmen vs. Americans." *The Nineteenth Century* 2: 621–28.

Perks, Thomas. 2007. "Does Sport Foster Social Capital? The Contribution of Sport to a Lifestyle of Community Participation." *Sociology of Sport Journal* 24: 378–401.

Perry, Timothy. 2012. "Sport in the Early Iron Age and Homeric Epic." In *Companion to Sport and Spectacle in Greek and Roman Antiquity*, edited by Paul Christesen and Donald Kyle, Malden, MA: Wiley-Blackwell.

Peterson, Robert. 1990. *Cages to Jump Shots: Pro Basketball's Early Years*. New York: Oxford University Press.

Pettersson, Michael. 1992. *Cults of Apollo at Sparta: The Hyakinthia, the Gymnopaidiai, and the Karneia*. Stockholm: Paul Åströms Förlag.

Pine, Lisa. 1997. *Nazi Family Policy, 1933–1945*. Oxford: Berg.

Pleket, H. W. 1973. "Some Aspects of the History of the Athletic Guilds." *Zeitschrift für Papyrologie und Epigraphik* 10: 197–227.

    1998. "Mass-Sport and Local Infrastructure in the Greek Cities of Roman Asia Minor." *Stadion* 24: 151–72.

Poliakoff, Michael. 1987. *Combat Sports in the Ancient World*. New Haven, CT: Yale University Press.

Pollard, Hugh. 1956. *Pioneers of Popular Education: 1760–1850*. London: Butler and Tanner.

Pomeroy, Sarah, Stanley Burstein, Walter Donlan, and Jennifer Tolbert Roberts. 2007. *Ancient Greece: A Political, Social, and Cultural History*. 2nd ed. New York: Oxford University Press.

Pope, S. W. 1996. "Amateurism and American Sports Culture: The Invention of an Athletic Tradition in the United States, 1870–1900." *International Journal of the History of Sport* 13: 290–309.

Portes, Alejandro. 1998. "Social Capital: Its Origins and Applications in Modern Sociology." *Annual Review of Sociology* 24: 1–24.

Powell, Barry. 1988. "The Dipylon Oinochoe Inscription and the Spread of Literacy in 8th-Century Greece." *Kadmos* 27: 65–86.

Prebish, Charles, ed. 1993. *Religion and Sport: The Meeting of Sacred and Profane.* Westport, CT: Greenwood Press.

Pritchard, David. 2003. "Athletics, Education, and Participation in Classical Athens." In *Sport and Festival in the Ancient Greek World*, edited by David J. Phillips and David Pritchard, 293–350. Swansea: Classical Press of Wales.

   2004. "Kleisthenes, Participation, and the Dithyrambic Contests of Late Archaic and Classical Athens." *Phoenix* 58: 208–28.

   2009. "Sport, War, and Democracy in Classical Athens." *International Journal of the History of Sport* 26: 212–45.

Putnam, Robert. 1995. "Bowling Alone: America's Declining Social Capital." *Journal of Democracy* 6: 65–78.

   2000. *Bowling Alone: The Collapse and Revival of American Community.* New York: Simon and Schuster.

Putnam, Robert, Robert Leonardi, and Raffaella Nanetti. 1993. *Making Democracy Work: Civic Traditions in Modern Italy.* Princeton, NJ: Princeton University Press.

Putney, Clifford. 2001. *Muscular Christianity: Manhood and Sports in Protestant America, 1880–1920.* Cambridge, MA: Harvard University Press.

Pyta, Wolfram. 2006. "German Football: A Cultural History." In *German Football: History, Culture, Society*, edited by Alan Tomlinson and Christopher Young, 1–22. London: Routledge.

Quint, Wilder Dwight. 1914. *The Story of Dartmouth.* Boston: Little, Brown, and Company.

Raaflaub, Kurt. 1997. "Soldiers, Citizens, and the Evolution of the Early Greek *Polis*." In *The Development of the Polis in Archaic Greece*, edited by Lynette Mitchell and P.J. Rhodes, 49–59. London: Routledge.

   1998. "A Historian's Headache: How to Read 'Homeric Society'?" In *Archaic Greece: New Approaches and New Evidence*, edited by Hans van Wees and Nick Fisher, 169–93. London: Duckworth.

   2007. "The Breakthrough of *Dêmokratia* in Mid-Fifth Century Athens." In *Origins of Democracy in Ancient Greece*, edited by Kurt Raaflaub, Josiah Ober, and Robert Wallace, 105–54. Berkeley: University of California Press.

Raaflaub, Kurt and Robert Wallace. 2007. "'People's Power' and Egalitarian Trends in Archaic Greece." In *Origins of Democracy in Ancient Greece*, edited by Kurt Raaflaub, Josiah Ober, and Robert Wallace, 22–48. Berkeley: University of California Press.

Rader, Benjamin. 2008a. *American Sports: From the Age of Folk Games to the Age of Televised Sports.* 6th ed. Englewood Cliffs, NJ: Prentice-Hall.

   2008b. *Baseball: A History of America's Game.* 3rd ed. Urbana: University of Illinois Press.

Raugh, Harold. 2004. *The Victorians at War, 1815–1914.* Santa Barbara, CA: ABC-CLIO.

Reed, Nancy. 1998. *More than Just a Game: The Military Nature of Greek Athletic Contests*. Chicago: Ares Publishers.

Reid, Douglas. 1990. "Beasts and Brutes: Popular Blood Sports c. 1780–1860." In *Sport and the Working Class in Modern Britain*, edited by Richard Holt, 12–28. Manchester: Manchester University Press.

Remijsen, Sofie. 2012. "Greek Athletics in Egypt: Status Symbol and Lifestyle." In *Companion to Sport and Spectacle in Greek and Roman Antiquity*, edited by Paul Christesen and Donald Kyle, Malden, MA: Wiley-Blackwell.

Révész, Miklos. 1997. "Opening Statement." In *European Conference on Sport and Local Authorities*, 7–8. Strasbourg: Council of Europe.

Richer, Nicolas. 2005. "Les Gymnopédies de Sparte." *Ktema* 30: 237–64.

Riess, Steven. 1995. *Sport in Industrial America, 1850–1920*. Wheeling, IL: Harlan Davidson.

———. 1999. *Touching Base: Professional Baseball and American Culture in the Progressive Era*. Rev. ed. Urbana: University of Illinois Press.

Rinehart, Robert. 1998. "Born-Again Sport: Ethics in Biographical Research." In *Sport and Postmodern Times*, edited by Geneviève Rail, 33–46. Albany: State University of New York Press.

Ritzer, George. 2008a. *Classical Sociological Theory*. 5th ed. Boston: McGraw-Hill Higher Education.

———. 2008b. *Sociological Theory*. 7th ed. Boston: McGraw-Hill Higher Education.

Rivers, Caryl. 1983. "God and the Free Throw." In *I'm On My Way Running: Women Speak of Coming of Age*, edited by Lyn Reese, Jean Wilkinson, and Phyllis Sheon Koppelman, 309-12. New York: Avon Books.

Roberts, William. 1831. *The Portraiture of a Christian Gentleman*. New York: T. and J. Swords.

Robinson, Richard. 1995. *Aristotle Politics Books III and IV*. New York: Clarendon Press.

Roebuck, Mary and Carl Roebuck. 1955. "A Prize Aryballos." *Hesperia* 24: 158–63.

Roller, Lynn. 1981. "Funeral Games for Historical Persons." *Stadion* 7: 1–18.

Romano, David. 1993. *Athletics and Mathematics in Archaic Corinth: The Origins of the Greek Stadion*. Philadelphia: American Philosophical Society.

Rouse, W. H. D. 1898. *A History of Rugby School*. New York: Charles Scribner's Sons.

Rubin, Sam. 2006. *Yale Football*. Mount Pleasant, SC: Arcadia Publishing.

Rubinstein, W. D. 1998. *Britain's Century: A Political and Social History 1815–1905*. London: Arnold.

Rudé, George. 1971. *The History of Hanoverian London 1714–1808*. Berkeley: University of California Press.

Ruskin, John. 1891. *Sesame and Lilies: Two Lectures by John Ruskin, LL.D*. New York: Charles E. Merrill and Co.

Russell, Gordon. 2008. *Aggression in the Sports World: A Social Psychological Perspective*. New York: Oxford University Press.

Sabin, Philip, Hans van Wees, and Michael Whitby, eds. 2007. *The Cambridge History of Greek and Roman Warfare*. 2 vols. Cambridge: Cambridge University Press.

Sage, George. 1998. *Power and Ideology in American Sport: A Critical Perspective*. 2nd ed. Champaign, IL: Human Kinetics.

2000. "Political Economy and Sport." In *Handbook of Sports Studies*, edited by Jay Coakley and Eric Dunning, 260–76. London: Sage Publications.

Sandiford, Keith. 1994. *Cricket and the Victorians*. Aldershot, Hants: Scolar Press.

Savage, Howard. 1929. *American College Athletics*. New York: Carnegie Foundation for the Advancement of Teaching.

Scanlon, Thomas. 1983. "The Vocabulary of Competition: *Agôn* and *Aethlos*, Greek Terms for Contest." *Arete* 1: 147–62.

2002. *Eros and Greek Athletics*. Oxford: Oxford University Press.

2008. "The Heraia at Olympia Revisited." *Nikephoros* 21: 159–96.

Scarborough, Vernon and David Wilcox, eds. 1991. *The Mesoamerican Ballgame*. Tucson: University of Arizona Press.

Schacht, Steven. 1996. "Misogyny On and Off the 'Pitch': The Gendered World of Male Rugby Players." *Gender and Society* 10: 550–65.

Scheidel, Walter, Ian Morris, and Richard Saller, eds. 2007. *The Cambridge Economic History of the Greco-Roman World*. Cambridge: Cambridge University Press.

Schilbach, Jürgen. 1992. "Olympia: Die Entwicklungsphasen des Stadions." In *Proceedings of an International Symposium on the Olympic Games*, edited by William Coulson and Helmut Kyrieleis, 33–37. Athens: Deutsches Archäologisches Institut Athen.

Sears, Edward. 2009. *Running through the Ages*. Jefferson, NC: McFarland.

Seippel, Ørnulf. 2002. "Volunteers and Professionals in Norwegian Sports Organizations." *International Journal of Voluntary and Nonprofit Organizations* 13: 253–70.

2006. "Sport and Social Capital." *Acta Sociologica* 49: 169–83.

2008. "Sports in Civil Society: Networks, Social Capital, and Influence." *European Sociological Review* 24: 69–80.

Seligman, Martin. 1975. *Helplessness: On Depression, Development, and Death*. San Francisco: W. H. Freeman.

Sherif, Muzafer, O. J. Harvey, B. Jack White, William R. Hood, and Carolyn W. Sherif. 1961. *Intergroup Conflict and Cooperation: The Robbers Cave Experiment*. Norman, OK: The University Book Exchange.

Shewman, Byron. 1995. *Volleyball Centennial: The First 100 Years*. Indianapolis, IN: Masters Press.

Shields, David, Brenda Bredemeier, Douglas Gardner, and Alan Bostrom. 1995. "Leadership, Cohesion, and Team Norms Regarding Cheating and Aggression." *Sociology of Sport Journal* 12: 324–36.

Shipley, Graham. 2000. *The Greek World after Alexander, 323–30 BC*. London: Routledge.

Shipley, Stan. 1989. "Boxing." In *Sport in Britain: A Social History*, edited by Tony Mason, 78–115. Cambridge: Cambridge University Press.

Shogan, Debra. 1999. *The Making of High-Performance Athletes: Discipline, Diversity, and Ethics*. Toronto: University of Toronto Press.

Silva, John III. 1983. "The Perceived Legitimacy of Rule Violating Behavior in Sport." *Journal of Sport Psychology* 5: 438–48.

Simon, Brian and Ian Bradley, eds. 1975. *The Victorian Public School*. Dublin: Gill and Macmillan.

Skinner, Ellen. 1996. "A Guide to Constructs of Control." *Journal of Personality and Social Psychology* 71: 549–70.

Skirstad, Berit. 1999. "Norwegian Sport at the Crossroad." In *Sports Clubs in Various European Countries*, edited by Klaus Heinemann, 269–92. Stuttgart: Hofmann Verlag.

Smiles, Samuel. 1861. *Self-Help, with Illustrations of Character and Conduct.* Boston: Ticknor and Fields.

1876. *Thrift.* Toronto: Belford Brothers.

Snyder, Thomas. 1993. *120 Years of American Education: A Statistical Portrait.* Washington, DC: U.S. Department of Education, Office of Educational Research and Improvement, National Center for Education Statistics.

Sønderskov, Kim Mannemar. 2011. "Does Generalized Trust Lead to Associational Membership? Unraveling a Bowl of Well-Tossed Spaghetti." *European Sociological Review* 27: 419–34.

Sontag, Susan. 1980. *Under the Sign of Saturn.* New York: Farrar, Straus & Giroux.

Spalding, Albert Goodwill. 1911. *America's National Game.* New York: American Sports Publishing Company.

Spiess, Adolf. 1860. *About Gymnastics in the Schools.* Translated by August Bernhard and Christian Biewend. Milwaukee, WI: Freidenker Publishing.

Spivey, Nigel. 2004. *The Ancient Olympics.* Oxford: Oxford University Press.

Sport Publishing House, People's. 1973. *Sports in China.* Beijing: Foreign Languages Press.

SportEngland. 1999. *The Value of Sport.* Retrieved from http://www.tool-kitsportdevelopment.org/html/resources/CD/CD24320F-E717-4A69-BA37-0E19E56B659F/best%20value%20through%20sport%20booklet.pdf.

Spreitzer, Elmer. 1994. "Does Participation in Interscholastic Athletics Affect Adult Development?" *Youth and Society* 25: 368–87.

Stanley, Arthur. 1845. *The Life and Correspondence of Thomas Arnold.* New York: D. Appleton.

Staunton, Howard. 1869. *The Great Schools of England.* London: Strahan and Co.

Stephens, W. B. 1998. *Education in Britain, 1750–1914.* London: MacMillan.

Stevenson, Betsey. 2007. "Title IX and the Evolution of High School Sports." *Contemporary Economic Policy* 25: 486–505.

2010. *Beyond the Classroom: Using Title IX to Measure the Return to High School Sports.* National Bureau of Economic Research Working Paper 15728. Retrieved from http://www.nber.org/papers/w15728.pdf.

Stone, Lawrence. 1965. *The Crisis of the Aristocracy 1558–1641.* Oxford: Clarendon Press.

Storr, F., ed. 1899. *Life and Remains of Rev. R. H. Quick.* Cambridge: The University Press.

Strachey, Lytton. 1918. *Eminent Victorians: Cardinal Manning, Florence Nightingale, Dr. Arnold, General Gordon.* New York: G. P. Putnam's Sons.

Strauss, Barry. 1996. "The Athenian Trireme, School of Democracy." In *Demokratia: A Conversation on Democracies, Ancient and Modern*, edited by Josiah Ober and Charles Hedrick, 313–25. Princeton: Princeton University Press.

Struna, Nancy. 1985. "In 'Glorious Disarray': The Literature of American Sport History." *Research Quarterly for Exercise and Sport* 56: 151–60.

Sugden, John and Alan Tomlinson. 2000. "Theorizing Sport, Social Class, and Status." In *Handbook of Sports Studies*, edited by Jay Coakley and Eric Dunning, 309–21. London: Sage Publications.

Suits, Bernard. 1978. *The Grasshopper: Games, Life, and Utopia*. Toronto: University of Toronto Press.

Sutherland, Gillian. 1990. "Education." In *The Cambridge Social History of Britain 1750–1950*, edited by F. M. L. Thompson, 3: 119–70. 3 vols. Cambridge: Cambridge University Press.

Sweet, Waldo. 1987. *Sport and Recreation in Ancient Greece*. New York: Oxford University Press.

Sztompka, Piotr. 1990. "R. K. Merton's Theoretical System: An Overview." In *Robert K. Merton: Consensus and Controversy*, edited by Jon Clark, Celia Modgil, and Sohan Modgil, 53–64. London: Falmer Press.

Tajfel, Henri. 1981. *Human Groups and Social Categories: Studies in Social Psychology*. Cambridge: Cambridge University Press.

Tarschys, Daniel. 1995. "Preface." In *The Significance of Sport for Society – Health, Socialisation, Economy: A Scientific Review*, edited by Ilkka Vuori, 5–6. Strasbourg: Council of Europe Press.

Taylor, Matthew. 2008. *The Association Game: A History of British Football*. Harlow: Pearson-Longman.

Theberge, Nancy. 2000. "Gender and Sport." In *Handbook of Sports Studies*, edited by Jay Coakley and Eric Dunning, 322–33. London: Sage Publications.

Thom, Walter. 1813. *Pedestrianism*. Aberdeen: D. Chalmers.

Thompson, E. P. 1963. *The Making of the English Working Class*. London: V. Gollancz.

   1995 (1978). *The Poverty of Theory, or, An Orrery of Errors*. London: Merlin Press.

Thompson, F. M. L., ed. 1990. *The Cambridge Social History of Britain, 1750–1950*. 3 vols. Cambridge: Cambridge University Press.

Thorley, John. 2004. *Athenian Democracy*. London: Routledge.

Tomlinson, Alan. 2004. "Pierre Bourdieu and the Sociological Study of Sport: Habitus, Capital, and Field." In *Sport and Modern Social Theorists*, edited by Richard Giulianotti, 161–72. New York: Palgrave Macmillan.

Tonts, Matthew. 2005. "Competitive Sport and Social Capital in Rural Australia." *Journal of Rural Studies* 21: 137–49.

Tranter, Neil. 1998. *Sport, Economy, and Society in Britain 1750–1914*. Cambridge: Cambridge University Press.

Trimborn, Jürgen. 2007. *Leni Riefenstahl: A Life*. Translated by Edna McCown. New York: Faber and Faber.

Tunis, John. 1941. *Democracy and Sport*. New York: A. S. Barnes.

Tyler, Moses Coit. 1869. *The Brawnville Papers*. Boston: Fields, Osgood, and Co.

Ulf, Christoph. 2011. "Ancient Greek Competition: A Modern Construction?" In *Competition in the Ancient World*, edited by Nick Fisher and Hans van Wees, 85–111. Swansea: Classical Press of Wales.

Underdown, David. 2001. *Start of Play: Cricket and Culture in Eighteenth-Century England*. London: Penguin.

United States, Anti-Doping Agency. 2011. *What Sport Means in America: A Study of Sport's Role in Society*. Retrieved from http://www.usada.org/uploads/usadaresearchreport.pdf.

Uslaner, Eric. 1999. "Democracy and Social Capital." In *Democracy and Trust*, edited by Mark Warren, 121–50. Cambridge: Cambridge University Press.

2002. *The Moral Foundations of Trust*. Cambridge: Cambridge University Press.

Vamplew, Wray. 1976. *The Turf: A Social and Economic History of Horse Racing*. London: Allen Lane.

1980. "Sports Crowd Disorder in Britain, 1870–1914: Causes and Controls." *Journal of Sport History* 7: 5–20.

1988. *Pay Up and Play the Game: Professional Sport in Britain, 1875–1914*. Cambridge: Cambridge University Press.

1989. "Horse-racing." In *Sport in Britain: A Social History*, edited by Tony Mason, 215–44. Cambridge: Cambridge University Press.

van Gennep, Arnold. 1960 (1906). *Rites of Passage*. Translated by Monika Vizedom and Gabrielle Caffee. Chicago: University of Chicago Press.

van Nijf, Onno. 2001. "Local Heroes: Athletics, Festivals, and Elite Self-Fashioning in the Roman East." In *Being Greek Under Rome: Cultural Identity, the Second Sophistic, and the Development of the Empire*, edited by Simon Goldhill, 306–34. Cambridge: Cambridge University Press.

van Wees, Hans. 2004. *Greek Warfare: Myth and Realities*. London: Duckworth.

van Wingerden, Sophia. 1999. *The Women's Suffrage Movement in Britain, 1866–1928*. New York: Palgrave Macmillan.

Veblen, Thorstein. 1912. *The Theory of the Leisure Class: An Economic Study of Institutions*. London: The MacMillan Company.

Voss, Thomas and Martin Abraham. 2000. "Rational Choice Theory in Sociology: A Survey." In *The International Handbook of Sociology*, edited by Stella Quah and Arnaud Sales, 50–83. Thousand Oaks, CA: Sage.

Wacquant, Loïc. 2004. *Body and Soul: Notebooks of an Apprentice Boxer*. Oxford: Oxford University Press.

Walker, Helen. 1989. "Lawn Tennis." In *Sport in Britain: A Social History*, edited by Tony Mason, 245–75. Cambridge: Cambridge University Press.

Walker, James and Elinor Ostrom. 2009. "Trust and Reciprocity as Foundations for Cooperation." In *Whom Can We Trust? How Groups, Networks, and Institutions Make Trust Possible*, edited by Karen Cook, Margaret Levi, and Russell Hardin, 91–124. New York: Russell Sage Foundation.

Walseth, Kristin. 2008. "Bridging and Bonding Social Capital in Sport – Experiences of Young Women with an Immigrant Background." *Sport, Education and Society* 13: 1–17.

Warre, Edmund. 1884. *Athletics; or Physical Exercise and Recreation*. London: William Clowes and Sons.

Warren, Mark. 1999. "Introduction." In *Democracy and Trust*, edited by Mark Warren, 1–21. Cambridge: Cambridge University Press.

2001. *Democracy and Association*. Princeton, NJ: Princeton University Press.

Wasson, Ellis. 2010. *A History of Modern Britain, 1714 to the Present*. Chichester: Wiley-Blackwell.

Watt, Bob. 2006. *UK Election Law: A Critical Examination*. London: Glass House Press.

Weber, Max. 1947. *The Theory of Social and Economic Organization*. Translated by A. M. Henderson and Talcott Parsons. New York: Oxford University Press.

1962. *Basic Concepts in Sociology*. Translated by H. P. Secher. New York: Kensington Publishing.

Weiler, Ingomar. 2004. "Theodosius I. und die Olympischen Spiele." *Nikephoros* 17: 53–75.

Weitlauf, Julie, Daniel Cervone, and Ronald Smith. 2000. "Generalization Effects of Coping-Skills Training: Influence of Self-Defense Training on Women's Efficacy Beliefs, Assertiveness, and Aggression." *Journal of Applied Psychology* 85: 625–33.

Welch, Paula. 2004. *History of American Physical Education and Sport.* 3rd ed. Springfield, IL: Charles Thomas.

Welford, Richard. 1884–87. *History of Newcastle and Gateshead.* 3 vols. London: Walter Scott.

Western Australia, Government of. 2008. *More than Winning: The Real Value of Sport and Recreation in Western Australia.* Department of Sport and Recreation. Retrieved from http://www.dsr.wa.gov.au//assets/files/Advocacy/More%20 than%20winning.pdf.

Whitney, Caspar. 1895. *A Sporting Pilgrimage.* London: Osgood, McIlvaine, and Co.

Wicks, Elizabeth. 2006. *The Evolution of a Constitution: Eight Key Moments in British Constitutional History.* Oxford: Hart Publishing.

Wiener, Martin. 2004. *English Culture and the Decline of the Industrial Spirit, 1850–1950.* 2nd ed. Cambridge: Cambridge University Press.

Wiggins, David. 1987. "A History of Organized Play and Highly Competitive Sport for American Children." In *Advances in Pediatric Sport Sciences: Volume 2: Behavioral Issues,* edited by Daniel Gould and Maureen Weiss, 1–24. Champaign, IL: Human Kinetics.

Williams, Jack. 1989. "Cricket." In *Sport in Britain: A Social History,* edited by Tony Mason, 116–45. Cambridge: Cambridge University Press.

Wilson, Peter. 2000. *The Athenian Institution of the Khoregia: The Chorus, the City, and the Stage.* Cambridge: Cambridge University Press.

Windelband, Wilhelm. 1894. "Geschichte und Naturwissenschaft." In *Rektoratsreden der Universität Strassburg,* 193–208. Strassburg: Heitz and Mündel.

Wingfield-Stratford, Esmé Cecil. 1959. *The Lords of Cobham Hall.* London: Cassell.

Wood, Walter. 1913. *The Playground Movement in America and Its Relation to Public Education.* London: Board of Education (of the United Kingdom).

Woolcock, Michael. 2001. "The Place of Social Capital in Understanding Social and Economic Outcomes." *ISUMA The Canadian Journal of Policy Research* 2: 11–17.

Worchel, Stephen and Dawna Coutant. 2001. "It Takes Two to Tango: Relating Group Identity to Individual Identity within the Framework of Group Development." In *Blackwell Handbook of Social Psychology,* edited by Miles Hewstone, Marilynn Brewer, Michael Hogg, and R. Scott Tindale, 3: 461–81. 4 vols. Malden, MA: Blackwell.

Wright, Thomas. 1867. *Some Habits and Customs of the Working Classes.* London: Tinsley Brothers.

    1868. *The Great Unwashed.* London: Tinsley Brothers.

Wrong, Dennis. 1961. "The Over-Socialized Conception of Man in Modern Sociology." *American Sociological Review* 26: 183–93.

    1994. *The Problem of Order.* New York: The Free Press.

Xiangjun, Cao and Susan Brownell. 1996. "The People's Republic of China." In *National Sports Policies*, edited by Laurence Chalip, Arthur Johnson, and Lisa Stachura, 66–88. Westport, CT: Greenwood Press.

Xu, Guoqi. 2008. *Olympic Dreams: China and Sports, 1895–2008*. Cambridge, MA: Harvard University Press.

Young, A. S. (Doc). 1963, September. "How Sports Helped Break the Color Line." *Ebony* 114–20.

Young, David. 1984. *The Olympic Myth of Greek Amateur Athletics*. Chicago: Ares Publishers.

Young, Michael. 1958. *The Rise of the Meritocracy, 1870–2023: An Essay on Education and Equality*. London: Thames and Hudson.

Zakus, Dwight, James Skinner, and Allan Edwards. 2009. "Social Capital in Australian Sport." *Sport in Society* 12: 986–98.

Zhihua, Lin. 2010, August 10. "Exercising on Air." *China Daily*. Retrieved from http://www.chinadaily.com.cn/life/2010–08/10/content_11126986.htm.

Zirin, Dave. 2005. *What's My Name, Fool? Sports and Resistance in the United States*. Chicago: Haymarket Books.

Index